ISBN: 9781313896887

Published by:
HardPress Publishing
8345 NW 66TH ST #2561
MIAMI FL 33166-2626

Email: info@hardpress.net
Web: http://www.hardpress.net

THE NATIONAL EDITION

This edition is strictly limited to seventeen hundred signed, numbered and registered sets.

Number

CURRENT LITERATURE PUBLISHING COMPANY

Adam Dingwall

Manager

THE PROCLAMATION OF EMANCIPATION

GREAT DEBATES IN AMERICAN HISTORY

*From the Debates in the British Parliament on the
Colonial Stamp Act (1764–1765) to the Debates
in Congress at the Close of the Taft
Administration (1912–1913)*

EDITED BY

MARION MILLS MILLER, Litt.D. (Princeton)

Editor of "The Life and Works of Abraham Lincoln," etc.

IN FOURTEEN VOLUMES

EACH DEALING WITH A SPECIFIC SUBJECT, AND CONTAINING A SPECIAL INTRODUC-
TION BY A DISTINGUISHED AMERICAN STATESMAN OR PUBLICIST

VOLUME SIX

The Civil War

With an Introduction by HENRY WATTERSON, LL.D.
Editor of the Louisville (Ky.) *Courier Journal*

CURRENT LITERATURE PUBLISHING COMPANY
NEW YORK

Press of J. J. Little & Ives Co., New York

CONTENTS OF VOLUME SIX

CONTENTS OF VOLUME SIX

ILLUSTRATIONS IN VOLUME SIX

INTRODUCTION

LINCOLN, THE INCARNATION OF THE UNION [1]

THE war of sections, inevitable to the conflict of systems but long delayed by the compromises of patriotism, did two things which surpass in importance and value all other things: it confirmed the Federal Union as a nation, and it brought the American people to the fruition of their manhood. Before that war we were a huddle of petty sovereignties held together by a rope of sand; we were as a community of children playing at government. Hamilton felt it, Marshall feared it, Clay ignored it, Webster evaded it. Their passionate clinging to the Constitution and the flag, bond and symbol of an imperfect if not tentative compact, confessed it. They were the intellectual progenitors of Abraham Lincoln. He became the incarnation of the brain and soul of the Union. "My paramount object," said he, "is to save the Union, and not either to save or destroy slavery. If I could save the Union without freeing any slave, I would do it; if I could save it by freeing all the slaves, I would do it; and if I could do it by freeing some and leaving others alone, I would do that."

In the sense of security which his travail and martyrdom achieved for us we are apt to forget that it was not a localized labor system but institutional freedom which was at stake; that African slavery was the merest

---
[1] Adapted from an article in the *Cosmopolitan*, March, 1909.

1

relic of a semi-barbarism shared in the beginning by all the people, but at length driven by certain laws of nature and trade into a corner, where it was making a stubborn but futile stand; that the real issue was free government, made possible by the Declaration of Independence and the Constitution of the United States, and inseparable from the maintenance of the Union. If the Union failed, freedom failed.

The trend of modern thought was definitely set against human slavery; but outside the American Union the idea of human freedom had gone no further than limited monarchy. Though he came to awaken the wildest passions of the time, the negro was but an incident —never a principal—to the final death-grapple between the North and the South.

No man of his time understood this so perfectly, embodied it so adequately, as Abraham Lincoln. The primitive Abolitionists saw only one side of the shield, the original secessionists only the other side. Lincoln saw both sides. His political philosophy was expounded in four elaborate speeches: one delivered at Peoria, Illinois, the 16th of October, 1854; one at Springfield, Illinois, the 16th of June, 1858; one at Columbus, Ohio, the 16th of September, 1859; and one at Cooper Institute, in New York City, the 27th of February, 1860. Of course he made many speeches and very good speeches, but these four, progressive in character, contain the sum and substance of his creed touching the organic character of the Government, and at the same time express his personal and party view of contemporary affairs. They show him to have been an old-line Whig of the school of Henry Clay, with strong emancipation leanings; a thorough anti-slavery man, but never an extremist or an Abolitionist. To the last he hewed to the line thus laid down.

It is essential to a complete understanding of Mr. Lincoln's relation to the time and of his place in the history of the country that the student peruse closely those four speeches: they underlie all that passed in the famous debate with Douglas, all that their author said and did after he succeeded to the presidency. They will always stand as masterpieces of popular oratory. The debate with Douglas, however—assuredly the most extraordinary intellectual spectacle in the annals of our party warfare—best tells the story and crystalizes it. Lincoln entered the canvass unknown outside the State of Illinois. He ended it renowned from one end of the land to the other.

Judge Douglas was himself unsurpassed as a ready debater, but in that campaign, from first to last, he was at a serious disadvantage. His bark rode an ebbing tide, Lincoln's a flowing tide. African slavery had become the single issue now; and, as I have said, the trend of modern thought was against slavery. The Democrats seemed hopelessly divided. The Little Giant had to face a triangular opposition embracing the Republicans, the Administration, or Buchanan, Democrats, and a remnant of the old Whigs, who fancied that their party was still alive and might hold some kind of a balance of power. Judge Douglas called the combination the "allied army," and declared that he would deal with it "just as the Russians dealt with the allies at Sebastopol; that is, the Russians did not stop to inquire, when they fired a broadside, whether it hit an Englishman, a Frenchman, or a Turk." It was something more than a witticism when Mr. Lincoln rejoined, "In that case I beg he will indulge us while we suggest to him that those allies took Sebastopol."

He followed this center-shot with volley after volley, of exposition so clear, of reasoning so close, of illustration so homely and sharp, and, at times, of humor so incisive, that, though he lost his election—though the allies did not then take Sebastopol—his defeat counted for more than Douglas's victory, for it made him the logical and successful candidate for President of the United States two years later.

What could be more captivating to an outdoor audience than Lincoln's description "of the two persons who stand before the people as candidates for the Senate," to quote his prefatory words? "Judge Douglas," he said, "is of world-wide renown. All the anxious politicians of his party . . . have been looking upon him as certainly . . . to be President of the United States. They have seen in his round, jolly, fruitful face post-offices, land-offices, marshalships, and cabinet appointments, chargeships, and foreign missions bursting and spreading out in wonderful exuberance, ready to be laid hold of by their greedy hands. And as they have been gazing upon this attractive picture so long they cannot, in the little distraction that has taken place in the party, bring themselves to give up the charming hope; but with greedier anxiety they rush about him, sustain him, and give him marches, triumphal entries and receptions, beyond what in the days of his highest prosperity they could have brought about in his favor. On the contrary, nobody has ever expected me to be President. In my poor, lean, lank face nobody has ever seen that any cabbages were sprouting."

As the debates advanced these cheery tones deepened into harsher notes; crimination and recrimination followed; the gladiators were strung to their utmost tension. They became dreadfully in earnest. Personal collision was narrowly avoided. I have recently gone over the entire debate, and with a feeling I can only describe as most contemplative, most melancholy.

I knew Judge Douglas well; I admired, respected, loved him. I shall never forget the day he quitted Washington to go to his home in Illinois to return no more. We sat down together in a doorway. "What are you going to do?" said he. "Judge Douglas," I answered, "we have both fought to save the Union; you in your great way and I in my small way; and we have lost. I am going to my home in the mountains of Tennessee, where I have a few books, and there I mean to stay." Tears were in his eyes, and his voice trembled like a woman's. He was then a dying man. He had burned the candle at both ends; an eager, ardent, hard-working, pleasure-loving man; and although not yet fifty the candle was burned out. His infirmities were no greater than those of Mr. Clay; not to be mentioned with those of Mr. Webster. But he lived in more exacting times. The old-style party organ, with its mock heroics and its dull respectability, its beggarly array of empty news columns and cheap advertising, had been succeeded by that unsparing, telltale scandal-monger, Modern Journalism, with its myriad of hands and eyes, its vast retinue of detectives, and its quick transit over flashing wires, annihilating time and space. Too fierce a light beat upon the private life of public men, and Douglas suffered from this, as Clay and Webster, Silas Wright, and Franklin Pierce had not suffered.

The presidential bee was in his bonnet, certainly; but its buzzing there was not noisier than in the bonnets of many other great Americans who have been dazzled by the presidential mirage. His plans and schemes came to naught. He died at the moment when the death of those plans and schemes was made more palpable and impressive by the roar of cannon proclaiming the reality of the "irrepressible conflict" he had refused to foresee and had struggled to avert. His lifelong rival was at the head of affairs. No one has found occasion to come to the rescue of his fame. No party interest has been identified with his memory. But when the truth of history is written it will be told that, no less than Webster and Clay, he, too, was a patriotic man, who loved his country and tried to save the Union. He tried to save the Union, even as Webster and Clay had tried to save it, by compromises and expedients. It was too late. That string was played out. Where they had succeeded he failed; but, for the nobility of his intention, the amplitude of his resources, the splendor of his combat, he merits all that any leader of a losing cause ever gained in the regard of posterity; and posterity will not deny him the title of statesman.

In those famous debates it was Titan against Titan; and, perusing them after the lapse of forty years, the philosophic critic will conclude which got the better of it, Lincoln or Douglas, much according to his sympathy with the one or the other. If Douglas had lived he would have become as Lincoln's right hand. Already, when he died, Lincoln was beginning to look to him and to lean upon him. Four years later they were joined together again on fame's eternal camping ground, each followed to the grave by a mourning people.

As I have said, Abraham Lincoln was an old-line Whig of the school of Henry Clay, with strong free-soil opinions, never an extremist or an Abolitionist. He was what they used to call in those old days "a Conscience Whig." He stood in awe of the Constitution and his oath of office. Hating slavery, he recognized its legal existence and its rights under the compact of the organic law. He wanted gradually to extinguish it, not to despoil those who held it as a property interest. He was so faithful to these principles that he approached emancipation not only with anxious deliberation, but with many misgivings. He issued his final proclamation as a military necessity; and, even then, so fair was his nature, he was meditating some kind of restitution.

Thus it came about that he was the one man in public life who could have taken the helm of affairs in 1861 handicapped by none of the resentments growing out of the anti-slavery battle. While Seward, Chase, Sumner, and the rest had been engaged in hand-to-hand combat with the Southern leaders at Washington, Lincoln, a philosopher and a statesman, had been observing the course of events from afar, and, like a philosopher and a statesman, his mind was irradiated and sweetened by the sense of humor. Throughout the contention that preceded the war, amid the passions inevitable to the war itself, not one bitter, proscriptive word escaped his lips or fell from his pen, while there was hardly a day that he was not projecting his great personality between some Southern man or woman and danger.

Had Lincoln lived! In that event it is quite certain that there would have been no era of reconstruction, with its repressive agencies and oppressive legislation. If Lincoln had lived there would have been wanting to the extremism of the time the bloody cue of his taking off to mount the steeds and spur the flanks of vengeance. For Lincoln entertained, with respect to the rehabilitation of the Union, the single wish that the Southern States—to use his familiar phraseology—"should come back home and behave themselves," and if he had lived he would have made this wish effectual as he made everything effectual to which he seriously addressed himself.

His was the genius of common sense. Of admirable intellectual aplomb, he sprang from a Virginia pedigree and was born in Kentucky. He knew all about the South, its institutions, its traditions, and its peculiarities. ''If slavery be not wrong,'' he said, ''nothing is wrong,'' but he also said, and reiterated it time and again: ''I have no prejudice against the Southern people. They are just what we would be in their situation. If slavery did not now exist among them they would not introduce it. If it did now exist among us we would not instantly give it up.''

The idea of paying the South for the slaves had been all along in his mind. He believed the North equally guilty with the South for the existence of slavery. He clearly understood that the irrepressible conflict was a conflict of systems, not merely a sectional and partisan quarrel. He was a considerate man, abhorring proscription. He wanted to leave the South no right to claim that the North, finding slave labor unremunerative, had sold its negroes to the South and then turned about and by force of arms confiscated what it had unloaded at a profit. He recognized slavery as property. In his message to Congress, of December, 1862, he proposed payment for the slaves, elaborating a scheme in detail and urging it with copious and cogent argument. ''The people of the South,'' said he, addressing a war Congress at that moment in the throes of bloody strife with the South, ''are not more responsible for the original introduction of this property than are the people of the North, and, when it is remembered how unhesitatingly we all use cotton and sugar and share the profits of dealing in them, it may not be quite safe to say that the South has been more responsible than the North for its continuance.''

This is the language not only of justice, but of far-reaching statesmanship.

Something more than two hundred and sixty years ago there arrived at the front of affairs in England one Cromwell. In the midst of monarchy he made a republic. It had no progenitor. It left no heirs at law. Why such cost of blood and treasure for an interval of freedom so equivocal and brief puzzled the wisest men and remained for centuries a mystery, though it is plain enough now and was long ago conceded, so that at last— dire rebel though he was—the name of Cromwell, held in execration through two hundred years, has a place in the history of the English-speaking races along with the names of William the Conqueror and Richard of the Lion Heart.

That which it took England two centuries to realize we in America have demonstrated within a single generation. Northerner or Southerner, none of us need fear that the future will fail to vindicate our integrity. When those are gone that fought the good fight, and philosophy comes to strike the balance sheet, it will be shown that the makers of the Constitution left the relation of the States to the Federal Government and of the Federal Government to the States open to a double construction. It will be told how the mistaken notion that slave labor was requisite to the profitable cultivation of sugar, rice, and cotton raised a paramount property interest in the Southern section of the Union, while in the Northern, responding to the impulse of modern thought and the outer movements of mankind, there arose a great moral sentiment against slavery. The conflict thus established, gradually but surely sectionalizing party lines, was wrought to bitter and bloody conclusion at Appomattox.

The battle was long though unequal. Let us believe that it was needful to make us a nation. Let us look upon it as into a mirror, seeing not the desolation of the past but the radiance of the present; and in the heroes of the new North and the new South who contested in generous rivalry up the fire-swept steep of El Caney and side by side reëmblazoned the national character in the waters about Corregidor Island and under the walls of Cavite, let us behold hostages for the old North and the old South blent together in a Union that recks not of the four points of the compass, having long ago flung its geography into the sea.

Henry Watterson

CHAPTER I

"The Union Is Perpetual"

[LINCOLN'S FIRST INAUGURAL AND THE DEBATE THEREON]

Speaking Tour of the President-elect on His Way to Washington—Remarks at Springfield, Ill., on "Divine Guidance"; at Indianapolis on "Preservation of the Union the People's Business, Not the President's"; to the Indiana Legislature on "The Union: Is It a Marriage Bond or a Free Love Arrangement?"; at Cincinnati on "Good Will to the South"; to the Ohio Legislature on "Nothing Is Going Wrong"; at Steubenville on "The Majority Should Rule"; at Pittsburgh on "Protection"; at Cleveland on "The Crisis Is Artificial"; at Buffalo on "Waiting for Developments"; at Albany on "President, Not Party Leader"; to the New York Legislature on "Reliance on the People"; at Poughkeepsie on "Standing by the Pilot"; at New York on "A Time for Silence" and "Save the Ship and Cargo—if Not Both, Then the Ship"; to the Senate of New Jersey on "The Liberty Inherited from the Fathers"; to the House of Representatives of New Jersey on "Putting the Foot Down Firmly"; at Philadelphia on "The Teachings of Independence Hall"; "The Principles of the Declaration," and "The Flag of the Union"; at Harrisburg on "The Men of Peace"; at Washington on "Misunderstanding Between the Sections"—His First Inaugural Address: "The Chorus of the Union"—Debate in the Senate upon the Address: Thomas L. Clingman [N. C.], Stephen A. Douglas [Ill.], Louis T. Wigfall [Tex.], James M. Mason [Va.]; Lafayette S. Foster [Conn.] Moves in the House to Expel Senator Wigfall; Motion Is Not Brought to Vote—The Senate Declares That the Seats of Senators from Seceded States Are Vacant.

ON February 11, 1861, the President-elect left his home at Springfield, Ill., to travel by a circuitous route to the national capital, there to be inaugurated on March 4. In a parting speech to his neighbors he expressed a solemn sense of his responsibility and a reliance upon "that Divine Being who ever attended Washington," the first President, upon whom rested a similar responsibility.

9

At Indianapolis, upon the same day, he addressed the citizens, saying: "To the salvation of the Union there needs but a single thing—the hearts of a people like yours." The preservation of the Union, he repeated, "is your business, not mine; not with Presidents, not with politicians, but with you is the question."

To the Indiana legislature he spoke on "The Union: Is it a Marriage Bond or a Free Love Arrangement?" claiming that the South regarded it as the latter. "Coercion," he said, could not properly be applied to the enforcement of Federal laws in South Carolina, but it could be so applied to the attempt of that State, being not one fiftieth part of the nation in soil and population, to break up the nation and force a proportionally larger subdivision of itself (the Union men in the State) into compliance with the act.

To the citizens of Cincinnati, on February 12, being on the border of the slave States, he expressed good will to the South, repeating a former speech which he had made in the city in 1859, in which he said: "We mean to treat you, as near as we possibly can, as Washington, Jefferson, and Madison treated you. We mean to leave you alone, and in no way to interfere with your institutions, to abide by all and every compromise of the Constitution."

On February 13 he addressed the Ohio legislature at Columbus, assuring them that he had not hitherto preserved silence on the state of the country from any want of real anxiety, as had been charged. Anxiety he felt, but not alarm, for "there is nothing going wrong." "Time, patience, and a reliance on that God who has never forsaken this people" would save the Union.

On February 14 he addressed the citizens of Steubenville, O., on the subject: "The Majority Should Rule." Where is there a judge to be found between the majority and the minority? Since one of the two, therefore, must rule, shall we submit to the minority? Would that be right? Would it be just or generous?

At Pittsburgh on February 15 he declared that the crisis was artificial, and, as if to minimize its importance, he spoke on the tariff, since, even in the stress which was threatening to tear the Union asunder, the citizens of Pennsylvania seemed to be primarily interested in that subject.

On the same day, at Cleveland, he returned to the theme that the crisis was an artificial one.

What they do who seek to destroy the Union is altogether artificial. What is happening to hurt them? Have they not all their rights now as they ever have had? Do not they have their fugitive slaves returned now as ever? Have they not the same Constitution that they have lived under for seventy-odd years? Have they not a position as citizens of this common country, and have we any power to change that position? [*Cries of "No!"*] What, then, is the matter with them? Why all this excitement? Why all these complaints? As I said before, this crisis is altogether artificial. It has no foundation in fact. It can't be argued up, and it can't be argued down. Let it alone, and it will go down of itself.

At Buffalo on February 16 he excused himself from telling his specific plans to save the Union.

When it is considered that these difficulties are without precedent, and have never been acted upon by any individual situated as I am, it is most proper I should wait and see the developments, and get all the light possible, so that when I do speak authoritatively I may be as near right as possible. When I shall speak authoritatively I hope to say nothing inconsistent with the Constitution, the Union, the rights of all the States, of each State, and of each section of the country, and not to disappoint the reasonable expectations of those who have confided to me their votes.

On February 18 he spoke to the citizens of Albany, saying that he intended to be the President, not of a party, but of the nation. On the same day he addressed the New York legislature, which had tendered him unanimous support, saying that he was the "humblest of all individuals that had been elevated to the Presidency"; and yet, with a more difficult task before him than had confronted any, Mr. Lincoln expressed confidence in the Almighty that, with the help of the people, these difficulties would be overcome.

On February 19 at Poughkeepsie, N. Y., he expressed the sentiment that, though he had not been the choice of all the people to "pilot the ship of State," he was confident that the defeated party were desirous of "running it through the tempest in safety," and would loyally support him in his endeavor to do so.

On the same day he spoke to the citizens of New York City on the theme, "There Is a Time for Silence." He would wait until the proper moment to announce details of his policy. For the present it sufficed to say that he would propose nothing in conflict with the Constitution, or the Union, or the perpetuation of the liberties of the people.

Replying to the reception accorded him by the mayor of the city, he returned to his former simile of the ship of state, saying that he would save, if possible, both ship and cargo, but, if necessary, the ship without the cargo.

He addressed the Senate and House of the New Jersey legislature at Trenton on February 21. Speaking to the Senate on the revolutionary memories aroused by the name of the State capital, he implored them to save the liberty inherited from the Fathers of the country. To the House he said, adverting to the fact that most of them were his political opponents, he would perform his duties in no partisan spirit.

I shall do all that may be in my power to promote a peaceful settlement of all our difficulties. The man does not live who is more devoted to peace than I am, none who would do more to preserve it, but it may be necessary to put the foot down firmly. [Here the audience broke out in cheers so loud and long that for some moments it was impossible to hear Mr. Lincoln's voice.] And if I do my duty and do right, you will sustain me, will you not? [Loud cheers and cries of "Yes, yes; we will."]

At Philadelphia on February 21 Mr. Lincoln addressed the citizens on "The Teachings of Independence

Hall," pledging himself never to do anything inconsistent with these. On the following day (Washington's birthday) he spoke in Independence Hall. Amplifying his remarks of the former day he said:

I have never had a feeling politically that did not spring from the sentiments embodied in the Declaration of Independence. I have often pondered over the dangers which were incurred by the men who assembled here and framed and adopted that Declaration. I have pondered over the toils that were endured by the officers and soldiers of the army who achieved that independence. I have often inquired of myself what great principle or idea it was that kept this confederacy so long together. It was not the mere matter of separation of the colonies from the motherland, but that sentiment in the Declaration of Independence which gave liberty not alone to the people of this country, but hope to all the world, for all future time. It was that which gave promise that in due time the weights would be lifted from the shoulders of all men, and that all should have an equal chance. Now, my friends, can this country be saved on that basis? If it can, I will consider myself one of the happiest men in the world if I can help to save it. If it cannot be saved upon that principle, it will be truly awful. But if this country cannot be saved without giving up that principle I was about to say I would rather be assassinated on this spot than surrender it.[1] Now, in my view of the present aspect of affairs, there is no need of bloodshed and war. There is no necessity for it. I am not in favor of such a course; and I may say in advance that there will be no bloodshed unless it is forced upon the Government. The Government will not use force unless force is used against it.

My friends, this is wholly an unprepared speech. I did not expect to be called on to say a word when I came here. I supposed I was merely to do something toward raising a flag. I may, therefore, have said something indiscreet. [Cries of "No, no."] But I have said nothing but what I am willing to live by, and, if it be the pleasure of Almighty God, to die by.

When the flag to which Mr. Lincoln referred was raised, he called attention to the new star which had been placed upon it for Kansas, admitted into the Union on January 29:

[1] Threats had been made that the President-elect would never take his seat.

I think we may promise ourselves that not only the new star placed upon that flag shall be permitted to remain there to our permanent prosperity for years to come, but additional ones shall from time to time be placed there until we shall number, as it was anticipated by the great historian, five hundred millions of happy and prosperous people.

On the same day, at Harrisburg, Pa., he replied to the welcome of Governor Andrew G. Curtin, saying:

Allusion has been made to the peaceful principles upon which this great commonwealth was originally settled. Allow me to add my meed of praise to those peaceful principles. I hope no one of the Friends who originally settled here, or who lived here since that time, or who lives here now, has been or is a more devoted lover of peace, harmony, and concord than my humble self.

While I have been proud to see to-day the finest military array, I think, that I have ever seen, allow me to say, in regard to those men, that they give hope of what may be done when war is inevitable. But, at the same time, allow me to express the hope that, in the shedding of blood, their services may never be needed, especially in the shedding of fraternal blood. It shall be my endeavor to preserve the peace of this country so far as it can possibly be done consistently with the maintenance of the institutions of the country. With my consent or without my great displeasure, this country shall never witness the shedding of one drop of blood in fraternal strife.

Later he addressed the State legislature in the same vein.

From Harrisburg Mr. Lincoln went secretly to Washington, since those who were managing his tour wished to guard against his assassination on the way, which had been threatened. On his arrival at the national capital he was welcomed by the mayor. Mr. Lincoln assured those present that he had as kindly feeling toward the slaveholding section as toward his own, and was confident that the enmity between the two was only the result of a misunderstanding. Replying to a serenade the next evening (February 28) he repeated his assurances of fair dealing toward the whole country.

On March 4 he delivered his inaugural address be-

fore a vast crowd of people assembled from all parts of
the country.

A tentative draft of this, the most important of his
utterances, Lincoln wrote and had privately printed
while at his home in Springfield, Ill.   On his way to
Washington he gave a copy to his friend, O. H. Browning, at Indianapolis, who suggested that the statement

LINCOLN AND SEWARD RUNNING THE UNION ENGINE

therein that Lincoln would "reclaim" the Federal property in the hands of the secessionists should be omitted,
as subject to construction as a threat, and as such unnecessarily aggravating to the South.   This suggestion
the President adopted.   On arriving at Washington Mr.
Lincoln gave a copy of the draft to William H. Seward,
his appointee as Secretary of State.   Mr. Seward suggested two important changes, one that was virtually
Mr. Browning's emendation, and the other the omission
of a statement that the President would follow the principles of the Republican platform.   Referring to the

latter, he reminded Lincoln that Jefferson, at a similar crisis when the opposing party sought to dismember the Government, "sank the partisan in the patriot in his inaugural address, and propitiated his adversaries by declaring: 'We are all Federalists, all Republicans.'" Most of Seward's other suggestions related to improvements in rhetoric. His "general remarks" were as follows:

The argument is strong and conclusive, and ought not to be in any way abridged or modified.

But something besides or in addition to argument is needful to meet and remove prejudice and passion in the South and despondency in the East.

Some words of affection—some of calm and cheerful confidence.

Mr. Seward submitted two paragraphs of his own as suggestions for closing the speech in a conciliatory and cheerful manner. The second was in that poetic vein which occasionally cropped out in Seward's speeches and writings, and over which Lincoln, on better acquaintance, was wont good-naturedly to rally him. Seward wrote:

I close. We are not, we must not be, aliens or enemies, but fellow countrymen and brethren. Although passion has strained our bonds of affection too hardly, they must not, I am sure they will not, be broken. The mystic chords which, proceeding from so many battlefields and so many patriot graves, pass through all the hearts and all hearths in this broad continent of ours, will yet again harmonize in their ancient music when breathed upon by the guardian angel of the nation.

Lincoln took this paragraph, and by deft touches which reveal a literary taste beyond that of any statesman of his time, transformed it into his peroration. More than anything else in the address, it was the tender spirit and chaste beauty of these closing words that convinced the people that Lincoln measured up to the high mental stature demanded of one who was to be their leader during the most critical period of the life of the nation.

The Chorus of the Union

President Lincoln's First Inaugural Address

The President began by assuring the people of the South that their peace would not be endangered, as they apprehended, by the accession of a Republican Administration. He quoted from one of his former speeches a declaration that he had neither the right nor the intention to interfere with slavery where it existed, and referred to a plank in the Republican platform showing that the same was true of his party.

I add, too, that all the protection which, consistently with the Constitution and the laws, can be given will be cheerfully given to all the States when lawfully demanded, for whatever cause—as cheerfully to one section as to another.

The return of fugitive slaves he regarded as a constitutional obligation which he and the national legislators were, by their unanimous oaths, bound to see executed. If Congressmen "would make the effort in good temper," he said, "could they not, with nearly equal unanimity, frame and pass a law by means of which to keep good that unanimous oath?"
It mattered little whether the surrender of fugitive slaves was by national or State authority.

If the slave is to be surrendered, it can be of but little consequence to him or to others by which authority it is done. And should anyone in any case be content that his oath shall go unkept on a merely unsubstantial controversy as to how it shall be kept?

However, abuses of the Fugitive Slave act should be remedied so that no free man should be delivered to slavery.

And might it not be well at the same time to provide by law for the enforcement of that clause in the Constitution which guarantees that "the citizen of each State shall be entitled to all privileges and immunities of citizens in the several States?"

He continued:

I take the official oath to-day with no mental reservations, and with no purpose to construe the Constitution or laws by any hypercritical rules. And, while I do not choose now to specify particular acts of Congress as proper to be enforced, I do suggest that it will be much safer for all, both in official and private stations, to conform to and abide by all those acts which stand unrepealed, than to violate any of them, trusting to find impunity in having them held to be unconstitutional.

He then turned to the question of secession.

I hold that, in contemplation of universal law and of the Constitution, the Union of these States is perpetual. Perpetuity is implied, if not expressed, in the fundamental law of all national governments. It is safe to assert that no government proper ever had a provision in its organic law for its own termination. Continue to execute all the express provisions of our National Constitution, and the Union will endure forever—it being impossible to destroy it except by some action not provided for in the instrument itself.

Again, if the United States be not a government proper, but an association of States in the nature of contract merely, can it, as a contract, be peaceably unmade by less than all the parties who made it? One party to a contract may violate it—break it, so to speak; but does it not require all lawfully to rescind it?

He argued from history that the Union is perpetual. It is older than the Constitution, having been formed by the Articles of Association in 1774, confirmed by the Declaration of Independence, and specifically plighted as perpetual in the Confederation.

But the Constitution was formed to secure ''a more perfect union.'' Therefore,

If the destruction of the Union by one or by a part only of the States be lawfully possible, the Union is less perfect than before the Constitution, having lost the vital element of perpetuity.

It follows, from these views, that no State, upon its own mere motion, can lawfully get out of the Union; that resolves and ordinances to that effect are legally void; and that acts of violence, within any State or States, against the authority of the United States, are insurrectionary or revolutionary, according to circumstances.

I therefore consider that, in view of the Constitution and the laws, the Union is unbroken; and to the extent of my ability I shall take care, as the Constitution itself expressly enjoins upon me, that the laws of the Union be faithfully executed in all the States. Doing this I deem to be only a simple duty on my part; and I shall perform it so far as prac-

COLUMBIA DEMANDS HER CHILDREN
From the collection of the New York Historical Society

ticable, unless my rightful masters, the American people, shall withhold the requisite means or in some authoritative manner direct the contrary. I trust this will not be regarded as a menace, but only as the declared purpose of the Union that it will constitutionally defend and maintain itself.

In doing this there needs to be no bloodshed or violence; and there shall be none, unless it be forced upon the national authority. The power confided to me will be used to hold, occupy, and possess the property and places belonging to the Government, and to collect the duties and imposts; but, beyond what may be necessary for these objects, there will be no invasion, no using of force against or among the people anywhere.

Where hostility to the United States in any interior locality shall be so great and universal as to prevent competent resident citizens from holding the Federal offices, there will be no attempt to force obnoxious strangers among the people for that object. While the strict legal right may exist in the Government to enforce the exercise of these offices, the attempt to do so would be so irritating, and so nearly impracticable withal, that I deem it better to forego for the time the uses of such offices.

The mails, unless repelled, will continue to be furnished in all parts of the Union. So far as possible, the people everywhere shall have that sense of perfect security which is most favorable to calm thought and reflection. The course here indicated will be followed unless current events and experience shall show a modification or change to be proper, and in every case and exigency my best discretion will be exercised according to circumstances actually existing, and with a view and a hope of a peaceful solution of the national troubles and the restoration of fraternal sympathies and affections.

That there are persons in one section or another who seek to destroy the Union at all events, and are glad of any pretext to do it, I will neither affirm nor deny; but, if there be such, I need address no word to them. To those, however, who really love the Union may I not speak?

Before entering upon so grave a matter as the destruction of our national fabric, with all its benefits, its memories, and its hopes, would it not be wise to ascertain precisely why we do it? Will you hazard so desperate a step while there is any possibility that any portion of the ills you fly from have no real existence? Will you, while the certain ills you fly to are greater than all the real ones you fly from—will you ask the commission of so fearful a mistake?

All profess to be content in the Union if all constitutional rights can be maintained. Is it true, then, that any right, plainly written in the Constitution, has been denied? I think not. Happily, the human mind is so constituted that no party can reach to the audacity of doing this. Think, if you can, of a single instance in which a plainly written provision of the Constitution has ever been denied. If, by the mere force of numbers, a majority should deprive a minority of any clearly written constitutional right, it might, in a moral point of view, justify revolution—certainly would if such a right were a vital one. But such is not our case. All the vital rights of minorities and of individuals are so plainly assured to them by affirmations and negations, guaranties and prohibitions, in the Constitution, that controversies never arise concerning them. But no organic law can ever be framed with a provision specifically applicable to every question which may occur in practical administration. No foresight can anticipate, nor any document of reasonable length contain, express provisions for all possible questions. Shall fugitives from labor be surrendered by national or by State authority? The Constitution does not expressly say, *May* Congress prohibit slavery in the Territories? The Constitution does not expressly say: *Must* Congress protect slavery in the Territories? The Constitution does not expressly say.

From questions of this class spring all our constitutional controversies, and we divide upon them into majorities and minorities. If the minority will not acquiesce, the majority must, or the Government must cease. There is no other alternative; for continuing the Government is acquiescence on one side or the other.

If a minority in such case will secede rather than acquiesce, they make a precedent which in turn will divide and ruin them; for a minority of their own will secede from them whenever a majority refuses to be controlled by such minority. For instance, why may not any portion of a new confederacy a year or two hence arbitrarily secede again, precisely as portions of the present Union now claim to secede from it? All who cherish disunion sentiments are now being educated to the exact temper of doing this.

Is there such perfect identity of interests among the States to compose a new Union as to produce harmony only and prevent renewed secession?

Plainly, the central idea of secession is the essence of anarchy. A majority held in restraint by constitutional checks and limitations, and always changing easily with deliberate changes of popular opinions and sentiments, is the only true sovereign of a free people. Whoever rejects it does, of necessity, fly to anarchy or to despotism. Unanimity is impossible; the rule of a minority, as a permanent arrangement, is wholly inadmissible; so that, rejecting the majority principle, anarchy or despotism in some form is all that is left.

I do not forget the position assumed by some that constitutional questions are to be decided by the Supreme Court; nor do I deny that such decisions must be binding, in any case, upon the parties to a suit, as to the object of that suit, while they are also entitled to very high respect and consideration in all parallel cases by all other departments of the Government.

And, while it is obviously possible that such decision may be erroneous in any given case, still the evil effect following it, being limited to that particular case, with the chance that it may be overruled and never become a precedent for other cases, can better be borne than could the evils of a different practice. At the same time the candid citizen must confess that if the policy of the Government upon vital questions affecting the whole people is to be irrevocably fixed by decisions of the Supreme Court the instant they are made, in ordinary litigation between parties in personal actions, the people will have ceased to be their own rulers, having to that extent practically resigned their government into the hands of that eminent tribunal. Nor is there in this view any assault upon the court or the judges. It is a duty from which they may not shrink to decide cases properly brought before them, and it is no fault of theirs if others seek to turn their decisions to political purposes.

One section of our country believes slavery is right and ought to be extended, while the other believes it is wrong and ought not to be extended. This is the only substantial dispute. The fugitive slave clause of the Constitution and the law for the suppression of the foreign slave trade are each as well enforced, perhaps, as any law can ever be in a community where the moral sense of the people imperfectly supports the law itself. The great body of the people abide by the dry legal obligation in both cases, and a few break over in each. This, I think, cannot be perfectly cured; and it would be worse in both cases after the separation of the sections than before. The foreign slave trade, now imperfectly suppressed, would be ultimately revived, without restriction, in one section, while fugitive slaves, now only partially surrendered, would not be surrendered at all by the other.

Physically speaking, we cannot separate. We cannot remove our respective sections from each other, nor build an impassable wall between them. A husband and wife may be divorced, and go out of the presence and beyond the reach of each other; but the different parts of our country cannot do this. They cannot but remain face to face, and intercourse, either amicable or hostile, must continue between them. Is it possible, then, to make that intercourse more advantageous or more satisfactory after separation than before? Can aliens make treaties easier than friends can make laws? Can treaties be more faithfully enforced between aliens than laws can among friends? Suppose you go to war, you cannot fight always; and when, after much loss on both sides and no gain on either, you cease fighting, the identical old questions as to terms of intercourse are again upon you.

This country, with its institutions, belongs to the people who inhabit it. Whenever they shall grow weary of the existing Government, they can exercise their constitutional right of amending it, or their revolutionary right to dismember or overthrow it. I cannot be ignorant of the fact that many worthy and patriotic citizens are desirous of having the National Con-

"DOMESTIC TROUBLES"

From the collection of the New York Historical Society

stitution amended. While I make no recommendation of amendments, I fully recognize the rightful authority of the people over the whole subject, to be exercised in either of the modes prescribed in the instrument itself; and I should, under existing circumstances, favor rather than oppose a fair opportunity being afforded the people to act upon it. I will venture to add that to me the convention mode seems preferable, in that it allows amendments to originate with the people themselves, instead of only permitting them to take or reject propositions originated by others not especially chosen for the purpose, and which might not be precisely such as they would wish to either accept or refuse. I understand a proposed amendment to the Constitution—which amendment, however, I have not seen—has passed

Congress, to the effect that the Federal Government shall never interfere with the domestic institutions of the States, including that of persons held to service. To avoid misconstruction of what I have said, I depart from my purpose not to speak of particular amendments so far as to say that, holding such a provision to now be implied constitutional law, I have no objection to its being made express and irrevocable.

The Chief Magistrate derives all his authority from the people, and they have conferred none upon him to fix terms for the separation of the States. The people themselves can do this also if they choose; but the Executive, as such, has nothing to do with it. His duty is to administer the present Government, as it came to his hands, and to transmit it, unimpaired by him, to his successor.

Why should there not be a patient confidence in the ultimate justice of the people? Is there any better or equal hope in the world? In our present differences is either party without faith of being in the right? If the Almighty Ruler of Nations, with his eternal truth and justice, be on your side of the North, or on yours of the South, that truth and that justice will surely prevail by the judgment of this great tribunal of the American people.

By the frame of the Government under which we live, this same people have wisely given their public servants but little power for mischief; and have, with equal wisdom, provided for the return of that little to their own hands at very short intervals. While the people retain their virtue and vigilance, no Administration, by any extreme of wickedness or folly, can very seriously injure the Government in the short space of four years. My countrymen, one and all, think calmly and well upon this whole subject. Nothing valuable can be lost by taking time. If there be an object to hurry any of you in hot haste to a step which you would never take deliberately, that object will be frustrated by taking time; but no good object can be frustrated by it. Such of you as are now dissatisfied still have the old Constitution unimpaired, and, on the sensitive point, the laws of your own framing under it; while the new Administration will have no immediate power, if it would, to change either. If it were admitted that you who are dissatisfied hold the right side in the dispute, there still is no single good reason for precipitate action. Intelligence, patriotism, Christianity, and a firm reliance on Him who has never yet forsaken this favored land are still competent to adjust in the best way all our present difficulty.

In your hands, my dissatisfied fellow countrymen, and not in mine is the momentous issue of civil war. The Government will not assail you. You can have no conflict without being yourselves the aggressors. You have no oath registered in heaven to destroy the Government, while I shall have the most solemn one to "preserve, protect, and defend it."

I am loath to close. We are not enemies, but friends. We must not be enemies. Though passion may have strained, it must not break our bonds of affection. The mystic chords of memory, stretching from every battlefield and patriot grave to every living heart and hearthstone all over this broad land, will yet swell the chorus of the Union when again touched, as surely they will be, by the better angels of our nature.

DEBATE UPON THE PRESIDENT'S INAUGURAL

SENATE, MARCH 4, 1861

President Buchanan had convened the Senate in special session on March 4 to receive and act upon such communications as might be made by his successor. It so met and was in session until March 28.

Upon motion made to print copies of the inaugural address of President Lincoln, Thomas L. Clingman [N. C.] took occasion to dissent from its views as leading to war with the seceded States.

The President declares expressly that he intends to treat those States as though they were still members of the Union; as though the acts of secession were mere nullities; and, as they claim to be independent, there can be no result except a collision. In plain, unmistakable language he declares that it is his purpose to hold, occupy, and possess the forts and arsenals in those States. We all know that he can hold them only by dispossessing the State authorities. He says, further, that it is his purpose to collect the revenue from those States. Surely I need not argue to any Senator that this must lead to a collision of arms. After we declared independence from Great Britain nobody supposed that the colonies were willing still to pay taxes or duties to the British Government. In point of fact, they refused to pay them even before the Declaration of Independence.

Stephen A. Douglas [Ill.] replied:

Mr. President, I cannot assent to the construction which the Senator from North Carolina [Mr. Clingman] has placed upon the President's inaugural. I have read it carefully, with a view of ascertaining distinctly what the policy of the Administration is to be. The inaugural is characterized by ability and by directness on certain points; but with such reservations and qualifications as require a critical analysis to arrive at its true construction on other points. I have made such an analysis, and come to the conclusion that it is a peace-offering rather than a war message. I think I can demonstrate that there is no foundation for the apprehension which has been spread through the country that this message is equivalent to a declaration of war; that it commits the President of the United States to recapture the forts in the seceded States, and to hold them at all hazards; to collect the revenue under all circumstances; and to execute the laws in all the States, no matter what may be the circumstances that surround him. I do not understand that to be the character of the message. On the contrary, I understand it to contain a distinct pledge that the policy of the Administration shall be conducted with exclusive reference to a peaceful solution of our national difficulties. True, the President indicates a certain line of policy which he intends to pursue, so far as it may be consistent with the peace of the country; but he assures us that this policy will be modified and changed whenever necessary to a peaceful solution of these difficulties.

The President declares that, in view of the Constitution and laws, the Union remains unbroken. I do not suppose any man can deny the proposition that, in contemplation of law, the Union remains intact, no matter what the fact may be. There may be a separation *de facto,* temporary or permanent, as the sequel may prove; but, in contemplation of the Constitution and the laws, the Union does remain unbroken. Let us see what there is in the address that is supposed to pledge the President to a coercive policy. He says:

"I shall take care, as the Constitution itself expressly enjoins upon me, that the laws of the Union be faithfully executed in all the States."

This declaration is relied upon as conclusive evidence that coercion is to be used in the seceding States; but take the next sentence:

"Doing this I deem to be only a simple duty on my part. I shall perform it, so far as is practicable, unless my rightful masters, the American people, shall withhold the requisite means, or in some other authoritative manner direct the contrary.''

This condition, on which he will not enforce the laws in the seceding States, is not as explicit as I could desire. When he alludes to his ''rightful masters, the American people,'' I suppose he means the action of Congress withholding the requisite means. Query: does he wish to be understood as saying that the existing laws confer upon him ''the requisite means''? or does he mean to say that, inasmuch as the existing laws do not confer the requisite means, he cannot execute the laws in the seceding States unless those means shall be conferred by Congress? The language employed would seem to imply that the President was referring to the future action of Congress as necessary to give him the requisite means to enforce obedience to the laws in the seceding States.

In a subsequent paragraph he says:

''The power confided to me will be used to hold, occupy, and possess the property and places belonging to the Government, and to collect the duties and imposts.''

What power? Does he mean that which has been confided or that which may be confided? Does he mean that he will exercise the power unless Congress directs the contrary or that he will exercise it when Congress confers it? I regret that this clause is understood by some persons as meaning that the President will use the whole military force of the country to recapture the forts and other places which have been seized without the assent of Congress. If such was his meaning, he was unfortunate in the selection of words to express the idea.

He says further:

''But, beyond what may be necessary for these objects, there will be no invasion, no using of force against or among the people anywhere.''

He will use the power confided to him to hold, occupy, and possess the forts and other property, and to collect the revenue; but beyond these objects he will not use that power. I am unable to understand the propriety of the distinction between enforcing the revenue laws and all other laws. If it is his duty to enforce the revenue laws, why is it not his duty to enforce the other laws of the land? What right has he to say that he will enforce those laws that enable him to raise revenue, to levy and collect taxes from the people, and that he will not enforce the laws which protect the rights of persons and property to the extent that the Constitution confers the power in those States? I reject the distinction; it cannot be justified in law or in morals.

The next paragraph is also objectionable. I will read it:

"Where hostility of the United States in any *interior* locality shall be so great and universal as to prevent competent resident citizens from holding the Federal offices, there will be no attempt to force obnoxious strangers among the people for that object."

I rejoice to know that he will not attempt to force obnoxious strangers to hold office in the interior places where public sentiment is hostile; but why draw the distinction between "interior localities" and exterior places? Why the distinction between the States in the interior and those upon the seaboard? If he has the power in the one case, he has it in the other; if it be his duty in the one case, it is his duty in the other. There is no provision of the Constitution or the laws which authorizes a distinction between the places upon the seaboard and the places in the interior.

This brings me to the consideration of another clause in the message which I deem the most important of all and the key to his entire policy.

After indicating the line of policy which he would pursue, if consistent with the peace of the country, he tells us emphatically that that course will be followed, unless modifications and changes should be necessary to a peaceful solution of the national troubles; and if in any case or exigency a change of policy should be necessary, it will be made "with a view and hope of a peaceful solution." In other words, if the collection of the revenue leads to a peaceful solution, it is to be collected; if the abandonment of that policy is necessary to a peaceful solution, the revenue is not to be collected; if the recapture of Fort Moultrie would tend to a peaceful solution, he stands pledged to recapture it; if the recapture would tend to violence and war, he is pledged not to recapture it; if the enforcement of the laws in the seceding States would tend to facilitate a peaceful solution, he is pledged to their enforcement; if the omission to enforce those laws would best facilitate peace, he is pledged to omit to enforce them; if maintaining possession of Fort Sumter would facilitate peace, he stands pledged to retain its possession; if, on the contrary, the abandonment of Fort Sumter and the withdrawal of the troops would facilitate a peaceful solution, he is pledged to abandon the fort and withdraw the troops.

Sir, this is the only construction that I can put upon this clause. If this be not the true interpretation, for what purpose was it inserted? The line of policy that he had indicated was stated vaguely; but there is not a pledge to use coercion.

I submit, then, to the Senate whether the friends of peace have not much to rejoice at in the inaugural address of the President. It is a much more conservative document than I had anticipated. It is a much more pacific and conciliatory paper than I had expected. I am clearly of the opinion that the Administration stands pledged by the inaugural to a peaceful solution of all our difficulties, to do no act that leads to war, and to change its policy just so often and whenever a change is necessary to preserve the peace.

Now, sir, far be it from me to intimate that the President, in these recommendations, has not been faithful to the principles of his party, as well as to the honor and safety of his country. Whatever departure from party platforms he has made in these recommendations should be regarded as an evidence of patriotism, and not an act of infidelity. In my opinion, if I have understood the inaugural right, he has sunk the partisan in the patriot, and he is entitled to the thanks of all conservative men to that extent. I do not wish it to be inferred, from anything I have said or have omitted to say, that I have any political sympathy with his Administration, or that I expect that any contingency can happen in which I may be identified with it. I expect to oppose his Administration with all my energy on those great principles which have separated parties in former times; but on this one question—that of preserving the Union by a peaceful solution of our present difficulties; that of preventing any future difficulties by such an amendment of the Constitution as will settle the question by an express provision —if I understand his true intent and meaning, I am with him.

Mr. President, if the result shall prove that I have put a wrong construction on the inaugural, I shall deplore the consequences which a belligerent and aggressive policy may inflict upon our beloved country, without being responsible in any degree for the disasters and calamities which may follow. I believe I have placed upon it its true interpretation. I know I have put the patriotic construction on it. I believe the action of the President will justify that construction. I will never relinquish that belief and hope until he shall have done such acts as render it impossible to preserve the peace of the country and the unity of the States. Sir, this Union cannot be preserved by war. It cannot be cemented by blood. It can be preserved only by peaceful means. And, when our present troubles shall have been settled, future difficulties can be prevented only by constitutional amendments which will put an end to all controversy by express provision. These remedies and preventives have been clearly marked out by the President in his inaugural. All I ask is that his Administration shall adhere to them and carry them out in good faith. Let this be done, and all who join in the good work will deserve, and they will receive, the applause and approbation of a grateful country. No partisan advantage can be taken, no political capital should be made out of a generous act of noble patriotism. While I expect to oppose the Administration upon all the political issues of the day, I trust I shall never hesitate to do justice to those who, by their devotion to the Constitution and the Union, show that they love their country more than their party.

LOUIS T. WIGFALL [Tex.].—It is impossible for the Senator from Illinois, or for any other Senator to rise here, and, by giving a commentary—a construction—of the inaugural to restore peace to the country. It is impossible for the Administration, by dealing in generalities, whether glittering or not, to give peace to the country. It is a fact that seven States have withdrawn from this Union; that they have entered into a new compact with each other; that they have established a government; and I suppose, though it may not have yet been officially announced, as it is a fact that is well known, I may allude to it, they have their representatives now here, prepared to reside near this court, and, waiving all questions of irregularity as to the existence of this Government, to enter into a treaty with it in reference to matters which must be settled, either by treaty or by the sword.

It is easy to indulge in general phraseology; it is easy to write so as to be misunderstood. It is very easy to talk of enforcing the laws; it is very easy to speak of holding, occupying, and possessing forts; but, when you come to holding, occupying, and possessing forts, bayonets and not words settle the question. This Administration will, by action, be forced to construe its inaugural. How will that inaugural be construed? Were it not for these facts which are pressing for solution, it might be that a Union party, both North and South, might be organized; and, were it not for these troublesome things called bayonets, platforms might be adopted to be construed differently on different sides of particular degrees of latitude; but, unfortunately for the Union-savers, these matters are practical, pressing for present solution; and this Government may leave Fort

Moultrie, Castle Pinckney, and Fort Johnson in the possession of the Confederate States, but the Confederate States will not leave Fort Sumter in the possession of this Government.

I am one of those who deny that this Union, as it formerly was, now exists legally, constitutionally. The Union has been disrupted. Seven of the high contracting powers have withdrawn from this Government (that now *de facto* exists at Washington) the powers heretofore exercised by them through this Government, and invested all those powers in their separate State governments first, and then entered into a new compact with each other.

These are facts. How are you going to deal with them? What is a remedy in one stage of a disease is no remedy in another. A blue-mass pill and a cup of coffee next morning will relieve the liver and prevent one from having a fever very frequently; but when the disease is on you, blistering and blood-letting may sometimes be necessary; and when the patient is dead, then it is necessary to have a coffin, a grave-digger, funeral services, and things of that sort; the only question is whether we shall have a decent, peaceable, quiet funeral or whether we shall have an Irish wake.

"Cannot preserve this Union by war!" Why, sir, there is no Union left. You may have reconstruction. The States that are now in the old Union may secede from it to the other, and come into the new Union, and, in the course of time, the thirty-four States may all be living under the same form of government again; but the seven States that have withdrawn from this Union are surely never coming back. If you were to give them a sheet of blank paper, and tell them to write their constitution on it, they would not come in again and live under this Administration. They are out; they have formed a union; they have a constitution, and it is satisfactory to them; and they will not secede again. Our doctrine of secession has been so belittled and so belied that we are beginning to have a downright contemptuous opinion of it ourselves; and we never intend to exercise it again. Other States that have not made the experiment may secede and come to us; Mohammed may come to the mountain, but the mountain will never come to Mohammed.

You have, therefore, to deal with all these things practically. What will you do? Getting up here and making constructions of Mr. Lincoln's message is not the remedy. To have persuaded the people of the seven seceded States at one time that the Republican party was a very conservative, Constitution-loving party might have prevented the act of secession; but it will do

no good now.   The act of secession has been committed; a new
government has been formed, and new remedies must be offered.   *Tempora mutantur, et nos mutamur in illis.*[1]   The question now is not of saving the Union, but of saving the peace of
the country.   Withdraw your troops; acknowledge the right of
self-government; make no futile attempt to collect tribute from
people who are no longer citizens of the United States; do these
things and you will have peace.   Send your flag into that
country with thirty-four stars upon it, and it will be fired at
and war will ensue.

The seceded States—having paid much of the money into
the Federal Treasury, with which your army was organized and
your navy built, with which your lighthouses and your buoys
were placed, your harbors cleaned out, and the public domain
acquired—send commissioners here to their former associates,
and ask them to enter into a fair arrangement for the division
of the public property and the assessment of the public debt.
Will you do that?   Or will you sit stupidly and idly gazing on
until there shall be a conflict of arms, because you cannot "compromise with traitors"—because you cannot recognize the independence of States that were States before this Government had
existence?

Senators, what is the meaning of this declaration?   It is that,
if we acknowledge ourselves to be slaves; if we will abandon the
right of self-government; if we will agree to be governed by
you, you promise us to govern us well.   We say first acknowledge our right of self-government; withdraw your troops; yield
to us the right of collecting our own revenues; divide fairly
the public property; give us our *pro rata* share of men-of-war
that are now afloat; send us our *pro rata* share of the army—
we want two, three, or four of the regiments; turn them over to
us; give us our share of the public domain—do these things,
and we will, *pro tempore*, enter into with you a treaty of commerce, of peace, and amity; and if you will reorganize your
own Government, and form such a one as suits us, we may
again confederate with you and enter into a compact of common defence and general welfare.   Refuse it and we will settle
this question by the sword.

There is no dodging these issues.   If you want war, you will
have it; if you want peace, we are anxious for it; but the time
has passed for party platforms; the time has passed for dema-
gogism to adopt compromises which mean nothing.   These are
plain, palpable issues, and they have to be met.

  [1] "Times change, and we change with them."

The President of the United States and the Senator from Illinois both misapprehend, utterly and wholly, the issues that are before the country. They seem to think that the whole difficulty is as to the question of the Wilmot proviso or squatter sovereignty in the Territories. These are dead issues; they are past; they were discussed; they have been decided upon; they are *res adjudicata*.

Seven States have withdrawn from the Union. What are the remaining States going to do? Preserve the Union you cannot, for it is dissolved. Conquer those States and hold them as conquered provinces, you may. Is the play worth the candle? Treat with them as a separate confederacy, and you have peace. Treat with them as States of this Union, and you have war. One or the other you must do. Which will you do? There is a very strong desire on the part of many to avoid the issue, to hold what are called the tobacco States still in the Union, and build up what is to be called a great Union party, composed of Free Soilism and Whiggery, and avoid a war with the cotton States; hold things as they are at home, get through the next succeeding three years, and elect somebody as President of the old Union upon the ground that he has been a great Union-saver. But, unfortunately, you cannot control facts, and making speeches will not do this thing. Mr. Abraham Lincoln has to remove those troops from Fort Pickens and from Fort Sumter or they will be removed for him. He has to collect the revenues in Charleston, Savannah, Mobile, New Orleans, or the Confederate States will collect their own revenues. He has no judiciary department, he has no custom house collectors, he has none of the machinery of government there. He has to appoint his custom house officers; he has to collect the revenues; and, when he attempts it, you know, and I know, that resistance will be made, and that a conflict of arms will ensue, and that war will be the result.

As to the States that remain, you can so amend the Constitution as to give them security for the future, if not indemnity for the past; but in doing that it will not be by dividing Territories. I say to you, though I do not represent those States, that it is useless to blind your eyes to these facts: that no compromise, no amendment of the Constitution, no arrangement that you enter into will be satisfactory to those States, Senators, unless you recognize the doctrine that slaves are property, and that you will protect that species of property as you do every other.

I have said so much in reply to the Senator from Illinois
VI—3

because I did not wish his speech to go out as an explanation of the meaning of the President of the United States. His speech was calculated to produce the impression that Mr. Lincoln meant to do nothing. Masterly inactivity is a policy that cannot now prevail. Action! action! action! as the great Athenian orator [Demosthenes] said, is now necessary. You cannot longer serve God and Mammon; you must declare ''under which king, Bezonian?''

SENATOR DOUGLAS.—The Senator from Texas is quite right in saying that the issue cannot be long postponed; words will not answer the purpose much longer; action must soon begin; and that action must be in the direction of peace or war. Which shall it be? I think the President means peace. His policy must be peace, or it is time that Congress was in session and two hundred thousand men ordered into the field and preparations made for war.

The Senator is unwilling to believe that Mr. Lincoln means peace. I rejoice in the belief that he does mean peace. The Senator and myself look at this question from different points of view. He has told us several times that he is here merely because you continue to call his name at the desk; but that to all intents and purposes he regards himself a foreigner. His affections are with his own country; mine are with my country.

SENATOR WIGFALL.—Mr. President, I have tried to explain, several times, the position which I occupy. I am not officially informed that the State which I represent here has abolished the office of United States Senator. When I am so advised officially I shall file at your desk that information; and then, if after being so informed, you shall continue to call my name, I will answer, probably, if it suits my convenience; and, if I am called on to vote, I shall probably give my reasons for voting; and, regarding this as a very respectable public meeting, continue my connection with it in that way. But, while I am up, I will ask the Senator, as he is speaking for the Administration —though not a part of it, nor a large part of it [laughter]— to say explicitly whether he would advise the withdrawal of the troops from Fort Sumter and Fort Pickens, the removal of the flag of the United States from the borders of the Confederate States, and that no effort should be made to levy tribute upon a foreign people?

SENATOR DOUGLAS.—Mr. President, as I am no part of the Administration, as I do not speak for them—although I hope that I speak the same sentiments which will animate them—as I am not in their counsels nor their confidence, I shall not tender them my advice until they ask it. I do not choose, either, to proclaim what my policy would be, in view of the fact that the Senator does not regard himself as the guardian of the honor and interests of my country, but he is looking to the interests of another, which he thinks is in hostility to this country. It would hardly be good policy or wisdom for me to reveal what I think ought to be our policy to one who may so soon be in the counsels of the enemy and the command of its armies.

There was much laughter and applause in the galleries at this hit at Senator Wigfall's reputed ambition to become a military leader of the Confederacy. Upon the Vice-President making the usual threat (which was never enforced) to clear the galleries if the applause were repeated, Senator Wigfall hoped that the applause would be permitted, as, the Union being dissolved, he considered the present occasion only a public meeting.

James M. Mason [Va.] denied that the President's message could be construed as a pronouncement of peace.

It is a declaration of the possession of political power, and a duty to exercise it, and a purpose to discharge that duty. Now, there are seven States out of the Union. You say they are not out; that the Constitution and laws are still extended over them. They say the contrary. You say you will execute the laws in all the States, including those that have abandoned the Union; and common sense tells us, if you attempt it, it will be resisted by force. Unless there be some men laboring under the hallucination to believe that secession is a mere stage trick to deceive and delude the Government from which these States have detached themselves, there can be no man who can tell me that the President does not intend war.

I am not quarreling with the President because of the interpretation that he puts upon his duty. The responsibility is with him; let him exercise it. But what I challenge him for is that he has not more explicitly told us what he means to do; that he has left it to inference, to construction, to interpretation that may possibly mislead these people as to his actual purpose. If the Senator from Illinois thinks that, because the President has a peaceful view of this armed invasion of a foreign territory, or a hope of a peaceful solution, notwithstanding the armed invasion which he declares he will exercise, I can only say to that Senator he is more credulous than any of those around him.

I say, sir, the message is silent only as to the question of the time when the President will use his powers. It is reported that Fort Sumter has provisions for only thirty days. No one doubts that this fort can never be reinforced by the Federal Government, who claim to be its owners, without a struggle of thousands and tens of thousands of armed men spilling their blood on the sands and on the sea; therefore, within the next thirty days, whatever of peace the Senator saw in this message will be converted into war, real war, stern war.

No, Mr. President, there is a solution of peace, one only—a solution that is not only not held out in this message, but that is carefully avoided, sedulously avoided; there is a solution of peace of this great question between the contending sections, and there is but one; and, so far from that being contained in this inaugural, it is repelled and repudiated by its whole tenor and purpose. That solution is to admit that the Union is broken; to yield to the existing fact; to admit that the Union is at an end by the separation of the seven States which have gone out; and, whether they are acknowledged as an independent power or not, to admit the fact of their separate and independent existence; and then withdraw the troops.

I can see no reason why that should be longer denied, even among those statesmen who look upon this Government, as the inaugural expresses it, as a thing so peculiar, God-given, or otherwise that it is insusceptible of being broken. The President says by the universal law it is presumed to be perpetual. What he means by the universal law I am quite as much at a loss to understand as I was the cabalistic meaning of a phrase used by a Senator from New York of a higher law. What is the universal law? I know what the law of the Constitution is; I know what the laws of the United States are; I know what the international law is; but what this universal law is, unless it be the law of the universe, the law which keeps the spheres in place, and directs their motions, and provides for their rotation upon their axes and in their orbits, I am at a loss to know. But it is by terms like these, not only general but unmeaning and inapplicable, that we are to be deluded into the idea that there is no mode by which this Government, as he calls it, however oppressive it may become, however odious to the people under it, however cruel in its exactions, however perverse in its infractions of constitutional duty, can be got rid of, because of some law of the universe.

I have thought it a matter of moment that the policy of this message should be eviscerated, wherever its meaning was indirect or dark, because my own people, the people in Virginia, who are yet in the Union, are banded together upon the fixed, unchangeable purpose of making themselves a party to that war when the first gun is fired.

On March 8 Lafayette S. Foster [Conn.] moved to expel from the Senate Louis T. Wigfall [Tex.] because of his declaration that he was a foreigner. On the 11th the matter came up for discussion. Thomas L. Clingman [N. C.] moved as a substitute:

Whereas, it is understood that the State of Texas has seceded from the Union and is no longer one of the United States; therefore be it resolved that she is not entitled to be represented in this body.

The motion in regard to Senator Wigfall's expulsion was not brought to vote.

On March 13 William P. Fessenden [Me.] moved that the names of Jefferson Davis [Miss.] and other Senators who had announced that they were no longer members of the Senate and had vacated their seats be stricken from the roll.

Senator Fessenden's motion was finally amended to "Whereas the seats of (the said Senators) have become vacant, resolved that the Secretary be directed to omit their names from the roll," and was passed in this form.

CHAPTER II

THE RIGHT OF SECESSION

Speech of Senator James A. Bayard, Jr., on ''The Right of Secession and the Propriety of Recognizing the Southern Confederacy''—The Confederate Peace Commission; It Is Not Received—The Fall of Fort Sumter—Secession of Virginia—Military Movements April-July, 1861—President Lincoln's First Message to Congress: ''The Sophistry of Secession.''

ON March 30, 1861, James A. Bayard, Jr. [Del.], introduced in the Senate a resolution to the effect that, whatever view be taken of the right of secession, seven States having withdrawn from the Union and the enforcement there of Federal laws by the magistracy being impracticable, the only alternative was civil war or recognition of their secession; and that, whereas war would not bring them back into the Union, their independence should be acknowledged and a treaty be made with them.

In support of his resolution Senator Bayard discussed the nature and right of secession and the causes which had led to its adoption by the Southern States in a speech which continued for three days.

THE RIGHT OF SECESSION

SENATOR BAYARD

The act of secession has been characterized in this body by some of its members as a constitutional right, as among the reserved rights of the States. By others it has been denounced as treason to the United States on the part of any of the actors. I agree with neither. It is not among the reserved rights of the States, but is a revolution by organized communities, by the authority of the people of the seceding States, in whom the ultimate power of sovereignty is vested. Its effect is the same, whether revolutionary or legal; it severs the State from the Union, and it suspends the operation of the laws of the Federal Government in the seceding States. It is, in the old Roman sense of the term, rebellion—the revolt of a nation— but not in the modern sense of the term rebellion.

All forms of republican government rest upon one great general principle which is recognized in America, and has been always recognized as the great basis, the only just basis, of all government, "the consent of the governed." Our fathers so declared it in the Declaration of Independence, but the mode of consent depends upon the character of the government. The consent of the governed as applied to the State governments, which are purely national, and to any purely national government, is but a political axiom called commonly the social compact, which assumes that there is an implied contract between each individual citizen by which that government is established. The law of that compact is, in theory and in practice, that the will of the majority of society shall be conclusive evidence of the consent of the whole; and, further, it has been denominated an inherent right in society and in the majority. It is still but an axiom. In practice, sex excludes one-half the governed from giving consent. Age excludes one-fourth. Age is arbitrary; it might be twenty-five; it is twenty-one. Further, in the origin of our Government, though the States were all national governments and all republican, an interest in the soil was essential for the purpose of giving consent. Nay, still, in many of the States, the prepayment of taxes is essential for the dissent or consent on the part of the individual, though he is bound under the axiom by the laws of the government established by his implied consent. Residence of greater or less duration is requisite in all the States; in some three months, in some six, in some a year, and at one time two years. Yet all the individuals who exist as inhabitants of that government or are within its jurisdiction are considered by the force of the axiom as consenting to the government and bound by its laws. In the State of Pennsylvania and in several other of the non-slaveholding States, I believe, race excludes many of the community from giving their actual consent, but their consent is implied and they are bound by the laws. No negro can vote in the State of Pennsylvania, and in others of the non-slaveholding States the same rule applies.

Yet the axiom is true and is a wise one; it is the foundation of government on the basis of the social compact, which is the will of society, evidenced by the determination of the majority of the great body of the people who are supposed to be competent to form government.

It is very evident, Mr. President, that revolution in a government founded upon such a basis could rarely, if ever, occur; because the majority, having it in their power to bring into accord with their opinions the legislative authority, could always change the form of government at will, without revolutionary action; and I understand revolution to mean a change of government against the will of the existing government. The word revolution is sometimes applied to any radical change of a government, whether with or without the will of the ultimate power of sovereignty; but, in the ordinary acceptation of the term, we mean, by revolution, a change against the consent of the existing government. The power of change, the right of change, exists in all governments, no matter what may be their form, and is vested of necessity where the ultimate power of sovereignty exists; in Russia, in an autocrat. No one doubts that the Emperor of Russia could change the form of government of Russia. In England it is in the King, Lords, and Commons. Being effected by the will of the existing government, the idea of force and resistance is precluded, and the change of government would be legal in all respects.

In the United States this ultimate power of government in each State is vested in the people under the social compact, and the majority in each State, having the ultimate sovereignty, have the right to change the form of government under which they live. This I suppose to be the established and uncontroverted principle derived from all the publicists, as to the theory on which purely national republics are founded, which all the States of this Union are. But it is very evident that the principle of the social compact cannot be applied to the United States as an aggregate nation. Could it be, of course a majority of the people of the United States could change the form of government by their will. The majority of one State would be carried into another State, and the majority of the aggregate nation would be competent to impose the form of government they desired over the people of all the States. Such is not the structure of the Federal Government.

The speaker here quoted in support of his views from the 39th number of "The Federalist," written by James Madison.

I think, if the present President of the United States had read this passage, he would have been able to understand the distinction between the relations of a county to a State and the relations of a State to the Federal Government. There exists, then, this broad distinction between the Federal and the State governments: the State governments exist by the consent of the governed, under the law of the social compact; but the Federal Government exists, not as the result of the implied compact which arises under that law, but by the *express* compact of the several States which were independent sovereignties at the time they created it. That compact specifies the extent of the powers delegated to the common Government, and without the compact it could have had no existence. Sir, whence came, or on what do we base, the power of the Federal Government to make or administer any laws? Has it any other basis than the consent given by the people of each State severally, by the adoption of the Constitution framed by the representatives of States and submitted to the people of each State for their several acceptance? Did unanimity in the State of Pennsylvania bring the State of Georgia within the operation of the Federal Constitution? Certainly not. The consent of the governed, the consent of the community, expressed under the social compact in the State (which is the basis of its government), forming, by express compact with the people of other States, a common government for all, with special delegated powers, is the only basis of the general Government of this Union.

Then, sir, what is the rule as to compacts of this kind? That they cannot be changed without the consent of all the parties to the compact. It matters not whether the compact is a treaty or creates a government; the law of the compacts of sovereignties is that no change can be made in terms except by the consent of all, unless it is otherwise provided in the instrument.

The Constitution contains no provision which authorizes a State by its own act to separate from the other States and withdraw from the Union. Had there been no provision as to amendments to the Federal Constitution, within the rule which governs the compacts of sovereignties, it would have been unalterable in any one particular; and it can only be altered in the mode which it provides. Neither a majority of the people of the United States can alter the Constitution on the basis on which it rests, nor a majority of the States; nor is the power expressly given to any State to withdraw at will from the confederation and establish herself as a separate nation. I hold, therefore, that the act of secession is a breach of the compact on the part of the seceding States; and that, being a breach of compact and against the will of the Federal Government, it is of necessity an act of revolution. But, Mr. President, it is a revolution inaugurated by a people in their collective capacity—a revolution and breach of the compact which, if groundless in morals and reason, gives just cause of war, but leaves no other remedy. You may quell insurrection, you may put down domestic violence by the operation of the law, but you cannot meet the collective action of a people in any other mode than by war or by peaceable negotiation; and that statesman will find that he makes a terrible mistake who is unable to distinguish between the collective action of a people and a mere temporary insurrection of factious individuals. Lord North made it, and he lost, under the plea of executing the laws, the brightest jewels of the British Crown. Concession might have led to a very different termination.

Mr. President, I can scarcely realize that it can be seriously urged that the States of this Union were not independent and sovereign States when they formed their original confederacy; that they did not, as independent and sovereign States, adopt, by the several action of their people, the present Federal Constitution; and that they did not reserve to the States and the people thereof all rights which were not ceded to the common Government by the Constitution which they adopted. But, sir, if the States were sovereign originally, what change was made in their relations by the formation of the present Constitution? The first and the most important change was the power to tax for the purpose of its support, which was given to the general Government, and which was the great defect of the old confederation. The next radical change was that the laws should operate upon the individual citizen, instead of operating upon the citizen through the action of the State. To that extent the alteration made the general Government a National Government. This change in the operation of the laws on individuals instead of communities was intended to strengthen and give stability to the Union by substituting for the coercion of arms—which existed in the Confederacy as against the State, but was practically a useless power—the coercion of the magistracy upon the individual. No more was intended, and the power it confers is quite sufficient for any federal government existing over independent communities, and founded upon opinion. But the coercion of a State in its collective capacity, even by the magistracy, which they inserted in the Constitution when it was originally adopted, was stricken out very soon afterward by amendment.

The inference seems irresistible. If the power was abrogated which, as first inserted in the Constitution, gave the means of coercion by the magistracy as against a State, on what principle can it be contended that the Federal Constitution gives the right of coercion by arms against a State, while the State remains in the Union? If the State, by secession, becomes alien, you have the same right of war or peace with her that you have with any other alien people; but, while you recognize her as a member of the Union, coercion by arms, or by the magistracy, against the State in its collective capacity, was neither given, nor intended to be given, by the Federal Constitution. The attempt to give the power in both shapes was made in the convention, and expressly voted down, both as to coercion by arms and coercion by the magistracy. It was given indirectly by the clause which gave jurisdiction to the Supreme Court in suits by individuals against a State; but that was stricken out, within a few years after its adoption, by amendment. The right of secession *at will,* with or without cause, was not given, because the insertion of such a clause in the Federal Constitution would but have been an invitation to dissolution. It was left unprovided for, as one of those exigencies in human affairs against which no government and no human foresight could provide.

Sir, coercion by the magistracy of the individual citizen gave all the strength and sanction to the laws of the Federal Government which were requisite; but it has no application to the collective action of the people in any State in their political capacity. Where a State, by the action of her people, declares herself out of the Union, or, in ordinary language, secedes, the necessary effect is that the magistracy is gone; there is no Federal officer to carry into execution the laws by means of the civil power, and of course the laws must cease to operate. It is the result of revolutionary action, I admit, because against the will of the existing common Government; but it is the action of an independent community in their collective capacity, and has precisely the same effect upon the relative condition of the people of that State and the rest of the Union that the abrogation of a treaty would have between independent nations. The treaty in such case is at an end; but if abrogated without sufficient cause the annulment gives just cause of war. The Union, however, stands; the Federal Government remains, as to all the other States, in its entirety, and with its laws and its Constittuion, as it stood before; but secession has abrogated the coercion of the magistracy within the States that have withdrawn by the action of the people thereof. Is not this action the consent of the governed? It is revolutionary; but, still, action had by the consent of the governed. Who adopted the Constitution? The people of Georgia, by the vote of their own people alone. If they decide to withdraw from that Union by the act of the same people—not of the legislature—on what principle, consistent with the Declaration of Independence, can it be denied that this same people can change their common as well as their State government, except on the ground that such change is a breach of the compact which they made with the people of other States, by adopting the Federal Constitution? If secession be, then, as I believe, a breach of compact, yet it would be justified by sufficient cause; if resulting from caprice without grave cause of discontent, or sense of insecurity, it gives just right of war; but it does not necessarily ensue, from the right of war, that war should follow. War is a question of morals and power combined, and always must be.

The military power in this country was never intended to be a primary power in the execution of the laws. It may be called in aid, under the mandate of the magistrate, as subsidiary to the civil power. By the express terms of the Constitution, you may, at the request of a State, use the military power in case of domestic violence; you may repress insurrection in the same mode; but this Government never was intended to be carried on by means of the military, as a substitute and primary power in place of the civil power—the action of the magistracy; and yet no other mode remains in which the laws can be enforced in the seceding States than by the military power, if their enforcement is insisted on. All laws require some sanction, or they are futile. There is but the sanction of the magistracy or the sanction of arms. Under the old Confederacy they had to depend entirely upon the sanction of arms, but never attempted its exercise, relying solely on the good faith of the States. The change made in constructing the present Government was by giving the power of coercion by the magistracy upon the individual citizen; but, of necessity, that is dependent upon the action of the people of the State in their collective capacity; and if they subvert and put an end to the magistracy the laws of the Union cannot be enforced, under our present Constitution, without a violation of its intent. The action of the seceding States was beyond human foresight, and one of those calamities against which no government, unless a military despotism, can guard.

When a State secedes by the action of her people, though its effect severs her from the Union and makes her an alien people, it is a breach of the compact which created this Government,

and is, in itself, just cause of war.   But the right of war arises
only as consequent upon the effect of the action of the people
of the State, having made the people thereof an alien to the rest
of the Union.   If still in the Union, you cannot make war upon
a State.   Such is the doctrine inculcated by Mr. Madison in
"The Federalist," as the law of the compact in all governments
founded upon the express compact of sovereignties, and not, as
this Federal Government certainly is not, upon the social compact.   It is the law, as laid down by all publicists, that the
breach of any one article absolves all the others from the engagements of the compact, *"unless they choose rather to compel
the delinquent party to repair the breach."*   I will not say that
the case might not be supposed, where a State, from mere
caprice, without any cause whatever, should withdraw from the
Federal Union, hostile measure, mingled with conciliation, might
have the effect of restoring her to the Union, of repairing the
breach.   Where the people were divided and the State small in
power, I can conceive that the use of hostile or coercive measures, mingled with affectionate consideration for her people,
might conduce to such a result without destroying the form of
our Government, though, in such a case, hostile measures would
be a stretch of constitutional power; but such supposition has no
relation to the case of a large section of country, having sufficient population and resources to exist as an independent nation, which chooses to throw off its allegiance to the Federal Government, and, by the action of the people, withdraw from any
further connection with it.   In such a case, you cannot restore
the Union by means of the power of arms.   Conciliation and
concession alone, and their consent, must bring back those States
to this Government, as by their separate consent they were originally incorporated among its members.

It has been said that the action of a State in seceding makes
all the actors guilty of treason if they attempt to support that
action by force of arms.   I am unable to appreciate the force
or the humanity of such a doctrine.   It may serve to excite; it
will never serve to deter.   It is not a practical question.   When
revolution comes, not insurrection, it overrides and cannot be
met by the law of treason.   The allegiance is due to the State
as well as to the Federal Government; and the allegiance to the
Federal Government is due through the State.   If the State, as a
political community, dissolves her connection with the Federal
Government, could there be a more revolting proposition than
that the individual man, who is domiciled in the State, and re-
siding there, shall be held in the position that he is guilty of

treason against the State if he does not side with her, and of treason against the general Government if he does? The law of domicile must necessarily govern the allegiance of the individual where the political action of the community has severed the State in which he is domiciled from the general Government. Humanity alone requires that such a doctrine should be enforced. But it is really not a practical question. The charge of treason only irritates; for the words "treason" and "traitor" are terms to which no man submits without a sense of indignation and a disposition to resistance. Practically you can never enforce the law of treason against the collective action of a people. It was threatened in the case of the revolution of our own ancestors in 1776. Was it ever enforced? Must it not always lead to retaliation where there is this collective action? Is there a possibility that where revolution occurs—and this is revolution on the part of the people of seven States in their collective capacity—that the law of treason can be enforced? Why, then, is the term applied unless, indeed, those who use it intend so to increase exasperation that neither reconciliation nor reunion, nor even peaceful separation, shall be practicable or possible.

But, sir, though the act of secession, which, for the reasons I have assigned, I believe to be revolutionary, is a revolutionary right, and is a right which the people of a State alone, in whom the ultimate sovereignty is vested, not the legislature, can exercise; and it is from the use of the words "the people," by our ancestors, to distinguish between the mere Government as an agent and the great body of the people in which, as possessing the ultimate sovereignty, the right to change the form of government reposes, that so many have been led into false views of the act of secession. They used the word "people" as representing the ultimate and true source of sovereignty in contradistinction to the mere Government. If the people of a State, acting in the same collective capacity in which they adopted the Constitution of the United States, as a distinct people, afterward choose to abrogate that Constitution, it seems clear, if they had the authority to adopt, they must have the sovereignty to rescind. The act is revolutionary, because it is against the will of the common Government, and a breach of the compact which created that Government. It becomes just cause of war, as in any case in which one nation abrogates a compact with another, and war alone must be the remedy or peaceful arrangement.

The remaining question, which I wish to discuss, is as to the power of the President and Senate, by treaty, to adjust all questions likely to give rise to difficulty and to collision between the new republic which has been formed and the Federal Government. I cannot entertain a doubt as to the existence of that power. It is not expressly given in those terms, but the treaty-making power is vested in the President and Senate. It is an indefinite power. The war power, contrary to the rule which exists in other nations, is in Congress, the legislative body, alone. The treaty-making power is confined to the President, and two-thirds of the Senate concurring with him in the negotiation of the treaty. One must necessarily, in the exigencies of a nation, be as broad as the other. What is there that prevents the United States from ceding a portion of territory not within a State, if the exigencies of the Government require it? You acquire territory by means of treaty, with no express power given for the purpose, because the external sovereignty of the Union is vested in the Federal Government alone; and for the same reason, if the general interests of the whole, where no particular State has jurisdiction or authority, require that you should cede territory of the United States to a foreign government, can anyone doubt that the cession could be made, not by Congress, but by the President and Senate, only by means of a treaty? You did it for the purpose of closing a boundary in the case of Maine, within a State, with the consent of the State. You were not able to run the line between Great Britain and the United States; and for the purpose of establishing a boundary and preventing collision and war between the nations you did cede a portion of the State of Maine, with the consent of the legislature of that State.

If one purpose will justify you in ceding a portion of the United States to a foreign nation, on what principle is it that, where seven States of this Union, by their consent and by the action of their people, have chosen to withdraw themselves from the Union and declare themselves out of the Union, you cannot accept their declaration and treat with them? You cannot doubt that you have the power of war against them, though not while they are States of the Union. If you once begin war, you treat them as an alien people. It is the necessary result of war. Will war give a power to the President and Senate to make a treaty, which they do not possess antecedent to the war? Is a baptism of blood necessary in order to give authority under the Constitution to the President and Senate of the United States to conclude peace? If such a doctrine be tenable, the result is that, if a collision of arms occurs with this new republic, and you fight for a period of eight or ten years, still you are powerless; the President and Senate cannot treat, peace can never be concluded, and eternal war must be the rule of your Government. No new power will be acquired by a collision of arms between you and this new republic. The power must exist now, or it exists never.

Mr. President, I do not see how this conclusion can be escaped; and why you should not have the power. The treaty-making power, beyond all question, is an indefinite power. It embraces all relations external to the Union. If any State had never become a party to the present Government, can anyone doubt that, such State remaining an independent state, you could have treated with her, and that every State of this Union had the right to part with any portion of her territory irrespective of the consent of the general Government, if she was not a party to that Government? It was part of their sovereignty and their independence, as it belongs to every other nation, to either acquire territory, which is one of the rights of sovereignty, or to diminish her territory by cession, where the public exigencies require it. Well, then, if a State, by the action of her people, declares herself out of the Union, what clause in the Constitution forbids your acceptance of her declaration, and excludes from the treaty-making power negotiation and treaty with her? If you, with her consent, can cede a portion of her territory to a foreign power, why can you not, with her consent, permit the whole State to withdraw from the Federal jurisdiction?

For the acquisition of territory by the United States, you find no express authority in the Constitution; but it results from the nature of your Government. It is forbidden to the States; it is permitted to the general Government, because the right of acquisition is incident to sovereignty.

The right to acquire territory implies the right to part with it. There is no limit, in fact, to the power of diminishing the territory of the Union, except in the States. As we have seen, the general Government, with the assent of the State concerned, did it for one purpose, in the case of the State of Maine, without even the action of the people.

In the case of the seven seceded States, the people in their original capacity, in whom the ultimate sovereignty rests according to our Declaration of Independence, have declared those States to be out of the Union by their representatives elected for that purpose, and they have dissolved their connection with the Federal Government. Have we not the right, has not this Government the power, to accept that declaration; not to destroy the Union, but to preserve it, and maintain peace with those States? You cannot escape from perpetual and eternal war, unless you come to this conclusion, that the President and the Senate have the power of negotiation with a State which secedes, if they see fit to exercise it. I admit freely that, on the other hand, the act of secession having the effect of severing the State from the Union, though revolutionary, and making her people an alien people, Congress has also the right of war, and just cause of war, if there is no cause for the withdrawal.

If you refuse to treat, if the relations between these two republics are left in their present unsettled condition, the danger of collision must be constantly existent. There is the loss also of prestige on the part of the Federal Government, if you assert your jurisdiction over the seceded States, and do not enforce your laws. In fact, non-action would amount to a virtual acknowledgment of the independence *de facto* of those States. Why not acknowledge it by treaty, by direct action, and thus avoid collision? Foreign governments will so act if you do not, and thus complicate the relations between the two republics.

But, sir, it cannot be doubted that war will be the inevitable result if the army or the navy is employed to execute the laws of the Federal Union within the seceded States. If you do mean war, it is a question of morals and of power. There is but one legitimate object for such a war, and that is the restoration of the seceded States to the Union. But you can never effect that result by a war of subjugation. Is it consistent with your form of government, if you could succeed in conquering those States, to hold them as subject provinces? You must either desolate them, if you succeed, or you must maintain your supremacy by an immense standing army, in order to keep them in subjection. Look at the condition of Venice and Austria. What myriads of troops is Austria obliged to maintain in order to keep an enervate people in a state of subjection against their will! Sir, the admiration of military glory is quite as strong a passion among the American people as with other nations. The permanent maintenance of a large standing army would necessarily foster and encourage that passion, and, in the end, some successful soldier would become the military autocrat of the Republic, and substitute the coercion of arms for the coercion of the magistracy, because the character of the people, under a war of one or two generations, would change, and the love of civil liberty that now exists throughout this nation would be seriously diminished, or, perhaps, entirely pass away.

You cannot conquer the South any more than the South could conquer the North. The first attempt at conquest would, of necessity, from the cause of contest, force other slaveholding

States into the Southern Confederacy, and this new republic, as it stands, has both the wealth and population to maintain a national existence. It would be no short war. The result of war, too, is always doubtful, and far beyond human foresight. Accident will often determine a decisive battle. The individual genius of leaders controls the events of war far beyond any control that can be exercised by human genius during a state of peace. The genius of Andrew Jackson secured the victory of New Orleans. Under another, though an able soldier, it might have been lost. The majority of numbers and resources will not insure success in war. On the plains of Marathon, ten thousand Greeks defeated the countless hosts of Xerxes, and a comparatively small number of deficiently armed Swiss mountaineers met the mailed chivalry of Charles of Burgundy, and defeated, utterly and disastrously, the best armed and organized army of Europe. Bannockburn must not be forgotten, and history is filled with similar illustrations.

Again, sir, a war of invasion—which, if the war commences, must be its character, if you attempt to effect your purpose under the pretext of enforcing the laws—is always in favor of the invaded country. Men will fight for their homes and their firesides as they will not fight for conquest, and will endure the utmost extent of privation and suffering, rather than yield to the invader; and disparity of force never insures the conquest of an invaded country. You have the illustration in our own contest with Great Britain.

Great Britain might possibly, under abler military men, have succeeded for the time; but after the first blood was shed she never could have retained her supremacy over this country. Conciliation might have saved her the colonies in the first instance, before independence was declared, but after its declaration the acknowledgment of their independence became an inevitable result, and was merely a question of time.

I trust the idea that it would be a legitimate act on the part of the Federal Government, for the purpose of effecting their subjugation, to incite servile insurrection in the States of this new republic, is not entertained. The act would be forbidden by common humanity and the indignant voice of the world. But if the spirit of malignity entertain such an idea, it will be disappointed. Servile insurrections may occur, and have occurred in the history of the world, but not at the call of an invader. Your own wars with Great Britain, in the Revolution and in 1812, illustrate this.

Is there, Mr. President, a point of honor? The Union is not

dissolved if we let these States go. The United States remain;
the Federal Government remains. We are a great and powerful
nation. Part of the dominions over which our laws extended
may be curtailed, and our jurisdiction over them lost, but we
remain with all the elements of a great nation, if we acknowledge the new republic. But it may be said that, if we sever in
consequence of this secession, arising from the anti-slavery sentiment, into two separate governments, the same sentiment will
produce collision between the independent governments by the
same interference which has led to secession from the common government. The answer is that the anti-slavery sentiment, with the masses at least, is an honest, though, as I
think, a mistaken conviction, founded in ignorance of the relations of race. They believe, also, that there is a moral responsibility on their part connected with the operations of the common government, in relation to this institution. That responsibility ceases if this new republic is acknowledged as a separate
nationality.

Mr. President, if so many separate and independent communities existing under a common government find that, from
dissonance of habits, of manners, of customs, or from antagonism of opinion, or any other cause, they can no longer remain
under that common government, and can agree by peaceful
action to separate into two republics, each pursuing its own destiny according to its own views and the will of its own people,
it will afford the most pregnant and conclusive evidence that
has ever been exhibited to the world of the capacity of man for
self-government. If, on the contrary, blood must flow, and war,
prolonged civil war, be consequent upon separation, then, indeed, will the columns that support this Federal Government be
scattered into fragments, and probably many petty and powerless governments arise upon their ruins. Years of conflict may
establish separate nationalities, but in that event the last hope
of the patriot, the philosopher, and the statesman, for the self-
government of man, will perish with the dissolution of the Federal Union.

NEGOTIATIONS WITH CONFEDERATE PEACE COMMISSION

Prior to the inauguration of Mr. Lincoln the Confederate Government had selected three commissioners
to adjust the ''differences'' which existed between the
two governments. They were Martin J. Crawford, a

former Democratic member of Congress from Georgia; John Forsyth, editor of a Democratic paper at Mobile, Ala., and Andrew B. Roman, a former Governor of Louisiana, and a Whig who had used all his influence to prevent disunion.

On the 13th of March, 1861, the commissioners sent a diplomatic dispatch to the Federal State Department informing the Federal Government that they had been appointed by the Confederate authorities as commissioners empowered to open negotiations for the settlement of all controverted questions between the two governments, and to conclude treaties of peace between "the two nations."

To this note no reply was returned, but Secretary William H. Seward made out a memorandum and filed it with the document, simply stating that the Government could not recognize the authority under which the alleged commissioners acted, nor reply to them. The memorandum stated that "it could not be admitted that the States referred to had, in law or fact, withdrawn from the Federal Union, or that they could do so in any other manner than with their consent, and the consent of the people of the United States, to be given through a national convention to be assembled in conformity with the provisions of the Constitution of the United States."

This memorandum was withheld until April 8, when it was at once telegraphed both to Montgomery, Ala., the Confederate capital, and Charleston, where it created great excitement.

In the meanwhile Chief-Justice Taney and Associate-Justices Campbell and Nelson had, of their own volition as good citizens, examined the legal question of the right of the President to coerce a State, and had concluded that there was no constitutional right so to do; and they gratuitously advised the several members of the Cabinet of the conclusions to which they had come, and recommended that terms of conciliation be proposed to the Confederate Government through the commissioners.

Secretary Seward was in favor of evacuating Fort Sumter, and he informed Judge Campbell, who was acting as mediator, that it would be evacuated, and Campbell so informed the Confederate commissioners, who in turn informed their Government. Mr. Lincoln was taking ample time to deliberate what to do, being uncertain as to the best policy. He was hopeful that Virginia would not secede, and that the Virginia convention, which was deliberating upon the question, would adjourn and so cease to be a menace to him.

On the 9th of April the Confederate commissioners sent a letter to the Secretary of State in which they proffered as their ultimatum of negotiation the evacuation of Sumter. Secretary Seward replied that he was not "at liberty to hold official intercourse with them."

Of this action the Confederate authorities were duly apprised, and the commissioners left Washington on April 11, and returned to Montgomery.

The Fall of Fort Sumter

President Lincoln, against the advice of a majority of his Cabinet, had finally resolved to send provisions to Fort Sumter, and an expedition sailed for this purpose on April 6.

Owing to a gale only the *Baltic* of the fleet arrived in time to be of service to Major Anderson, and that only to bear away the surrendered garrison. The Confederate Government heard of the coming of the provisioning expedition and, considering the capture of the fort necessary to the life of the rebellion, ordered General Pierre G. T. Beauregard, who was in charge of the investment, to procure its surrender, or, failing in this, to bombard it. On the 11th Beauregard sent to Major Anderson a summons to surrender, offering to him, in case of compliance, facilities to remove the troops, and to the garrison the privilege of saluting their flag. To this Anderson replied that he would surrender the fort on the 15th if supplies did not reach him by that time, or if he did not before then receive orders to the contrary from his Government.

These conditions did not suit the Confederates, and on Friday, April 12, at 3 a. m., they gave Anderson notice that their batteries would open on the fort in an hour. At 4:30 the bombardment began, and continued throughout that day and into the next.

Anderson then accepted the conditions of surrender offered, and on the following day, Sunday, April 14, the garrison sailed northward in the *Baltic*.

THE VIRGINIA CONVENTION

Since February 13 Virginia had been holding a convention to consider its policy in the crisis. The Union delegates were in a majority. An ordinance of secession was voted down on March 17 by a majority of ninety to forty-five, and a similar proposition was defeated on April 4, but still the convention declined to adjourn. Mr. Lincoln therefore caused a letter to be sent to George W. Summers of Charleston, Va., the most talented of the Union men in his State, requesting that he come to Washington for conference. Summers was kept by timidity from accepting the President's invitation, but he sent John B. Baldwin in his place.

The interview was held on the morning of April 4. Baldwin returned to the convention reporting that his conference with the President was inconclusive; that Mr. Lincoln had characterized the convention as a "standing menace which embarrassed him very much," and therefore he desired that it adjourn *sine die,* but that he had given no promise of what return he would make to it for compliance with his wishes. John Minor Botts, another member of the convention, called on the President two days afterward, and held a conversation in which Mr. Lincoln gave an account of the interview with Baldwin which, as remembered by Mr. Botts, differed materially from Baldwin's report. The President, said Botts, spoke of the fleet in New York harbor preparing to sail that afternoon to provision Fort Sumter. "Now," said Mr. Lincoln, "your convention in Richmond has been sitting for nearly two months, and all it has done has been to shake the rod over my head (threatening to secede if coercion should be used to bring back South Carolina into the Union). If the Union majority in the Virginia convention will adjourn it without its passing an ordinance of secession, this fleet shall be kept from sailing, and, instead, Fort Sumter shall be evacuated. I think it is a good swap to give a fort for a State any time.''

As a result of Baldwin's report, the Virginia convention remained in session, and on April 8 appointed another delegation, consisting of William Ballard Preston, Alexander H. H. Stuart, and George W. Randolph, to wait on President Lincoln, and ask him to communicate to the convention ''the policy which the Federal Executive intends to pursue in regard to the Federal States.''

The committee had an audience with the President at Washington on April 13, the day after Fort Sumter had been fired upon by the South Carolinian secessionists. He referred the convention to the policy expressed in his inaugural address:

As I then and therein said, I now repeat: ''The power confided to me will be used to hold, occupy, and possess the property and places belonging to the Government, and to collect the duties and imposts; but beyond what is necessary for these objects there will be no invasion, no using of force against or among the people anywhere.'' . . . In case it proves true that Fort Sumter has been assaulted, as is reported, I shall perhaps cause the United States mails to be withdrawn from all the States which claim to have seceded, believing that the commencement of actual war against the Government justifies and possibly demands this. . . .

Whatever else I may do for the purpose, I shall not attempt to collect the duties and imposts by any armed invasion of any part of the country; not meaning by this, however, that I may not land a force deemed necessary to relieve a fort upon a border of the country.

The report of this committee, followed as it was by the President's call of April 15 for 75,000 militia to suppress the rebellion and to be raised by the several States of the Union, which included Virginia, caused the convention, on April 17, to pass an ordinance of secession.

This was followed by a similar ordinance in Arkansas on May 6, and a military league with the Confederacy in Tennessee on May 7.

The Confederate Government established its capital at Richmond, Virginia, on the 21st of May, and North Carolina, being surrounded by secession territory, seceded the same day.

THE CALL FOR TROOPS

On April 15, the day after the surrender of Fort Sumter, the President issued a proclamation calling forth the militia of the several States of the Union to the aggregate number of 75,000 to suppress combinations which existed in the seceding States for the purpose of opposing and obstructing the enforcement of Federal laws, and which were "too powerful to be suppressed by the ordinary course of judicial proceedings, or by the powers vested in the marshals by law." The concluding paragraph of the proclamation convened Congress to meet on July 4 "to consider and determine such measures as, in their wisdom, the public safety and interest might seem to demand."

The call for troops was really signed on Sunday, April 14, though dated April 15. On the evening of the 14th Senator Stephen A. Douglas called upon President Lincoln and was closeted with him for two hours. He went forth from the conference to publish by telegraph to the country the declaration that he was "prepared to sustain the President in the exercise of all his constitutional functions to preserve the Union, and maintain the Government, and defend the Federal capital." On April 25, before the Illinois legislature, he made, in behalf of the Union, the most eloquent speech of his life. Unfortunately for the cause which had become the paramount passion of his soul, he died a little more than a month thereafter, on June 3, at his home in Chicago. Even measured by his few weeks of service, his place is secure in American history as the first and greatest of "War Democrats."

The governors of all the free States responded to the

call for troops with enthusiasm, offering more men than were required or could be armed. The governors of the border States, however, indignantly refused the call. Governor Jackson of Missouri said, "Not one man will Missouri furnish to carry on such an unholy crusade." Governor Magoffin of Kentucky said, "I say emphatically, Kentucky will furnish no troops for the wicked purpose of subduing her sister Southern States," and Governor Harris of Tennessee said, "Tennessee will not furnish a man for coercion, but 50,000 for the defence of our Southern brothers."

MILITARY MOVEMENTS OF THE CONFEDERACY

As an answer to Lincoln's call for troops, Jefferson Davis, President of the Southern Confederacy, issued a proclamation on April 17, offering letters of marque and reprisal to privateers desiring to prey upon the commerce of the United States. Two days later President Lincoln replied by proclaiming a blockade of all the Confederate ports, and giving notice that privateering would be treated as piracy.

General Beauregard was ordered by President Davis into northern Virginia to assume command of the forces gathering there from the Gulf States.

MILITARY MOVEMENTS OF THE UNION

On May 3 the President issued a proclamation calling for 42,034 more volunteers from the several States, and an increase in the regular army of 22,714 men, and in the navy of 18,000.

The first efforts of the Government were to hold the border States in the Union. Major Robert Anderson, the hero of Fort Sumter, was sent to his native State of Kentucky to recruit volunteers. Captain Nathaniel Lyon, an ardent anti-slavery man, who was in charge of the St. Louis arsenal, was ordered to enlist 10,000 loyal Missourians, and, if necessary, to proclaim martial law in the State. Later, he was put in charge of the military department in which Missouri was situated, replacing General William H. Harney, a conservative, who had been cajoled into making a compact with the State government, which was attempting to take Missouri into the Confederacy, to refrain from military movements, since these were apt to ''create excitements and jealousy.'' General Lyon at once went into action, and on June 17 defeated the State (really Confederate) troops under General Sterling Price at Booneville. The

THE BATTLE OF BOONEVILLE, OR THE GREAT MISSOURI LYON HUNT

From the collection of the New York Historical Society

governor, Claiborne F. Jackson, was forced to flee from place to place in the State while keeping up the pretence of a government. Missouri, under Jackson, was recognized as a part of the Confederacy by the Davis Government.

General George B. McClellan entered West Virginia from Ohio and occupied it for the Union. A Michigan regiment under Colonel Elmer E. Ellsworth entered Virginia from Washington and occupied Alexandria. Ellsworth, as he was cutting down a rebel flag on a hotel there, was assassinated by the proprietor.

The capture of Alexandria inaugurated open conflict

between the Confederacy and the Union in Virginia. General Pierre G. T. Beauregard, who was looked upon by the South as the hero of Fort Sumter, was sent on May 31 to command the Confederate forces centering about Manassas. General Joseph E. Johnston was in command at Winchester, having fallen back from Harper's Ferry before a superior Union force under General Robert Patterson. On June 19 President Lincoln called his Cabinet and the leading generals to a council of war, at which it was decided that General Irvin McDowell should lead the Union forces against Beauregard, while Patterson should remain confronting Johnston in the Shenandoah Valley, following him in a rear attack if he should attempt to join Beauregard.

This was the situation when Congress met in special session July 4 and listened to the President's message.

The message was in effect an answer to Senator Bayard's speech on the right of secession.

The Sophistry of Secession

First Message of President Lincoln to Congress

In his message President Lincoln described the state of affairs at the time of his inauguration; the suspension of all functions of the Federal Government, save those of the postoffice, in South Carolina, Georgia, Alabama, Mississippi, Louisiana, and Florida; the seizure by the several governments of these States of forts and other Federal property, and the organization of these States into a Confederation which "was already invoking recognition, aid, and intervention from foreign powers." The President recounted his forbearance in pursuing the policy expressed in his inaugural address of exhausting all peaceful measures before resorting to stronger ones.

He then lucidly recited the story of the assault upon Fort Sumter by South Carolina, demonstrating that it was in no sense an act of defence, but on the contrary of deliberate aggression, designed to force the hand of the Federal Government.

That this was their object the Executive well understood; and having said to them, in the inaugural address, "You can have no conflict without being yourselves the aggressors," he took pains not only to keep this declaration good, but also to keep the case so free from the power of ingenious sophistry that the world should not be able to misunderstand it. By the affair at Fort Sumter, with its surrounding circumstances, that point was reached. In this act, discarding all else, they have forced upon the country the distinct issue, "immediate dissolution or blood."

And this issue embraces more than the fate of the United States. It presents to the whole family of man the question whether a constitutional republic or democracy—a government of the people by the same people—can or cannot maintain its territorial integrity against its own domestic foes. It presents the question whether discontented individuals, too few in numbers to control administration according to organic law in any case, can always, upon the pretences made in this case, or on any other pretences, or arbitrarily without any pretence, break up their government, and thus practically put an end to free government upon the earth. It forces us to ask: "Is there, in all republics, this inherent and fatal weakness?" "Must a government, of necessity, be too strong for the liberties of its own people, or too weak to maintain its own existence?"

So viewing the issue, no choice was left but to call out the war power of the Government; and so to resist force employed for its destruction by force for its preservation.

The President then discussed the action of the border States, particularly Virginia, pursuant to the attack on Sumter.

The course taken in Virginia was the most remarkable—perhaps the most important. A convention elected by the people of that State to consider the very question of disrupting the Federal Union was in session at the capital of Virginia when Fort Sumter fell. To this body the people had chosen a large majority of professed Union men. Almost immediately after the fall of Sumter, many members of that majority went over to the original disunion minority, and with them adopted an ordinance for withdrawing the State from the Union. Whether this change was wrought by their great approval of the assault upon

Sumter or their great resentment at the Government's resistance to that assault is not definitely known. Although they submitted the ordinance for ratification to a vote of the people, to be taken on a day then somewhat more than a month distant, the convention and the legislature (which was also in session at the same time and place), with leading men of the State not members of either, immediately commenced acting as if the State were already out of the Union. They pushed military preparations vigorously forward all over the State. They seized the United States armory at Harper's Ferry, and the navy yard at Gosport, near Norfolk. They received—perhaps invited—into their State large bodies of troops, with their warlike appointments, from the so-called seceded States. They formally entered into a treaty of temporary alliance and coöperation with the so-called "Confederate States," and sent members to their congress at Montgomery. And, finally, they permitted the insurrectionary government to be transferred to their capital at Richmond.

The people of Virginia have thus allowed this giant insurrection to make its nest within her borders; and this Government has no choice left but to deal with it where it finds it. And it has the less regret as the loyal citizens have, in due form, claimed its protection. Those loyal citizens this Government is bound to recognize and protect, as being Virginia.

The attitude of "armed neutrality" adopted by Kentucky the President characterized as "disunion completed."

Figuratively speaking, it would be the building of an impassable wall along the line of separation—and yet not quite an impassable one, for under the guise of neutrality it would tie the hands of Union men and freely pass supplies from among them to the insurrectionists, which it could not do as an open enemy. . . . It recognizes no fidelity to the Constitution, no obligation to maintain the Union; and, while very many who have favored it are doubtless loyal citizens, it is, nevertheless, very injurious in effect.

The President proceeded to justify his orders to Lieutenant-General Scott authorizing him at discretion to suspend the writ of *habeas corpus,* an order which had been harshly criticised as arbitrary and unconstitutional.

The provision of the Constitution that ''the privilege of the writ of *habeas corpus* shall not be suspended, unless when, in cases of rebellion or invasion, the public safety may require it,'' is equivalent to a provision—is a provision—that such privilege may be suspended when, in case of rebellion or invasion, the public safety does require it. It was decided that we have a case of rebellion, and that the public safety does require the qualified suspension of the privilege of the writ which was authorized to be made. Now it is insisted that Congress, and not the Executive, is vested wth this power. But the Constitution itself is silent as to which or who is to exercise the power; and, as the provision was plainly made for a dangerous emergency, it cannot be believed the framers of the instrument intended that in every case the danger should run its course until Congress could be called together, the very assembling of which might be prevented, as was intended in this case, by the rebellion.

The President concluded his message proper with an appeal to Congress to pass those measures which would enable him to suppress the rebellion quickly and decisively:

It is now recommended that you give the legal means for making this contest a short and decisive one: that you place at the control of the Government for the work at least four hundred thousand men and $400,000,000. That number of men is about one-tenth of those of proper ages within the regions where, apparently, all are willing to engage; and the sum is less than a twenty-third part of the money value owned by the men who seem ready to devote the whole. A debt of $600,000,000 now is a less sum per head than was the debt of our Revolution when we came out of that struggle; and the money value in the country now bears even a greater proportion to what it was then than does the population. Surely each man has as strong a motive now to preserve our liberties as each had then to establish them.

A right result at this time will be worth more to the world than ten times the men and ten times the money. The evidence reaching us from the country leaves no doubt that the material for the work is abundant, and that it needs only the hand of legislation to give it legal sanction, and the hand of the Executive to give it practical shape and efficiency. One of the greatest perplexities of the Government is to avoid receiving troops faster than it can provide for them. In a word, the people will save their Government if the Government itself will do its part only indifferently well.

The latter half of the message was in its nature an address to the country upon the fallacies of secession

THE AMERICAN EAGLE SCOTCHING THE SNAKE OF SECESSION
[Cover picture of "Vanity Fair," May 4, 1861]
From the collection of the New York Public Library

and the constitutional duty imposed upon the President to suppress it by arms. The movers of secession, said Mr. Lincoln, in order to undermine the loyalty of the South to the Union, "invented an ingenious sophism, which, if conceded, was followed by perfectly logical steps through all the incidents to the complete destruction of the Union. The sophism itself is that any State in the Union may, consistently with the national Constitution, withdraw from the Union without the consent of the Union or of any other State. The little disguise that the supposed right is to be exercised only for just cause, themselves to be the sole judges of its justice, is too thin to merit any notice.''

This sophism, said Mr. Lincoln, is based upon the false doctrine of State sovereignty. ''Our States,'' he said, ''have neither more nor less power than that reserved to them in the Union by the Constitution—no one of them ever having been a State out of the Union. . . . The States have their *status* in the Union, and they have no other legal *status*. If they break from this, they can only do so against law and by revolution. The Union, and not themselves separately, procured their independence. . . . The Union is older than any of the States, and, in fact, it created them as States.''

The rights of the States reserved to them by the Constitution, argued Mr. Lincoln, are obviously administrative powers, and certainly do not include a power to destroy the Government itself. ''This relative matter of national power and State rights, as a principle, is no other than the principle of generality and locality. Whatever concerns the whole should be confined to the whole—to the general Government, while whatever concerns only the State should be left exclusively to the State.

''The nation purchased with money,'' continued Mr. Lincoln, ''the countries out of which several of these States were formed; is it just that they shall go off without leave and without refunding? . . . The nation is now in debt for money applied to the benefit of these so-called seceding States in common with the rest; is it just that . . . the remaining States pay the whole? . . . Again, if one State may secede, so may another, and when all shall have seceded none is left to pay the debts. . . . The principle itself is one of disintegration, and upon which no government can possibly endure.''

It may be affirmed, without extravagance, that the free institutions we enjoy have developed the powers and improved the condition of our whole people beyond any example in the world. Of this we now have a striking and an impressive illustration. So large an army as the Government has now on foot was never before known without a soldier in it but who had taken his place there of his own free choice. But, more than this, there are many single regiments whose members, one and another, possess full practical knowledge of all the arts, sciences, professions, and whatever else, whether useful or elegant, is known in the world; and there is scarcely one from which there could not be selected a President, a Cabinet, a Congress, and perhaps a Court, abundantly competent to administer the Government itself. Nor do I say this is not true also in the army of our late friends, now adversaries in this contest; but if it is, so much better the reason why the Government which has conferred such benefits on both them and us should not be broken up. Whoever, in any section, proposes to abandon such a government, would do well to consider in deference to what principle it is that he does it; what better he is likely to get in its stead; whether the substitute will give, or be intended to give, so much of good to the people? There are some foreshadowings on this subject. Our adversaries have adopted some declarations of independence, in which, unlike the good old one, penned by Jefferson, they omit the words, "all men are created equal." Why? They have adopted a temporary national constitution, in the preamble of which unlike our good old one, signed by Washington, they omit, "We, the people," and substitute, "We, the deputies of the sovereign and independent States." Why? Why this deliberate pressing out of view the rights of men and the authority of the people?

This is essentially a people's contest. On the side of the Union it is a struggle for maintaining in the world that form and substance of government whose leading object is to elevate the condition of men; to lift artificial weights from all shoulders; to clear the paths of laudable pursuits for all; to afford all an unfettered start and a fair chance in the race of life. Yielding to partial and temporary departures, from necessity, this is the leading object of the Government for whose existence we contend.

I am most happy to believe that the plain people understand and appreciate this. It is worthy of note that, while in this, the Government's, hour of trial, large numbers of those in the army and navy who have been favored with the offices have resigned and proved false to the hand which had pampered them, not one common soldier or common sailor is known to have deserted his flag.

Great honor is due to those officers who remained true, despite the example of their treacherous associates; but the greatest honor, and most important fact of all, is the unanimous firmness of the common soldiers and common sailors. To the last man, so far as known, they have successfully resisted the traitorous efforts of those whose commands but an hour before they obeyed as absolute law. This is the patriotic instinct of plain people. They understand, without an argument, that the destroying the Government which was made by Washington means no good to them.

Our popular Government has often been called an experiment. Two points in it our people have already settled—the successful establishing and the successful administering of it. One still remains—its successful maintenance against a formidable internal attempt to overthrow it. It is now for them to demonstrate to the world that those who can fairly carry an election can also suppress a rebellion; that ballots are the rightful and peaceful successors of bullets; and that, when ballots have fairly and constitutionally decided, there can be no successful peal back to bullets; that there can be no successful appeal, except to ballots themselves, at succeeding elections. Such will be a great lesson of peace; teaching men that what they cannot take by an election neither can they take by a war; teaching all the folly of being the beginners of a war.

It was with the deepest regret that the Executive found the duty of employing the war power in defence of the Government forced upon him. He could but perform this duty or surrender the existence of the Government. No compromise by public servants could, in this case, be a cure; not that compromises are not often proper, but no popular government can long survive a marked precedent that those who carry an election can save the government from immediate destruction only by giving up the main point upon which the people gave the election. The people themselves, and not their servants, can safely reverse their own deliberate decisions.

As a private citizen the Executive could not have consented that these institutions shall perish; much less could he, in betrayal of so vast and so sacred a trust as the free people have confided to him. He felt that he had no moral right to shrink, nor even to count the chances of his own life in what might follow. In full view of his great responsibility he has, so far, done what he has deemed his duty. You will now, according to your own judgment, perform yours. He sincerely hopes that your views and your actions may so accord with his as to assure all faithful citizens who have been disturbed in their rights of a certain and speedy restoration to them, under the Constitution and the laws.

And having thus chosen our course without guile and with pure purpose, let us renew our trust in God, and go forward without fear and with manly hearts.

CHAPTER III

The War-making Power: Does It Lie in the President or Congress?

General George B. McClellan's Victories in Western Virginia—Union Defeat at Manassas [Bull Run], Va.—Demoralization of the Country—Lincoln's War Measures—War Acts of Congress—Debate in the House on "Constitutionality of the President's Acts''; Against the Acts, Clement L. Vallandigham [O.]; in favor, William S. Holman [Ind.]—Debate on the Same in the Senate; Against the Acts, John C. Breckinridge [Ky.]; in Favor, Edward D. Baker [Ore.]; Kinsley S. Bingham [Mich.], Henry S. Lane (Ind.)—Anti-Secession Resolutions of Representative John J. Crittenden [Ky.] and Senator Andrew Johnson [Tenn.]; Carried—Lyman Trumbull [Ill.] Introduces in the Senate Bill to Suppress Insurrection (Virtually to Make War)—Debate on the Bill: in Favor, Senator Trumbull, Edward D. Baker [Ore.]; Opposed, James A. Bayard, Jr. [Del.], William P. Fessenden [Me.], John C. Breckinridge [Ky.], Jacob Collamer [Vt.]; Bill Is Not Pressed.

TEN days after the President had promulgated his enheartening message, Congress, as well as the Northern people, were rejoiced by the victories of General McClellan at Rich Mountain and Carrick's Ford, whereby western Virginia was secured to the Union. A week later, however, their joyful anticipation of an early and complete conquest of the seceded States was turned into dismay; instead of this easy victory perhaps it was the North which would be invaded; the national capital might fall, and the Southern Confederacy dictate from the halls of Congress terms for its recognition as a separate republic, and, indeed, the dominant one on the continent.

Battle of Bull Run [Manassas]

On July 21 the Confederate troops under Generals P. G. T. Beauregard and Joseph Johnston defeated the

68

Union troops under General Irwin McDowell at Manassas [Bull Run] Va. The Union retreat became a disorderly flight back to Washington. Many civilians had gone to see the battle, and these, mingling with the retreating soldiers, contributed to the confusion. One Congressman was captured by the rebels—a salutary

"WE WANT PEACE"

Benjamin Wood, of the New York *Daily News* (pro-South), and Horace Greeley, of the *Tribune* (anti-slavery)

From the collection of the New York Public Library

lesson to his colleagues of the evil effects of over-confidence.

The entire country was thrown into a panic, from which it was some time in recovering. On July 29, "after seven sleepless nights," Horace Greeley wrote a despairing letter to Lincoln, in which he advised the President that, if, in his opinion, the recent disaster was fatal, he should not shrink even from making peace with the rebels at once, and on their own terms.

Lincoln had spent sleepless nights, not in selfish

nursing of grief, but in planning for the salvation of the Republic. He placed General McClellan in chief com-mand at Washington, with power to organize a new army out of the three years' regiments beginning to pour in upon the capital, and he devised plans for a vigorous offensive campaign in the West.

Congress, which, during the days of victory, had up-held the President in granting him the legislation he asked, did not falter in the days of defeat, but was, if anything, more whole-hearted in its support, passing more drastic measures than it otherwise might have done, to exert the full military power of the Republic in order to preserve its honor and integrity.

War Acts of Congress

It authorized a loan of $250,000,000; it passed laws to define and punish treason; it superseded the "Morrill Tariff," enacted during the previous session, by a "War Tariff" in which increases of rate of duty were made wherever these would result in increases of revenue; it passed an income tax; it authorized the Presi-dent to close Southern ports in cases where collec-tion of duties was impossible, to call out 500,000 volunteers if necessary, and to confiscate the property of secessionists, including slaves (where these were em-ployed against the Government), and, in a section of the act of August 6 to increase the pay of the army, it vali-dated all the President's preceding acts to suppress the rebellion, such as calling out troops, blockading Southern ports, and suspending the writ of *habeas corpus*.

In the discussion upon the President's message and the acts passed by Congress in accordance with his recommendations, strenuous opposition was manifested by "State Rights" Democrats to what they considered to be "executive usurpation."

On July 10, 1861, Clement L. Vallandigham [Dem.], of Ohio, replied in the House to the President's message. On July 16 William S. Holman [Dem.], of Indiana, re-plied to him.

Constitutionality of the President's Acts

House of Representatives, July 10-16, 1861

Mr. Vallandigham.—Holding up the shield of the Constitution, and standing here in the place and with the manhood of a representative of the people, I propose to myself to-day the ancient freedom of speech used within these walls.

Mr. Chairman, the President, in the message before us, demands the extraordinary loan of $400,000,000—an amount nearly ten times greater than the entire public debt, State and Federal, at the close of the Revolution in 1783, and four times as much as the total expenditures during the three years' war with Great Britain, in 1812.

Sir, that same Constitution which I hold up, and to which I give my whole heart and my utmost loyalty, commits to Congress alone the power to borrow money and to fix the purposes to which it shall be applied, and expressly limits army appropriations to the term of two years. Whenever this House shall have become but a mere office wherein to register the decrees of the Executive, it will be high time to abolish it.

Sir, it has been the misfortune of the President from the beginning that he has totally and wholly underestimated the magnitude and character of the revolution with which he had to deal, or surely he never would have ventured upon the wicked and hazardous experiment of calling thirty millions of people to arms among themselves, without the counsel and authority of Congress. But when at last he found himself hemmed in by the revolution, and this city in danger, as he declares, and waked up thus, as the proclamation of the 15th of April proves him to have waked up, to the reality and significance of the movement, why did he not forthwith assemble Congress, and throw himself upon the wisdom and patriotism of the representatives of the States and of the people, instead of usurping powers which the Constitution has expressly conferred upon us? aye, sir, and powers which Congress had, but a little while before, repeatedly and emphatically refused to exercise, or to permit him to exercise?

At twelve o'clock on the 4th of March last, from the eastern portico of this Capitol, and, in the presence of twenty thousand of his countrymen, but enveloped in a cloud of soldiery which no other American President ever saw, Abraham Lincoln took the oath of office to support the Constitution, and delivered his inaugural—a message, I regret to say, not written in the direct and straightforward language which becomes an American President and an American statesman, and which was expected from the plain, blunt, honest man of the Northwest, but with the forked tongue and crooked counsel of the New York politician [Secretary Seward], leaving thirty millions of people in doubt whether it meant peace or war. But, whatever may have been the secret purpose and meaning of the inaugural, practically for six weeks the policy of peace prevailed; and they were weeks of happiness to the patriot and prosperity to the country. Business revived; trade returned; commerce flourished. Never was there a fairer prospect before any people. Secession in the past languished and was spiritless and harmless; secession in the future was arrested and perished. By overwhelming majorities, Virginia, Kentucky, North Carolina, Tennessee, and Missouri all declared for the old Union, and every heart beat high with hope that, in due course of time, and through faith and patience and peace, and by ultimate and adequate compromise, every State would be restored to it.

Mr. Vallandigham then claimed that *party necessity* caused the change from this pacific policy to one of coercion.

The peace policy was crushing out the Republican party. Under that policy, sir, it was melting away like snow before the sun. The general elections in Rhode Island and Connecticut, and municipal elections in New York and in the Western States, gave abundant evidence that the people were resolved upon the most ample and satisfactory constitutional guaranties to the South as the price of a restoration of Union. And then it was, sir, that the long and agonizing howl of defeated and disappointed politicians came up before the Administration. The newspaper press teemed with appeals and threats to the President. The mails groaned under the weight of letters demanding a change of policy; while a secret conclave of the Governors of Massachusetts, New York, Ohio, and other States assembled here promised men and money to support the President in the irrepressible conflict which they now invoked. And thus it was, sir, that the necessities of a party in the pangs of dissolution, in the very hour and article of death, demanding vigorous measures, which could result in nothing but civil war, renewed secession, and absolute and eternal disunion, were preferred and hearkened to before the peace and harmony and prosperity of the whole country.

Another cause for the change of policy, said Mr. Vallandigham, was "the passage of an obscure, ill-considered, ill-digested, and unstatesmanlike high protective tariff act, known as the Morrill tariff." The Confederate Government had adopted the old United States revenue tariff of 1857, the lower duties of which began to turn trade southward.

Political association and union, it was well known, must soon follow the direction of trade and interest. The City of New York, the great commercial emporium of the Union, and the Northwest, the chief granary of the Union, began to clamor now loudly for a repeal of the pernicious and ruinous tariff. Threatened thus with the loss of both political power and wealth or the repeal of the tariff, and at last of both, New England—and Pennsylvania, too, the land of Penn, cradled in peace—demanded now coercion and civil war, with all its horrors, as the price of preserving either from destruction. And, sir, when once this policy was begun, these self-same motives of waning commerce and threatened loss of trade impelled the great City of New York, her merchants and her politicians and her press, with here and there an honorable exception, to place herself in the very front rank among the worshipers of Moloch. Much, indeed, of that outburst and uprising in the North which followed the proclamation of the 15th of April, as well, perhaps, as the proclamation itself, was called forth, not so much by the fall of Sumter—an event long anticipated—as by the notion that the "insurrection," as it was called, might be crushed out in a few weeks, if not by the display, certainly, at least, by the presence of an overwhelming force.

I will not venture now to assert, what may yet some day be made to appear, that the subsequent acts of the Administration, and its enormous and persistent infractions of the Constitution, its high-handed usurpations of power, formed any part of a deliberate conspiracy to overthrow the present form of Federal republican government, and to establish a strong centralized government in its stead. No, sir; whatever their purposes now, I rather think that, in the beginning, they rushed heedlessly and headlong into the gulf, believing that, as the seat of war was then far distant and difficult of access, the display of vigor in reinforcing Sumter and Pickens, and in calling out seventy-five thousand militia upon the firing of the first gun, and, above all, in that exceedingly happy and original conceit of commanding the insurgent States to "disperse in twenty days," would not, on the one hand, precipitate a crisis, while, upon the other, it would satisfy its own violent partisans, and thus revive and restore the falling fortunes of the Republican party.

I can hardly conceive, sir, that the President and his advisers could be guilty of the exceeding folly of expecting to carry on a general civil war by a mere *posse comitatus* of three

"I PROMISE TO SUBDUE THE SOUTH IN TWENTY DAYS—A. LINCOLN."

months' militia. It may be, indeed, that, with wicked and most desperate cunning, the President meant all this as a mere entering wedge to that which was to rive the oak asunder ; or possibly as a test, to learn the public sentiment of the North and West. But, however that may be, the rapid secession and movements of Virginia, North Carolina, Arkansas, and Tennesseee, taking with them, as I have said elsewhere, four millions and a half of people, immense wealth, inexhaustible resources, five hundred thousand fighting men, and *the graves of Washington and Jackson,* and bringing up, too, in one single day the frontier from the Gulf to the Ohio and the Potomac, together with the abandonment by the one side and the occupation by the other of Har·

per's Ferry and the Norfolk navy yard, and the fierce gust and
whirlwind of passion in the North, compelled either a sudden
waking up of the President and his advisers to the frightful
significancy of the act which they had committed in heedlessly
breaking the vase which imprisoned the slumbering demon of
civil war, or else a premature but most rapid development of
the daring plot to foster and promote secession, and then to
set up a new and strong form of government in the States which
might remain in the Union.

But, whatever may have been the purpose, I assert here to-
day, as a Representative, that every principal act of the Administration since has been a glaring usurpation of power and
a palpable and dangerous violation of that very Constitution
which this civil war is professedly waged to support. Sir, I
pass by the proclamation of the 15th of April summoning the
militia—not to defend this capital; there is not a word about
the capital in the proclamation, and there was then no possible
danger to it from any quarter; but to retake and occupy forts
and property a thousand miles away. The militia thus called
out, with a shadow, at least, of authority, were amply sufficient
to protect the capital against any force which was then likely
to be sent against it—and the event has proved it—and ample
enough also to suppress the outbreak in Maryland. Every other
principal act of the Administration might well have been postponed, and ought to have been postponed, until the meeting of
Congress; or, if the exigencies of the occasion demanded it,
Congress should forthwith have been assembled.

But, sir, Congress was not assembled. The entire responsibility of the whole work was boldly assumed by the Executive,
and all the powers required for the purposes in hand were
boldly usurped from either the States or the people, or from
the legislative department; while the voice of the judiciary, that
last refuge and hope of liberty, was turned away from with
contempt.

Sir, the right of blockade—and I begin with it—is a belligerent right, incident to a state of war, and it cannot be exercised
until war has been declared or recognized; and Congress alone
can declare or recognize war. But Congress had not declared
or recognized war. On the contrary, they had but a little while
before expressly refused to declare it, or to arm the President
with the power to make it. And thus the President, in declaring a blockade of certain ports in the States of the South, and
in applying to it the rules governing blockades as between independent powers, violated the Constitution.

But if, on the other hand, he meant to deal with these States as still in the Union, and subject to Federal authority, then he usurped a power which belongs to Congress alone—the power to abolish and close up ports of entry; a power, too, which Congress had also but a few weeks before refused to exercise. And yet, without the repeal or abolition of ports of entry, any attempt by either Congress or the President to blockade these ports is a violation of the spirit, if not the letter, of that clause of the Constitution which declares that ''no preference shall be given by any regulation of commerce or revenue to the ports of one State over those of another.''

Jackson, sir! the great Jackson! did not dare to do this without authority of Congress; but the mimic Jackson of to-day blockades not only Charleston harbor, but the whole Southern coast, three thousand miles in extent, by a single stroke of the pen.

Next after the blockade, sir, in the catalogue of daring executive usurpations, comes the proclamation of the 3d of May, and the orders of the War and Navy Departments in pursuance of it—a proclamation and usurpation which would have cost any English sovereign his head at any time within the last two hundred years. Sir, the Constitution not only confines to Congress the right to declare war, but expressly provides that ''Congress (not the President) shall have power to raise and support armies''; and to ''provide and maintain a navy.'' And yet the President, of his own mere will and authority, and without the shadow of right, has proceeded to increase, and has increased, the standing army by twenty-five thousand men; the navy by eighteen thousand; and has called for and accepted the services of forty regiments of volunteers for three years, numbering forty-two thousand men, and making thus a grand army or military force, raised by executive proclamation alone, without the sanction of Congress, without warrant of law, and in direct violation of the Constitution and of his oath of office, of eighty-five thousand soldiers enlisted for three and five years, and already in the field. And yet the President now asks us to support the army which he has thus raised; to ratify his usurpations by a law *ex post facto,* and thus to make ourselves parties to our own degradation and to his infractions of the Constitution. Meanwhile, however, he has taken good care not only to enlist the men, organize the regiments, and muster them into service, but to provide in advance for a horde of forlorn, wornout, and broken-down politicians of his own party, by appointing, either by himself or through the governors of the

States, major-generals, brigadier-generals, colonels, lieutenant-colonels, majors, captains, lieutenants, adjutants, quarter-masters, and surgeons, without any limit as to numbers, and without so much as once saying to Congress, "By your leave, gentlemen."

Beginning with this wide breach of the Constitution, this enormous usurpation of the most dangerous of all powers—the power of the sword—other infractions and assumptions were easy; and, after public liberty, private right soon fell. The privacy of the telegraph was invaded in the search after treason and traitors; although it turns out, significantly enough, that the only victim, so far, is one of the appointees and especial pets of the Administration. The telegraphic dispatches, preserved under every pledge of secrecy for the protection and safety of the telegraph companies, were seized and carried away without search warrant, without probable cause, without oath, and without description of the places to be searched or of the things to be seized, and in plain violation of the right of the people to be secure in their houses, persons, *papers,* and effects against unreasonable searches and seizures. One step more, sir, will bring upon us search and seizure of the public mails; and finally, as in the worst days of English oppression—as in the times of the Russells and the Sydneys of English martyrdom—of the drawers and secretaries of the private citizen; though even then tyrants had the grace to look to the forms of the law, and the execution was judicial murder, not military slaughter.

But who shall say that the future Tiberius of America shall have the modesty of his Roman predecessor, in extenuation of whose character it is written by the great historian, *avertit oculos, jussitque scelera non spectavit!* [1]

Sir, the rights of property having been thus wantonly violated, it needed but a little stretch of usurpation to invade the sanctity of the person; and a victim was not long wanting. A private citizen of Maryland, not subject to the rules and articles of war—not in a case arising in the land or naval forces, nor in the militia when in actual service—is seized in his own house, in the dead hour of night, not by any civil officer nor upon any civil process, but by a band of armed soldiers, under the verbal orders of a military chief, and is ruthlessly torn from his wife and his children and hurried off to a fortress of the United States—and that fortress, as if in mockery, the very

---

[1] "He averted his eyes that he might not see the crimes which he ordered."

one over whose ramparts had floated that star-spangled banner immortalized in song by the patriot prisoner who,

"By the dawn's early light,"

saw its folds gleaming amid the wreck of battle, and invoked the blessings of Heaven upon it, and prayed that it might long wave—

"O'er the *land of the free* and the home of the brave."

And, sir, when the highest judicial officer of the land, the Chief Justice of the Supreme Court, upon whose shoulders, "when the judicial ermine" fell, it touched nothing not as spotless as itself, the aged, the venerable, the gentle and pure-minded Taney, who but a little while before had administered to the President the oath to support the Constitution and to execute the laws, issued, as by law it was his sworn duty to issue, the high prerogative writ of *habeas corpus*—that great writ of right, that main bulwark of personal liberty, commanding the body of the accused to be brought before him that justice and right might be done by due course of law, and without denial or delay; the gates of the fortress, its cannon turned toward and in plain sight of the city where the court sat, and frowning from the ramparts, were closed against the officer of the law, and the answer returned that the officer in command has, by the authority of the President, *suspended* the writ of *habeas corpus*. And thus it is, sir, that the accused has ever since been held a prisoner without due process of law; without bail; without presentment by a grand jury; without speedy or public trial by a petit jury of his own State or district, or any trial at all; without information of the nature and cause of the accusation; without being confronted with the witnesses against him; without compulsory process to obtain witnesses in his favor; and without the assistance of counsel for his defence.[1] And this is our boasted American liberty? And thus it is, too, sir, that here, here, in America, in the seventy-third year of the Republic, that great writ and security of personal freedom which it cost the patriots and freemen of England six hundred years of labor and toil and blood to extort and to hold fast from venal judges and tyrant kings; written in the great charter at Runnymede by the iron barons, who made the simple Latin and uncouth words of the times, *nullus liber homo*,[2] in

[1] This case is known as *ex parte* Merryman, and is found in 9 Amer. Law Reg. 524; 1 Taney's, Dec. 246.
[2] "No free man."

the language of Chatham, worth all the classics; recovered and confirmed a hundred times afterward, as often as violated and stolen away, and finally and firmly secured at last by the great act of Charles II, and transferred thence to our own Constitution and laws, has been wantonly and ruthlessly trampled in the dust. Ay, sir, that great writ, which no English judge, no English minister, no king or queen of England, dare disobey; that writ brought over by our fathers and cherished by them as a priceless inheritance of liberty, an American President has contemptuously set at defiance. Nay, more, he has ordered his subordinate military chiefs to suspend it at their discretion! And yet, after all this, he coolly comes before this House and the Senate and the country, and pleads that he is only preserving and protecting the Constitution; and demands and expects of this House and of the Senate and the country their thanks for his usurpations of power; while outside of this Capitol his myrmidons are clamoring for impeachment of the Chief Justice, as engaged in a conspiracy to break down the Federal Government!

Sir, however much necessity—the tyrant's plea—may be urged in extenuation of the usurpations and infractions of the President in regard to public liberty, there can be no such apology or defence for his invasions of private right. What overruling necessity required the violation of the sanctity of private property and private confidence? What great public danger demanded the arrest and imprisonment, without trial by common law, of one single private citizen, for an act done weeks before, openly, and by authority of his State? If guilty of treason, was not the judicial power ample enough and strong enough for his conviction and punishment? What, then, was needed in his case but the precedent under which other men, in other places, might become the victims of executive suspicion and displeasure?

As to the pretence, sir, that the President has the constitutional right to suspend the writ of *habeas corpus,* I will not waste time in arguing it. The case is as plain as words can make it. It is a legislative power; it is found only in the legislative article; it belongs to Congress only to do it. Subordinate officers have disobeyed it; General Wilkinson disobeyed it, but he sent his prisoners on for judicial trial; General Jackson disobeyed it and was reprimanded by James Madison; but no President, no body but Congress, ever before assumed the right to suspend it. And, sir, that other pretence, of necessity, I repeat, cannot be allowed. It had no existence in fact. The

Constitution cannot be preserved by violating it. It is an offence to the intelligence of this House and of the country to pretend that all this, and the other gross and multiplied infractions of the Constitution and usurpations of power, were done by the President and his advisers out of pure love and devotion to the Constitution. But if so, sir, then they have but one step further to take, and declare, in the language of Sir Boyle Roche in the Irish House of Commons, that such is the depth of their attachment to it that they are prepared to give up, not merely a part, but the whole of the Constitution, *to preserve the remainder*. And yet, if indeed this pretext of necessity be well founded, then let me say that a cause which demands the sacrifice of the Constitution and of the dearest securities of property, liberty, and life cannot be just; at least, it is not worth the sacrifice.

Sir, the power and rights of the States and the people, and of their Representatives, have been usurped; the sanctity of the private house and of private property has been invaded; and the liberty of the person wantonly and wickedly stricken down; free speech, too, has been repeatedly denied; and all this under the plea of necessity. Sir, the right of petition will follow next—nay, it has already been shaken; the freedom of the press will soon fall after it; and let me whisper in your ear that there will be few to mourn over its loss, unless, indeed, its ancient high and honorable character shall be rescued and redeemed from its present reckless mendacity and degradation. Freedom of religion will yield too, at last, amid the exultant shouts of millions, who have seen its holy temples defiled and its white robes of a former innocency trampled now under the polluting hoofs of an ambitious and faithless or fanatical clergy. Meantime national banks, bankrupt laws, a vast and permanent public debt, high tariffs, heavy direct taxation, enormous expenditure, gigantic and stupendous peculation, anarchy first and a strong government afterward, no more State lines, no more State governments, and a consolidated monarchy or vast centralized military despotism, must all follow in the history of the future, as in the history of the past they have, centuries ago, been written.

Sir, I have spoken freely and fearlessly to-day, as became an American Representative and an American citizen; one firmly resolved, come what may, not to lose his own constitutional liberties, nor to surrender his own constitutional rights in the vain effort to impose these rights and liberties upon ten millions of unwilling people. I have spoken earnestly, too, but yet not as one unmindful of the solemnity of the scenes which surround us upon every side to-day. Sir, when the Congress of the United States assembled here on the 3d of December, 1860, just seven months ago, the Senate was composed of sixty-six Senators, representing the thirty-three States of the Union, and this House of two hundred and thirty-seven members— every State being present. It was a grand and solemn spectacle; the embassadors of three and thirty sovereignties and of thirty-one million people, the mightiest republic on earth, in general Congress assembled. The new wings of the Capitol had then but just recently been finished, in all their gorgeous magnificence, and, except a hundred marines at the navy yard, not a soldier was within forty miles of Washington.

Sir, the Congress of the United States meets here again to-day; but how changed the scene. Instead of thirty-four States, twenty-three only, one less than the number forty years ago, are here or in the other wing of the Capitol. Forty-six Senators and a hundred and seventy-three Representatives constitute the Congress of the now United States. And of these, eight Senators and twenty-four Representatives, from four States only, linger here yet as deputies from that great South which, from the beginning of the Government, contributed so much to mold its policy, to build up its greatness, and to control its destinies. The vacant seats are, indeed, still here; and the escutcheons of their respective States look down now solemnly and sadly from these vaulted ceilings. But the Virginia of Washington and Henry and Madison, of Marshall and Jefferson, of Randolph and Monroe, the birthplace of Clay, the mother of States and of Presidents; the Carolinas of Pinckney and Sumter and Marion, of Calhoun and Macon; and Tennessee, the home and burial place of Jackson; and other States, too, once most loyal and true, are no longer here. The voices and the footsteps of the great dead of the past two ages of the Republic linger still, it may be in echo, along the stately corridors of this Capitol; but their descendants from nearly one-half of the States of the Republic will meet with us no more within these marble halls. But in the parks and lawns, and upon the broad avenues of this spacious city, seventy thousand soldiers have supplied their places; and the morning drumbeat from a score of encampments within sight of this beleaguered capital gives melancholy warning to the Representatives of the States and of the people that AMID ARMS LAWS ARE SILENT.

Sir, some years hence, I would fain hope some months hence, the present generation will demand to know the cause of all

VI—6

this; and some ages hereafter the grand and impartial tribunal of history will make solemn and diligent inquest of the authors of this terrible revolution.

At the close of his speech Mr. Vallandigham, merely to record his position, presented a resolution to the effect that the Federal Government, being the agent of the States, should be sustained by the people in the exercise of its constitutional powers for the preservation of the Union.

Mr. Holman, in his reply to Mr. Vallandigham, declared that a pacific policy could no longer be pursued by the Government; indeed at no time since the secession of the Confederate States would it have availed.

South Carolina, Florida, and Mississippi declared the separation to be eternal. It was not an apprehension of encroachment on their constitutional rights that induced secession; for, from the very beginning of this Administration the opposition would have controlled every measure of its policy. No, sir; the triumph of the Republican party was not the cause, but the pretence and the occasion, for dissolving the Union.

Thus, by the intemperate ambition of the leaders of public opinion in the South, war became inevitable; for upon the part of the secession leaders it is war—war with all its violence and hatred and malignity and bitterness. What, then, sir, on the part of the loyal men of the nation, is the object of the war?

It is not vengeance; for, in the midst of these vast preparations, the public indignation at the wanton wickedness of this attempt to overthrow the Constitution is softened by shame and sorrow, and the very bitterness of grief. It is not for the purpose of conquest or subjugation; not to enlarge the powers of the Government or increase its territorial limits; not to establish the supremacy of the one section of the Union, or to diminish the social or political rights of the other. But I say, sir, here in my place, in the presence of the Representatives of the people, on the authority of a well-defined public opinion, that the sole and only purpose of the people of the United States in this appeal to arms IS TO MAINTAIN THE UNION UNDER THE COMPACTS AND SAFEGUARDS OF THE CONSTITUTION. The popular instincts are not to be deceived. But for this high purpose, not a farmer would have left his field or a mechanic his shop; not a sword would have been withdrawn from its scabbard. Not only has this single purpose summoned your army into the field, but if it were possible that any other purpose should be developed —as the invasion of any constitutional right or the usurpation of political power—your army would either, with irresistible fury, hew down the new enemies of the Constitution or, overwhelmed with grief, abandon the tented field in despair. I tell you, sir, that, for purity of purpose, unselfishness of patriotism, intelligence, and cultivation, the army of the Republic may challenge the history of the world for a parallel.

A generation unaccustomed to arms, and in the enjoyment of unexampled blessings of peace, trampling on every selfish consideration, is almost in a moment transformed into a nation of soldiers; peaceful cities and towns and villages and the scenes of rural life, unused to even the tones of martial music, except in celebrating the achievement of a past generation, became the camps of gathering armies. The hereditary feuds of party, bitter as they may have been, are silenced, and the landmarks of political opinion, apparently indelible in the growth of more than half a century, are, at least for the moment, swept away. One sentiment animates every bosom: "The Union must be preserved."

No people have ever so clearly comprehended the necessity of an appeal to arms. The whole people understand the origin and immediate cause of our misfortunes. The unbridled ambition of a few men, unfortunately too great in the confidence of the South, indulging in the delusive hope of a great Southern empire, and, by new commercial relations, making the cities of Charleston and Savannah and New Orleans the commercial rivals of New York and Philadelphia and Boston, suggested the policy of a Southern Confederacy; and the leading statesmen, whose power was to be increased, seizing upon the intemperate opinions of a few fanatical men of the North on the question of slavery, inspired the Southern mind with the belief that the North meditated an assault on the domestic policy of the South and an invasion of their constitutional rights, and thus ensnared the Southern people into the whirlpool of revolution, and aroused such a storm of public rage as might only be satiated by overturning a Union which they themselves and their fathers, for more than three generations, had believed to be the very palladium of their safety.

To recognize secession or acquiesce in the right of peaceful revolution is an end of the Government, destroying the foundation of public faith on which it rests. What State would aid in the construction of forts and arsenals, or other works of national necessity, within the limits of other States, with the right of secession or acquiescence in revolution the established policy of the Government? To maintain the Union by an appeal to arms, or submit to total national ruin, is the only alternative. Could a brave and free people, controlled by sentiments of justice and honor, hesitate in their choice?

In my judgment an overwhelming majority of the people of the free States would not only have defended the constitutional rights of the South while in the Union, but would have made sacrifice upon sacrifice, even of opinion, to preserve the old fraternal relations and save us from the horrors of civil war, but secession has left us no alternative. It has appealed to the sword; and bitter as may be our grief, dark and gloomy as may be the future, we cannot escape the issue. The sword must decide the contest. A generation, twelve months ago the most happy and peaceful and prosperous that the world has ever seen, may be sacrificed by the mad ambition of the hour. But, if public liberty shall be upheld, the sacrifices of this generation, its shame and sorrow and tears, may redound to the stability and enduring honor of the Republic. As generations of the past have been, so ours may be sacrificed for the happiness and prosperity of the future.

But, sir, I cannot suppress my astonishment that a Representative of any part of the people of the great West, whose interests are so indissolubly united with the free navigation of the Mississippi River, should doubt the overwhelming necessity of maintaining the Union at every hazard.

Recognize the Southern Confederacy, and you place the navigation of the Mississippi, and with it the prosperity of the whole West, at the mercy of a foreign government. It may be said that mutual interests will produce treaties of mutual advantage. But a right existing in nature, sustained by every consideration of justice, and sanctioned by national compacts, cannot be the further subject of treaty. It is a right which the brave men of the West, following the example of their fathers, will hold, if it must be, by the tenure of the sword, and not by the arts of diplomacy. They will not pay one cent for the right to navigate the Mississippi River or any of its tributaries. If the South persists in the obstruction of this right, as she must do if she would maintain her separate nationality, the universal sentiment will be, "millions for war, but not one cent for tribute." If the Government shall hesitate in the vindication of this right, the people will vindicate it for themselves, and will never desist until the great river of the West, from its springs to the Gulf, shall be as free to their commerce as the ocean is to the commerce of the world.

So far, then, as the great West is concerned, there can be but one sentiment—*there can be no compromise at the expense of the Union;* there can be no settlement of pending difficulties except on the basis of the Constitution and the union of the States. The constitutional rights of no loyal citizen are to be impaired. The domestic and social policy of no State is to be invaded. The constitutional powers of the general Government are to be sustained, not to be enlarged. It is war for the Union, and not for the subjugation of States. As a Democrat and a citizen of the dominant section, I would hail with joy any proposition for compromise and peace coming from the people of the States the wild ambition of whose leaders has plunged the nation into the horrors of civil war, and for the time crushed the Union sentiment of the South. I would insist that the Government should meet such propositions, springing from a returning sense of patriotism and honor, in a spirit of magnanimity, of conciliation, and kindness. I would only demand, sir, that the misguided people of the South should submit, not to the supremacy of the North, or to the force of military power, or to new forms of government, but to the majesty of the Constitution—the Constitution as it was made by their and our fathers; and until that auspicious hour shall come, sir, the army of the Union, following the flag of the Republic wherever it shall be unfurled, cannot with honor return their swords to their scabbards or turn their thoughts upon the sweet blessings of peace.

In the Senate on July 16 John C. Breckinridge [Ky.] attacked the acts of the President as unconstitutional and denied the power of Congress to validate them. Edward D. Baker [Ore.], Kinsley S. Bingham [Mich.], and Henry S. Lane [Ind.] replied to him.

CONSTITUTIONALITY OF THE PRESIDENT'S ACTS

SENATE, JULY 16, 1861

SENATOR BRECKINRIDGE.—I deny, Mr. President, that one branch of this Government can indemnify any other branch of the Government for a violation of the Constitution or the laws. The powers conferred upon the general Government by the people of the States are the measure of its authority. Those powers have been confided to the different departments and the boundaries of those departments determined with perfect exactitude, and I deny that one can encroach upon another, or can indemnify it for a usurpation of powers not confided to it by the Constitution. Sir, Congress, by a joint resolution, has no more right, in my opinion, to make valid a violation of the Constitution and the laws by the President than the President would have by an entry upon the executive journal to make valid a usurpation of the executive power by the legislative department. Congress has no more right to make valid an unconstitutional act of the President than the President would have to make valid an act of the Supreme Court of the United States encroaching upon executive power; or than the Supreme Court would have the right to make valid an act of the Executive encroaching upon the judicial power.

On the contrary, I think that the acts of the President were usurpations, and that, so far from a resolution being passed ratifying and approving them, I think the Chief Magistrate of the country—and I have a right in my place to say it—should be rebuked by the vote of both Houses of Congress.

The President of the United States, first, has established a blockade of the whole Southern coast and an interior blockade of the chief rivers. By what authority has he done it? Where is the clause of the Constitution that authorized him? An attempt was made at the last session of Congress to confer the authority by bill. It did not pass. Congress refused to grant this authority by law in face of the fact that seven States had then withdrawn from the Federal Union. Will any Senator say that the power exists, under the Constitution, upon the part of the President to establish a blockade? It is an incident of war, sir; it is the exercise of the war power; and the Constitution of the United States declares that Congress shall pass an act to declare war, or exercise that power.

In this connection the speaker quoted from remarks made by Daniel Webster during the troubles in South Carolina in 1832-33, when it was suggested that President Jackson would blockade the port of Charleston.

"For one, I raise my voice beforehand against the unauthorized employment of military power, against superseding the authority of the laws by an armed force, under pretence of putting down nullification. The President has no authority to blockade Charleston; the President has no authority to employ military force, till he shall be duly required so to do, by law, and by the civil authorities. His duty is to cause the laws to be executed. His duty is to support the civil authority.''

It is proposed, continued the speaker, to make valid the act of the President in enlisting men for three and five years. I ask you by what authority of Constitution or law he has done this act? The power is not conferred in the Constitution; it has not been granted by the law. It is, therefore, an unconstitutional and illegal act of Executive power. The President, of his own will —and that is one of the acts enumerated in this joint resolution which it is proposed to approve and ratify—has added immensely to the force of the regular army. The Constitution says that Congress shall raise armies, and a law now upon your statute book limits the number of the regular force, officers and men. Hence, sir, that is an act in derogation both of the Constitution and of the laws.

The President has added immensely to the navy of the United States. The Constitution says that Congress shall provide and maintain a navy, and there is now a law upon the statute book limiting the number of men to be employed in the navy. That, like the rest, sir, will not bear argument.

Mr. President, it needs no elaborate argument to show that the Executive authority of the United States has no right to suspend the writ of *habeas corpus.* I content myself here, unless some defence be offered upon this floor, with referring to the fact that the privilege to suspend the writ in case of rebellion or invasion is classed among the legislative powers of the Constitution. That article of the Constitution which refers to the powers of the President, executive powers, touches not the question. I may add that upon no occasion has it ever been asserted in the Congress of the United States, as far as I recollect our history, that this power exists upon the part of the Executive. On one memorable occasion in our history, Jefferson thought a period had arrived when, perhaps, that writ might properly be suspended. He did not undertake to do it himself. He submitted the question to Congress. He did not even recommend that it should be done; and in the long debates that occurred in this and the other branch of Congress upon the question of suspending the writ, which finally was not suspended, not one intimation was given by any speaker in either House, as far as I remember, that the power existed on the part of the President.

What part of the Constitution is it, sir, which confers upon the President the right to do this act more than upon any other officer, executive or judicial, of the Government? Surely it is not that portion of the Constitution which declares that he shall take care that the laws be faithfully executed. The most eminent commentators on the Constitution of the United States concur in saying that it is purely a legislative act. Justice Story, one of the most eminent judicial lights of New England, in his "Commentaries on the Constitution," declares it to belong to the legislature and not to the Executive. The Supreme Court of the United States have determined that Congress alone can suspend the privilege of the writ. Upon a recent occasion, in a case which arose in Maryland,[1] the present Chief Justice [Roger B. Taney], in an opinion which has never been answered, and which never will be answered, exhausts the argument, and makes all other reference to the subject idle and superfluous.

You propose to make valid the President's suspension of the writ, without making a defence of his act either upon constitutional or legal grounds. What will be the effect, sir? In approving what the President has done in this regard in the past, you invite him to do the like in the future; and the whole country will lie prostrate at the feet of executive power when, in the opinion of the President, the time shall have come to suspend the rights of individuals and to have substituted military power for judicial authority.

I enumerate what I regard as usurpations of the Executive to go upon the record as a protest of those of us who are not willing to see the Constitution subverted and the public liberty trampled under foot, under whatever pretext of necessity or otherwise.

The Constitution declares that Congress alone shall have power "to declare war." The President has made war. Congress alone shall have power "to raise and support armies." The President has raised and supported armies on his own authority. Congress shall have power "to provide and maintain a navy." The President has provided an immense navy and maintains it without authority of law. The Constitution declares that no money shall be taken from the treasury except in pursuance of appropriations made by law. The President has taken money from the treasury without appropriations made by law for the purpose of carrying out the preceding unconstitutional acts. One of the amendments to the Constitution declares that—

[1] See page 77.

"A well-regulated militia being necessary to the security of a free State, the right of the people to keep and bear arms shall not be infringed."

They have been disarmed, and disarmed without criminal charge and without warrant. One of the amendments to the Constitution declares that—

"The right of the people to be secure in their persons, houses, papers, and effects, against unreasonable searches and seizures, shall not be violated; and no warrants shall issue but upon probable cause, supported by oath or affirmation, and particularly describing the place to be searched and the persons or things to be seized."

The people have not been exempt from unreasonable searches and seizures. Their property has been taken from them; their houses have been searched without authority of law, and by a pure military authority.

"No person"—

says one of the amendments to the Constitution—

"shall be held to answer for a capital or otherwise infamous crime, unless on a presentment or indictment of a grand jury."

Many persons have been held to answer for infamous crimes without presentment or indictment, and without warrant, by military authority. The same amendment continues:

"Nor shall be compelled in any criminal case to be a witness against himself, nor be deprived of life, liberty, or property, without due process of law."

Citizens have, by military authority, been deprived of liberty and property without due process of law.

These great and fundamental rights, sir, the sanctity of which is the measure of progress and of civilization, which have been carefully guarded and locked up in your Constitution, have been trampled under foot by military power, are being now every day trampled under foot by military power here and hereabouts in the presence of the two Houses of Congress; and yet, so great upon the one side is the passion of the hour, and so astonishing the stupid amazement on the other, that we receive it as natural, as right, as of course. We are rushing, and with rapid strides, from a constitutional government to a military despotism.

The Constitution says the freedom of speech and of the press shall not be abridged. Three days ago, in the city of St. Louis, a military officer, with four hundred soldiers—that was his warrant—went into a newspaper office of that city, removed the types, and declared that it should no longer be published, giving, among other reasons, that it was fabricating reports injurious to the United States soldiers in Missouri. We are told in the same dispatch that the proprietors of the paper submitted, and intended to make their appeal—where, and to whom? To the judicial authorities? No, sir; but to Major-General Frémont when he should reach St. Louis; to appeal from General Lyon to General Frémont. The civil authorities of the country are paralyzed, and a practical martial law is being established all over the land. The like never happened in this country before, and would not be tolerated in any country in Europe which pretends to the elements of civilization and regulated liberty. George Washington carried the thirteen colonies through the war of the Revolution without martial law. The President of the United States cannot conduct the Government three months without resorting to it.

Then, Mr. President, the Executive of the United States has assumed legislative powers. The Executive of the United States has assumed judicial powers. The executive power belongs to him by the Constitution. He has, therefore, concentrated in his own hands executive, legislative, and judicial powers, which, in every age of the world, has been the very definition of despotism, and exercises them to-day, while we sit in the Senate Chamber and the other branch of the legislative authority at the other end of the Capitol. What is the excuse; what is the justification; what is the plea? Necessity. Necessity? I answer, first, there was no necessity. Was it necessary, to preserve the visible emblems of Federal authority here, that the Southern coast should have been blockaded? Did not the same necessity exist when Congress, at its last session, refused to pass the force bill, that existed at the time the President assumed these powers? Was it necessary, until Congress should meet, to the existence of the Union of these States, and of its Constitution, that powers not conferred by the instrument should be assumed? Was there any necessity for overrunning the State of Missouri? Was there a necessity for raising the largest armies ever assembled upon the American continent, and fitting out the largest fleets ever seen in an American harbor? Will any Senator point out the necessity for the occurrences which are now taking place every day of arresting individuals without warrant of law? If that be a necessity in the present condition of affairs, and when Congress is in session here, what a long necessity we have before us and impending over us! Sir, let Congress adjourn, approving and ratifying these acts, and the same character of necessity precisely, even stronger, perhaps, will justify the President in superseding the laws in every State of this Union where, in his opinion, it should be done; and, sir, there will not be a vestige of civil authority left to rise after the passing tread of military power.

But, Mr. President, I deny this doctrine of necessity. I deny that the President of the United States may violate the Constitution upon the ground of necessity. The doctrine is utterly subversive of the Constitution; it is utterly subversive of all written limitations of government; and it substitutes, especially where you make him the ultimate judge of that necessity, and his decision not to be appealed from, the will of one man for a written constitution. Mr. President, the Government of the United States, which draws its life from the Constitution, and which was made by that instrument, does not rest, as does the constitution in many other countries, upon usage or upon implied consent. It rests upon express written consent. The Government of the United States may exercise such powers, and such only, as are given in this written form of government and bond which unites the States; none others. The people of the States conferred upon this agent of theirs just such powers as they deemed necessary, and no more; all others they retained. That Constitution was made for all contingencies; for peace and for war.

Mr. President, is this contest to preserve the Constitution? If so, then it should be waged in a constitutional manner. Is the doctrine to obtain that the provisions of the Federal Constitution are to be entirely subordinated to the idea of political unity? Shall the rallying cry be, "the Constitution and the Union," or are we prepared to say, "the Constitution is gone, but the Union survives"? What sort of Union would it be? Let this principle be announced, let us carry on this contest with this spirit, and wink at or approve violations of this sacred instrument, and, sir, the people will soon begin to inquire what will become of their liberties at the end of the strife. The pregnant question, Mr. President, for us to decide is whether the Constitution is to be respected in this struggle; whether we are to be called upon to follow the flag over the ruins of the Constitution. Without questioning the motives of any, I believe that the whole tendency of the present proceedings is to establish a government without limitations of powers, and to change radically our frame and character of government.

Sir, in proof of my statement that the disposition is to conduct this contest without regard to the Constitution, witness the remarks that fell the other day from the able and very eloquent Senator from Oregon [Edward D. Baker]. He is a constitutional lawyer; he knows what the Constitution of his country is—no man better. He declared, in the presence of the Senate and the country, that he meant direct war, and that for that purpose nothing was so good as a dictator; he therefore was for conferring upon the President of the United States almost unlimited powers. I heard no rebuke administered to that eminent gentleman. Upon the contrary, I saw warm congratulations from more than one Senator, apparently upon the sentiments and the character of the address.

In the course of the same speech to which I have referred that eminent Senator declared that not only must that country be ravaged by armies, but that unless the people of those States paid willing and loyal obedience to the Federal Government, their State form must be changed, and they must be reduced to the condition of Territories; to be governed by governors sent from Massachusetts and Illinois.

SENATOR BAKER.—On the contrary, I spoke against giving too much power to the President. I was occupying my usual constitution guarded position against the increase of a standing army. I gave, as an excuse for voting for an army at all, the present condition of public affairs; and, in that light and with that purpose, I did say that, in order to save the Union, I would take some risk of despotism. I repeat that now: I will risk a little to save all.

Again: I expressed my sincere hope—perhaps I may have added my conviction—that in a better and not a very distant day the Southern States would not only return to their allegiance, but would become loyal in sentiment as well as opinion. But I declared then what no comment of his will drive me from, that if, contrary to that hope, they did not do it, if they would not send members here to govern them, it was better, for the sake of ultimate peace, for freedom, civilization, humanity, that they should be governed as Territories are governed, rather than permit perpetual anarchy, confusion, discord, and civil war. [Manifestations of applause in the galleries.] I did say that and I do believe that now; and I think the events of the next six months will show that it would be better for the country and the world and the Senator himself if he believed it. [Applause in the galleries.]

SENATOR BRECKINRIDGE.—Mr. President, I did not misunderstand the position of the Senator from Oregon, and I think that I stated it in substance as he has stated it himself. The Senator reaffirms upon this floor that, if it should become necessary in the opinion of Congress, he would be in favor of reducing these States to a territorial condition. Well, sir, if they are out of the Union, I suppose we have the power to make war on them under that general power which exists in all people to make war, and conquer them and do as we please with them; but, if they are regarded as still being States in this Union, and to be treated according to the provisions and the powers conferred by the Federal Constitution, there is no pretence of argument, none will be made, that the instrument contains any authority to reduce them to the territorial condition. It is an additional proof of the statement I made that the Constitution of the United States is put aside in this contest. I want the people to know it. Let them determine. They will determine as they think best for their own interest and their own destiny. Perhaps, sir, they will pause and consider what is likely to become of their own liberties after this spirit shall have worked out itself.

I consider it not only subversive of the Constitution, but I consider it subversive of the public liberty, to clothe any man with dictatorial powers, and to undertake, under a republican form of government, to govern ten million people as if they were in a territorial condition.

Mr. President, as a further proof, I will accumulate two or three more. The excellent Senator from Connecticut [James Dixon], heretofore always regarded as one of the most moderate and conservative in the political organization to which he is attached, said in substance that, if the institution of African slavery stood in the way of the Union, it must be abolished.

Let us pause one moment, Mr. President, and consider to what that leads. Men who love the Constitution and the Union of the States as sincerely and cordially as the Senator himself could possibly do consider the Union not an end, but a means—a means by which, under the terms of the Constitution, liberty may be maintained, property and personal rights protected, and general happiness secured. The substance of what is declared by the Senator is that the unity of the Government shall survive not only the Constitution, but all rights both of persons and of property.

The institutions of the Southern States existed before the Constitution was formed, and were intended to be secured by it. Their property of any other description is no more sacred in view of the Constitution, or of their own laws, than the description of property to which the Senator referred. To declare that this contest shall be prosecuted, if necessary, to the abolition of slavery in the Southern States is in principle to declare that, if it becomes necessary, it shall be prosecuted to the total subversion of all State authority, to the total overthrow of all rights, personal and political, and to the entire subversion of their liberties, possibly of ours. The conclusions are not too large which I draw from the principle announced by the Senator; and taken in connection with the declaration of the Senator from Oregon, taken in connection with the acts which are treated in this joint resolution, and the other acts which I have enumerated, it proves what I fear, and what I desire the country to understand, that the Constitution of the United States is no longer to be held as the measure of power on one side and of obedience on the other, but that it is to be put aside to carry out the purposes of the majority.

I hold, sir, that it is no legitimate mode to preserve the Union of the States by trampling the Constitution under foot; and I do not believe that the people of the adhering States are willing to go into this strife with vast armies, make war, abolish institutions and political communities themselves, struggling simply for the idea of territorial integrity and national unity, and finding, when they come out of the contest, the Constitution gone and themselves at sea as to the character of the institutions with which they shall emerge from it.

Mr. President, I regret to say that what may be called the more extreme, violent, and resolute men of the Republican organization appear to have control of its destiny at this time, and all efforts are being made for the purpose of preventing any return to peace, and of inflaming the public passions against the institutions of the South. I heard a bill read at that table this morning by its title, ''A bill to suppress the slaveholders' rebellion.''[1] If it had had a title, ''A bill to provide for the execution of the laws,'' or any other parliamentary title known heretofore in American legislative proceedings, of course I should not have been astonished; but when I see in a deliberative body an attempt made, through the very heading of a bill, to create odium and prejudice against a particular interest, which is equally protected with others under the Constitution of your country, it shows a frame of mind which leads all thoughtful men to despair both of the Constitution and the country, if such a spirit can prevail.

[1] Introduced by Samuel C. Pomeroy [Kan.].

OPPONENTS OF THE "UNNATURAL AND FRATRICIDAL WAR"

[Satire on Breckinridge's Petition]

From the collection of the New York Public Library

Senator Bingham.—I wish to ask the Senator if he denies that the present rebellion is a slaveholders' rebellion?

Senator Breckinridge.—I do, sir. I have no doubt that the question of slavery, and their rights as connected with that institution, as they understand them, had a great deal to do first with the controversies which preceded the separation, and then with the act of separation itself; but it is perfectly manifest that, whereas the proportion of slaveholders to non-slaveholders is very small in the seceded States, the sentiments of the population are almost unanimous. Allow me to ask the Senator a question. Does he approve the title of that bill?

Senator Bingham.—I do.

Senator Breckinridge.—I regret to hear that answer; but it serves to bring the mind of the country to consider the actual condition of affairs, and the danger which is impending over us.

My colleague has this moment handed me the bill referred to. The enacting clause, as might have been anticipated from the title, reads as follows:

Be it enacted, That from and after the passage of this act, there shall be no slavery or involuntary servitude in any of the States of this Union that claim to have seceded from the Government and are in open and armed resistance to the execution of the laws and the provisions of the Constitution of the United States.

I believe that is to be carried out by a proclamation of the President.

And be it further enacted, That immediately after the passage of this act, the President of the United States shall cause his proclamation to be issued, setting forth the immediate and unconditional emancipation of all persons held as slaves in any of the aforesaid States under the laws thereof, and also ordering all officers to give protection to all such emancipated slaves, and to accept the services of all who may tender them in behalf of the Government, if, in the judgment of such officers, such services shall be useful or necessary to the prosecution of this war.

It is not only a congressional act of emancipation, but it is intended to arm the slaves against the masters. It is not only to confiscate the whole property, but it is to foment a servile war. That is a proposition offered in the Senate of the United States! Sir, I shall find myself denounced in the newspapers to-morrow morning as a man who was uttering treason here for speaking a word in favor of the Constitution; but not one word will be uttered against a Senator who deliberately proposes to trample that Constitution under his feet, and to plunge the country into all the horrors of civil and of servile war.

I shall trouble the Senate no longer. I know that argument and appeal are all in vain. The Senate pants for action. I am quite aware that, in the present temper of Congress, one might as well oppose his uplifted hand to the descending waters of Niagara as to reason or to appeal against the contemplated proceedings. The few of us left here who are faithful to our convictions can only look with sadness upon the melancholy drama that is being enacted before us. We can only hope that this flash of frenzy may not assume the form of chronic madness, and that in any event Divine Providence may preserve for us and for posterity, out of the wreck of a broken Union, the priceless principles of constitutional liberty and of self-government. [Applause in the galleries.]

Senator Lane.—Gentlemen take a technical objection against the action of the President, and say that he has violated the Constitution of the United States. I remember an incident, I think in Roman history, where an African pro-consul was required to swear that he had not violated the laws of Rome; instead of which, with uplifted hand, he swore that he had saved the Roman republic. And, whatsoever differences of opinion may this day exist in reference to the action of the President, I take it for granted that every intelligent patriot in the land not only believes but knows that the President has saved the Republic by his energetic and patriotic action since the 4th of March. I sanction and approve everything that the President has done during the recess of Congress, and the people sanction and approve it, and there is no power this side of Heaven that can reverse that decision of the American people. I not only sanction all that they have done, but I sanction all that they are soon to do. When your victorious and conquering columns shall sweep treason out of old Virginia; when they shall make that old commonwealth a fit residence for the patriotic descendants of her revolutionary fathers, I shall sanction and approve that. I sanction and approve the use of force now, at once, immediately; and I would shake that traitorous commonwealth as with an earthquake tread of a hundred thousand armed men.

What is it that the President has done since the last meeting of Congress? First, he has declared a blockade of the Southern ports, and gentlemen tell us there is no constitutional authority for that. It is the first duty of the President to see that the laws are faithfully executed. We have a tariff law imposing duties upon foreign importations. That has been disregarded by the seceding States; they have assumed to pass a tariff act different from ours. That law of Congress cannot be enforced by the ordinary course of procedure under your collections of revenue at the proper ports established by law. There is no higher power in the Constitution of the United States delegated to the President than the power to "take care that the laws be faithfully executed." These high and extraordinary powers, although not perhaps technically granted in the Constitution, result as an incident to the war power, which is invoked, and constitutionally invoked, under that provision of the Constitution which authorizes the President to use force to suppress insurrection and to put down rebellion. I sanction, then, the proclamation establishing a blockade.

The next objection is to the declaration of martial law, by which the writ of *habeas corpus* was suspended. I only regret that when the writ was suspended the *corpus* of Baltimore treason was not "suspended" too. It is necessary to the enforcement of the laws and to the preservation of the Union that this writ of *habeas corpus* should be suspended; and the Constitution of the United States says, in express terms, it may be suspended in case of rebellion and insurrection. Then the whole question comes to this: Who is to judge? Where is the discretion lodged? Clearly with the President of the United States; and it can be safely lodged nowhere else. Suppose an insurrection breaks out during the recess of Congress: the President is sworn to uphold the law and the Constitution; he finds armed rebellion; has he no power to put it down? May he not use all proper power to put down armed rebellion? I approve, then, the suspension of the writ of *habeas corpus*.

What more does the honorable Senator from Kentucky say? That General Washington prosecuted the Revolutionary War to a successful termination without ever suspending the writ of *habeas corpus*. That is true. He was in a contest with a foreign foe. Here we are engaged in entirely a different war, where our enemies are in our midst. What would gentlemen have the President do? Suppose my distinguished friend from Kentucky had been elected President, and seven States had seceded and levied war against the United States, and were with an embattled host threatening to take and capture the capital: what would have been his action? Would he have folded his arms? No, no. He, I doubt not, would have made a blow to defend the Union and the Constitution of the United States. Then what else could he have done than President Lincoln has done? If, as I suppose he does, the distinguished Senator from Kentucky echoes public opinion in Kentucky or intends to echo public opinion there, I have no doubt that that proud commonwealth would have sanctioned and approved and advised the very step the President has taken to vindicate the laws and to defend the Constitution of the United States.

But another charge which he made against this Administration—that private papers were seized. I suppose the honorable and distinguished Senator from Kentucky refers to telegraphic dispatches. They were seized, but not quite soon enough, as I think; and still they have proven a California placer of treason. It was right and proper to seize them. It was right to seize the dispatches to vindicate the character of honorable Senators on this floor.

Another count in this indictment is that citizens have been imprisoned without any authority of law, which amounts to precisely the former charge that martial law has been declared under the proclamation of the President in some few localities where it was eminently necessary. Citizens of Baltimore have been imprisoned under military authority, and, as I believe, have been rightfully imprisoned. When a New England regiment cannot march through the city of Baltimore to defend the capital without being attacked and shot down by a mob, it is time that the military authority should do what the civil authority was not able to do—suppress and put down that unauthorized mob. I sympathize with the true and loyal citizens of Baltimore. I sympathize with the patriotic soldiery of Massachusetts who were coming to defend the capital. I have no sympathy to waste upon armed traitors and rebels. I leave others to pronounce their eulogy and to show them sympathy.

Another charge is that the President has violated the Constitution of the United States in this: that he has disarmed citizens; refused them the privilege, under the Constitution, of bearing arms. Sir, it is true that he has refused traitors the privilege of using arms against the Government of the country. General Lyon, of Missouri, and the gallant Frank Blair, and their associates, did disarm some fifteen hundred rebels at Camp Jackson, near St. Louis; and for that we are told they are violators of the Constitution. The President has not only guaranteed by his action the right to bear arms, but he has invited the patriotic citizens of the United States to bear arms for the only noble purpose for which men can take arms—in defence of the Constitution and liberties of the people. Is the right to bear arms in Kentucky so sacred that it may never be violated? Then why do you not bear arms in defence of the Constitution and liberties of the Republic? There is a right to bear arms that is worth something. Does Kentucky stand upon the right to bear arms? Why is she not bearing arms upon the battlefield to-day, beside Massachusetts and Indiana and Ohio, and the loyal States? Why does she not insist upon her right to bear arms, when traitors are seeking to tear down the Government under which we live? The right to bear arms, forsooth, is a forgotten right in the chivalric old commonwealth of Kentucky. I have listened for her voice in this war; I have heard it not; and why? Because her action is, as I believe, paralyzed by the course of her State authorities; but on the first Monday of next August the true voice of old Kentucky will be heard, and you will have a two-thirds majority in favor of loyalty to the Union, and the places that know her distinguished governor now will soon know him no more forever.

Another count in this indictment against the Administration is that they have put down treasonable newspapers. The Administration have shown a forbearance beyond all parallel in history. There is no government of constituted authority upon earth that would have tolerated either the treasonable utterance or publications of these traitors. I say that I not only approve of the destruction of that St. Louis paper, but I rejoice at it as an evidence of returning common sense in those who are to defend the Government of the country.

One word, before I forget it, on the subject of this war and the object of the war. There is no war levied against any State, or against any State institutions. The President has called out troops to suppress insurrection and put down rebellion. These are the objects for which your troops have been called into the field. The abolition of slavery is no object contemplated for which this war is to be prosecuted. But let me tell gentlemen that, although the abolition of slavery is not an object of the war, they may, in their madness and folly and treason, make the abolition of slavery one of the results of this war. That is what I understand to be precisely the position of the Administration upon the subject of this war.

The gentleman closes his very able and eloquent speech with the assumption of a position and doctrine that I do not for one moment admit; and that is that the States made this National Union of ours. I have read wrongfully, and to little purpose, the history of the convention that formed the Constitution if that is historically corect. I understand the people of the United States to have made this Constitution; and so Webster understood it.

This doctrine of State rights, as opposed to the rights of

the general Government, under the Federal Constitution, is a most dangerous and pestilent heresy, which underlies this whole controversy. Out of that idea, and one other idea, the present disastrous state of things has been brought upon the country. The idea of social, political inequality among the respective members of the Confederacy underlies this war at its very foundation. We are to teach them, I hope, a lesson of respect for the North; we are to teach them a lesson of equality. Whatever else this war may do, it will teach a lesson of equality for a thousand years; nay, more, it will add a thousand years to the glorious lifetime of this, the only republic upon the earth.

So much for these objections to what the President of the United States has done. But the closing argument, after all, and that upon which the gentleman places most stress, is that an effort was made at the last session of Congress to give to the President this very power, and that the Congress of the United States refused to pass that bill. That is true; and why? Because the vacant seats around us were then filled by traitors, many of whom are now in arms against the Republic. For that reason, and that alone, we failed to confer this power upon the President of the United States.

But the gentleman says he is glad that the people have their attention now directed to the true posture of American politics. I am glad that the people have their eye turned in the same direction. In the last sixty days four hundred thousand troops have volunteered to defend the Stars and Stripes and to defend the Constitution. There is no parallel in all human history to the widespread enthusiasm which has pervaded the whole people. The nearest parallel is when Peter the Hermit preached a crusade for the recovery of the Holy Sepulcher; and our cause is little less sacred than that for the recovery of the grave of the Savior of mankind, for we propose a crusade in defence of the Constitution, the rights of man, and the liberties of the American people.

I understand by coercion a right to march troops wheresoever the Government desires to march them. You hear much said about the invasion of a sovereign State. Who can invade a State? The home government or a foreign government? Virginia is to-day as much a part of the United States as Indiana, and the President has as much right to march troops there, and I hope is now engaged in marching troops there for the purpose of crushing out rebellion. Let us stand by the compromises of the Constitution. Let us hereafter send all our pacific messages to traitors at the mouth of the cannon. Let the politicians reflect honestly the will of the people, and your volunteer soldiers will crush out this rebellion without leaders and without officers. They have determined to do this very thing.

But gentlemen say how, from the ruins, will you reconstruct the Republic? We do not contemplate any destruction of the Republic which involves a reconstruction. We intend to protect the Union men of the border States, to foster the Union sentiment, to get up a counter revolution, which will lay all secession and treason in ruins. We expect soon to readmit Tennessee into the Union, as we have recently readmitted old Virginia; we expect soon to readmit North Carolina; and we expect to present in six months an unbroken front to all foreign powers, no single star erased, the light of no star obliterated by treason in any part of the country. When we get the seceding States properly represented upon the floor of the Congress of the United States, then we shall have nothing to do but to punish the last remains and remnants of this most disgraceful rebellion; and the remedy, after all, is a Kentucky remedy; we propose—hemp. That is the remedy for treason; not under mob law, but under indictments in courts. We propose to have courts and judges sworn to support the law, and who will abide by that sacred oath. When this is done, I promise you that treason and rebellion will be buried forever.

ANTI-SECESSION RESOLUTIONS

The day after the Union defeat at Bull Run, John J. Crittenden [Ky.], who had retired from the Senate to enter the House of Representatives, introduced in the House a resolution confirming the President's theory of secession, namely, that war had been forced on the Government by the Southern disunionists; that it was waged by the Government not for subjugating the seceded States, nor interfering with their rights and institutions, but to maintain the supremacy of the Constitution, the dignity and integrity of the Union, and the equality of all the States; and that, so soon as these objects were accomplished, the war ought to cease.

This was passed by the House on July 22 with only two dissenting votes, those of Henry C. Burnett [Ky.] and John W. Reid [Mo.], other opponents of the

J. J. Crittenden

measure, such as Clement L. Vallandigham [O.], not voting. On July 24 the Senate passed a resolution to the same effect (introduced by Andrew Jackson of Tennessee) with only five dissenting votes, John C. Breckinridge [Ky.] being among the number.

On July 17 Lyman Trumbull [Ill.] introduced in the Senate a bill to suppress insurrection in places proclaimed by the President, by giving the military authorities power in their respective districts to suspend the writ of *habeas corpus* by proclamation, arrest persons on the charge of sedition and try them by court-martial, compel suspected persons to take the oath of allegiance, etc. This came up for discussion on July 30.

MARTIAL LAW BY LEGISLATIVE ENACTMENT

SENATE, JULY 30-AUGUST 1, 1861

Senator Trumbull supported his resolution. He said:

I wish to premise by saying that I am as much for standing by the Constitution of the country and for putting down this rebellion in a constitutional and legal way as any gentleman here. I will not yield to the Senator from Kentucky [Mr. Breckinridge] or any other Senator in my veneration for the Constitution of the United States. I believe that that instrument was intended by its framers to be perpetual. I believe it contains all the power necessary to suppress even this gigantic rebellion; and the object of this bill is to confer the necessary power on the military authorities, in cases of insurrection and rebellion, to suppress them, and to regulate, as far as practicable, by law the exercise of those powers. The object of the bill is to provide for putting down rebellion in a constitutional and legal manner.

When the Constitution gives authority to call forth the militia for the purpose of enforcing the laws of the Union it is not a meaningless authority, and whatever authority it may be necessary to exercise to accomplish that object I say your militia and your army may lawfully exercise. If it be necessary to suspend the writ of *habeas corpus*, if it be necessary to ravage the country and plunder towns, if it be necessary to slay persons, to search houses, to do anything that men in time of war may do, then that authority is given in the Constitution.

You will find, by reference to the works upon international law, that it is laid down by all writers that whenever an insurrection assumes such formidable proportions as to be recognized by the Government, and whenever the civil authority is unable to put it down and the military is called out, then all the incidents which, according to the laws of nations, may be done by an army follow your army called out for that purpose.

The Supreme Court of the United States has so decided this very question [Luther *vs*. Borden and others, in 1849, reported in 7 Howard]. Judge Woodbury dissented from the opinion of the court, and placed his dissent chiefly upon the ground that a State had not this power, admitting that the Government of the United States might exercise it.

Here is an express decision that the military power may interfere in a case where the civil authorities are overborne, and may arrest anyone when they have reasonable grounds to believe that he is engaged in the insurrection, and may enter houses for that purpose; and the court say that, if this were not so, the military array of the Government would be mere parade, and rather encourage than repel attack. Shall it then be said, when express power is given by the Constitution of the United States to call out the militia to enforce the laws of the country, that they are merely to make a parade? What more has your military power done in this instance than was done in the State of Rhode Island? Have they done anything more in Baltimore than to arrest persons suspected of favoring this insurrection? Nothing. The writ of *habeas corpus* cannot relieve them; the courts cannot interfere; and this power, the court say, is essential to the preservation of order and free institutions and the existence of every government, and they would draw the power from the nature of government itself if it were not expressly given in the Constitution.

That case covers, in my judgment, every feature of the bill now under consideration.

James A. Bayard, Jr. [Del.], considered the bill "exceedingly dangerous to the personal liberties and rights of every citizen of the United States, and also entirely unnecessary for the purpose of carrying on this war with the seceded States." In order that it might have grave consideration he moved its postponement until next day.

William P. Fessenden [Me.] wished the bill settled

at once, or to be postponed indefinitely; with his present impressions he would vote against it.

John C. Breckinridge [Ky.] concurred with the Senator from Maine. He said:

If there is a serious intention to pass it, at some time before the vote is taken I may briefly express my opposition to it. I content myself now with saying that it appears to me to combine in eleven sections everything most atrocious which has been resisted, fought against, and trampled down by a free people for the last five hundred years; and that I think the introduction of such a bill into the American Senate is the most gloomy commentary we could have upon the degenerate character of the times.

After some discussion the bill was postponed until next day, and, when it then came up, until the day following (August 1).

Jacob Collamer [Vt.] opposed the bill as a usurpation by Congress of the powers of the President.

Mr. President, it is quite useless for men to talk about Congress having the war-making power. All there is in that argument is this: Among the powers enumerated in the Constitution is that Congress shall have power to declare war; that is to say that that department of the Government which can initiate a war in this country is Congress; but that has nothing to do with a war made upon us. If a war be waged and declared by another nation upon this nation, I take it, it needs no declaration of Congress about it; it is a state of war. The difficulty that arose in my mind was this: War has been declared by those whom we do not recognize as a sovereign power. We do not regard it as a regularly declared war. Therefore, in order to avoid all doubt about the fact that an insurrection existed, in order to give to that insurrection in this country, by whatever name called, a local and legal existence, recognized by us, we passed a law in the early part of this session by which we authorized the President, wherever the insurrection existed in a State, and especially if it claimed to do so by State authority, and the State authority did not disclaim it, to declare the people of that State, or any section of it, where the insurrection existed, in a state of war. This is what we have done in order to give it all formal sanction.

Now, Mr. President, the war, I take it, exists. It has been suggested by some gentlemen here that that war cannot be legally prosecuted after Congress meets; that though it might be, from the necessity of the case, prosecuted by the President, iu the exercise of the powers that ordinarily belong to the prosecution of war, until Congress met, yet when Congress did meet he could do nothing but what Congress authorized. I utterly disclaim any such principle in our Government. Why, sir, since we have met and during the three or four weeks we have been sitting here, the President, or those acting under him, have sent down twenty, thirty, or forty thousand of our own citizens into Virginia, and have killed hundreds of people. Is this murder? Where is your law to authorize it? Look through your acts and through all your statutes, and where do you find any authority of that kind? Has it been done by any action of Congress? Not at all. Sir, we may as well come to it first as last: the power to prosecute war and the manner of carrying on that war is entirely executive—it is so in every country everywhere—and the laws that govern those who thus prosecute that war are the laws of war, not the laws of municipalities.

They are not the laws of Congress, nor of Parliament, nor of the National Assembly of France: they are the laws of war; and no war can be prosecuted in auy other way. The President, or the general of our armies, in the prosecution of this war, is to conduct it just the same as any other. I desire no resentments or irritations about it; but they do not derive their authority from Congress. Not only do they not derive their authority from that source, but they cannot. The laws of war are laws between the belligerents. When you capture a spy you can execute him, according to the laws of war. Those laws are recognized, and do not come out of legislation by anybody.

Again, Mr. President, the mere powers which are absolutely necessary to the prosecution of a war are many of them powers which Congress, in the express words of the Constitution, is forbidden to adopt. Now, take one feature of the bill before us which recognizes the trying of people and punishing them capitally, executing them, by court-martial. The Constitution provides expressly that all crimes shall be tried by a jury, unless they are offences committed by those who are members either of the army or navy. That is the provision of the Constitution. Now it is not with that clause as it may be with the *habeas corpus*. That clause may be suspended; but the provision in regard to trial by jury Congress has no power to suspend anywhere.

I mention that as one illustration. I can find a number of others similar to it, wherein the prohibitions of the Constitution—prohibitions upon the action of Congress—are of that character that shows it is not possible to give, by any action of Congress, those powers which everybody recognizes as the rights of war, under the laws of war. Therefore, without occupying any further time about it, the war now being in legal existence, and, if any more particular locality should be given to it, it is by presidential proclamation, under the statute we have already passed; my idea is that the rights of war, the power of prosecuting it, and the mode of carrying it on, with all its limitations, are to be derived from what are known in the world as the laws of war. They are entirely in the executive administration, not derived from Congress, and, I think, ought not to be undertaken to be legislated about in Congress, because, as I before said, the very attempt to legislate upon them is to negative the idea that they have any other power; and we should want more time and more forethought and foresight to provide for the various exigencies which may present themselves in war than we should ever be able to give to the subject. Therefore, I think it better to leave it to the laws of war, where it properly belongs.

SENATOR TRUMBULL.—The Senator from Vermont asserts that this is war; that you cannot regulate a war by Congress; it is the law of nations that regulates war; and he wants to know, if this is a bill providing for war, why you do not provide for spies, and why you do not make other provisions? He goes on to say that it is directly against the Constitution of the United States to try a man by court-martial, because a man is entitled to a jury trial. Why, sir, did the learned Senator from Vermont never read the acts of Congress? It is provided by the act of 1806, in force to-day, that—

"Whoever shall be convicted of holding correspondence with, or giving intelligence to, the enemy, either directly or indirectly, shall suffer death, or such other punishment as shall be ordered by the sentence of a court-martial."

The Senator says we cannot regulate the proceedings during a time of war; that Congress has no power over them. The statute is full of regulations of the army in time of war; and this very act, the very case he puts, provides the punishment for a spy.

The statute is full of provisions controlling and governing the army in time of war. Express authority is given to Con-

gress by the very words of the Constitution to make the rules
and regulations for the government of the army; and yet, forsooth, we are told by the Senator from Vermont Congress cannot
make any laws at all; war is declared, and the President can
carry on the war just as he pleases. Now, sir, I deny his very
premises. I deny that this is a war in the sense in which he
speaks. There is a rebellion. We have treated it as a rebellion.
The Executive has treated it as a rebellion. The Senator wants
to know if it was murder when our army went over to Virginia
a few days ago and killed several hundred persons? Certainly
not. It was not necessary to write down in the statute book
that our army should have authority to go into Virginia and
shoot men; but what has Congress done? Congress has recognized this existing state of things. It has voted hundreds of
millions of money and hundreds of thousands of men to put
down the rebellion. It has authorized the calling out of the
militia for the purpose of enforcing the laws; and the courts
have decided that when the militia are called out for that purpose they may use all the means necessary to accomplish the
object; and the provision of the Constitution which provides
for trial by jury has no application. When the military authority is called out to enforce the laws and suppress rebellion, they
have all the authority necessary to accomplish the end for which
that power is given; and if it be necessary to level houses, to
ravage the country, and to shoot men, they have the authority.
The military power is not called out as a display. Nor is this a
war in the sense the Senator from Vermont would intimate.
His doctrine would recognize these Southern rebels as a government. He wants to provide for an exchange of prisoners, and
he asks why that is not in the bill.

SENATOR COLLAMER.—I disclaimed that they were a government. I said the reason we passed a law to authorize the President to issue his proclamation was because we did not recognize
such a power on earth.

SENATOR TRUMBULL.—Then, if he does not recognize this as
a war in that sense, why undertake to apply to it the rules of
war? Is a war existing in my State? By virtue of the military
authority men in the State of Illinois have been arrested. Is
war existing in Baltimore? By what authority are you arresting
men in the city of Baltimore and holding them in custody? Is
the Senator from Vermont, or is anybody in this country, for
leaving the power in the hands of the President, or, rather, in
the hands of your commanding general, just when he pleases,
without proclamation, to march to any locality, arrest men, put

them in prison, and do what he pleases with them? Shall we be told that Congress has no power, although the express authority to make rules and regulations for the government of every officer is vested here in Congress and nowhere else? Our power is omnipotent over this army; and they ought to have rules and regulations by which to be governed. And, let me tell Senators, it is no new feature for courts-martial, in time of rebellion, insurrection, and civil war, to bring men before them and try them, sentence them, and shoot them without the intervention of any grand or petit jurors.

SENATOR BRECKINRIDGE.—I endeavored, Mr. President, to demonstrate a short time ago that the whole tendency of our proceedings was to trample the Constitution under our feet and to conduct this contest without the slightest regard to its provisions. Everything that has occurred since demonstrates that the view I took of the conduct and tendency of public affairs was correct. Already both Houses of Congress have passed a bill virtually to confiscate all the property in the States that have withdrawn. Nothing can be more apparent than that that is a general act of emancipation.

Again, sir: to show that all these proceedings are characterized by an utter disregard of the Federal Constitution, what is happening around us every day?

The police commissioners of Baltimore were arrested by military authority without any charges whatever. In vain they have asked for a specification. In vain they have sent a respectful protest to the Congress of the United States. In vain the House of Representatives, by resolution, requested the President to furnish the Representatives of the people with the grounds of their arrest. He answers the House of Representatives that, in his judgment, the public interest does not permit him to say why they were arrested, on what charges, or what he has done with them—and you call this liberty and law and proceedings for the preservation of the Constitution! They have been spirited off from one fortress to another, their locality unknown, and the President of the United States refuses, upon the application of the most numerous branch of the national legislature, to furnish them with the grounds of their arrest, or to inform them what he has done with them.

Well might the Senator from Delaware [Willard Saulsbury] say that this bill contains provisions conferring authority which never was exercised in the worst days of Rome, by the worst of her dictators. I have wondered why the bill was introduced. I have sometimes thought that possibly it was introduced for the purpose of preventing the expression of that reaction which is now evidently going on in the public mind against these procedures so fatal to constitutional liberty. The army may be thus used, perhaps, to collect the enormous direct taxes for which preparation is now being made by Congress; and, if in any part of Illinois, or Indiana, or New York, or any State, North or South, there shall be difficulty or resistance the President, in his discretion, may declare it to be in a state of insurrection, all the civil authorities may be overthrown, and his military commander may make rules and regulations, collect taxes, and execute the laws at his pleasure.

Mr. President, gentlemen talk about the Union as if it was an end instead of a means. They talk about it as if it was the union of these States which alone had brought into life the principles of public and of personal liberty. Sir, they existed before, and they may survive it. Take care that in pursuing one idea you do not destroy, not only the Constitution of your country, but sever what remains of the Federal Union. These eternal and sacred principles of public and of personal liberty, which lived before the Union and will live forever and ever somewhere, must be respected; they cannot with impunity be overthrown; and, if you force the people to the issue between any form of government and these priceless principles, that form of government will perish; they will tear it asunder as the irrepressible forces of nature rend whatever opposes them.

The Senator from Vermont [Mr. Collamer] says that all these proceedings are to be conducted according to the laws of war; he adds that these laws require many things to be done which are absolutely forbidden in the Constitution; which Congress is prohibited from doing, and all other departments of the Government are forbidden from doing by the Constitution; but that they are proper under the laws of war, which must alone be the measure of our action now. I desire the country, then, to know this fact: that it is openly avowed upon this floor that constitutional limitations are no longer to be regarded; but that you are acting just as if there were two nations upon this continent, one arrayed against the other; some eighteen or twenty millions on one side and some ten or twelve millions on the other, as to whom the Constitution is nought, and the laws of war alone apply.

Sir, if the Constitution is really to be put aside, if the laws of war alone are to govern, and whatever may be done by one independent nation at war with another is to be done, why not act upon that practically? I do not hold that the clause of the Constitution which authorizes Congress to declare war applies to any internal difficulties. I do not believe it applies to any of the political communities bound together under the Constitution in political association. I regard it as applying to external enemies. Nor do I believe that the Constitution of the United States ever contemplated the preservation of the Union of these States by one half the States warring on the other half. It details particularly how military force shall be employed in this Federal system of government, and it can be employed properly in no other way; it can be employed in aid of the civil tribunals. If there are no civil tribunals, if there is no mode by which the laws of the United States may be enforced in the manner prescribed by the Constitution, what follows? The remaining States may, if they choose, make war, but they do it outside of the Constitution; and the Federal system, as determined by the principles and terms of that instrument, does not provide for the case. It does provide for putting down insurrections—illegal uprisings of individuals—but it does not provide, in my opinion, either in its spirit or in its terms, for raising armies by one half of the political communities that compose the Union for the purpose of subjugating the other half; and the very fact that it does not is shown by the fact that you have to avow on the floor of the Senate the necessity for putting the Constitution aside and conducting the whole contest without regard to it and in obedience solely to the laws of war.

Then, if we are at war, if it is a case of war, treat it like war. Practically it is being treated like war. The prisoners whom the United States have taken are not hung as traitors. The prisoners which the other States have taken are not hung as traitors. Is it war? The Senator is right in saying it is war; but, in my opinion, it is not only an unhappy but an unconstitutional war. Why, then, all these proceedings upon the part of the Administration, refusing to send or to receive flags of truce; refusing to recognize the actual condition of affairs; refusing to do those acts which, if they do not terminate, may at least ameliorate the unhappy condition in which we find ourselves placed?

So much, then, we know. We know that admitted violations of the Constitution have been made and are justified. We know that we have conferred by legislation, and are, perhaps, still further by legislation to confer, authority to do acts not warranted by the Constitution of the United States. We have it openly avowed that the Constitution of the Union, which is the bond of association, at least, between those States that still adhere to the Federal Union, is no longer to be regarded. It is not enough to tell me that it has been violated by those communities that have seceded. Other States have not seceded; Kentucky has not seceded; Illinois has not seceded; some twenty States yet compose the Federal Union, nominally under this Constitution. As to them, that instrument, in its terms and in its spirit, is the bond of their connection under the Federal system. They have a right, as between themselves and their comembers of the Union, to insist upon its being respected. If, indeed, it is to be put aside, and we are to go into a great continental struggle, they may pause to inquire what is to become of their liberties and what their political connections are to be in a contest made without constitutional warrant and in derogation of all the terms of the instrument? How can this be successfully controverted? Though you may have a right to trample under foot the Constitution and to make war (as every power has a right to make war) against the States that have seceded, have you a right to violate it as to any of the adhering States who insist upon fidelity to its provisions? No, sir.

EDWARD D. BAKER [Ore.].—Will the gentleman be kind enough to tell me what single particular provision there is in this bill which is in violation of the Constitution of the United States?

SENATOR BRECKINRIDGE.—They are all, in my opinion, so equally atrocious that I dislike to discriminate. The Senator can select which he pleases.

SENATOR BAKER.—Let me try, then, if I must generalize as the Senator does, to see if I can get the scope and meaning of this bill. It is a bill providing that the President of the United States may declare, by proclamation, in a certain given state of fact, certain territory within the United States to be in a condition of insurrection and war; which proclamation shall be extensively published within the district to which it relates. That is the first proposition. I ask him if that is unconstitutional? He will not dare to say it is.

SENATOR BRECKINRIDGE.—The State of Illinois, I believe, is a military district. The State of Kentucky is a military district. In my judgment, the President has no authority, and, in my judgment, Congress has no right to confer upon the President authority, to declare a State in a condition of insurrection or rebellion.

SENATOR BAKER.—The bill does not say a word about States.

SENATOR BRECKINRIDGE.—Does not the Senator know, in fact,

that those States compose military districts? It might as well have said "States" as to describe what is a State.

SENATOR BAKER.—The objection certainly ought not to be that the President can declare a part of a State in insurrection and not the whole of it. In point of fact, the Constitution of the United States, and the Congress of the United States acting upon it, are not treating of States, but of the territory comprising the United States; and I submit once more to his better judgment that it cannot be unconstitutional to allow the President to declare a county or a part of a county, or a town or a part of a town, or part of a State or the whole of a State, or two States, or five States in a condition of insurrection, if, in his judgment, that be the fact.

In the next place the bill provides that, that being so, the military commander in that district may make and publish such police rules and regulations as he may deem necessary to suppress the rebellion and restore order and preserve the lives and property of citizens. I submit to him, if the President of the United States has power, or ought to have power, to suppress insurrection and rebellion, is there any better way to do it, or is there any other? The gentleman says do it by the civil power. Look at the fact. The civil power is utterly overwhelmed; the courts are closed; the judges banished. Is the President not to execute the law? Is he to do it in person, or by his military commanders? Are they to do it with regulation, or without it? That is the only question.

Mr. President, the honorable Senator agrees with the Senator from Vermont that there is a state of war. What then? There is a state of public war; none the less war because it is urged from the other side; not the less war because it is unjust; not the less war because it is a war of insurrection and rebellion. It is still war; and I am willing to say it is public war—public as contradistinguished from private war. What then? Shall we carry that war on? Is it his duty as a Senator to carry it on? If so, how? By armies, under command; by military organization and authority, advancing to suppress insurrection and rebellion. Is that wrong? Is that unconstitutional? Are we not bound to do with whoever levies war against us as we would do if he was a foreigner? There is no distinction as to the mode of carrying on war; we carry on war against an advancing army just the same, whether it be from Russia or from South Carolina. Will the honorable Senator tell me it is our duty to stay here, within fifteen miles of the enemy seeking to advance upon us every hour, and talk about nice questions of constitutional construction as to whether it is war or merely insurrection? No, sir. It is our duty to advance, if we can; to suppress insurrection; to put down rebellion; to dissipate the rising; to scatter the enemy; and, when we have done so, to preserve, in the terms of the bill, the liberty, lives, and property of the people of the country by just and fair police regulations. When we took Mexico did we not do it there? Is it not a part, a necessary, an indispensable part of war itself, that there shall be military regulations over the country conquered and held? Is that unconstitutional?

It is true that the Constitution of the United States does adopt the laws of war as a part of the instrument itself during the continuance of war. The Constitution does not provide that spies shall be hung. Is it unconstitutional to hang a spy? There is no provision for it in terms in the Constitution; but nobody denies the right, the power, the justice. Why? Because it is part of the law of war. The Constitution does not provide for the exchange of prisoners; yet it may be done under the law of war. Indeed the Constitution does not provide that a prisoner may be taken at all; yet his captivity is perfectly just and constitutional. It seems to me that the Senator does not, will not, take that view of the subject.

Again, sir, when a military commander advances, as I trust, if there are no more unexpected great reverses, he will advance, through Virginia, and occupies the country, there, perhaps, as here, the civil law may be silent; there perhaps the civil officers may flee as ours have been compelled to flee. What then? If the civil law is silent, who shall control and regulate the conquered district—who but the military commander? As the Senator from Illinois has well said, shall it be done by regulation or without regulation? Shall the general, or the colonel, or the captain be supreme, or shall he be regulated and ordered by the President of the United States? That is the sole question. The Senator has put it well.

I agree that we ought to do all we can to limit, to restrain, to fetter the abuse of military power. Bayonets are at best illogical arguments. I am not willing, except as a case of sheerest necessity, ever to permit a military commander to exercise authority over life, liberty, and property. But, sir, it is part of the law of war; you cannot carry in the rear of your army your courts; you cannot organize juries; you cannot have trials according to the forms and ceremonial of the common law amid the clangor of arms, and somebody must enforce police regulations in a conquered or occupied district. I ask the Senator from Kentucky again respectfully, is that unconstitutional; or, if, in the nature of war, it must exist, even if there be no law passed by us to allow it, is it unconstitutional to regulate it? That is the question, to which I do not think he will make a clear and distinct reply.

I would ask the Senator what would you have us do now— a Confederate army within twenty miles of us, advancing, or threatening to advance, to overwhelm your Government; to shake the pillars of the Union; to bring it around your head, if you stay here, in ruins? Are we to predict evil and retire from what we predict? Is it not the manly part to go on as we have begun, to raise money and levy armies, to organize them, to prepare to advance; when we do advance, to regulate that advance by all the laws and regulations that civilization and humanity will allow in time of battle? Can we do anything more? To talk to us about stopping is idle; we will never stop. Will the Senator yield to rebellion? Will he shrink from armed insurrection? Will his State justify it? Will its better public opinion allow it? Shall we send a flag of truce? What would he have? Or would he conduct this war so feebly that the whole world would smile at us in derision? What would he have? These speeches of his, sown broadcast over the land, what clear, distinct meaning have they? Are they not intended for disorganization in our very midst? Are they not intended to dull our weapons? Are they not intended to destroy our zeal? Are they not intended to animate our enemies? Sir, are they not words of brilliant, polished treason, even in the very Capitol of the Confederacy? [Manifestations of applause in the galleries.]

What would have been thought if, in another capitol, in another republic, in a yet more martial age, a Senator as grave, not more eloquent or dignified than the Senator from Kentucky, yet with the Roman purple flowing over his shoulders, had risen in his place, surrounded by all the illustrations of Roman glory, and declared that advancing Hannibal was just and that Carthage ought to be dealt with in terms of peace? What would have been thought if, after the battle of Cannæ, a Senator there had risen in his place and denounced every levy of the Roman people, every expenditure of its treasure, and every appeal to the old recollections and the old glories? Sir, a Senator, himself learned far more than myself in such lore [Mr. Fessenden], tells me, in a voice that I am glad is audible, that he would have been hurled from the Tarpeian rock. It is a grand commentary upon the American Constitution that we permit these words to be uttered. I ask the Senator to recollect, too, what, save to send aid and comfort to the enemy, do these predictions of his amount to? Every word thus uttered falls as a note of inspiration upon every Confederate ear. Every sound thus uttered is a word (and falling from his lips, a mighty word) of kindling and triumph to a foe that determines to advance. For me, I have no such word as a Senator to utter. For me, amid temporary defeat, disaster, disgrace, it seems that my duty calls me to utter another word, and that word is: bold, sudden, forward, determined war, according to the laws of war, by armies, by military commanders clothed with full power, advancing with all the past glories of the Republic urging them on to conquest.

I do not stop to consider whether it is subjugation or not. It is compulsory obedience, not to my will, not to yours, sir, not to the will of any one man, not to the will of any one Senate; but compulsory obedience to the Constitution of the whole country. When we subjugate South Carolina what shall we do? We shall compel its obedience to the Constitution of the United States; that is all. We do not mean, we have never said, any more. If it be slavery that men should obey the Constitution their fathers fought for, let it be so. If it be freedom, it is freedom equally for them and for us. We propose to subjugate rebellion into loyalty; we propose to subjugate insurrection into peace; we propose to subjugate Confederate anarchy into constitutional Union liberty. When the Confederate armies are scattered; when their leaders are banished from power; when the people return to a late repentant sense of the wrong they have done to a Government they never felt but in benignancy and blessing, then the Constitution made for all will be felt by all, like the descending rains from heaven which bless all alike. Is that subjugation? To restore what was as it was for the benefit of the whole country and of the whole human race is all we desire and all we can have.

Sir, how can we retreat? Sir, how can we make peace? Who shall treat? What commissioners? Who would go? Upon what terms? Where is to be your boundary line? Where the end of the principles we shall have to give up? What will become of constitutional government? What will become of public liberty? What of past glories? What of future hopes? Shall we sink into the insignificance of the grave—a degraded, defeated, emasculated people, frightened by the results of one battle and scared at the visions raised by the imagination of the Senator from Kentucky upon this floor? No, sir; a thou-

sand times, no, sir! We will rally—if, indeed, our words be
necessary—we will rally the people, the loyal people, of the
whole country. They will pour forth their treasure, their
money, their men, without stint, without measure. The most
peaceable man in this body may stamp his foot upon this Senate chamber floor, as of old a warrior and a Senator did, and
from that single tramp there will spring forth armed legions.
Shall one battle determine the fate of empire, or a dozen? the
loss of one thousand men or twenty thousand, or $100,000,000
or $500,000,000? In a year's peace, in ten years, at most, of
peaceful progress, we can restore them all. There will be some
graves reeking with blood, watered by the tears of affection.
There will be some privation; there will be some loss of luxury;
their will be somewhat more need for labor to procure the necessaries of life. When that is said, all is said. If we have the
country, the whole country, the Union, the Constitution, free
government—with these there will return all the blessings of
well-ordered civilization; the path of the country will be a career
of greatness and of glory such as, in the olden time, our fathers
saw in the dim visions of years yet to come, and such as would
have been ours now, to-day, if it had not been for the treason
for which the Senator too often seeks to apologize.

SENATOR BRECKINRIDGE.—The Senator asks me: "What
would you have us do?" I would have us stop the war. We
can do it. I have tried to show that there is none of that inexorable necessity to continue this war which the Senator seems
to suppose. I do not hold that constitutional liberty on this
continent is bound up in this fratricidal, devastating, horrible
contest. Upon the contrary, I fear it will find its grave in it.
The Senator is mistaken in supposing that we can reunite these
States by war. He is mistaken in supposing that eighteen or
twenty million upon the one side can subjugate ten or twelve
million upon the other; or, if they do subjugate them, that you
can restore constitutional government as our fathers made it.
You will have to govern them as Territories, as suggested by the
Senator, if ever they are reduced to the dominion of the United
States. Sir, I would prefer to see these States all reunited upon
true constitutional principles to any other object that could be
offered me in life; and to restore, upon the principles of our
fathers, the Union of these States, to me the sacrifice of one un-
important life would be nothing; nothing, sir. But I infinitely
prefer to see a peaceful separation of these States than to see
endless, aimless, devastating war, at the end of which I see the
grave of public liberty and of personal freedom.

The Senator asked if a Senator of Rome had uttered these things in the war between Carthage and that power, how would he have been treated? Sir, the war between Carthage and Rome was altogether different from the war now waged between the United States and the Confederate States. I would have said —rather than avow the principle that one or the other must be subjugated, or perhaps both destroyed—let Carthage live and let Rome live, each pursuing its own course of policy and civilization.

The Senator says that these opinions which I thus expressed, and have heretofore expressed, are but brilliant treason; and that it is a tribute to the character of our institutions that I am allowed to utter them upon the Senate floor. Mr. President, if I am speaking treason I am not aware of it. I am speaking what I believe to be for the good of my country. If I am speaking treason, I am speaking it in my place in the Senate, By whose indulgence am I speaking? Not by any man's indulgence. I am speaking by the guaranties of that Constitution which seems to be here now so little respected. And, sir, when he asked what would have been done with a Roman Senator who had uttered such words, another Senator on this floor replies in audible tones: "He would have been hurled from the Tarpeian rock." Since, in ancient Rome, (while the defenders of the public liberty were sometimes torn to pieces by the people, yet their memories were cherished in grateful remembrance,) to be hurled from the Tarpeian rock was ever the fate of usurpers and tyrants, this remark is an insult which ought not to be offered on the floor of the Senate chamber to a Senator who is speaking in his place.

Senator Trumbull's bill was not brought to a vote, owing to the opposition of such influential Republicans as Senators Fessenden and Collamer, who thought it both unnecessary and of doubtful constitutionality.

Senator Breckinridge soon after left the Senate to become a general in the Confederate army. Senator Baker also shortly resigned his seat to become a Union officer. He was killed while gallantly leading his regiment in a hopeless charge at the battle of Ball's Bluff, Va., on October 21, 1861.

CHAPTER IV

Military Emancipation

Gen. Benjamin F. Butler Declares Slaves Employed on Confederate Works "Contraband of War"; the Doctrine Is Upheld by the President and Congress—Gen. John C. Frémont Issues an Order of Military Emancipation; It Is Revoked by the President, Who Is Criticized Therefor by Anti-Slavery Radicals—His Reply to Sen. Orville H. Browning [Ill.]—Frémont Is Removed—Gen. Henry W. Halleck Is Put in Charge of Department of Missouri—He Excludes Fugitive Slaves from the Army—Henry Wilson [Mass.] Introduces in the Senate a Bill to Punish Army Officers for Returning Fugitives—Debate: in Favor, Jacob Collamer [Vt.], Sen. Wilson; Amendment to Punish Officers for Enticing Slaves to Run Away, Supported by Willard Saulsbury [Del.], James A. Pearce [Md.]—Francis P. Blair, Jr. [Mo.] Makes a Similar Proposition in the House—Debate: in Favor, Mr. Blair, John A. Bingham [O.]; Opposed, Robert Mallory [Ky.), Charles A. Wickliffe [Ky.], Henry Grider [Ky.]—Bill Passed by House and Senate—Gen. David Hunter's Proclamation of Military Emancipation; It Is Revoked by the President.

SLAVES employed on the earthworks of General John B. Magruder [Conf.], in May, 1861, ran away to Fortress Monroe, Va., which was held by Union troops under Benjamin F. Butler, and General Butler refused to give them up to their owners on the ground that, Virginia claiming to be a foreign State, its citizens who endorsed this claim (as did the owners) could not assert as their right a duty of the Federal Government which extended only to its citizens.

This reasoning led to an even more advanced position which was concisely summed up in a single phrase, viz., that negroes employed in aid of rebellion were "contraband of war, and so subject to confiscation." Since the Southerners regarded slaves as chattels they could not consistently except to this conclusion.

The Government heartily approved General Butler's

119

course. On May 30 Secretary Cameron of the War
Department gave him a formal order authorizing him
to pursue the policy he had adopted. Even the border-
State Union men did not voice any objections, for to do
so would impeach their loyalty. The public generally
applauded Butler.

Congress, as we have seen (page 70), declared that
all negroes employed upon fortifications, etc., by the
Confederates, should not, if taken by the Union troops,
be returned to their owners, and in this it was supported by public opinion in the North and even in the
border States.

When, however, Major-General John C. Frémont,
in command of the Western Department, consisting of

"CONTRABANDS"

An envelope cut during the Civil War

Illinois and all the region between the Mississippi and
the Rocky Mountains, attempted to gain a similar popular acclaim by issuing on his own responsibility a proclamation confiscating all property of persons in rebellion,
and emancipating their slaves, neither the Administration nor the country as a whole supported him, although
the Abolitionists hailed it as the most important act thus
far of the war.

To President Lincoln and his military advisers the
previous course of General Frémont had been most dis-
appointing. His neglect to reënforce the brave General
Lyon, isolated at Springfield in southwestern Missouri
among gathering rebel forces, had led to the defeat
and death of Lyon at Wilson's Creek on August 10, and
his egotism in refusing to consult with the civil authorities and his subordinate officers had thoroughly demoralized his entire department.

President Lincoln therefore was watching for danger in that quarter, and, as soon as he was informed of Frémont's proclamation on August 30 of military emancipation, wrote him on September 2 to modify it so that it should conform to the act of Congress confiscating property used for insurrection, giving as a reason for his objection that the liberation of slaves would alarm Southern Unionists, and perhaps precipitate Kentucky into the Confederacy.

Before Lincoln received a reply to this he wrote to General David Hunter a letter full of shrewd foresight and delicate diplomacy:

> September 9, 1861.
> MY DEAR SIR: General Frémont needs to have by his side a man of large experience. Will you not, for me, take that place? Your rank is one grade too high to be ordered to it; but will you not serve the country and oblige me by taking it voluntarily?

Two days later he received an answer from Frémont to his letter of September 2. It was full of excuses and self-justification. Mrs. Frémont brought it in person. She adopted a hostile attitude toward the President, and, insinuating that there was a conspiracy against her husband, demanded a copy of the President's Missouri correspondence. Lincoln courteously but firmly replied:

> I do not feel authorized to furnish you with copies of letters in my possession, without the consent of the writers. No impression has been made on my mind against the honor or integrity of General Frémont, and I now enter my protest against being understood as acting in any hostility toward him.

The situation precipitated by General Frémont's proclamation was most critical. The border States, for whose adherence to the Union Lincoln had thus far most successfully played, seemed about to escape from his control. Besides, soldiers from the Northern States, who had enlisted to save the Union and not to free the negro, were greatly disaffected by Frémont's proclamation. On the other hand events had rapidly developed many conservative Northerners into anti-slavery radicals, and these, together with the original Abolitionists, made a hero of General Frémont. Such persons had to be treated with utmost consideration.

One of these was an old friend and adviser of Lincoln, Orville H. Browning, who had succeeded Stephen A. Douglas in the Senate. On September 17 he wrote to the President objecting to his attitude toward Frémont's proclamation. To this letter Lincoln replied on the 22d:

MY DEAR SIR: Yours of the 17th is just received; and, coming from you, I confess it astonishes me. That you should object to my adhering to a law which you had assisted in making and presenting to me less than a month before is odd enough. But this is a very small part. General Frémont's proclamation as to confiscation of property and the liberation of slaves is purely political and not within the range of military law or necessity. If a commanding general finds a necessity to seize the farm of a private owner for a pasture, an encampment, or a fortification he has the right to do so, and to so hold it as long as the necessity lasts; and this is within military law, because within military necessity. But, to say the farm shall no longer belong to the owner, or his heirs forever, and this as well when the farm is not needed for military purposes as when it is, is purely political, without the savor of military law about it. And the same is true of slaves. If the general needs them, he can seize them and use them; but, when the need is past, it is not for him to fix their permanent future condition. That must be settled according to laws made by law-makers, and not by military proclamations. The proclamation on the point in question is simply "dictatorship." It assumes that the general may do anything he pleases—confiscate the lands and free the slaves of loyal people as well as of disloyal ones. And, going the whole figure, I have no doubt, would be more popular with some thoughtless people than that which has been done! But I cannot assume this reckless position, nor allow others to assume it on my responsibility.

You speak of it as being the only means of saving the Government. On the contrary, it is itself the surrender of the Government. Can it be pretended that it is any longer the Government of the United States—any government of constitution and laws—wherein a general or a president may make permanent rules of property by proclamation? I do not say Congress might not with propriety pass a law on the point just such as General Frémont proclaimed. I do not say I might not, as a member of Congress, vote for it. What I object to is, that I, as President, shall expressly or impliedly seize and exercise the permanent legislative functions of the Government.

So much as to principle. Now as to policy. No doubt the thing was popular in some quarters, and would have been more so if it had been a general declaration of emancipation. The Kentucky legislature would not budge till that proclamation was modified; and General Anderson telegraphed me that, on the news of General Frémont having actually issued deeds of manumission, a whole company of our volunteers threw down their arms and disbanded. I was so assured as to think it probable that the very arms we had furnished Kentucky would be turned against us. I think to lose Kentucky is nearly the same as to lose the whole game. Kentucky gone, we cannot hold Missouri, nor, as I think, Maryland. These all against us, and the job on our hands is too large for us. We would as well consent to separation at once, including the surrender of this capital. On the contrary, if you will give up your restlessness for new positions, and back me manfully on the grounds upon which you and other kind friends gave me the election and have approved in my public documents, we shall go through triumphantly. You must understand I took my course on the proclamation because of Kentucky. I took the same ground in a private letter to General Frémont before I heard from Kentucky.

There has been no thought of removing General Frémont on any ground connected with his proclamation. . . . I hope no real necessity for it exists on any ground.

Frémont's continued inaction, however, compelled the President at last to supersede him with General David Hunter. A few months later Frémont was placed in charge of the Mountain Department [western Virginia and eastern Kentucky and Tennessee].

On November 9, 1861, General Henry W. Halleck was placed in charge of the Department of Missouri [Missouri, Arkansas, western Kentucky, Iowa, Minnesota, Wisconsin, and Illinois], and Hunter put in command of the Department of Kansas [Kansas, Nebraska, Colorado, Dakota, and Indian Territory].

General Halleck set himself at once to settle the vexatious problem of the relation of the army to fugitive slaves. Contrary to Frémont's policy he issued an order on November 20 excluding these fugitives from the army lines on the ground that they conveyed information to the enemy. For this order he was violently attacked by the anti-slave press and Congressmen, who averred that, on the contrary, the.fugitives brought in valuable information about the enemy.

During the session of December, 1861–July, 1862, several bills were proposed in both the Senate and the House to punish officers and privates of the army and navy for aiding owners to recover fugitive slaves. That of Henry Wilson [Mass.] was reported on January 6, 1862, in the Senate. On January 17 it came up for discussion.

RETURN OF FUGITIVE SLAVES BY ARMY OFFICERS

CONGRESS, JANUARY 6-MARCH 10, 1862

Jacob Collamer [Vt.] said:

It is a perversion entirely to undertake to use soldiers as a mere *posse comitatus*, or as a mere police force, or to use them in any way in the enforcement of the laws of any particular section into which they may be marched. They have nothing to do with that; their business is to suppress the rebellion, and disperse the insurgents wherever they may be found in arms. I believe we are generally agreed that there is great impropriety in military men exercising military authority within the States in relation to their internal and municipal affairs; it is very likely to produce collisions that ought to be avoided.

Willard Saulsbury [Del.] moved to amend the resolution by making it punish soldiers for enticing slaves from their masters or harboring them. This amendment was amended by limiting the cases to slaves of loyal masters.

Senator Wilson was opposed to any amendment. James A. Pearce [Md.] supported the amendment.

The bill without it is an invitation to all slaves in the vicinity to resort to the lines of the army as a harbor of refuge where they can be safe from the operation of the undoubted legal rights of the owner. It is an invitation to the whole body of such people within a loyal State, such as Maryland, to accomplish their freedom by indirection. It is not an act of emancipation in its terms; but, so far as it can operate and does operate, it leads directly to that result. I know that fact that the slaves of masters whose titles are undoubted and their loyalty unquestioned have resorted to camps, and the officers sometimes have been very unwilling and have positively refused to take any step whatever in the matter? What is the result of that? A great many of these soldiers come from States where they hold this whole system of domestic servitude in such dislike that they will not permit the master to exercise his undoubted, valid rights, even though he goes accompanied by an officer of the law. He cannot exercise his rights except at the peril of personal ill treatment from these soldiers, who are not to be restrained by a military officer and who, therefore, will make their will the law of the case. Sir, I do not think that is right. I think that is making a camp of the United States army a refuge for runaway negroes. I think we are violating the rights of loyal masters in loyal States.

As for its operation in seceded States the bill will have no operation there anyway. Its effect is to take away the property of the people of Maryland, and of the loyal people of Maryland too. If it does not have that effect it will have none. I think, therefore, the amendment ought to be retained and that equal justice demands it. If it is not retained we of Maryland shall have to consider that our rights in this species of property are set aside, so far as this Government can set them aside by such an act.

The bill was kept from a vote by the tactics of the Democrats aided by a few conservative Republicans.

In the House, however, Francis P. Blair, Jr. [Mo.], of the Military Committee, on February 25, reported the substance of the Wilson resolution in an additional Article of War. The article was strongly opposed by Robert Mallory [Ky.], who argued with great ability that the army was intended to aid the Government in enforcing its laws, of which the Fugitive Slave Act was one, and, if the articles were not intended to repeal this act, it was a denial to the State where that law was sought to be enforced by the aid of the general Government in its enforcement.

"If it be the intention to repeal that law I wish gentlemen of the House to say so candidly and at once, and to let us know what we are to expect in regard to this matter."

Mr. Blair refused to decide whether his bill was a virtual repeal of the Fugitive Slave Act, contenting himself with saying that in common with a great many others he believed that "the army of the United States has a great deal better business than returning fugitive slaves."

John A. Bingham [O.], however, took it upon himself to declare that:

"it is impossible by any fair construction to make the bill imply any interference with the administration of civil justice in this country, either under the legislation of 1850 or under any act that has ever been passed by this Government. Sir, the bill simply provides that your officers in the army and navy, and those under them, shall not exercise in the future, as in the past, the functions which belong alone and exclusively to the civil magistrates of the country, upon the penalty of being tried by a court-martial, and, upon conviction, of being dismissed from the service thus abused and disgraced."

Mr. Mallory, while granting the high legal attainments of the gentleman from Ohio, was

"very suspicious of the accuracy of the working of his mind upon questions of this character. [Laughter.] Upon this question, at any rate, I cannot concur with him in opinion upon the construction he gives to this bill."

Charles A. Wickliffe [Ky.], referring to General Grant's return to their owners of slaves captured at Fort Donelson [February 16, 1862], asked the gentleman from Ohio if the bill would prevent a military commander from the exercise of such a power hereafter?

Henry Grider [Ky.], stating that the Rebel army had run off with $300,000 worth of slaves in three counties of Kentucky, asked the gentleman if the bill proposed that these should not be intercepted and returned, and whether he would make the military power paramount to every other consideration, even of constitutional obligation, and turn these negroes free.

Mr. Bingham replied that the prevalent practice of officers in the army returning without trial slaves to those claiming to be their owners was in direct violation of the carefully guarded provisions of the Fugitive Slave act, and this practice the bill was intended to prevent.

This practice is a military despotism that the American people should not tolerate for a moment, nor lose a moment in ending by the enactment of this bill into a law. Mr. Speaker, if I had my way, instead of having this bill provide, as it does simply provide, that persons in the United States military or naval service thus offending should, upon conviction by court-martial, be dismissed from the service, I would have the bill provide that such offenders should, by the sentence of a court-martial, be shot as kidnappers and as invaders of the rights of persons, as violators of justice and of the very sanctuary of justice.

Mr. Mallory said that he did not ask that slaves be returned where there was doubt as to their ownership. The laws of his State, indeed, forbade it.

Mr. Bingham replied:

There is always a doubt, a doubt imposed by law upon the conscience of every civil magistrate, in favor of the party brought before him and attempted to be deprived of his liberty—a doubt which should bind the magistrate to stand by the party who is thus sought to be deprived of his liberty until that doubt is overcome by lawful evidence. But, sir, no man in the military or naval service of this country has the right to hear evidence or to determine that question of doubt. I go further. The presumption of law is that every man in this land is entitled to his liberty until the contrary shall be made to appear. I want to know by what authority any officer in the naval or military service of the United States has the right to assume for himself to hear evidence and to determine against that presumption?

Mr. Mallory.—I understand my friend from Ohio to admit

in a case where there is no doubt either in law or in fact, where the officer knows the party is the slave of the loyal master who claims him, that he is willing that the slave should be restored to the master by the United States officer.

MR. BINGHAM.—The gentleman will pardon me; I admit no such thing.

MR. MALLORY.—Does the gentleman deny that in that case it becomes the duty of the officer to restore the slave to his loyal master?

MR. BINGHAM.—I do deny it. I deny that he has the right to entertain the question. I deny that he has the right, where no offence is charged, to clothe himself with authority to sit upon the right of any human being in this land to his liberty. One of the strongest utterances of the Declaration of Independence may be repeated upon this floor this day in favor of the enactment of this very bill. That utterance was: that "the King," whose character is thus marked by every act which may define a tyrant, "has affected to render the military independent of, and superior to, the civil power."

That is what is so offensive in this practice which has ob-tained in your camps, from the shores of the Potomac to the shores of the Mississippi—the attempt by the military power to assume and exercise civil authority in contempt of the civil power of the land. Some of your military officers of high and low degree have been detailing their men for the purpose of seizing, and have seized, persons not accused of crime, but *suspected* of the virtue of preferring liberty to bondage. Are we to revive here in this land the hated rule of the Athenian ostra-cism, by which men were condemned, not because they were charged with crime or proved guilty of crime, but because they were *suspected* to possess and practice the virtues of justice and patriotism in such degree as rendered their presence in the state dangerous to republican equality? Aristides was condemned because he was just, and Themistocles because he was the savior of the city.

These alleged fugitive slaves, who are subjected to this in-tolerable military despotism, are seized, not upon the charge or the proof that they have stolen anybody's goods, not that they have invaded anybody's rights, but upon the suspicion that they have been guilty of asserting their right of personal lib-erty, and of running away from a cruel and unjust bondage. Some of your officers, according to the practice of late, assume the right to sit in judgment upon the delicate question of the liberty of these suspected persons, to seize them, to condemn them as slaves, and to surrender them over to stripes and punishment.

I have read in the papers, and I believe it is true, that one of these persons *suspected* of escaping from bondage to liberty swam across the Ohio River, making for an encampment upon the Indiana shore, where he saw the banner of liberty flying which he fondly looked upon as consecrating that place, at least, as sacred to the rights of person, and where even the rights of a hunted bondman would be respected. After having been beaten about, bruised, and mangled against the rocks in the channel of the river, to whose rushing waters he committed his life that he might regain his liberty, he reached the opposite shore. Somebody went into the camp and reported that this man was suspected of the crime of having run away from chains and slavery. A company of soldiers, it is said, were detailed to seize him, and did seize and return him as a slave to the man who claimed him. If that practice is to be pursued by the army and navy under the American flag it ought to cover with midnight blackness every star that burns upon its field of azure, and with everlasting infamy the men who dare to desecrate it to such base uses.

What are we fighting for in this land? For the supremacy of the laws; for the administration of justice according to law; for liberty regulated and sheltered by law. We are fighting for the principle, among others, that no man shall be deprived of his liberty in this land without a hearing before the only tribunals authorized by law to hear and determine the question. The bill now under consideration proposes to provide against interfering with that right, sacred as any other, guarded and protected by the very letter and spirit of the Constitution. And it surprises me that any gentleman should stand here to-day objecting to the enactment of such a law.

The bill was passed by a substantially party vote— yeas, 83; nays, 44. Coming before the Senate on March 4 it was vehemently opposed by the Democrats, and as stoutly supported by the Republicans, and on March 10 was passed by 29 yeas to 9 nays—a party vote, with the exception that James A. McDougall [Dem.] of California voted for it.

The capture of Port Royal, S. C., on November 7, 1861, opened the way to the Federal occupation of the coast of South Carolina, Georgia, and Florida, which was formed into the military department of the South, General Hunter being called from Kansas to command it.

General Hunter's Emancipation Proclamation

On May 9, 1862, General David Hunter issued a proclamation on the ground that, martial law having been declared in it (on April 25), slavery and martial law were "altogether incompatible in a free country."

On May 19 the President revoked the order, saying that he "had no knowledge, information, or belief" of an intention on General Hunter's part to issue it, nor had the general nor any other commander or person authority from the Government to declare the slaves of any State free.

I further made known that, whether it be competent for me, as commander-in-chief of the army and navy, to declare the slaves of any State or States free, and whether, at any time, in any case, it shall have become a necessity indispensable to the maintenance of the government to exercise such supposed power, are questions which, under my responsibility, I reserve to myself, and which I cannot feel justified in leaving to the decision of commanders in the field. These are totally different questions from those of police regulations in armies and camps.

CHAPTER V

Abolition of Slavery in the District of Columbia

Sen. Wilson Introduces Bill in Senate for Abolition of Slavery in the District of Columbia—Debate: in Favor, John P. Hale [N. H.], Sen. Wilson, James Harlan [Ia.], Charles Sumner [Mass.]; Opposed, Garrett Davis [Ky.], Waitman T. Willey [Va.], Anthony Kennedy [Md.], Willard Saulsbury [Del.]; Bill Is Passed in Senate and House—Points Made by Representative Benjamin F. Thomas [Mass.]—The President Signs the Bill, with Remarks.

IN his first annual message (December 2, 1861) President Lincoln recommended that steps be taken to colonize the "contraband" freedmen and other free negroes in a congenial climate.

To carry out the plan of colonization may involve the acquiring of territory and also the appropriation of money beyond that to be expended in the territorial acquisition. Having practiced the acquisition of territory for nearly sixty years, the question of constitutional power to do so is no longer an open one with us. The power was questioned at first by Mr. Jefferson, who, however, in the purchase of Louisiana, yielded his scruples on the plea of great expediency. If it be said that the only legitimate object of acquiring territory is to furnish homes for white men, this measure effects that object; for the emigration of colored men leaves additional room for white men remaining or coming here. Mr. Jefferson, however, placed the importance of procuring Louisiana more on political and commercial grounds than on providing room for population.

On this whole proposition, including the appropriation of money with the acquisition of territory, does not the expediency amount to absolute necessity—that, without which the Government itself cannot be perpetuated?

On February 13, 1862, a bill drawn by Henry Wilson [Mass.] was reported in the Senate from the Committee

131

on the District of Columbia abolishing slavery in the District. It provided for compensation to the owners, which was fixed by commissioners appointed by that purpose, but with limitation of an average of $300 per slave to each owner, for the punishment of kidnapping of such freedmen and other negroes as felony, and appropriated $100,000 to be expended under direction of the President for colonizing these and other negroes of the District, if they so desired, in tropic countries outside of the United States.

The bill came up for discussion on March 12, six days after the receipt of a special message from the President proposing compensated emancipation in any State so desiring it (see page 163).

ABOLITION OF SLAVERY IN THE DISTRICT OF COLUMBIA

SENATE, MARCH 12-APRIL 3, 1862

Garrett Davis [Ky.] objected to the bill; he first attacked the voluntary colonization feature as impracticable.

Not one slave in a hundred will consent to be colonized when liberated. The liberation of the slaves in this District, and in any State of the Union, will be just equivalent to settling them in the country where they live; and whenever that policy is inaugurated, especially in the States where there are many slaves, it will inevitably and immediately introduce a war of extermination between the two races. Free negroes are notoriously worthless. A negro's idea of freedom is freedom from work as a general rule. Where you have a few free negroes in a white community, and the negroes have but a small association and the examples all around them are the examples of diligence, industry, and thrift, this outward influence will force them to a modicum of labor and of thrift, too. But whenever you settle negroes in large numbers, or liberate them in large numbers, and they become a society to themselves, you will have a thriftless, worthless, indolent, inefficient population.

The negroes that are now liberated, and that remain in this city, will become a sore and a burden and a charge upon the white population. They will be criminals; they will become paupers. They will be engaged in crimes and in petty misdemeanors. They will become a charge and a pest upon this society, and the power which undertakes to liberate them ought to relieve the white community in which they reside, and in which they will become a pest, from their presence.

Mr. President, whenever any power, constitutional or unconstitutional, assumes the responsibility of liberating slaves where slaves are numerous they establish as inexorably as fate a conflict between the races that will result in the exile or the extermination of the one race or the other. I know it. We have now about two hundred and twenty-five thousand slaves in Kentucky. Think you, sir, that we should ever submit to have those slaves manumitted and left among us? No, sir; no, never; nor will any white people in the United States of America where the slaves are numerous. If, by unconstitutional legislation, you should, by laws which you shrink from submitting to the test of constitutionality in your courts of justice, liberate them, without the intervention of the courts, the moment you reorganize the white inhabitants of those States as States of the Union, they will reduce those slaves again to a state of slavery, or they will expel them and drive them upon you, or south of you, or they will hunt them down like beasts and exterminate them. They will not do this from choice, but they will do it from necessity. Emancipation will produce such a conflict between the races as will render extermination inevitable, and there will be no escape from it.

I maintain that it is a matter of humanity to the negro in this city, and of justice to the white population of this city, that, when you turn three or four thousand negroes who are now in a state of slavery free, you should relieve them from the curse of such a population, from its expense, from its burdens upon this community in every form; you ought to assume the philanthropy and the justice—the philanthropy to the negro race and the justice to the white race—to remove these people from the District. You may refuse to do it. If you do, a few years' experience will tell you what a mistake you made. I shall speak, though, on this subject at more length on another occasion. I will only say now that, when the negroes are liberated in the cotton States, it is giving up the cotton States to the negro race, and it is expelling, in a very short time, by inevitable necessity, the white population from that country, or it is introducing war between the two races that will result in the exile or expulsion of one or the other.

I know what I talk about. Mr. President, the loyal people of the slave States are as true to this Union as any man in the

Senate chamber, or in any of the free States; but never, never will they submit by unconstitutional laws to have their slaves liberated and to remain domiciled among them; and the policy that attempts it will establish a bloody La Vendée in the whole of the slave States, my own included. If, at the time you commenced this war, you had announced as the national policy that was to prevail the measures and visionary schemes and ideas of some gentlemen on this floor, you would not have had a solitary man from the slave States to support you. Whenever you seek to carry those measures into operation you unite the slave States as one man. They will tell you that in resisting such schemes they are fighting for the Union and the Constitution; and they will tell you so truly. They will tell you that your system of policy is no less aggressive and destructive upon the Union and the Constitution than that of the rebels of Secescia themselves; and they will tell you so truly. They will feel it as incumbent on them as men and as freemen to resist your unconstitutional policy, by which you will overturn and trample under your feet the principles of the Constitution, as they feel it to be their duty to resist the war which the secessionists have made upon the Union.

On March 18 John P. Hale [N. H.] replied to Senator Davis.

Of all the forms skepticism ever assumed the most insidious' and the most fatal is that which suggests that it is unsafe to perform plain and simple duty for fear that disastrous consequences may result therefrom.

This question of emancipation, wherever it has been raised in this country, has rarely ever been argued upon the great and fundamental principles of right, but upon what are to be the consequences. Men entirely forget to look at the objects that are to be effected by the bill, in view of the inherent rights of their manhood, in view of the great questions of humanity, of Christianity, and of duty; but what is to be its effect upon the price of sugar, tobacco, cotton, and other necessaries and luxuries of life? The honorable Senator from Kentucky looks upon it in that point of view entirely. Now, it does not become me to venture my opinions against the opinions of that Senator who has lived among the population of which he speaks; but it is as much my prerogative as it is the honorable Senator's to read a little of history, and to know what is its teaching upon this question, and by that test to compare the predictions of the honorable Senator with some other predictions of a different character that have been made elsewhere on other occasions.

The Senator here discussed the situation of Jamaica. He admitted that a steady decline had occurred there in its staple industries, particularly sugar, but showed from official British statistics that this deterioration had begun long before emancipation [1838], and was therefore due to other causes, the chief of which, he declared, was the system of great estates operated not by the owners, but by overseers.

But, sir, since emancipation the island has been divided into small proprietorships, and the proprietors of these estates have got up a system of exports of other things, such as cocoanuts, etc., which now amount to a very considerable sum.

But, sir, Jamaica is almost the only island that shows a comparative decrease of wealth from the effect of emancipation. It is different in the island of Barbadoes. That island has increased in its exports, in its value, in its wealth more than double since emancipation. Similar progress has been made in the Leeward Islands, Antigua, Dominica, Nevis, Montserrat, and St. Kitts.

I hope that it will be gratifying to the humane feelings of the honorable Senator from Kentucky to find that he is altogether mistaken as to the effects that emancipation will produce upon this laboring class of population. I hope that it will do something to expel from his mind that skepticism which makes him shrink from looking at this measure in the light in which an enlightened and philanthropic statesman ought to look at it, and that is in regard to its bearings upon the great question of human rights.

Mr. President, it seems to me that in the good providence of God He presents to this nation to-day an opportunity never presented before. If the rebellion which is now rending this Republic, and which is strewing our plains with the dead of our young men who have gone out to do battle on the field, has horrors, if it has miseries, if it has everything or almost everything to make humanity weep, it is not without some aspects that relieve the dark shade of the picture. If this rebellion—I trust ere long to be crushed out—shall, in the progress of the great injury that it is doing, afford this Republic, these United States, the opportunity of trying here, in this little District of less than ten miles square, the experiment which other nations are trying upon a great scale; and if we are enabled to show to the world that it is sometimes safe to do right, and not always inexpedient; then, sir, we shall have achieved something at which humanity will rejoice and something for which our posterity, to the latest generations, will bless us.

Sir, the governments of the world the world over are trying this experiment. The Emperor of Russia [Alexander II] over his vast dominions is now striking the bands of oppression from his long trodden down millions of serfs. The ameliorating influences of better principles and purer Christianity than have yet prevailed in the monarchies of the Old World are melting those iron despotisms and carrying into practical effect that great lesson of Christianity: "to loose the bands of wickedness" and "let the oppressed go free"; and it would be a reproach that ought to mantle the cheek of every citizen of this Republic with burning shame, if, at this day and this hour, when the monarchies of the earth are waking up to the great questions of human rights and making Christianity, instead of being a barren speculation, a practical and efficient principle of their government, this nation, at a time when the providence of God presents this opportunity to it, should, from any skepticism or fear of consequences, fail to meet the question and do justice by the oppressed.

Sir, I do not ask that the Government of the United States should trample upon the Constitution in any one of its provisions. I believe that, up to a very late period in our history, it was the conceded doctrine of this Republic, by statesmen North and South, that the constitutional power to legislate upon the subject of slavery in this District existed in Congress. I know that in late years that has been questioned and even denied. I know that within the last ten or twelve years this nation has been rent upon a new dogma, which denied the constitutional power of Congress to legislate for the Territories; and, while that question was rending the country, while it was tearing political parties in twain, dividing churches, bringing itself home to the hearts and consciences of this people, the Supreme Court of the United States undertook, with their puny efforts, to throw themselves in the way of the great question by the Dred Scott decision, and to say to the surging waves of humanity that, while washing out the stains of oppression from our history, they should go thus far and no further. The Supreme Court will find out ere long how much that has effected. Whether it has done more to wipe out the controversies that they wanted to crush

out, or to obliterate whatever of respect there was remaining
in the public heart for themselves, they will find out before the
issue is settled.

But, sir, while by this decision the Territories of the United
States were taken theoretically from the management of the
Federal Government, I believe, though I never read the Dred
Scott decision in reference to that particular view of it, it did
not go to the extent of saying that Congress had no constitutional
power to legislate in the District of Columbia. I am glad they
did not. I think they would if they had thought of it. [Laugh-
ter.] But, sir, that is left to us. Over this little spot of ten
miles square, or what there is left of it after the retrocession of
the part ·ceded by Virginia, we have confessedly the right of
legislation; and here in our midst, and by our laws, this system
of human slavery exists, and we are called upon to-day to
abolish it, to repeal the laws upon which it rests, and to the
most limited extent to try what will be the effect of emancipation upon the few slaves that are in this District.

When the midnight clock ushered in the 1st of August,
1838, the last manacle fell from the last slave in the British West
India Islands. This population knew it, and what was the aspect they exhibited? Riots, drinking, acts of degradation and
crime; such scenes as you might expect from what the Senator
from Kentucky said when he predicted that they would become
pests to society? Was there anything of that kind exhibited?
No, sir; but on the preceding night almost the whole population
gathered themselves together in their churches, in their places
of worship, and when the hour of twelve struck, which told
them that the slaves had been converted into British freemen,
they rose and sent up one united shout of thanksgiving to Almighty God for the great boon He had conferred upon them;
and the conduct that these emancipated slaves have exhibited
in most, if not all, the islands since has been such as indicates
not only the wisdom and the justice but the expediency of this
measure.

Mr. President, there is nothing on earth that is more unjust.
nothing more unkind, than for this boasted white Caucasian
race to enslave the colored race, to keep them in a state of
ignorance, to keep them in a state where it is a penal offence to
teach them to read so much out of the Bible as that they may
learn that God made them and Christ died to redeem them;
I say it is cruel and unjust to such a people, denied the right
of bringing a suit in court, denied the right of testifying as
to their own personal rights and wrongs, the whole intelligence

of the world shut out by the bar of an inexorable penal statute from enlightening their understandings; to pronounce them as degraded, ignorant, incapable of representation, because under the crushing weight of all these disabilities they have not made such progress as to enable them to step at once on an equality into a condition which their masters have enjoyed for many years. It is cruel. The injustice of it cannot be winked out of sight. It is as unjust as it would be to put out the eyes of a man and then taunt him with his blindness, as unjust as it would be to reproach any man with a personal deformity. It is as unjust as it is possible for perverted human intellect to be. Take off these burdens, give them a fair chance, let the light of science shine into their minds, make it no longer a crime punishable with imprisonment to open to them the pages of God's eternal truth, let them read something of the world that is about them, and something of the hope which leads to the world beyond them, give them the elevating influence of some of the motives that have elevated you, and then, if against all that, they fail to rise and fail to improve, then, and not till then, will it be time to reproach them with their inability to cope and contend with their white masters.

On March 20 Waitman T. Willey [Va.] opposed the measure.

Sir, this bill is a part of a series of measures, already initiated, all looking to the same ultimate result—the universal abolition of slavery by Congress. The consequences, in my judgment, involve the lives of thousands of my fellow-citizens and the happiness of all the loyal people of all the border slaveholding States. Perhaps I should be justified in saying that they involved in most serious peril the restoration of the Union and the Constitution.

Mr. President, I shall not trouble the Senate with any argument respecting the constitutional power of Congress to pass laws emancipating slaves. The arguments already made against this power by Congress in the States where slavery exists have not been answered, and, I believe, they never will be. But I do not think the argument against the expediency and practicability of such laws has been exhausted. Sir, I admit that the rebels, especially the leaders of the rebellion, should be punished. They ought, in some manner, to be made to bear the burdens of the war they have forced upon the country, as far as is possible, and to indemnify loyal men for the injuries inflicted upon them by the rebellion. But this punishment should be according to law. To punish treason by unconstitutional penalties is to be guilty of virtual treason ourselves, to say nothing of the inconsistency and danger of such a procedure. And it is worthy of remark, that no measure of emancipation yet proposed contains any indemnity for injuries received by the Government or individuals. Simply to emancipate the slave of the rebel may be a punishment to him, but it affords no relief to the loyal man who has suffered by the rebellion. Nay, one of the fundamental provisions of the confiscation bill of the Senator from Illinois [Mr. Trumbull] is to make the loyal people of the Union contribute of their means to transport and colonize the emancipated slaves of rebels. I cannot understand either the justice or expediency of such a policy. It seems to me to involve a manifest inconsistency. It punishes the traitor, indeed, but it only increases the burdens and taxes of the loyal people.

The agitation of these questions, under existing circumstances, must be positively mischievous. Will it not create strife and divisions here? Will it not disturb the country? Above all, will it not afford aid and comfort to the enemy? I am sure it will. It will be used by the leaders of the rebellion to "fire the Southern heart." The people of the South have been taught to believe that the object and design of the Republican party are to abolish slavery in all the States. These propositions will be seized upon as evidence of this intention. They will say: "Look at their unconstitutional confiscation laws, making no safe nor practical discrimination between Union men and secessionists. Look at the bill to abolish slavery in the District of Columbia; it is a stepping-stone to further encroachments." Especially will they point to the sweeping resolutions of the great apostle of abolition, the Senator from Massachusetts [Mr. Sumner], which, by one dash of the pen, deprive every Southern man of his slaves. No recruiting officer will have such power to replenish the thinned ranks of the rebel army as these propositions. No financial skill of Southern statesmen will have such power to replenish the depleted treasury of the rebel Government. Thus will these measures advance the cause of rebellion in the South; and so, consequently, will they prolong the horrors of war on our part, increase our expenditures, and augment the burdens of taxation. Worse than all, they will destroy that Union settlement in the South on which we hope to reorganize the State governments and restore the authority of the Constitution. They will not only encourage our enemies in the South, but they will dishearten our friends there. Thus do the claims of our common humanity, deprecating the evils of war, suggest the impolicy of such legislation at this time.

There is no necessity for driving the secessionists to such desperate extremities. Justice, moderation, generosity will meet a joyful response in many a Southern heart. They love the old flag; they love the old Union. Show them that their rights under the Constitution—their prejudices of education and habit, if you please to say so—are to be respected, and you will strike a blow more fatal to the rebel cause than a score of such victories as that at Fort Donelson. And this will be a victory without bloodshed. It destroys no valuable lives. It wastes no resources of the country's wealth. It makes no widows nor orphans. It desolates no homes. Why should not the North be generous and forbearing? Are not moderation and forbearance the invariable characteristics of a great people?

I understand Mr. Lincoln himself to be actuated by such principles. I understand that, in reference to this very matter of abolishing slavery in the District of Columbia, he was in 1858, and I hope is still, governed by the same considerations of expediency. If in 1858 considerations of expediency were enough to cause the Republican party to pause in their course at that day, now with the storm and tempest of war upon us, and an accumulating debt pressing down the people, should we not also hearken to the suggestions of expediency?

Why may we not to-day conquer a peace, and, after that, in the language of Mr. Douglas just before he died, settle all these difficulties? I will quote his words:

"When we shall have rescued the Government and country from its perils, and seen its flag floating in triumph over every inch of American soil, it will then be time enough to inquire as to who and what has brought these troubles upon us. Let him be marked as no true patriot who will not abandon all such issues in times like these."

Again, I ask Senators to consider what may be the effect of these extreme measures upon the public sentiment of the loyal States. There is but one sentiment there now, but one mind, one purpose. Therein consist our strength and the surest guaranty of our success. But this unity of sentiment and purpose is predicated on the distinctly declared purpose of the war, to wit, the suppression of the rebellion and the restoration of the Constitution and the Government as they were prior to the rebellion, without change or modification. Sir, let it be understood that there is a different object to be accomplished—such as is indicated by some, if not all, of the measures to which I have alluded—and that unity and harmony of public sentiment will be instantly destroyed. We shall thereafter in the loyal States be "a house divided against itself." Distraction will disturb our proceedings here, division will enter the army, and the cause of constitutional liberty will be imperiled with defeat and disgrace. Already are there indications of dissatisfaction in the public mind lest Congress should depart from the avowed purpose hitherto announced as the only object of the war.

Mr. President, what must be the practical effects of these measures of emancipation upon the welfare of the slave? You cannot enact the slave into a freeman by bill in Congress. A charter of his liberty may be engrossed, enrolled, and passed into a law, with all the formalities of legislation, and still he must remain, virtually, a slave. The servile nature of centuries cannot be eradicated by the rhetoric of Senators, nor by an act of Congress. You may call "spirits from the vasty deep," but they will not come. A freeman has the right of locomotion; he has the right of going into any State and of becoming the citizen of any State. Let me ask the Senators from Illinois and Indiana whether, if I set my slave free, they will allow him to come to these States. Sir, the constitutions of both of those States prohibit free negroes from becoming citizens of those States, or even residents thereof; and that is the liberty which you propose for the slave. Other States are agitating the question whether they will enact similar interdicts.

In how many States is the free negro entitled to the right of suffrage or to be a juror, or a judge, or to a seat in the legislature; to make, interpret, or execute the laws of the State in which he lives? I understand there are some negroes living in the North who possess large estates, are well educated, and of good morals and manners. Do you receive them into your families on terms of equality? Do you give them your daughters in marriage?

We must take things as they actually exist and, legislating for the slave, we must conform to his actually existing character and condition—moral, intellectual, and physical. We shall not deserve the name of statesmen if we do not; nor shall we entitle ourselves to the character of philanthropists if we disregard such considerations. Sir, would you recommend the Chinese to adopt a republican form of government? Would you advise the native Africans, cannibals and all, to organize a government on the model of the Constitution of the United States? The idea is preposterous.

And now, sir, candidly considering the ignorance, degradation, and helplessness of the slaves in the South, can you desire their immediate emancipation? Think of four millions of these degraded, helpless beings, without a dollar of money, without an acre of land or an implement of trade or husbandry, without house or home, thrust out upon the community to maintain themselves! Sir, they would starve to death, or they would steal, or they would murder and rob. Better drive them into the Gulf of Mexico and end their sufferings at once than perpetrate such a monstrous cruelty as this upon them.

We heard from the honorable Senator from New Hampshire [Mr. Hale] in regard to the prosperity of the British West Indies and of the French West Indies. I shall rejoice in the perfect success of those efforts to elevate the African race. But did not the Senator know how different was the position of the slaves in those states from that of the slaves in the United States? There were but few white men in those islands; the soil was all their own; implements of husbandry were put into their hands; and, with the moral influence and watchfulness of great Christian nations standing beside them and breathing upon them encouragement and words of good will, affording them moral and physical aid and protection; and yet, with all these advantages; with a soil all their own; with no white men to overshadow them; with a government of their own; with the moral influence and aid of these Christian patrons that had set them free, it is to-day, after so many years, a question whether it will not be a failure rather than a success. God grant that it may be a perfect success!

And now you, men of the North, I beg to ask, what would be the consequences of this wholesale emancipation on your own communities? How long would it be until this miserable population, like the frogs of Egypt, would be infesting your kitchens, squatting in your gates, and filling your almshouses? Sir, are you willing to receive them? If you set them free you must receive them. Will your operatives extend to them the right hand of fellowship and receive them as coequals and colaborers in your fields and shops? Meantime, what will become of the cotton fields of the South, and the cotton factories of the North? While you are increasing the number of your laborers, you will be destroying the sources of their employment. You will ruin the industrial interests of the South and bring serious detriment on the labor of the North.

The answer to all this is: transport and colonize the emancipated slaves in some tropical country. What then? Whither shall they be sent? Where shall we find a tropical territory for four millions of inhabitants? And where shall we find the money to pay for a territory sufficient to settle four millions of inhabitants? How much will it cost? I say nothing of constitutional difficulties in the way. Let them pass, along with the suspension of the *habeas corpus, et id omne genus.*[1] Where is the money to come from? Rhetoric and philanthropic platitudes will not purchase territory nor furnish the cost of transportation and the cost of the outfit and the cost of houses to be built for the reception of four millions of people, and the cost of implements of husbandry and tools of trade, and the cost of food and clothing for the first year, at the least. And then, sir, our task is just commenced. We must provide for their continued supervision, direction, and protection. And how long must all this continue? How long will it be before this mass of ignorant and servile population will become capable of self-government and self-subsistence? How many generations will it require to divest the slave of his servility and to clothe him with the independence of the freeman? Who can pay the debt? The accumulating millions of the current war debt, now rising mountain high, and resting with the weight of mountains upon the people, sink into mole-hills before the Atlas-like dimensions of the sum that will be required for the accomplishment of this stupendous scheme of philanthropy.

Mr. President, if slavery shall suffer from the incidental and necessary effects upon it of this war, let it be so; I shall not regret it. I am no pro-slavery man. I wish there were no slavery. I believe that slavery is doomed. I believe the time is coming when it will be abolished. Heaven hasten the day when, under the regenerating and reforming influences of Christian civilization, the slave shall be qualified for the enjoyment of freedom, and when it shall be practicable and humane to strike the fetters from the limbs of the last bondman of our race. But let us abide the appointed time of divine Providence. Let us not, in our eagerness to avenge the wrongs, real or imaginary, of the slave, repeat the folly of Samson, and in the frenzy of an indiscreet zeal pull down the pillars of the Constitution and involve both the slave and ourselves in the ruins of our country.

On March 4 Senator Davis spoke again upon the bill.

An honorable member of the other House has proclaimed, audaciously proclaimed, that he has attended and harangued

[1] And the like.

negro meetings here, that he has told them they had the same right to their masters' labor that the masters had to theirs; that they had the same right to sell their masters as their masters had to sell them; that they had the same right to sell their masters' children as the masters had to sell their children. Are these the dogmas, destructive to society, that you intend to preach and establish in this District? Was there anything in British oppression upon the colonial inhabitants of this country at all comparable in grievance, in real wrong and outrage, to what you are endeavoring now to force upon the people of this District? Have they not as much right to say they will have slaves as you to say that you will not have slaves? If you will not allow them that privilege, will you not allow them the poor privilege of voting whether free negroes shall stay here among them or not, a curse to the soil, a blight upon this small and poverty-stricken society?

If you are so humane, so benevolent, buy the slaves of the poor helpless widows in this city at fair prices with your money and take them to your homes, and there make them your neighbors, if you choose, your equals in politics and in the social circle. When you do this the world will give you credit for benevolence and philanthropy, but now it is all cant, it is all ambition. You and the men in the South are trying to make the same use of the slavery question. The business of both parties is to agitate, agitate, and never cease to agitate, because it becomes an element of political power by which individuals or parties may vault into office. Out, out with such benevolence and philanthropy as that!

It is not for the advantage of the white man in the agricultural States that slavery exists. It is expensive labor; it would be better for the country if it had never been there. I am no friend to slavery as an abstract question. If now I could decide whether slavery should exist or not, or whether it should cease with the colonization of all the negroes, I would colonize them all. If my own will could prevail I would put into operation in my own State a system of gradual emancipation that it would take about a hundred years to consummate and the thing should die out so gradually that nobody would be injured by it. But I say, in relation to this District and these people, give them a fair compensation for their slaves, and, when you get them, remove them from the country; let the races be separated; let the negro go to a land where, when he is buried, memory may raise some trophies over his tomb. None, none can ever be raised over his tomb in this land.

On March 25 Senator Wilson spoke in defence of his bill. He referred to certain laws in regard to slavery in the District as barbarous in the extreme, such as the act of May 31, 1827, that all negroes, except they proved the contrary, were presumed to be absconding slaves, and were to be committed to jail as such.

In what age of the world, in what land under the whole heavens, can you find any enactment of equal atrocity to this iniquitous and profligate statute—this "legal presumption" that color is evidence that man, made in the image of God, is an "absconding slave"?

This monstrous doctrine, abhorrent to every manly impulse of the heart, to every Christian sentiment of the soul, to every deduction of human reason which the refined, humane, and Christian people of America have upheld for two generations, which the corporation of Washington enacted into an imperative ordinance has borne its legitimate fruits of injustice and inhumanity, of dishonor and shame. Crimes against man, in the name of this abhorred doctrine, have been annually perpetrated in this national capital which should make the people of America hang their heads in shame before the nations, and in abasement before that Being who keeps watch and ward over the humblest of the children of men. Men and women of African descent, no matter in what State they were born, no matter what rights and privileges they possessed under the laws and institutions of the States from whence they came, have annually been seized, imprisoned, fined, and sometimes sold into perpetual servitude.

This doctrine, that color is presumptive evidence of slavery—this ordinance, consigning its victims to imprisonment, offers a tempting bribe to the base, the selfish, the unprincipled, to become men-stealers and kidnappers. This bribe has converted Government officials, justices of the peace, constables, and police officers into manufacturers of slaves. This bribe has annually filled your jail with its victims, making it the workshop where the selfish, the base, the ignoble have plied their trade in the souls and bodies of men. Hundreds, aye, thousands of men of African descent have been seized, arrested, imprisoned since the District of Columbia became the seat of the national capital.

The men of New England, New York, and Pennsylvania of that generation were responsible before God for these deeds of inhumanity.

But, sir, we of this age in America are not guiltless of like enormities.

VI—10

Here the Senator referred to the numerous negroes, many of them claiming to be free, that were incarcerated as fugitive slaves in Washington jails as late as the foregoing December.

In this national capital lurks a race of official and unofficial man-hunters, greedy, active, vigilant, dexterous, ever ready by falsehood, trickery, or violence to clutch the hapless black man who carries not with him a title-deed to freedom. Only a few days ago these harpies of the land, more merciless than the wreckers of the seas, pounced upon and hurried to your jail two men your officers in the field had sent to Washington to give important intelligence to your generals. For these deeds of inhumanity and injustice the intelligent, patriotic, and Christian freemen of America are responsible before man and before God! And if we, their representatives, who now for the first time have the power, do not end these crimes against man forever, the guilt and shame will rest upon our souls, and we shall be consigned to the moral indignation of Christendom.

Justice to a wronged and oppressed race demands that this corrupt and corrupting doctrine, that color is presumptive evidence of slavery in the capital of the Republic, shall be condemned, disowned, repudiated by the Government of the United States. For two generations it has pressed with merciless force upon a race who mingled their blood with the blood of our fathers on the stricken fields of the war of independence. In those days of trial black men, animated by the same mighty impulse, fought side by side with our fathers to win for America a place among the nations. They rallied at the tap of the drum on the morning of the 19th of April, 1775, to meet the shock of the first battle of the Revolution. They poured their unerring shots into the bosom of the veteran troops of England as they moved up the slopes of Bunker Hill. They met, and three times, by their steady valor repulsed the charges of British veterans on the battlefield of Rhode Island, which La Fayette pronounced "the best fought battle of the Revolution." They fought and fell by the side of Ledyard at Fort Griswold. They shared in the glorious defence and victory of Red Bank, which will live in our history as long as the Delaware shall flow by the spot made immortal by their valor. They endured with our fathers uncomplainingly the toils and privations of the battlefields and bivouacks of the seven years' campaigns of the Revolution, from Lexington to Yorktown, to found in America a Government which should recognize the rights of human nature. For more than sixty years, unmindful of their rights and ungrateful for their services in our hour of weakness, we have recognized in the capital of the nation the wicked and insulting dogma which writes ''slave'' on the brow of all who inherit their blood. Let us of this age hasten to atone for this great wrong by erasing that word from the brow of this proscribed race here, and making manhood, here at least, forever hereafter presumptive evidence of freedom.

What wrongs, what outrages may not be perpetrated upon a race of men where ''color is legal presumption of slavery,'' where they ''may be arrested as absconding slaves,'' where their oath cannot be received as ''good and valid evidence in law,'' where ''every person seizing and taking up runaways shall receive two hundred pounds of tobacco or the value thereof,'' where, ''if any slave strikes a white person, he may, upon the oath of the person so struck, have one of his ears cropped''? What wrongs, what outrages may not be perpetrated upon a race where, upon ''information to any justice of the peace that any free negro or mulatto is going at large without any visible means of subsistence such justice is required to issue his warrant to any constable directing him to apprehend such free negro or mulatto; and, if such free negro or mulatto shall fail to give security for his good behavior, or to leave the State within five days, or if, after leaving the State, he shall return again within six months, such justice may commit said free negro or mulatto to the common jail; and, if such offender so committed shall not, within twenty days thereafter, pay his or her prison charges, the sheriff, with the approbation of any two justices of the peace, may sell such free negro or mulatto to serve six calendar months?''

The speaker here enumerated other oppressive laws against free negroes in the District, such as the punishment by whipping, fine, or imprisonment of frequenters of night assemblies and the fine or imprisonment of negroes found in the streets after 10 p. m.

Since I have held a seat in the Senate I have known colored men, trusted and employed by the Government, while quietly hastening to their homes after ten o'clock from their duties in the public service, to be arrested under color of this ordinance. An ordinance so oppressive, so barbarous should be annulled by the Congress of the United States.

Another act requires every free colored person to furnish the mayor of the city of Washington evidence of his or her title to freedom, and to give bonds annually for his or her orderly conduct, and, failing so to do, to be sent to the workhouse; this places ten thousand free persons of color at the mercy of the corporation officials of this city, who may exercise, under color of this law, the most oppressive acts of petty tyranny.

Another act fines frequenters of religious meetings after 10 p. m.

The Christian men of New England, of the central States, of the West, must not forget that they are not free from responsibility for the existence, in their national capital, of a statute which imposes a fine of five dollars upon Christian men and women who may be found in a religious meeting after the hour of ten o'clock at night; that in the capital of this Christian Republic it is made the duty of police constables, under penalties of fine and disfranchisement, to enter a religious meeting after the hour of ten at night and disperse Christian men and women listening to the story of salvation, or offering up to Him who made the humblest of the race in His own image the praises and gratitude of contrite hearts.

The corporation of the city of Washington, from 1829 to 1841, enacted cruel and brutal laws for the punishment of slaves within the limits of the city by whipping on the bare back for breaking street lamps, exploding fire-crackers, etc.

Do Senators believe that there can be in the laws and ordinances of any Christian nation on the globe enactments so brutal, degrading, inhuman, indecent? It is time these bloody statutes for lashing men and lashing women should be obliterated from the laws and ordinances of the capital city of the Republic.

In spite, however, of these oppressive and cruel enactments which have pressed with merciless force upon the black race, bond and free, slavery, for more than half a century has grown weaker, and the free colored stronger, at every decade. Within the last half century the free colored population of the District of Columbia has increased from four to twelve thousand. In spite of the degrading influences of oppressive statutes, and a perverted public sentiment, this free colored population, as it has increased in numbers, has increased also in property, in churches, schools, and all the means of social, intellectual, and moral development. This despised race, upon which we are wont to look down with emotions of pity, if not of contempt or of hate, are industrious and law-abiding, loyal to the Government and its institutions. To-day the free colored men of the

District of Columbia possess hundreds of thousands of dollars of property, the fruits of years of honest toil; they have twelve churches, costing some $75,000, and eight schools for the instruction of their children. They are compelled to pay for the support of public schools for the instruction of the white children from which their own children are excluded by law, custom, and public opinion. Some of these free colored men are distinguished for intelligence, business capacity, and the virtues that grace and adorn men of every race. Some of these men have in possession considerable property, real and personal. The passage of this bill by the Congress of the United States will not, cannot, disturb for a moment the peace, the order, the security of society. Its passage will excite in the bosoms of the enfranchised, not wrath nor hatred nor revenge, but love, joy, and gratitude. These enfranchised bondmen will be welcomed by the free colored population with bounding hearts, throbbing with gratitude to God for inspiring the nation with the justice and the courage to strike the chains from the limbs of their neighbors, friends, relatives, brothers, and lifting from their own shoulders the burdens imposed upon them by the necessities, the passions, and the pride of slaveholding society.

This bill, to give liberty to the bondman, deals justly, ay, generously, by the master. The American people, whose moral sense has been outraged by slavery and the black codes enacted in the interests of slavery in the District of Columbia, whose fame has been soiled and dimmed by the deeds of cruelty perpetrated in their national capital, would stand justified in the forum of nations if they should smite the fetter from the bondman, regardless of the desires or interests of the master. With generous magnanimity this bill tenders compensation to the master out of the earnings of the toiling freemen of America. In the present condition of the country the proposed compensation is full, ample, equitable.

But the Senator from Kentucky [Mr. Davis] raises his warning voice against the passage of this measure of justice and beneficence. He assumes to speak like one having authority. He is positive, dogmatic, emphatic, and prophetic. The Senator predicted, in excited, if not angry, tones, that the passage of this bill, giving freedom to three thousand bondmen, will bring into this District beggary and crime, that the "liberated negroes will become a sore, a burden, and a charge"; that they "will be criminals"; that "they will become paupers"; that "they will be engaged in crimes and petty misdemeanors"; that "they will become a charge and a pest upon this society." Assured, confident, defiant, the Senator asserts that "a negro's idea of freedom is freedom from work"; that after they acquire their freedom they become "lazy," "indolent," "thriftless," "worthless," "inefficient," "vicious," "vagabonds."

The Senator from Kentucky, who speaks with so much assurance, may have the right to speak in these terms of emancipated slaves in Kentucky; but he has no authority so to speak of the twelve thousand free colored men of the District of Columbia. Under the weight of oppressive laws and a public opinion poisoned by slavery they have by their industry, their obedience to law, their kindly charities to each other, established a character above such reproaches as the Senator from Kentucky applies to emancipated bondmen.

But the Senator from Kentucky, upon this simple proposition to emancipate in the national capital three thousand bondmen, with compensation to loyal masters, chooses to indulge in the vague talk about "aggressive and destructive schemes," "unconstitutional policy," the "horrors of the French Revolution," the "heroic struggle of the peasants of La Vendée," and the "deadly resistance" which the "whole white population of the slaveholding States, men, women, and children, would make to unconstitutional encroachments." Why, sir, does the Senator indulge in such allusions? Have not the American people the constitutional right to relieve themselves from the guilt and shame of upholding slavery in their national capital? Would not the exercise of that right be sanctioned by justice, humanity, and religion? Does the Senator suppose that we, the representatives of American freemen, will cowardly shrink from the performance of the duties of the hour before these dogmatic avowals of what the men and the women of the slaveholding States will do? Sir, I tell the Senator from Kentucky that the day has passed by in the Senate of the United States for intimidation, threat, or menace, from the champions of slavery.

I would remind the Senator from Kentucky that the people, whose representatives we are, now realize in the storms of battle that slavery is, and must ever be, the relentless and unappeasable enemy of free institutions in America, of the unity and perpetuity of the Republic. Slavery—perverting the reason, blinding the conscience, extinguishing the patriotism of vast masses of its supporters, plunged the nation into the fire and blood of rebellion. The loyal people of America have seen hundreds of thousands of brave men abandon their peaceful avocations, leave their quiet homes and their loved ones, and follow the flag of their country to the field, to do a soldier's duties, and fill, if need be, soldiers' graves, in defence of their periled country; they have seen them fall on fields of bloody strife beneath the folds of the national flag; they have seen them suffering, tortured by wounds or disease, in camps and hospitals; they have seen them return home maimed by shot or shell, or bowed with disease; they have looked with sorrowful hearts upon their passing coffins, and gazed sadly upon their graves among their kindred, or in the land of the stranger; and they know—yes, sir, they know—that slavery has caused all this blood, disease, agony, and death. Realizing all this—ay, sir, knowing all this, they are in no temper to listen to the threats or menaces of apologists or defenders of the wicked and guilty criminal that now stands with uplifted hand to strike a death blow to the national life. While the brave and loyal men of the Republic are facing its shots and shells on the bloody fields their representatives will hardly quail before the frowns and menaces of its champions in these Chambers.

Anthony Kennedy [Md.] opposed the bill on the ground that it would tend to make his State, already containing the highest ratio of free negroes to population of any State in the Union," the great free negro colony of the country."

What must be the embittered state of feeling in Maryland when they find that this Congress, departing from every principle of good faith and of constitutional obligation to the compact of the Union, interferes to throw more of this class of free negroes in direct competition with the white labor of our own State?

Speaking of the proposition of the President for gradual compensated emancipation in Maryland he said that "it would produce an exodus of such of the slave-holding population from my State as can leave, and would force those who cannot emigrate either to manumit or to take the little pittance that is proposed."

But, sir, the worst of it all is that you will produce an exodus of that class of people upon whom the State of Maryland has rested more than all others for her great material prosperity —I mean her great mechanical and manufacturing class. Instead of the city of Baltimore being, as she has been heretofore, the third commercial emporium of this country, I fear that the day is to come when the grass may grow in her streets and her vessels lie rotting at her wharves.

This Government was created to promote domestic tranquility and to insure the general welfare. The passage of this bill does not promote either the general welfare or insure the domestic tranquility of my State; it will create strife in our borders as a forerunner of that other question, which is shortly to become a leading and important question in the future discussions and organizations of parties, and that is the emancipation policy of the President. You can show me no possible way by which emancipation can be effected without colonization. If you do not carry with emancipation colonization at the same time, if you emancipate these eighty-seven thousand slaves in the State of Maryland, making one hundred and seventy-five thousand colored people to remain there, one race or the other will ultimately perish; and scenes of blood and carnage that we have little idea of will result from it.

Sir, I am constrained to submit to the people of Maryland, if this measure passes, how far good faith has been kept with their trusting confidence; how far their honor and devotion to principle have been respected in the taunts and low flings which have been made at various times in both branches of Congress against their loyalty to constitutional obligations. Sir, I may speak warmly, for I feel deeply. I feel that whatever of consideration my State has had heretofore she has lost it; that while we of Maryland avoided the rock of secession, still clinging to the Constitution upon which we were embarked, we may find ourselves fast drifting into the dark and overwhelming whirlpool of a relentless, unyielding, and reckless sectional policy, which will end forever, in my humble judgment, the last hope of bringing together the dismembered and broken ties that bound this great and prosperous nation in one fraternal bond of union and power? In the name of my State I protest against this measure.

Willard Saulsbury [Del.], referring to Northern missionaries going to Port Royal, S. C. (captured by the Federal army and navy), and these embracing the negroes as brothers and sisters, said Senators should carry their principles to the logical conclusions and take negroes to their bosoms.

James Harlan [Ia.] opposed the charge that miscegenation would result from emancipation, or that the white people would rise and murder the freedmen. He therefore opposed colonization.

Do you find white gentlemen and white ladies marrying the free negroes that are now in this District? Do Senators find that the amalgamation of the white and the negro race is in progress in the States they represent? And, if so, does it progress more rapidly in the free than in the slave States? I have known of but three cases in my own State, and all three of those men married to wenches have been residents of slave States, where, I doubt not, they acquired their tastes. [Laughter.] Liberating the negroes carries with it no obligation to marry their wenches to white men. Gentlemen may follow their tastes afterward as now.

It is here in a slave District and in the slave States that men learn to associate familiarly as laborers and mechanics with the colored population; and, as a result of that familiar association at the daily toils of life, there is less reluctance at receiving them into their embrace, so handsomely described by the Senator from Delaware but a moment since. You will find in every slaveholding community a much larger number of mulattoes than in the free States.

But, then, what is to be done with these fifteen hundred liberated slaves? If they are to be liberated we are told they must be expatriated; they must be sent into some other country, into a strange community, and there compelled to provide in a land of strangers for the supply of their daily wants? Where are they now? In the bosom of the families of this metropolis. They are the house servants and the field hands of those who now claim to be their owners. Whence, then, a necessity for expatriating them? It does not increase their number to liberate them. If their labor is now necessary for the industrial purposes and comfort of the people of this District, will it not be as necessary after they shall have been liberated? If they are now needed as house servants and hotel servants, laborers and mechanics, in shops and fields, will they not be as necessary afterward? The only change in this regard that I can perceive is that after their liberation, those who now enjoy their labor gratuitously will, if their services are continued, be compelled to pay them reasonable compensation, the Government paying them a bonus of $300 each to relinquish the supposed right to their labor without the payment of wages. This is the only wrong that will have been inflicted on those who now own them. They now employ them, and give them food and raiment and shelter for their services, without reference to their own wishes, coercing obedience with the lash when found necessary. Afterward they will be compelled to consult the will and wishes of the employed, and to pay them probably stipulated wages, with which the servant will provide his own supplies. No injury is inflicted on society, no change is wrought on its organization, and no change is made in the political condition of the emancipated. They will have acquired no political rights or franchises. They will have acquired simply the right to enjoy as they choose the proceeds of their own labor. But if you confer this right on fifteen hundred more negroes now slaves in this District, we are gravely warned by Senators, in most eloquent and pathetic strains, that we will thus inaugurate a war of extermination between the white and black race! Rather than pay the negroes just compensation for their services their former masters, who have lived on the proceeds of their unpaid toil, will take down their rifles and shoot them! A war of extermination is to arise!

It is declared on the floor of the American Senate, in the face of a Christian nation, that, if men are to be liberated from a slavery that is more galling and degrading than any that has ever existed on the face of the earth from the commencement of time down to this moment, the people will rise and murder the poor freedmen. Senators say so without expressing so much as a regret. They thus approve and justify this savage feeling—if it exists; but, sir, it does not exist; I will defend the people of Kentucky, of Maryland, of Delaware, and of this District from any such slanderous aspersion. They entertain no such purpose on their part as the indiscriminate murder of the colored population, if they should become free. I doubt not but that the public sentiment that now exists, induced by the slaveholders themselves, in the State to which I have referred, is bitterly opposed to the liberation of the slaves; but if these slaves should be set free it will be effected by their own legislatures; and, if thus set free, no such savage war would arise.

You say that if two races are thrown together as freemen they will necessarily engender a war of extermination. Such a war never did commence between two races of free people; and, until the laws of the human mind and the human heart change, never will. To say that men of different, so called, races are natural enemies to each other, and will commence and wage a war of extermination when brought into contact, is a libel on humanity. It is a libel on the Author of the human race. The Almighty never implanted such feelings in the human heart. They never have been cultivated by an enlightened people. Wars of extermination exist only among savages; and with them only between belligerent tribes.

On March 31 Charles Sumner [Mass.] made an exhaustive and carefully prepared speech on the bill.

Mr. President, with unspeakable delight I hail this measure and the prospect of its speedy adoption. It is the first installment of that great debt which we all owe to an enslaved race, and will be recognized in history as one of the victories of humanity. At home, throughout our own country, it will be welcomed with gratitude; while abroad it will quicken the hopes of all who love freedom.

In early discussions of this question it was part of the tactics of slavery to claim absolute immunity. Indeed, without such immunity it had small chance of continued existence. Such a wrong, so utterly outrageous, could find safety only where it was protected from inquiry. Therefore, slave masters always insisted that petitions against its existence at the national capital were not to be received; that it was unconstitutional to touch it even here within the exclusive jurisdiction of Congress; and that, if it were touched, it should be only under the auspices of the neighboring States of Virginia and Maryland. On these points elaborate arguments were constructed; but it were useless to consider them now. Whatever may be the opinions of individual Senators the judgment of the country is fixed. The right of petition, first vindicated by the matchless perseverance of John Quincy Adams, is now beyond question, and the constitutional power of Congress is hardly less free from doubt. It is enough to say on this point that, if Congress cannot abolish slavery here, then there is no power anywhere to abolish it here, and this wrong will endure always, immortal as the capital itself.

But as the moment of justice approaches we are called to meet a different objection, inspired by generous sentiments. It is urged that since there can be no such thing as property in man, especially within the exclusive jurisdiction of Congress, therefore all now held as slaves at the national capital are justly entitled to freedom, without price or compensation of any kind to their masters; or, at least, that any money paid should be distributed according to an account stated between masters and slaves. Of course, if this question were determined according to divine justice, so far as we may be permitted to look in that direction, it is obvious that nothing can be due to the masters, and that any money paid belongs rather to the slaves, who for generations have been despoiled of every right and possession. But, if we undertake to audit this fearful account, pray what sum shall be allowed for the prolonged torments of the lash? What treasure shall be voted to the slave for wife ravished from his side, for children stolen, for knowledge shut out, and for all the fruits of labor wrested from him and his fathers? No such account can be stated. It is impossible. If you once begin the inquiry all must go to the slave. It only remains for Congress, anxious to secure this great boon, and unwilling to embarass or jeopard it, to act practically according to its finite powers, in the light of existing usages, and even existing prejudices, under which these odious relations have assumed the form of law; nor must we hesitate at any forbearance or sacrifice, provided freedom can be established without delay.

The clear-headed Senator from Kansas [Mr. Pomeroy] has asked, *first, has slavery any constitutional existence at the national capital? and, secondly, shall money be paid to secure its abolition?* The answer to these two inquiries will make our duty clear. If slavery has no constitutional existence here, then more than ever is Congress bound to interfere, even with money; for the scandal must be peremptorily stopped, without any postponement or any consultation of the people on a point which is not within their power.

It may be said that, whether slavery be constitutional or not, nevertheless it exists, and therefore this inquiry is superfluous. True, it exists as a monstrous fact; but it is none the less important to consider its origin, that we may understand how, assuming the form of law, it was able to shelter itself beneath the protecting shield of the Constitution.

It is true, there can be no such thing as property in man. If this pretension is recognized anywhere it is only another instance of the influence of custom, which is so powerful as to render the idolator insensible to the wickedness of idolatry, and the cannibal insensible to the brutality of cannibalism. To argue against such a pretension seems to be vain; for the pretension exists in open defiance of reason as well as of humanity. It will not yield to argument; nor will it yield to persuasion. It must be encountered by authority. It was not the planters in the British islands or in the French islands who organized emancipation, but the distant governments across the sea, far removed from the local prejudices, who at last forbade the outrage. Had

these planters been left to themselves they would have clung to
this pretension as men among us still cling to it. Of course,
in making this declaration against the idea of property in man,
I say nothing new. An honored Senator from Maryland, whose
fame as a statesman was eclipsed, perhaps, by his more remarkable fame as a lawyer—I mean William Pinkney, whom Chief
Justice Marshall called the undoubted head of the American bar
—in a speech before the Maryland House of Delegates, spoke as
statesman and lawyer when he said:

> "Sir, by the eternal principles of natural justice no master in the
> State has a right to hold his slaves in bondage for a single hour."

And Henry Brougham spoke not only as statesman and lawyer,
but as orator also, when, in the British Parliament, he uttered
these memorable words:

> "Tell me not of rights—talk not of the property of the planter in his
> slaves. I deny the right—I acknowledge not the property. The principles,
> the feelings of our common nature, rise in rebellion against it. Be the
> appeal made to the understanding or to the heart, the sentence is the same
> that rejects it. In vain you tell me of laws that sanction such a claim.
> There is a law above all the enactments of human codes—the same through-
> out the world, the same in all times: it is the law written by the finger of
> God on the heart of man; and by that law, unchangeable and eternal, while
> men despise fraud and loathe rapine and abhor blood they will reject with
> indignation the wild and guilty phantasy that man can hold property in
> man."

It has often been said that the finest sentence of the English
language is that famous description of law with which Hooker
closes the first book of his "Ecclesiastical Polity"; but I cannot
doubt that this wonderful denunciation of an irrational and inhuman pretension will be remembered hereafter with higher
praise; for it gathers into surpassing eloquence the growing and
immitigable instincts of universal man.

Of course, here in the national capital, which is under the
exclusive jurisdiction of Congress, the force which now maintains this unnatural system is supplied by Congress. Therefore does it behoove Congress to act in order to relieve itself of
this painful responsibility.

But this responsibility becomes more painful when it is considered that slavery exists at the national capital absolutely
without support of any kind in the Constitution. Nor is this all.
Situated within the exclusive jurisdiction of the Constitution,
where State rights cannot prevail, it exists in open defiance of
most cherished principles. Let the Constitution be rightly in-

terpreted by a just tribunal, and slavery must cease here at once. The decision of a court would be as potent as an act of Congress. If authority could add to the force of irresistible argument it would be found in the well-known opinion of the late Mr. Justice McLean, in a published letter, declaring the constitutional impossibility of slavery in the national Territories, because, in the absence of express power under the Constitution to establish or recognize slavery, there was nothing for the breath of slavery, as respiration could not exist where there was no atmosphere. The learned judge was right, and his illustration was felicitous. Although applied at the time only to the Territories, it is of equal force everywhere within the exclusive jurisdiction of Congress; for within such jurisdiction there is no atmosphere in which slavery can live.

Under the Constitution Congress has ''exclusive jurisdiction in all cases whatsoever'' at the national capital. But Congress can exercise no power except in conformity with the Constitution. Now, looking at the Constitution, we shall find, first, that there are no words authorizing Congress to establish or recognize slavery; and, secondly, that there are positive words which prohibit Congress from the exercise of any such power. The argument, therefore, is twofold: first, from the absence of authority, and, secondly, from positive prohibition.

Of course, a barbarism like slavery, having its origin in force, and nothing else, can have no legal or constitutional support except from positive sanction. It can spring from no doubtful phrase. It must be declared by unambiguous words incapable of a double sense. In asserting this principle I simply follow Lord Mansfield, who, in the memorable case of Sommersett, said: ''The state of slavery is of such a nature that it is incapable of being introduced on any reasons, moral or political, but only by *positive law*. It is so odious that nothing can be suffered to support it but positive law.'' (Howell's ''State Trials,'' Vol. 20, p. 82.) This principle has been adopted by tribunals even in slaveholding States. (See Horey *vs.* Decker, Walker's R., 42; Rankin *vs.* Lydier, 2 Marshall, 470.) But I do not stop to dwell on these authorities. Even the language, ''exclusive jurisdiction in all cases whatsoever,'' cannot be made to sanction slavery. It wants those positive words, leaving nothing to implication, which are obviously required, especially when we consider the professed object of the Constitution, as declared in its preamble, ''to establish justice and secure the blessings of liberty.'' There is no power in the Constitution to make a king, or, thank God, to make a slave, and the absence of all such power is hardly more clear in one case than in the other.   The word king nowhere occurs in the Constitution, nor does the word slave.   But, if there be no such power, then all acts of Congress sustaining slavery at the national capital must be unconstitutional and void.   The stream cannot rise higher than the fountain head; nay, more, *nothing can come out of nothing;* and, if there be nothing in the Constitution authorizing Congress to make a slave, there can be nothing valid in any subordinate legislation. It is a pretension which has thus far prevailed simply because slavery predominated over Congress and courts.

To all who insist that Congress may sustain slavery in the national capital I put the question, where in the Constitution is the power found?   If you cannot show where, do not assert the power.   So hideous an effrontery must be authorized in unmistakable words.   Do not insult human nature by pretending that its most cherished rights can be sacrificed without solemn authority.   Remember that every presumption and every leaning must be in favor of freedom and against slavery.   Do not forget that no nice interpretation, no strained construction, no fancied deduction, can suffice to sanction the enslavement of our fellowmen.   And do not degrade the Constitution by foisting into its blameless text the idea of property in man.   It is not there; and if you think you see it there, it is simply because you make the Constitution a reflection of yourself.

A single illustration will show the absurdity of this pretension.   If under the clause which gives to Congress "exclusive legislation" at the national capital slavery may be established, if under these words Congress is empowered to create slaves instead of citizens, then, under the same words, it may do the same thing in "the forts, magazines, arsenals, dock-yards, and other needful buildings" belonging to the United States, wherever situated, for these are all placed within the same "exclusive legislation."   The extensive navy-yard at Charlestown, in the very shadow of Bunker Hill, may be filled with slaves, whose enforced toil shall take the place of that cheerful, well-paid labor whose busy hum is the best music of the place.   Such an act, however consistent with slaveholding tyranny, would not be regarded as constitutional near Bunker Hill.

A court properly inspired, and ready to assume that just responsibility which dignifies judicial tribunals, would at once declare slavery impossible at the national capital, and set every slave free—as Lord Mansfield declared slavery impossible in England, and set every slave free.[1]   The two cases are parallel;

[1] The famous Sommersett case; see Index.

but, alas! the court is wanting here. But the good work which courts have thus far declined remains to be done by Congress.

But the question is asked, shall we vote money for this purpose? I cannot hesitate. And here there are two considerations, which with me are prevailing. First, the relation of master and slave at the national capital has from the beginning been established and maintained by Congress, everywhere in sight, and even directly under its own eyes. The master held the slave; but Congress, with strong arm, stood behind the master, looking on and sustaining him. Not a dollar of wages has been taken, not a child has been stolen, not a wife has been torn from her husband, without the hand of Congress. If not a partnership, there was a complicity on the part of Congress, through which the whole country has become responsible for the manifold wrong. Though always protesting against its continuance, and laboring earnestly for its removal, yet gladly do I now accept my share of the promised burden. And, secondly, even if we are not all involved in the manifold wrong, nothing is clearer than that the mode proposed is the gentlest, quietest, and surest in which the beneficent change can be accomplished. It is, therefore, the most practical. It recognizes slavery as an existing fact and provides for its removal. And when I think of the unquestionable good which we seek; of all its advantages and glories; of the national capital redeemed; of the national character elevated; and of a manganimous example which can never die; and when I think, still further, that, according to a rule alike of jurisprudence and morals, *liberty is priceless*, I cannot hesitate at any appropriation within our means by which all these things of incalculable value can be promptly secured.

Let this bill pass, and the first practical triumph of freedom, for which good men have longed, dying without the sight—for which a whole generation has petitioned, and for which orators and statesmen have pleaded—will at last be accomplished. Slavery will be banished from the national capital. This metropolis, which bears a venerated name, will be purified; its evil spirit will be cast out; its shame will be removed; its society will be refined; its courts will be made better; its revolting ordinances will be swept away; and even its loyalty will be secured. If not moved by justice to the slave, then be willing to act for your own good and in self-defence. If you hesitate to pass this bill for the blacks, then pass it for the whites. Nothing is clearer than that the degradation of slavery affects the master as much as the slave; while recent events testify that, wherever slavery exists, there treason lurks, if it does not flaunt. From the beginning of this rebellion slavery has been constantly manifest in the conduct of the masters, and even here in the national capital it has been the traitorous power which has encouraged and strengthened the enemy. This power must be suppressed at every cost, and, if its suppression here endangers slavery elsewhere, there will be a new motive for determined action.

Amid all present solicitudes the future cannot be doubtful. At the national capital slavery will give way to freedom; but the good work will not stop here. It must proceed. What God and nature decree rebellion cannot arrest. And as the whole widespread tyranny begins to tumble, then, above the din of battle, sounding from the sea and echoing along the land, above even the exultations of victory on well-fought fields, will ascend voices of gladness and benediction, swelling from generous hearts wherever civilization bears sway, to commemorate a sacred triumph, whose trophies, instead of tattered banners, will be ransomed slaves.

The bill was passed on April 3 by 29 yeas to 14 nays, the Senators from the border and Pacific States and Joseph A. Wright of Indiana voting in the negative.

The bill was sent to the House and there debated on April 10-11, the discussion including the right of secession, the power of Congress to confiscate property and to emancipate slaves in the seceded States.

Judge Benjamin F. Thomas [Mass.], a conservative Republican, was the leading speaker on these subjects. He delivered a profound legal argument showing that there could be no secession of States, but only of citizens, and that the acts of these were rebellion and not war; that confiscation of the property of the rebels was unconstitutional, unjust, and impolitic; and that emancipation of slaves could be justified only as a military necessity.

The bill was passed upon this day (April 11), and signed by the President on April 16. In his message to the House communicating his act the President said:

I have never doubted the constitutional authority of Congress to abolish slavery in this District, and I have ever desired to see the national capital freed from the institution in some satisfactory way. Hence there has never been in my mind any question upon the subject, except the one of expediency, arising in view of all the circumstances. I am gratified that the two principles of compensation and colonization are both recognized and practically applied in the act.

One curious result of the act was that under it a District negro (free) claimed and received compensation for his wife and their six children, whom he had previously purchased from their white master.

CHAPTER VI

Compensated Emancipation

D
URING the debates on abolition of slavery in the District of Columbia the President sent a special message to Congress on *compensated emancipation* in the States so desiring it.

Compensated Emancipation

Special Message of President Lincoln, March 6, 1862

I recommend the adoption of a joint resolution by your honorable bodies, which shall be substantially as follows:

"*Resolved,* That the United States ought to coöperate with any State which may adopt gradual abolishment of slavery, giving to such State pecuniary aid, to be used by such State, in its discretion, to compensate for the inconveniences, public and private, produced by such change of system."

If the proposition contained in the resolution does not meet the approval of Congress and the country, there is the end; but if it does command such approval I deem it of importance that the States and people immediately interested should be at once distinctly notified of the fact, so that they may begin to consider whether to accept or reject it.

The Federal Government would find its highest interest in such a measure, as one of the most efficient means of self-preservation. The leaders of the existing insurrection entertain the hope that this Government will ultimately be forced to acknowledge the independence of some part of the disaffected region, and that all the slave States north of such part will then say, "The Union for which we have struggled being already gone, we now choose to go with the Southern section." To deprive them of this hope substantially ends the rebellion; and the initiation of emancipation completely deprives them of it as to all the States initiating it.

The point is not that the States tolerating slavery would very soon, if at all, initiate emancipation; but, that while the offer is equally made to all, the more Northern shall, by such initiation, make it certain to the more Southern that in no event will the former ever join the latter in their proposed confederacy. I say "initiation" because, in my judgment, gradual and not sudden emancipation is better for all. In the mere financial or pecuniary view any member of Congress, with the census tables and treasury reports before him, can readily see for himself how very soon the current expenditures of this war would purchase, at fair valuation, all the slaves in any named State. Such a proposition on the part of the general Government sets up no claim of a right by Federal authority to interfere with slavery within State limits, referring, as it does, the absolute control of the subject in each case to the State and its people immediately interested. It is proposed as a matter of perfectly free choice with them.

In the annual message, last December, I thought fit to say, "The Union must be preserved, and hence all indispensable means must be employed." I said this not hastily, but deliberately. War has been made, and continues to be, an indispensable means to this end. A practical reacknowledgment of the national authority would render the war unnecessary, and it would at once cease. If, however, resistance continues, the war must also continue; and it is impossible to foresee all the incidents which may attend and all the ruin which may follow it. Such as may seem indispensable, or may obviously promise great efficiency, toward ending the struggle, must and will come.

The proposition now made, though an offer only, I hope it may be esteemed no offence to ask whether the pecuniary consideration tendered would not be of more value to the States and private persons concerned than are the institution and property in it, in the present aspect of affairs?

While it is true that the adoption of the proposed resolution would be merely initiatory, and not within itself a practical measure, it is recommended in the hope that it would soon lead to important practical results. In full view of my great responsibility to my God and to my country, I earnestly beg the attention of Congress and the people to the subject.

LINCOLN'S CONFERENCE ON COMPENSATED EMANCIPATION WITH BORDER STATE DELEGATES

On March 10 the President held a conference with delegates from the border slave States. One of the delegates, John W. Crisfield [Md.], reported the substance of the conference.

The President disclaimed any intent to injure the interests or wound the sensibilities of the slave States. On the contrary, he declared that his purpose was to protect the one and respect the other. We were, he said, engaged in a terrible, wasting, and tedious war; immense armies were in the field, and must continue there as long as the war should last; these armies came of necessity into contact with slaves in the States we represented, and, as they advanced, would be brought into contact with the slaves of other States. Slaves came, and would continue to come, to the camps, thus keeping up continual irritation. He was constantly annoyed by conflicting and antagonistic complaints. On the one side a certain class complained if the slave was not protected by the army; persons were frequently found who, participating in these views, acted in a way unfriendly to the slaveholder. On the other hand, slaveholders complained that their rights were interfered with, their slaves were induced to abscond and were protected within the lines. These complaints were numerous, loud, and deep. They were a serious annoyance to him, and embarrassing to the progress of the war. They kept alive a spirit hostile to the Government in the States we represented; they strengthened the hopes of the Confederates that at some day the border States would unite with them, and thus tend to prolong the war; and he was of opinion, if this resolution should be adopted by Congress and accepted by our States, that these causes of irritation and these hopes would be removed, and more would be accomplished toward shortening the war than could be hoped from the greatest victory achieved by Union armies. He made this proposition in good faith, and desired it to be accepted, if at all, voluntarily, and in the same patriotic spirit in which it was made. Emancipation was a subject exclusively under the control of the States, and must be adopted or rejected by each for itself; he did not claim, nor had this Government any right, to coerce them for that purpose.

The President disclaimed that he had any ulterior purpose, such as emancipation by Federal authority. He should lament the refusal of the States to accept compensated emancipation, but had no designs beyond their refusal.

In respect to the constitutionality of the proposition he said that it presented no difficulties, proposing as it did simply to co-operate with any State by giving it pecuniary aid. It was the expression of a sentiment, rather than the presentation of a constitutional issue. In any scheme to get rid of slavery the North as well as the South was morally bound to do its equal share. He thought that the institution was wrong and that it ought never to have existed; but yet he recognized the rights of property which had grown out of it, and he would respect those rights as fully as similar rights in any other property; he recognized that property can exist, and does legally exist, in slavery; he would get rid of the odious law, not by violating the right, but by encouraging the proposition and offering inducements to give it up.

Compensated Emancipation

House of Representatives, March 10-11, 1862

On March 10 Roscoe Conkling [N. Y.] introduced the President's bill in the House. He said:

This resolution is in the exact words of the President of the United States, as sent here with the message in which he recommends its passage. It relates to a subject in regard to which almost every member, if not every one, has made up his mind; and those who have not made up their minds will not have their conclusions settled by any discussion which may occur on this resolution.

William A. Richardson [Dem.], of Illinois, replied:

The gentleman from New York says that we ought to have our minds made up on the subject of this resolution. Why, sir, there is no subject which will engage the attention of this Congress of more magnitude. I venture to say that not one half of the members on this side of the House have had time to consider it. We have had no time to communicate with our people.

But I am prepared to say one thing in regard to that message of the President. So far as it recommends the doctrine of the rights of the States in this matter I recognize its force. My objection to it is not of that character; I object to it upon another ground altogether. I do not believe my people are prepared to enter upon this proposed work of purchasing the slaves of other people and turning them loose in our midst. I have long entertained the idea that this class of negroes in our country are incapable of becoming the repository of freedom or government.

In reference to another point embraced in that message I have but a single word to offer. Without the Constitution and the Union there is no liberty—no government—and whatever stands in the way of their preservation I am prepared to strike down or to yield up. Whatever stands in the way of our Government and its integrity must be destroyed. But I do not propose to go beyond the Constitution. I do not know why a single article of property should be singled out and made an exception.

But, sir, I am satisfied that gentlemen are not prepared to vote upon this question to-day. It is a subject which requires consideration; and I move, therefore, that it be postponed to this day week.

JOHN A. BINGHAM [O.].—I hope the motion to postpone will not prevail. If gentlemen propose to entertain the proposition of the President they can have but little, if any, difficulty in coming to a just conclusion upon it, as it involves no principle save the power of the Government of the United States to contribute in aid of the gradual abolition of slavery in any State which, of its own motion, may initiate that policy. That is all there is of the resolution.

The President has told us that he deems it important, if the resolution meets the approval of Congress, that the people immediately interested should be *at once* distinctly notified of the fact, so that they may begin to consider whether they will accept or reject the proposition. The adoption of the resolution imposes upon no State any obligation to act in the premises. It interferes with no right of any State by intendment or otherwise.

CHARLES A. WICKLIFFE [Ky.].—The gentleman is learned in the Constitution of the United States. Will he tell me under what clause of the Constitution he finds the power in Congress to appropriate the treasure of the United States to buy negroes, or to set them free? Is it under the head of "the general welfare"?

MR. BINGHAM.—I supposed, Mr. Speaker, that that question was settled long ago by those who made the Constitution. If the gentleman will pardon me, I beg leave to remind him again of the words of Madison, that

"It is in vain to oppose constitutional barriers to the impulse of self-preservation. It is worse than in vain!"

And, says Hamilton:

"Congress have an unlimited discretion to make requisitions of men and money."

DANIEL W. VOORHEES [Dem.], of Indiana.—I shall vote against any postponement of this question. I, for one, as a member of this House, am fully prepared to act upon it now. If this measure is to be pressed, and to become a part of the policy of the Government, I think it is right and proper that the people should know it soon; that, while groaning under almost untold burdens, while trembling under the weight of taxation upon their shoulders, if this additional burden is to come upon them they may prepare in season their sad and oppressed hearts and almost broken bodies to bear it.

I will say one thing further: that if there is any border slave State man here who is in doubt whether he wants his State to sell its slaves to this Government or not, I represent a people that is in no doubt as to whether they want to become the purchasers. It takes two to make a bargain; and I repudiate, once and forever, for the people whom I represent on this floor, any part or parcel in such a contract. Slavery, wherever it exists under the Constitution, I and my constituents will recognize and respect in its legal rights; the *slave trade*, either domestic or foreign, we are opposed to, and it is no favorite of the Constitution. If *emancipation* means *taxation* on the free States, now lavishing their all for the Union and the Constitution, and ever ready to do so, I am opposed to that cause; and I here take my stand in the name of the people I represent against it.

Thaddeus Stevens [Rep.], of Pennsylvania, was in favor of postponing the bill in order to give every member time to consider it.

I have read it over; and I confess I have not been able to see what makes one side so anxious to pass it or the other side so anxious to defeat it. . I think it is about the most diluted, milk and water gruel proposition that was ever given to the American nation. [Laughter.] The only reason I can discover why any gentleman should wish to postpone this measure is for the purpose of having a chemical analysis made to see whether there is any poison in it. [Laughter.]

The House adjourned with the motion to postpone the bill before it. The discussion was resumed on the following day (March 11). The motion to postpone was decided in the negative—yeas, 67; nays, 71.

Charles A. Wickliffe [Ky.] opposed the bill on constitutional grounds, stating that the only color of its justification was to be found in the "general welfare" clause in the preamble of the Constitution.

Under this pretence of power, Congress might think that it would be advancing the interests of the general Government to dot the whole country over with turnpikes, railroads, and bridges, or with schools and colleges, or to do anything or everything that a legislative body, unrestrained by a constitution, may do for the benefit of the people. I thought that this idea of a general welfare power had long since been exploded by our statesmen and jurists and courts whenever it was attempted to be asserted in the State or Federal tribunals. If you were to allow that to be taken as a granting power in the Constitution, then there is no limit to which the Federal Government or Congress may not go.

But we are told that this measure is to be consummated under the war power. It is alleged that we are now in a state of war, and we are told that the Constitution is, therefore, to be disregarded. It is said that whatever is *necessary* to carry on this war to a successful conclusion may be done with perfect freedom under the license and authority, not of the Constitution, but as a military necessity. I deny that a state of war, and especially the present state of war, enlarges the power of Congress. What will be the result of that military necessity which, it is said, enables us to lay aside the Constitution? What is it, and what has caused this line of executive and military action? I greatly fear there are many who desire more the emancipation of the slaves of the South than the restoration of the Union of the States. If it had not been for that strong desire I think that we would never have heard of this military-necessity power.

I suspect, sir, that these old-fashioned opinions of mine may be taken as evidence of my want of loyalty. I have not as yet seen any necessity why we should violate the Constitution in order that we should do what is required of us, and that is to furnish the men and money necessary to the restoration of the Union—I deny that a state of war increases or enlarges the powers of Congress.

Furthermore, the proposition is unwise. If the measures which now seem to be the particular and favorite ones urged to our consideration shall be carried out, if you proclaim to these people extermination or subjugation, and the confiscation of private property, you will have a war that will last longer than the life of any man upon this floor. You may conquer battles, and gain victories; but you will not in that way secure the re-establishment of the Government and the restoration of the Union. How do you expect to maintain the Union and to re-establish the laws of the United States over the seceded States? How do you expect to induce the people of those States to aid and assist you in the restoration of the Union and of the Government? How do you expect to do that if you drive every man from his homestead under the threat you make here of utter destruction or subjugation? You destroy all hope of peace. Leave the peaceful non-combatants at rest; let them know that they have the pledge of their security by this Government. If that be done, when the war is over you will find a nucleus of Union men in the slave States around which the inhabitants of those States can rally, and then the Union may be restored. But if they are to be alarmed by threats of confiscation of estates of non-combatants, then their homesteads will be abandoned and burned either by themselves or the enemy. You see already the madness of the leaders of the rebellion. They urge the population of the South to burn their homesteads, and to destroy all their crops, in order to keep them out of the possession of what they term their enemies. You have taken possession of a portion of the South. I was glad when I heard of it. You have alarmed the population. They have now run off and left their slaves unprotected. What is proposed here? One gentleman has proposed that we shall have a land office in the South, and that the lands of the nabobs shall be distributed to the slaves that have been abandoned. There are other projects equally as absurd, and in violation of the laws of civilized war.

Suppose you emancipate the whole of the black population of the Southern seceded States, something over three millions, what do you intend to do with them? Have you provided any colony to which you can send them? Do you intend to leave them in the South where they are? Or do you intend to locate them in the free States? One plan was before us, I think, in a bill this morning. It is proposed that the Congress of the United States shall open cotton plantations in the South, upon lands now in the possession of the army. Is that a *military necessity?* Is it a military necessity that we should employ, at the public expense, many agents (I do not know that they are called over-seers, as they are in the South; that would not sound well), sub-agents or superintendents? They are none of them to be called *overseers,* that would sound too much like the agent of a Southern slaveholder. There was a peculiar provision in it—this bill to which I refer. They were to *force* these creatures to work —they were to use *"humane and Christian force,"* I believe. What do you mean by that? You are to send a parcel of men to superintend the negroes on the cotton plantations as over-seers for the United States.

I ask the gentlemen who are advocating these propositions if it is a "military necessity" that this Government, with a debt now of upward of seven hundred millions of dollars, should commence the business of cotton planting in South Carolina and Georgia or elsewhere? I ask where are the power and authority in the Government of the United States to go into the business of farming—for it amounts to that practically? Where is the authority for the Government of the United States to send a parcel of men South to engage in the business of cotton-growing who, when they get there, will know as much about raising cotton as I do about preaching the Gospel, and not as much, for I have heard the Gospel preached, and they never saw a stalk of cotton growing. [Laughter.] If you carry out your plan it will be the finest position for one of your modern honest men to steal that you can find in the United States, not excepting army contracts.

What is to be the effect of this resolution upon the war? There seems to be an intimation, if I understand it, that there is danger that the border slave States, as they are termed, unless this measure shall be inaugurated, may wish to join the slave States of the South, not while the war is going on, but when the

Southern Confederacy, composed of the cotton States, shall have gained its independence. Sir, I can see how this message of the President and the vote of this House may be understood abroad greatly to our prejudice. The inference will be inevitably drawn there that you from the North who advocate this resolution look to the utter impossibility of carrying out your favorite scheme of emancipation and confiscation, and the liberation of the slaves of the South; that you do not desire Union until slavery is abolished; and that you are willing to give up the cotton States, provided you can get the border States to emancipate their slaves.

In Kentucky and all these border States the great difficulty that we have had to encounter from the influence of the South, and those of our own citizens who acted with the South, was to convince them that the Federal Government did not mean to interfere with slavery. I do not mean this to apply to the man alone who owns the slave; for it is a strange fact that the non-slaveholding portion of the population are most against emancipation.

The speaker concluded with declarations of the Administration, Congress, and the officers of the army, made at the beginning of difficulties and up to this time, that the war, being forced upon the United States, is to be prosecuted for the maintenance of the Constitution and the restoration of the Union as it was. He said:

To give it now a different purpose, to wage it for the destruction of the States, the abolition of slavery, would be a fraud so infamous that it would call down upon its authors the anathemas of all good and honest men.

Alexander S. Diven [N. Y.] believed that the reason which urged the President to his recommendation was that President Jefferson Davis of the Confederacy had issued a proclamation implying that the Confederate forces would be concentrated for the defence of the cotton States, and that the border States would be abandoned to the Union, thus inducing the United States Government to acknowledge the independence of the cotton States.

The rebels, he said, hugged the idea that we care but little for these States, if we could only get the border States—the most valuable in a commercial point of view—and believe that with the Union thus broken, with that holy devotion broken which the whole country has ever had for the Union of Washington, Jefferson, and Madison, the loyalty for the Union would be broken. It was then hoped that a petty annoyance would be waged against the border States until they would be driven, one by one, to join that confederation of the Gulf States. They would thus add to their power, and secure what they now find they cannot secure by force of arms. Seeing that they were clinging to that hope, the President is desirous to strip them of their last hope of refuge, and to show them that, even though they should succeed in their rebellion, they will be disappointed in their expectation of drawing the border States with them. Disappointed in it by this, by a noble, just, fair proposition upon the part of the Government not to interfere with any of the reserved rights of these States; not, under the Constitution or above the Constitution, to meddle with any of their institutions; not to assume to pass laws, if we have the right to pass them, which could interfere with their reserved rights; but a magnanimous proposition to them, that if they would stand by the Union no injustice should be done to them. If the possession of their slaves should become intolerable they might have an opportunity to rid themselves of them without crushing them out and breaking them down. In a spirit of magnanimity the President of the United States recommended that this Congress should adopt this resolution, looking to an ultimate resort in case any of the States at any time find it necessary, for the protection of their rights, to adopt that ultimate resort.

When they pass a law for the emancipation of their slaves, if they ever do pass such an act, they will make it conditional that Congress shall pay a portion of the loss. If that condition be not complied with they lose nothing by their law. If it be complied with by Congress they gain. There is, I repeat, no tampering with their rights, no infringement upon their rights.

The gentleman from Indiana [Mr. Voorhees] has thought proper in the discussion of this proposition to refer to the expense that would be incurred. Why, sir, half a day's expense of this war will pay for the emancipation of all the slaves in Delaware. The cost of sustaining this war for half a month will pay for the emancipation of all the slaves in Kentucky. The cost of maintaining this war for a month would pay for the emancipation of the slaves in Missouri and Kentucky. And if we can cut off from these rebels their last hope, and in my judgment this is their last hope, for they have already been obliged to surrender the hope to which they have so fondly clung of the intervention of European countries; and now if you will cut off this last desperate hope which the rebel leaders still entertain, you will do more to accelerate the termination of this rebellion than any other congressional measure that can possibly be adopted.

Abraham R. Olin [N. Y.] replied to Mr. Wickliffe.

It is not true that either this House or the people of this country have any other motive in the prosecution of this war than they had in August last. They are fighting this war for the maintenance of the Constitution and the Union. I know that there is a difference of opinion upon another question, and that is as to the means to be employed for the prosecution of this war. I know that some gentlemen, and perhaps my friend from Illinois [Owen Lovejoy] for one, think that the best way is, like the Dutch governor of New York, to fight it by proclamations, to proclaim liberty throughout the land to captives. Another gentleman would say, let the negro question alone.

Mr. LOVEJOY.—I beg the gentleman's pardon for interrupting him; but I simply desire to say that I want to fight with bayonets and bullets, and not with proclamations.

Mr. OLIN.—I am happy to hear that, and it will enlighten the House upon that point, I have no doubt.

Now, there is, as I have observed, a difference of opinion upon this subject. But every intelligent man in the free States as well as in the slave States knows—the whole world knows—that this institution of slavery, never very palatable to the free States of the Union, has been the cause of this accursed rebellion. Mr. Speaker, you remember Toombs said that that institution could only exist as long as slaveholders controlled this Government, and that, when they were deprived of the power and patronage of the Government to uphold it, that institution must fall. Slaveholders having been deprived of that power, this rebellion is the consequence. Now, gentlemen from slave States must treat with a little forbearance my friends upon this side of the House. I beg you remember they, together with all the world, know that this war has been brought upon us by men who sought to control the destinies of this country by wielding the influence of slavery. It is not to be wondered at that the people of the free States do not feel very kindly disposed toward that institution, or that every opportunity is sought within the constitutional limits of the Government to strike a blow at slavery, which, if it shall not destroy that institution forever, will leave it in such a situation that it will never hereafter be a disturbing power in the administration of this Government.

Now, I am desirous to see this war prosecuted within the strict limits of the Constitution. I think that this Government is released from no obligation to my friend from Kentucky by reason of this rebellion; that the Government is bound to protect all his rights of property and everything that is dear to him in his social and political relations, and I wish to see the war prosecuted successfully, if it may be, with a most sacred regard to all the rights of every citizen. In my humble judgment the whole strength of this accursed rebellion rests in an entire delusion on the part of the Southern people. Every gentleman who has held a seat on the floor of this House as long as I have knows one fact, and that is that there has been for years a strenuous, constant, and persistent effort on the part of some Southern men in this House, and out of it, to imbue the entire Southern mind with the idea that the party now in power, if they ever did attain power, would, by force and violence, if necessary, emancipate their slaves; and it is that belief that now adds strength to their army. If that delusion could be dispelled this rebellion would melt away like frost-work before the sun. I believe as sincerely that that is so as I believe any truth revealed from above.

What, then, is obviously the policy of the Government in respect to this measure? Why, I think—though, perhaps, my opinion upon that subject is not worth much—that the President is pursuing a wise and prudent course, and I think that my friend from Kentucky is unnecessarily alarmed at the introduction of this resolution. What is it, in its whole scope and extent? Why, simply that if you gentlemen of the slave States are willing to get rid of slavery the general Government will aid you to do it by giving you a compensation for any loss that you may sustain; and, although I am not worth much, God knows I would divide my last crust of bread to aid our Southern friends to get rid of slavery, and let us live in peace and harmony together. If these gentlemen say, ''we cannot afford to make the sacrifice of manumitting our slaves,'' the President says, ''very well; the general Government will aid you to accomplish it.'' That is the magnanimous, the great, the God-like policy of the Administration. But, while it says that, it says to you and it says to the world, ''we do not propose to force this question of emancipation upon you; you are perfectly free to accept or to reject the offer. We disclaim entirely the right to constrain you in the matter."

But the gentleman from Kentucky [Mr. Wickliffe] says that the offer to aid in the emancipation of the slaves is an interference with this institution. Merciful God! Does this institution make you mad? Must you close your eyes to what is going on all over the civilized world? Look, I beseech you, at this matter! Conduct your army in the best way you can, with the most sacred regard to every right, and when it overruns a State, as it has overrun Missouri, what is the result? Where have gone to-day her slave population? Nearly two-thirds of them have fled either North or South; and, if our army marches successfully through Kentucky and Tennessee, to some extent this same result will be produced there. Nay, more. As they march through other States, as they are now marching through South Carolina, thousands upon thousands of these poor negro slaves will flock to the standard of the Union—the slaves of rebel masters, the slaves of men who have taken up arms to subvert this Government, a Government such as was never founded by man. And do you think, I pray you, that any power of this Government, judicial, military, or executive, can ever be induced to surrender those men to those rebel masters? Oh, no; you are touching there a chord that vibrates through the whole Northern heart, and it says we never will consent that property of this description shall be returned to men thus arrayed against the Government by the strong arm of the Government.

John J. Crittenden [Ky.] construed the proposition as asking the border States to give up their "domestic institution" of slavery as a pledge of loyalty to the Union.

What right have you to suppose now that old Kentucky will abandon her faith in the Constitution of the United States, and unite herself with the South? None at all. The way to conciliate Kentucky is not by pressing these questions upon her. The way to conciliate her is to let her alone. That is the way to show your confidence in her—your confidence that she will always, and under all circumstances, do her duty. That will make the old State proud. But when you demand of her a revolution in her domestic policy, when you make a demand of that sort upon her, I am apprehensive it may not have the good effect you suppose. The cardinal principle upon which our whole system of Government is founded is that matters of a local and domestic character shall be under the exclusive control of the State governments, and national and external matters under the control of the general Government. If you begin now to trench upon that paternal and patriarchal jurisdiction which belongs to the States by taking one domestic subject from under its control, what will be the result in the future?

I do not know how this proposition will be received by my constituents. It is suddenly brought before them. It relates to a subject about which they are very sensitive. I fear they will think that they ought to be let alone on this subject. You urge them to take a further step in proof of their loyalty. They will say: "Is this the way the other States of the Union treat us? The moment we come within their grasp, the moment we join hands with them, and take up the sword in defence of the Constitution, they desire that we shall modify our institutions in accordance with their wishes."

Do you demand of us a surrender of a part of our constitutional rights, while you are professing to support the whole Constitution?

MR. LOVEJOY.—I desire to ask the gentleman if he thinks it would be unconstitutional if Kentucky should emancipate her slaves, on condition that the Federal Government shall pay her a certain amount of money?

MR. CRITTENDEN.—I am not prepared to say that it would be unconstitutional. But the gentleman looks at the matter in a very limited way. When this Government makes a proposition of this sort, it is equivalent to an invitation, and by such an invitation agitation may be introduced at a time when we want no agitation.

But gentlemen say that this will break the hopes of the rebellion, and that otherwise the South will compel you to recognize her independent government. So says my friend from New York [Mr. Diven] ; and this measure proposed is only to prevent Kentucky and the border States from acceding to that independent Southern government when it shall force itself upon our acknowledgment. Sir, I hope that that day is never to come. It is too remote a possibility to found any argument upon. If that time ever does come, when these twenty millions of people shall be content to see this great Government broken up ; and if, looking forward beyond that infamous and disgraceful day, we shall be told that there is a fear on the part of the North that the border States will then join the Southern Confederacy, if you permit that day to come I shall not want to be with you. Are we recreantly to submit to have this country broken into pieces, and then dare to think of things that are to happen afterward? No, sir; there is no thereafter; there is no future beyond that. I will not look into it. And yet the argument used here to-day is that we shall, without consideration, without knowing what will happen to this measure in Kentucky or the other border States, base this measure only upon things that may happen in the future, that may happen after that day of infamy. My policy does not reach so far, nor will I act upon any supposition of the sort.

Sir, we are in the habit of saying a great many things in the ardor of our feelings which we would like to recall. My friend from New York [Mr. Olin] has said so many admirable things that he will excuse me for alluding to one extravagance of this sort in the remarks which he has just made. He says that when it shall be necessary for the preservation of the country he would be willing to see the negro armed and servile war made in the South by Southern negroes upon Southern planters—a war of the black man upon the white man.

How can it ever become necessary for a nation to do what, in the sight of God and man, is condemnable under all circumstances? I will not suppose such a case. It is the very *argumentum* which ranges through the long series of resolutions here for confiscation and emancipation—that you have a right to do anything to weaken your enemy and to strengthen yourself. A doctrine more at war with every principle of ethics, of morals, and of religion cannot be proclaimed.

In the name of God, what are we fighting for this day? Are we not fighting to uphold the Government; to uphold humanity; to put down those who violate law, who would induce to disorder, homicide, and crime? And are you to say that you have a right to commit all manner of crimes for the purpose of accomplishing your object? No matter what your enemy was, he could not be worse than you are, if that is your morality. In a cause like ours, a glorious cause, which seeks to maintain justice and liberty and right among men, let not us, its chosen defenders, sink ourselves down to the level of those who have called forth this effort on our part to subdue them. This is a great contest. I want to see it waged on principles that become it; that are lofty as the subject itself is. It is not necessary for us to do wrong. It is only necessary for us to behave dutifully toward our country, and to enforce our laws. We shall thus do our whole duty, and shall have nothing to upbraid ourselves with when the war is over.

John Hickman [Pa.], a radical Republican, said that
he would vote for the bill, although he thought it of
little practical importance.

It does not possess any great intrinsic merit, for the reason
that its adoption would not constitute legislation. It would be
better distinguished as a plank in the platform of a political
party. If carried through this House it will not even bind the
present House to pass a law, much less a House that shall be
convened in the future. It is, in my judgment, simply a declaration of opinion as to a policy, and nothing more. As I look
at it is is rather a compensation to the North for disappointed
hopes, and a warning to the people of the border slave States.
The President of the United States cannot be ignorant of the
fact that he has, thus far, failed to meet the just expectation of
the party which elected him to the office he holds, and his friends
are to be comforted, not so much by the resolution itself as by
the body of the message, while the people of the border slave
States will not fail to observe that with the comfort to us is
mingled an awful warning to them.

The paper is somewhat of an assurance—slight, I admit—
that the President still has convictions upon the great question
of freedom and slavery, and that in a certain event the interests
of slavery, which he seems anxious to protect, may be prostrated;
and that, therefore, it is better for the border States to put
themselves in a position to meet a great crisis. It is, therefore,
rather a palliative and caution than an open and avowed policy;
it is rather an excuse for non-action than an avowed determination to act. Neither the message nor the resolution is manly and
open. They are both covert and insidious. They do not become
the dignity of the President of the United States. The message
is not such a document as a full-grown independent man should
publish to the nation at such a time as the present, when positions should be freely and fully defined.

Sir, any man who sits down and carefully reads this message
cannot fail to understand just what it was the President had in
his mind at the time he penned it. In the first place, he says
to the Republican party: "Gentlemen, I am not such a great
defender of the institution of slavery as you would make the
country believe I am. I am willing that the institution of
slavery shall be sustained, and especially in the border States,
but in case a dissolution of the Union, to any extent, shall occur,
I will see, as far as my official influence extends, that those
border States shall affiliate with the States of the North." In

the second place, he says to those border States: ''Gentlemen, I give you warning in time that in the prosecution of the war a policy may eventually become necessary on the part of this Administration which will lead to the destruction of the slave interest in these States.''

I am satisfied that I cannot be mistaken as to the points in the mind of the President. He does look, and we look, and you gentlemen from the slave States look to a contingency in which extreme war measures may become necessary. If this Union and Constitution are deserving of the eulogiums which have been passed upon them by gentlemen from all sections they are worth more than the pecuniary interests involved in any single local or domestic institution; and if you are possessed of the patriotic feelings which I suppose you to be possessed of, and which I am willing to admit you are possessed of, you will regard the preservation of the Constitution and the Union as paramount to the pecuniary interests involved in any domestic institution, not excepting slavery. That man who is not willing to save the Constitution and the Union by the sacrifice of a private interest is already a rebel, and I care not upon whose ear that declaration may fall with harshness; and, sir, when, a few weeks since, in a running discussion in this Hall, I propounded the question to gentlemen from the border slave States whether they would sustain the Constitution and the Union, although it might be necessary to sacrifice slavery to save them, there was but a solitary and a very feeble voice came up in affirmative response. Now, sir, although the North has magnanimity, the North has not too much patience. I proclaim here a fact which has studiously been concealed, as it seems to me, that the border States are not in this Union because they love freedom. They are in it because they fear force.

What means the action of Kentucky maintaining neutrality in the hour when the Union required friends? If a man professes to be a friend of mine I expect him to show his active friendship in the hour of my trial and my sufferings. Kentucky, proud, magnanimous Kentucky, as she has been designated here this morning—and I have nothing to say against either attribute —in that hour of trial and danger stood on the ground of perfect neutrality. But when the passage of our troops to the national capital had been secured, when the integrity of the Union had been put out of danger for the time being, and when the safety of Kentucky was imperiled, then she was the proud and magnanimous State to declare herself on the side of the Union.

And, sir, I do not hesitate to say that, from all I can see, there is no slave State population that has not the well-being of slavery so much at heart, and into the composition of whose hearts slavery does not enter to such an extent that they love human slavery, with its christianizing and republican influences, its separations of husbands and wives, of parents and children, its days of toil without recompense, its servility and utter degradation, its life without hope, and its death without knowledge, as much as they love the Government. Why, sir, I have found but one among the Representatives of slave constituencies on this floor who, when the Union was in the hour of its direst peril, was ready to make the open and distinct avowal that, if the Union and slavery could not both be saved, he would save the Union in preference to slavery.

Now, sir, but one word more. Mr. Lincoln has found himself between two swords—the sword of the party looking to a particular policy, to be pursued toward a rebellion springing from slavery, and the sword in the hands of the border States, who insist all the time that the war shall be prosecuted in such a way as to save their peculiar, divine, and humanizing institution. The President of the United States, if he has any recollection— and I do not know whether he has or not, for I do not perceive any evidence of the fact—if he has any recollection he will remember that he was taken up by a party, sustained and carried into his high position by a party whose very life was dedicated to the maintenance of the Constitution and the Union; and they had the right to expect the adoption of such measures, not inconsistent with the laws of war, as would be most likely to crush treason at the earliest moment. And when I say to this House that the nation at large has been somewhat disappointed in its reasonable expectation, I may be open to a charge of indiscretion, but not to one of misrepresentation.

I say, further, that the nation has felt a great lack of confidence, not only in the President, but in those military leaders put in the highest position by the President. He knows this well, and has made some changes. He knows, further, that the people of the Northern States regard this Government as sacred, and will never allow the sacrilegious hand to touch it without striking it off, and that its downfall cannot precede Northern desolation and death. No matter what interests may perish, no matter what lives may be sacrificed, they will command that the war shall be prosecuted with the greatest vigor, and that the Government shall be reëstablished, even if it be but over smoldering cities and wasted lands.

I speak for myself alone; I do not speak for organizations, political or otherwise, and I assume the responsibility. That may be my misfortune.

> "Never mind!
> My words, at least, are more sincere and hearty
> Than if I sought to sail before the wind.
> He who has naught to gain can have small art; he
> Who neither wishes to be bound nor bind
> May still expatiate freely, as will I,
> Nor give my voice to slavery's jackal cry."

The bill passed the House on March 11 by a vote of 89 to 31. It came up in the Senate on March 24.

COMPENSATED EMANCIPATION

SENATE, MARCH 24-APRIL 2, 1862

Willard Saulsbury [Del.] denounced the bill as in effect an interference with slavery in the States by fomenting agitation upon the subject, and by holding out inducements for the abolition of the institution. Whether force or bribery was used to accomplish this end, it was an infraction of the solemn pledge of the Republican party not to touch slavery in the States.

On March 26 James A. McDougall [Dem.], of California, opposed the bill on the ground that it would be ineffectual—indeed, would defeat the very end aimed at by arousing antagonism to emancipation through agitating the question.

I have seen the time when I hoped Missouri would soon provide for the gradual emancipation of her slaves, and it would have been done but for agitation. The same thing has been known in the history of Kentucky, Virginia, Maryland, and Delaware. I believe that by the just administration of the Government of its own affairs the legitimate course of events will accomplish all these results yet; but they never will be accomplished by legislation. We may have this subject agitated session after session, year after year, Congress after Congress, angry discussions, expensive discussions, profitless discussions— Federal legislation cannot cure this evil; it cannot be reached by any such medicine; for favorable times, circumstances, events, we may hope; but if we here undertake the management of this great social problem we will find that we are not merely antici- pating, but that we are usurping the ways of Providence, and assuming an office higher than any to which we have been yet elected.

Lazarus W. Powell [Ky.] regarded the measure as "a pill of arsenic, sugar-coated," its object being to inaugurate Abolition parties in the border States.

I happened a few nights ago, through curiosity, to go to the Smithsonian Institution, to hear a man of some distinction as an orator and lecturer in this country. There I heard this man, Wendell Phillips, for half an hour, and he distinctly announced, after eulogizing the President very highly for this message, that the interpretation of it was simply saying to the border slave State men: "Gentlemen, if you do not take this we will take your negroes anyhow." That was the interpretation given to it by some gentlemen of the House of Representatives, and that, in my opinion, is the plain, distinct, and proper interpretation of the message, when you take it as a whole.

Lot M. Morrill [Me.] defended the proposition of the President as generous and just. He could not con- ceive how it could possibly be offensive to any man who had not made up his mind to hold slavery supreme above the Constitution and the integrity and welfare of the Union.

John B. Henderson [Dem.], of Missouri, supported the bill (and, indeed, thereafter acted as an emancipa- tionist).

It has been urged with a great deal of power in the border slaveholding States that the design of the bill is to effect the emancipation of the slaves in the border slaveholding States, and then to consent to a dissolution of the Union. I have no idea that any such thing is really contemplated.

The institution of slavery in the State of Missouri has not been sufficient, notwithstanding it has been deemed by Senators here to be sufficient in a great many of the States—because slavery has been charged to be the cause of all our troubles— to withdraw the people of my State from their allegiance to the

Federal Government. There are other interests in Missouri besides the interests of slavery of equal, if not superior, importance. One of the great reasons inducing them to remain firm and fixed to the Union is that they will never consent to surrender their right to the Mississippi River, over every inch of it, from the borders of Missouri to the Gulf of Mexico; and, sir, if they lose all idea that that is to be an object of the majority here, it will inevitably affect their feelings in the future.

We of the South have been annually frightened by some imaginary plot for the overthrow of slavery in the United States. We have been regularly informed by a race of politicians, whose watchful and jealous regard for our true interests has been about equal to that of the Abolitionist for the negro, that unless they were continued in power the whole institution would be immediately upset, the owner robbed of his property, and the negro made equal, if not superior, to the white man. We have listened to these stories, and been made alike to fear and hate the most unsubstantial and harmless thing on earth.

Why was this war forced upon us, and who are its authors? However opposed I may be to some radical measures which have been introduced in Congress, and which, no doubt, are largely attributable to the feelings engendered by this unjustifiable war, yet candor compels the Union men of the border States to do justice to the President, and even to his friends in Congress. This terrible revolution was brought about by Mr. Yancey and his confederates, by inflaming the Southern mind against the dangers of Abolition, which they knew to be false. They drove the South to madness, to self-destruction.

Now, sir, what has been the result of this unnecessary strife upon my State. In 1860 our slave population was one hundred and fourteen thousand nine hundred and sixty-five. Our white population at the same period was upward of one million. How is it now? I doubt whether there are fifty thousand slaves in the State.

The true value of real and personal property in Missouri in 1860 was $501,214,398. Aside from the depreciation of value, which no man can now estimate, and beyond the loss of slaves to which I have referred, I think it safe to say that ten per cent. of this vast amount of property has been destroyed and forever lost to the owners in consequence of this war—an amount equal to the aggregate value of all the slaves in the State at the commencement of hostilities.

If I were to add to this the loss occasioned to the people of the State by the utter prostration of its agricultural, commercial, and manufacturing interests for the last twelve months I might add fifty millions more to the sum already named.

Looking, then, to my own State, I am not disposed to take issue with the President in regard to the future results of the war. I regard his expression as a prophecy, and not as a threat —a prophecy that I feel will be realized if this war continues. It is a new pledge of faith by the representatives of the people that this vexed question shall be left with the people of each State. It comes not in the spirit of arrogance, demanding conformity with the views of others, but with humility acknowledging if slavery be an evil it is a sin for which we are all responsible, and for the removal of which we are willing to come with practical benevolence. It means more than all this. It intimates to the States that the nation would prefer gradual to immediate emancipation, and that the measures now pending in Congress, looking to such results, should be superseded by one of conciliation and good will.

If this spirit had been more largely cultivated in days gone by we would not this day be forced to witness a ruined South and a deeply oppressed North. Why, sir, ninety-six days of this war would pay for every slave, at full value, in the States of Kentucky, Missouri, Maryland, Delaware, and the District of Columbia. Nine months of the expenditures of this strife would have purchased all the slaves in the States named, together with those in Arkansas, Tennessee, Mississippi, and Louisiana, thus preserving in peace the whole of the Mississippi to the Gulf. Less than two years of these expenditures would have paid for every slave that treads the soil of the nation. If Northern men had treasured these things, and learned that kind words can accomplish more than wrath, and if Southern men had resolved to look upon slavery as upon other questions of moral and political economy, and both had determined to examine this as all other subjects, in calmness and deliberation, we would have been spared the evils that now oppress us.

Mr. President, I have made up my mind to cast my vote for the resolution, and to leave it with the people of my State. I am indifferent as to the result upon myself. I feel that it is altogether a change from what we have witnessed for the last number of years on the floor of this and the other House. Instead of that wrangling controversy, instead of those rushing waves of tumult, of ill feeling, and of anger that have been engendered in the discussion of this question, it marches up and takes hold of the slavery question as a practical one, worthy of the calm, cool, and deliberate judgment of those in whom the nation has trusted its prosperity and its future greatness. Then, sir, I shall cast my vote for it. I regard it as no insult to the people of my State; I regard it as no threat; but I regard it as a measure that is conciliatory, and looks to the future peace and harmony of the country, and to the early restoration of the Union.

On April 2 John Sherman [O.] spoke in behalf of the bill, closing the debate.

It is said that the resolution of the President now before us looks to an interference with slavery in the States. I do not so construe it. It does not assert the power or advise us to interfere with slavery in the States. On the contrary, it, by necessary implication as strong as express denial, denies the power. If the State of Maryland should, in its wisdom, see fit to commence a system of gradual emancipation of slaves, would they not have the right by this bill to call upon us for aid and assistance? We here announce beforehand that we will give them pecuniary aid, but not until they call for it. It is right that we should announce that doctrine. It is right that they should inaugurate that system; and I believe that in the providence of Almighty God the system will be inaugurated more rapidly even than we now hope for.

Why should we not give this aid? By it we accomplish great purposes. We banish from the Halls of Congress a disturbing element which in some form or other will permeate this body and every political organization in this country. It is for the peace and quiet and comfort of our people we should aid any State desiring to emancipate their slaves.

Besides, the policy of emancipation would tend to develop the resources of the States in a wonderful degree. Why, sir, I visited the other day the Chesapeake Bay, James River, and York River. It surprises me beyond expression that that magnificent region, with resources unrivaled in this country, is not now peopled by a million of men. When I look upon those deep bays, those fertile fields, requiring only energetic labor to develop them, when I see those marts of commerce in the very center of our Atlantic coast, I wonder in amazement that a million of men are not now crowded there, delving and striking and working with honest toil for an honest reward. But, sir, there is no other cause for this lack of development except simply that labor, upon which all civilization depends; labor which has built up New York, New England, and the West, is there degraded by the presence of slaves, so that the master must live on the labor of the slaves, and the slaves must work for the master without hope of reward.

Sixty years ago Ohio was a wilderness, now she has two and a half millions of people. I believe that if Virginia was a free State now, in thirty years from this time she would contain three or four millions of people. Therefore I say that, if I were a citizen of a border State, I would at once raise the banner of gradual emancipation; I would call on the general Government for aid, and, for one, if I should happen to be a member of this body, I will give that aid cordially and freely.

But it is said that Congress by giving this aid would interfere with slavery. The resolution of the President does not say that Congress shall render this aid, but that the United States ought to coöperate. It may be necessary to call upon the States; and I think I can say in advance that, if Kentucky should free her slaves, Ohio would gladly respond to anything that Kentucky would ask. She would gladly pay the debt she owes from the war of 1812 by any aid that Kentucky might ask of her.

The policy and the effect of emancipation in the border States would undoubtedly be to induce the slaves to go southward. They would commence a kind of hegira southward, and free people from the Old World and from the Northern States would go down to the border States. I have no doubt that the tide of emigration, having now met the vast plains and deserts of the West, will gradually seek a home southward. If you will welcome it, avail yourself of it, use that labor to develop your resources, it will make the people of Kentucky and of these border States rich, prosperous, and happy. The owner of seventeen hundred acres of land will be worth three times as much as his lands and his slaves are now worth. Labor makes everything and not the mere possession of land.

I am willing, therefore, to adopt the policy of the President in regard to slavery in the States, to abolish slavery in this District, to promote a system of voluntary colonization. I am also in favor of confiscation; I think such a measure should be passed promptly. We must seize upon the property of these men who have taken up arms against the Government. Our people, when they come to pay taxes, will demand it. These men know it. They themselves are confiscating all the property of their own citizens who will not take up arms. You must in war adopt the laws and policy of war. I am, therefore, in favor of the most rigid law of confiscation against the leaders of this rebellion; but I would, as an act of wisdom, of amnesty, of wise forbearance, and moderation, authorize the President at any time to proclaim an amnesty to the great masses of the rebels. As to those who have led, the captains of companies, the members of Congress, the leaders in the rebellion, all those who have staked their property upon it, men of intelligence and character, I would, without mercy, prosecute the laws of confiscation and war against them to the furthest extent. Let us adopt this policy, guided by wise moderation, controlled by a manly earnestness and a determination to stand by each other, and I believe the Republican party will not only save the country, but will put the country in a march of prosperity of which we have heretofore had no example. If, on the contrary, any useless measures of legislation, looking to extreme means, be adopted, prejudicing the great mass of the people of the Southern States, destroying their rights as citizens of those States, or reducing the States to Territories, it will only exasperate the people of those States more and more, will make conquest impossible, and a reunion of all the States utterly futile. I believe that by a wise system we may, one by one, gather these States again into the folds of the Union; and if the Republican party, through its wisdom and ability, shall carry the country through this revolution, I do not fear for the verdict of the popular will. I have heard some of my friends express a doubt, and say, ''let us do this now, because after a while we may not have the power.'' I will do what I think is right, and I have an abiding confidence in the people of the United States that they will stand by those who follow their convictions of duty with moderation and good sense.

The bill was then passed by a vote of 32 yeas, including Henderson, Garrett Davis [Ky.], and Waitman T. Willey [Va.], to 10 nays, mostly from the border States.

Abolition of Slavery in the Territories

On March 24, 1862, Isaac N. Arnold [Ill.] introduced in the House a bill abolishing slavery without compensation in every existing Territory, and prohibiting it in all which might be formed in the future. It was referred to the Committee on Territories. On May 1 it was reported from the committee by Owen Lovejoy [Ill.]. The bill was bitterly opposed by the Democrats: Samuel

S. Cox [O.] called it a complete justification of the charges of the secessionists that the Republicans had never intended to abide by the pledges of the Chicago platform, and therefore that its title should be "A Bill for the Benefit of Secession and of Jeff. Davis." John W. Crisfield [Md.] characterized the bill as "a palpable violation of the rights of the States, and an unwarrantable interference with private property—a fraud upon those States which have made cessions of land to the Government, and a violation of the Constitution." Judge Benjamin F. Thomas [Mass.] ably opposed the bill because of the lack of compensation to slaveholders in it, and to remove this objection the feature of compensation was added. The bill was then passed by vote of 85 yeas, including all the Republicans and two Democrats, William T. Sheffield [R. I.] and Judge Thomas, to 50 nays.

The bill was reported in the Senate by Orville H. Browning [Ill.] on May 15, and on June 9 it was passed by a strict party vote of 28 yeas to 10 nays. On June 19 it was approved by the President.

Lincoln's Appeal to the Border States

On July 12 President Lincoln read to the border State Representatives in Congress an appeal that their States adopt compensated emancipation.

If the war continues long, as it must if the object be not sooner attained, the institution of slavery in your States will be extinguished by mere friction and abrasion—by the mere incidents of the war. It will be gone, and you will have nothing valuable in lieu of it. Much of its value is gone already.

I am pressed with a difficulty which threatens division among those who, united, are none too strong. An instance of it is known to you. General Hunter is an honest man. He was, and I hope still is, my friend. I valued him none the less for his agreeing with me in the general wish that all men everywhere could be free. He proclaimed all men free within certain States, and I repudiated the proclamation. He expected more good and less harm from the measure than I could believe would follow. Yet, in repudiating it, I gave dissatisfaction, if not offence, to many whose support the country cannot afford to lose. And this is not the end of it.   The pressure in this direction is still upon me, and is increasing.   By conceding what I now ask you can relieve me, and, much more, can relieve the country, in this important point.

In his annual message of December 1, 1862, the President was forced to report on his favorite project of colonization that no countries were willing to accept the freedmen as citizens except Liberia and Hayti, and to these the freedmen were unwilling to migrate.

He had, however, a more favorable report to present of State action in regard to compensated emancipation, a number of loyal slave States having initiated legislation looking to this end.

The passage of the Thirteenth Amendment abolishing slavery superseded Federal action in regard to compensation.

CHAPTER VII

Punishment of Treason

Thomas D. Eliot [Mass.] Introduces in the House, and Lyman Trumbull
[Ill.] in the Senate, a Bill to Confiscate Property of Rebels—Speeches
against the Bill by Sen. Edgar Cowan [Pa.] and Sen. James R. Doolittle [Wis.]—Daniel Clark [N. H.] Introduces in Senate Bill to Emancipate Slaves of Rebels, Garrett Davis [Ky.] Opposes It—Mr. Eliot Introduces Confiscation and Emancipation Bills in the House—Debate:
in Favor, Mr. Eliot; Opposed, Benjamin F. Thomas [Mass.], Samuel
S. Cox [O.], John Law [Ind.]—Conference of Senate and House Reports Combined Confiscation and Emancipation Bill—It Is Passed—No
Punishments Inflicted for Treason.

THE policy of punishing treason by confiscation of
the property of rebels, at least their slaves, had
been timidly suggested in the extra session of
Congress (July-August, 1861), but no action was then
taken to this end. Early in the present session it was
more definitely proposed: on December 2, 1861, by
Thomas D. Eliot [Mass.] in the House; and on December 5, by Lyman Trumbull [Ill.] in the Senate. The
proposition with various amendments, sometimes including other property than slaves, was hotly discussed in
both Houses throughout the session in intervals of other
measures, and in connection with these when they dealt
with the question of emancipation. By all the Democrats, and by some of the more conservative Republicans,
the proposition was denounced as utterly and glaringly
in antagonism to the Constitution and the pledges of
the dominant party, and as calculated to extinguish the
last vestige of Unionism in the seceded States, and to
imperil it in the loyal border States. Thus Edgar Cowan
[Rep.], a Senator from Pennsylvania, said, on March
4, 1862:

AGAINST CONFISCATION OF REBEL PROPERTY

SENATOR COWAN

We are standing now squarely face to face with questions of most pregnant significance. Shall we stand or fall by the Constitution, or shall we leave it and adventure ourselves upon the wide sea of revolution? Shall we attempt to liberate the slaves of the people of the rebellious States, or shall we leave them to regulate their domestic institutions the same as before the rebellion? Shall we go back to the doctrine of forfeitures which marked the middle ages, and introduce feuds which intervening centuries have not yet sufficed to quiet? These are great questions, and they are in this bill, every one of them.

This bill proposes, at a single stroke, to strip four millions of people of all their property, real, personal, and mixed, of every kind whatsoever, and reduce them at once to absolute poverty; and that, too, at a time when four hundred thousand of them are in the field opposing us desperately.

Now, sir, it does seem to me that, if there was anything in the world calculated to make that four millions of people and their four hundred thousand soldiers in the field now and forever hostile to us and our Government, it would be the promulgation of a law such as this. Will they yield to us sooner in view of such a result to them? What would we be likely to do if they were to threaten us with a similar law? Would we ever, under any circumstances, yield on terms like those? I need hardly ask that question to men descended from sires who refused to pay the tax on teas, and from grandsires who rose in rebellion and overturned a monarchy rather than pay twenty shillings ship money—for that, I believe, was the sum demanded from Hampden, and which cost Charles I his head.

The English conquerors of Ireland, in their long series of forfeitures and confiscations, from the time of Strongbow down to the rebellion of 1798, never, at any time, ventured upon such a sweeping measure as this; their attainders exhausted themselves upon the Irish nobility, and they never were rash enough to strip the Irish people.

I do not know the value of the property forfeited by this bill; I cannot even approximate it, except to say that it is enormous—to be computed by billions. But, sir, the bill goes further, and forfeits a vast amount of property of the rebels which, when forfeited, cannot be confiscated or put into the coffers of the conquerors—I mean their property in negro slaves.

This bill would liberate, perhaps, three millions of slaves; surely the most stupendous stroke for universal emancipation ever before attempted in the world; nay, I think it equivalent, if carried out, to a virtual liberation of the whole four millions of slaves in the Union.

Now, I do not mean to stop here to discuss their right to this species of property; it is enough for me to say that all the people of the slave States, loyal and rebellious, seem to agree as

WHAT THE THIRTY-SEVENTH CONGRESS HAS DONE
[Confiscation Act and Bankrupt Act]
From the collection of the New York Public Library

to this with a wonderful unanimity, and to resent with an excessive sensibility any interference with it whatever. And, although in the bitterness of the feuds engendered by the civil war now raging among them, the loyalists there would be glad to join in inflicting upon the rebels even the severest punishments, yet this one they abhor and refuse, because they aver that it would be equally injurious to them as to their enemies.

But what is to be the effect of it upon the war? Will we be stronger after it than before; or will we find we have doubled the number of those in arms against us? They have now no cause of war; will not this measure furnish them one, and one they think more just and holy than any other? Let the loyal

VI—13

men who know them also answer this question. I will abide their answer.

Those who favor this astounding bill seem determined to bewilder and blind us still more by an additional project of greater magnificence and, if possible, of greater difficulty; and that is, in the duty it imposes upon the President, of procuring a home for these emancipated millions in some tropical country, and of transporting, colonizing, and settling them there, if they desire to go, with guaranties for their rights as freemen! Surely, sir, we must have been recently transported away from the sober domain of practical fact, and set down in the regions of eastern fiction, if we can for a moment entertain this proposition seriously. Do the advocates of the scheme propose to confer upon the President the gold-making touch of Midas? One would think the universal menstruum or the philosophers' stone had been at last discovered. Certainly, nothing short of the ring and lamp of Aladdin, with their attendant genii, would enable us in our present condition to assure the President of his ability to enter upon such a task, unless, indeed, it is conceived the treasury note is of equal potency in this behalf. If so, the sovereign of the tropical country and the transportation companies ought to be consulted in regard to the legal tender clause. I suppose it is not expected that the exodus can be supported on the way by quails and manna; and yet, I am free to say, it will need the miraculous interposition of Heaven quite as much as did that of the Israelites of old.

Then there is a further consideration involved in this bill of still greater moment than even those I have already glanced at; and that is its direct conflict with the Constitution of the United States, requiring us, indeed, should we pass it, to set aside and ignore that instrument in all its most valuable and fundamental provisions; those which guarantee the life, liberty, and property of the citizen, and those which define the boundaries between the powers delegated to the several departments of the Government.

Pass this bill, sir, and all that is left of the Constitution is not worth much. Certainly it is not worth a terrible and destructive war, such as we now wage for it. And it must be remembered that that war is waged solely for the Constitution, and for the ends, aims, and purposes sanctioned by it, and for no others.

I am aware, however, that some think the Constitution is a restraint upon the free action of the nation in the conduct of the war, which they suppose could be carried on a great deal better without it, etc. Now, sir, I have no hesitation in saying that no greater mistake ever was made in the world than is made by such people, because, under the Constitution, we have full and ample power delegated to the general Government to enable it to do, in war as well as peace, everything which a Government ought to be allowed to do; while, at the same time, it has laid down accurately upon its charts all those rocks upon which other governments have been split and wrecked heretofore, with the proper prohibitions to prevent us from seeking our destruction upon them. And I will venture to say that there is not a restraint it imposes which is not salutary, and which, if thrown off, will not prove most destructive. The real danger consists in the fact that the prohibited measures are all of them at first sight most plausible; they are not roaring breakers, obvious to all, but sunken rocks in a calm sea, where the chart of experience is most necessary to guide the political pilot, if he is prudent enough to take the warning.

Congress cannot forfeit the property of rebels for longer than their lives, by the enactment of any law whatever, for the following reasons:

1. Those persons now in rebellion, having levied war against the United States, are guilty of treason within the exact definition of that crime contained in the third section of the third article of the Constitution, in which it is declared that

"Treason against the United States shall consist only in levying war against them, or in adhering to their enemies, giving them aid and comfort."

Hence, as soon as the rebels are arrested and brought within the power of any law we may pass, they become *eo instanti* [1] traitors, and obnoxious to the punishment which is imposed by our statute for treason. As long, however, as the rebel is at large, or in the hands of the military, he cares nothing for the law, and is not amenable to it, because the military power cannot try him under the law—that must be done by the courts. But the second clause of that same section provides further, that

"The Congress shall have power to declare the punishment of treason, but no attainder of treason shall work corruption of blood or forfeiture, except during the life of the person attainted."

Therefore any law made for the guidance of the courts must conform to this provision, and no other or greater penalty could

---

[1] "In that instant."

be imposed than it would warrant. If, therefore, the law was to enact an absolute forfeiture of the estates of the traitor, it would be bad for the excess, and the judges would be obliged to make the sentence constitutional, either by cutting down the statutory penalty to a forfeiture of his estates for life, or by omitting to forfeit them at all. All this seems to me so obvious as not to be doubted.

2. The power assumed in this bill is also obnoxious to the provisions of the Constitution, if it be assumed that Congress can legislate an effectual forfeiture of the estates of rebels, as such, without allowing them an opportunity or means of trial in the courts. Because,

By the fifth amendment to the Constitution, it is provided:

"No person shall be held to answer for a capital or otherwise infamous crime, unless on a presentment or indictment of a grand jury, except in cases arising in the land or naval forces, or in the militia when in actual service, in time of war or public danger; nor shall any person be subject, for the same offence, to be twice put in jeopardy of life or limb; nor shall be compelled in any criminal case to be a witness against himself; nor be deprived of life, liberty, or property, without due process of law; nor shall private property be taken for public use without just compensation."

Here it is attempted to deprive a large class of persons of all their estates and property, without any arrest, without any presentment by a grand jury, without any trial by a petit jury, without, indeed, any trial at all in any court. This would be to deprive them of their property in the very face of the provision requiring that it shall only be done "by due process of law," which, all commentators and all lawyers agree, means proceedings according to the course of the common law.

I am aware that this will seem strange to some people who think that, as we are at war with the rebels, we ought of course to be able to enact any law we pleased, inflicting upon them punishment befitting their crimes. Such people, however, will do well to remember that our Government is not one of absolute powers—it is in no respect omnipotent or restrained only by its own sense of propriety or policy. On the contrary, its powers are limited to those expressly delegated to it, and are not to be implied from any supposed necessity that they ought to be there, or that it was intended to confer them. Besides this, the powers actually delegated are also distributed and divided to and among the several departments of the Government which are to exercise them. These, too, must confine themselves severally to their functions as fixed by the terms of the grant. Congress has its part, the President has his part, and the courts their part. Now Congress, for instance, has no power to punish anybody (except for contempts), and to-day, if we had half a dozen of the worst rebels caged here in this Chamber, we could inflict upon them no punishment. We could not order the sergeant-at-arms to hang or behead them, no matter how certain we might be of their guilt. Nay, more, the President himself and all his army could not lead them away from this hall to execution. The only way they could be punished at all would be to deliver them over to the judges—the proper judges—because no one judge might have a right to try all of them. Nay, it is possible every one of them might have to be tried by his separate judge, in his separate court and district. There, again, the functions of the judges, in such cases, are limited—a jury shares them, and its members are the exclusive judges of the facts, while, after the condemnation and judgment, the sheriff or marshal would be the only person having the right to execute the judgment.

I may also further remark that it is in this limitation of the powers of the Government, and their distribution after the manner of the Constitution, that its great merit consists. On those accounts we love, cherish, and revere it; and because it has such features we are now at war with all our force and treasure to defend and preserve it. Had we no Constitution limiting its powers, defining its agencies, fixing the boundaries of their rights and duties under it, nobody would lift a hand for it; and if you make it usurp powers not granted at all, not granted to the usurping department, then our war for it is a great mistake if not a great wickedness.

Again, this is further guarded against in the ninth section of the first article and third clause, as follows:

"No bill of attainder or *ex post facto* law shall be passed."

A bill of attainder was a mode of proceeding resorted to in England, as well as in some of the United States during the Revolution, to condemn and punish traitors, by Parliament or the legislature, in cases where they were out of the reach of the process of the courts; nay, indeed, in many cases even after they were dead. In such cases the law-making branch of the Government supplied the want of due process of law by blending together in one statute the law and the application of the law to particular persons named therein, or to a class of persons by description. Bills of attainder condemned the accused to death (if not dead already), forfeited their estates, and corrupted the inheritable blood of their children and heirs, so that no one could take any estate either from or through them. Bills, however, like the one under consideration, which does not propose to inflict capital punishment, or corrupt the blood of the offenders, but imposed other penalties of lesser grade, were called "bills of pains and penalties."

It may be said the latter are not within the prohibition, and therefore allowable here. It is true they are not within the letter of it, but being equally within the mischief, which was that the legislature should in any case attempt to usurp and exercise the functions of the courts; and construing the fifth amendment in connection, I have no doubt they are also prohibited. Indeed, no one can come to any other conclusion but that the convention which framed the Constitution intended to remove every possibility of the usurpation, by Congress, of the power to punish anybody without "due process of law."

Besides, to grant our power of passing bills of pains and penalties is to nullify the whole effect of the clause, inasmuch as it is easy, by passing several of these against the same person, to make their aggregate result precisely the same as a bill of attainder. Such a construction would defeat the provision instead of making it avail, as intended.

We are not left, however, without authority as to this point, if any were needed to give force to the reason adduced for it, because Judge Story, in his "Commentary on the Constitution," at section 1344, says:

"But in the sense of the Constitution, it seems that bills of attainder include bills of pains and penalties; for the Supreme Court have said, 'A bill of attainder may affect the life of an individual, or may confiscate his property, or both.' "

And for this he cites Fletcher *vs.* Peck, 6 Cranch's Reports, 137; 1 Kent's Commentaries, sec. 19, p. 382; and this was well shown by the honorable Senator from California [James A. McDougall].

This, then, being, in the language of the Supreme Court, a bill of attainder, and in the stricter language of the common law a bill of pains and penalties, is clearly within the prohibition contained in the clause read; and nothing which I can say is so apposite as the remainder of the section quoted from Judge Story, and from it all may see the view taken of such laws as this by a jurist so eminent—one, too, sitting calmly in his closet and free from all those exciting influences which, in troubled times like ours, are so apt to warp our judgments and blind our reason to the truth:

"The injustice and iniquity of such acts, in general, constitute an irresistible argument against the existence of the power. In a free government it would be intolerable; and, in the hands of a reigning faction, it might be, and probably would be, abused, to the ruin and death of the most virtuous citizens. Bills of this sort have been most usually passed, in England, in times of rebellion, or of gross subserviency to the Crown, or of violent political excitements—periods in which all nations are most liable (as well the free as the enslaved) to forget their duties, and to trample upon the rights and liberties of others."

I now propose to go further and argue that the exercise of such a power, even if it had been granted, would now be mischievous and impolitic, and that our fathers did wisely and well in refusing it. By their just leniency they showed that they looked beyond the hour of conflict to the better day of reconciliation, and offered a bounty to the heirs of the guilty that they might be loyal. I may say, too, that the civilized world, at least in all christendom, have come to this same conclusion, and have generally purged their statute-books of such a relic of angry barbarism:

"The reasons commonly assigned for these severe punishments, beyond the mere forfeiture of the life of the party attainted, are these: by committing treason the party has broken his original bond of allegiance, and forfeited his social rights. Among these social rights, that of transmitting property to others is deemed one of the chief and most valuable. Moreover, such forfeitures, whereby the posterity of the offender must suffer, as well as himself, will help to restrain a man, not only by the sense of his duty and dread of personal punishment, but also by his passions and natural affections; and will interest every dependent and relation he has to keep from offending. But this view of the subject is wholly unsatisfactory. It looks only to the offender himself, and is regardless of his innocent posterity. It really operates as a posthumous punishment upon them, and compels them to bear, not only the disgrace naturally attendant upon such flagitious crimes, but takes from them the common rights and privileges enjoyed by all other citizens, where they are wholly innocent, and however remote they may be in the lineage from the first offender. It surely is enough for society to take the life of the offender, as a just punishment of his crime, without taking from his offspring and relatives that property which may be the only means of saving them from poverty and ruin. It is bad policy, too; for it cuts off all the attachments which these unfortunate victims might otherwise feel for their own government, and prepares them to engage in any other service, by which their supposed injuries may be redressed, or their hereditary hatred gratified. Upon these and similar grounds it may be presumed that the clause was first introduced into the original draft of the Constitution; and after some amendments it was adopted without any apparent resistance. By the laws since passed by Congress, it is declared that no conviction or judgment, for any capital or other offences, shall work corruption of blood, or any forfeiture of estate. The history of other countries abundantly proves that one of the strong incentives to prosecute offences as treason has been the chance of sharing in the plunder of the victims. Rapacity has been thus stimulated to exert itself in the service of the most corrupt tyranny; and tyranny has been thus furnished with new opportunities of indulging its malignity and revenge, of gratifying its envy of the rich and good, and of increasing its means to reward favorites, and secure retainers for the worst deeds.''—Story's "Commentaries on the Constitution," Sec. 1300.

In the light of this exposition let us follow the consequences of this bill into detail, and let us suppose its provisions fully carried out. Our armies have overrun the whole territories of the Confederate States; resistance has entirely ceased; and the President and his officers being masters of the country, they have time to finish the residue of their work by gathering in the balance of the property of the rebels not already taken to supply the "military necessities" of the suppression. The rebels themselves are homeless, houseless, and propertyless; and the question arises, have you made them loyal by your severity? Are you assured their love for the Union will return again after this chastisement? Have you thought how they would shout at the sight of the glorious old banner—"the stars and stripes"— which brought them such deliverance?

Mr. President, these people are to be again our brethren and kinsmen, if such a thing is possible; but it does seem to me that, by such laws as this, you will make that possibility a very remote one. Will not their women and children hate you, and their children's children hate and curse you down to the latest generation; and whenever they get a chance will they not rebel against you? Have you not sown the seeds of many rebellions by this one ill-advised act? All this might make little or no difference if they were of hostile race and alien enemies, and if we were making war upon them for conquest and subjugation. But that is not the fact. We have here in these Halls of Congress solemnly declared that the war was for no such purpose, but that it was for the purpose of compelling obedience to the Constitution and the laws; and I am for standing upon that declaration.

The Constitution and the laws being restored and obedience tendered, is this law one of them? Now, we suppose that a large number of people everywhere in the Confederate States were constrained, even by force, to join in the rebellion—are these to suffer upon the same scaffolds with the willing traitor; and is there no difference to be made between the general who betrayed his country and the soldier he has compelled to march at his bidding at the head of a rebel column? · This bill makes none; and, if it did, it makes no provision to try it and determine its value when it is found; the officers have seized the property, and the victim of force in the beginning ends by being the victim of wrong and injustice. To him the Constitution and laws are not yet restored. Again: thousands of these people have been duped into rebellion by being told that we of the North were all Abolitionists—intent, when we had the power, to wield it for the emancipation of their slaves, and the destruction of their social system. What does your bill do with these—these men, who believed the falsehood because it was first asserted by Southern demagogues and then proved and corroborated by Northern knaves? Is there no difference here, again, between the wily traitor and his simple dupe? This bill makes none, but includes within its terms the whole rebel population, of every state and degree, from the lordly planter down to the negro laborer; and the broad acres of the one, as well as the narrow hovel of the other, are alike forfeit under it.

But the President and his officers are to dispose of these confiscated estates. Who will buy them? What kind of neighborhood will exist between the former owner or his heirs and your alienees or their heirs? How the delights of this society will enhance the value of those estates to the purchasers, especially when they reflect that the forfeiture will never be forgotten in the family of the rebel, and that, if they have no other, they can transmit this inheritance to their descendants unimpaired for centuries! The tradition of it will sit continually by the hearthstone of that family a hideous specter, deathless for ages, prompting to revenge and inciting to rebellion. Sir, your thrifty purchasers will not like incumbrances such as these hanging over your forfeited estates; and you might as well try to attract them and their capital to your vendue by promising they should be entitled, as appurtenant to the land offered for sale, to an Irish feud in perpetuity or a Corsican vendetta in fee to them and their heirs forever. Such titles have never been desirable. In the French Revolution, even when its success seemed well assured the holders of the *assignats* refused to buy the public domain with them, although at that time (August, 1793) the *franc assignat* had so depreciated that the metal franc was worth nine of them. Sir, you might as well expect capital to seek the margin of an extinct volcano before the lava had cooled for investments in real estate. The only purpose forfeitures ever served in ancient times was to furnish a means of payment to the hardy soldier who achieved their conquest; his title was in his sword, and he could maintain it. That which is taken in war must be kept in war. Every hill must have its castle, and every march its wardens. But surely this is not one of the "dispositions" the President and his officers are to make of this property.

As a Republican, standing upon the Constitution as construed by that party, I protest against this bill as being a total and entire departure from the principles of that instrument, most mischievous at this time, because it uselessly distracts, divides, and weakens the friends of the country when they ought to be united and of one accord in action, if ever such were needed before. In addition to this, it would make us do of all things in the world that which would most gratify and strengthen our enemies everywhere—worth to-day more than a hundred thousand armed men to the traitors of the South, and worth more than five hundred thousand votes to the would-be traitors of the North; thus enabling the latter again to get control of the Government, to wield it as they have wielded it before. No, sir; pass that bill by this Congress and every falsehood uttered and every design charged upon us in six years of desperate struggle is verified by our deliberate act, an act as useless to the country and to the cause in which we are engaged (apart from other objections) as would be a law against serfdom in Russia passed here.

Sir, I hope and trust some other and better way than this will be found to punish those concerned in this rebellion after it shall have been suppressed, and that the method adopted, whatever it may be, will not be one which will furnish cause for future revolts. Those who are to be punished at all ought to be punished effectually under the Constitution, and according to the laws they have violated; and those who are to be forgiven ought to be forgiven fully and freely as it becomes the majesty of a great nation to forgive. Having rescued the revolted States, and restored the dominion over them to the loyal people within them, I would have the traitors dealt with in such way as not to endanger in the future either the happiness or safety of such as have remained faithful through the terrible ordeal to which they have been subjected. In this I should consult their wishes and defer much to their better judgment; but certainly I would not do that which, in their opinion, would leave them worse with the Union restored than they would be with the Confederacy sustained. I would not offer bounties to make them rebels, neither would I impose penalties or conditions having the like effect. I look upon this bill as a measure of the latter kind—the natural consequence of which would be to give to the rebels the energy of despair, and to take from the loyalists every motive for fidelity. Pass this bill and the same messenger who carries it to the South will come back to us with the news of their complete consolidation as one man. We will then have done that which treason could not do; we, ourselves, will then have dissolved the Union; we shall have rent its sacred charter and extinguished the last vestige of affection for it in the slave States by our blind and passionate folly.

I am well aware, sir, of the object of this second clause—emancipating the slaves of the rebels—and I know there are many who think that ought to be done, because they think slavery the only cause for the rebellion. In considering this it is well to remember that there are now in the world, and always will be, many great evils which God, in His wisdom and for His own purposes, has put out of the reach of remedy except in His own way and at His own time, and then His means are always adequate and very generally apparent. Four millions of negro slaves are now in bondage in the United States. Where are the signs of their emancipation? Have not hundreds of thousands of these everywhere had ample opportunities to throw off their chains within the last few months? Have they done so? And, if they have not done so, can you compel them to exchange voluntary servitude for involuntary freedom? I thought the world was old enough by this time to know that they who are entitled to freedom themselves must strike the blow which is to secure it. What blow has the negro struck for himself in this his fairest opportunity? His rebel master, with a madness to all other men incomprehensible, engaged himself in revolt, broke up the society in which he lived, liberated all its elements, so that they are free to act, and thus tacitly invited him to assert his manhood? How has he availed himself of it? Why, sir, just in the way one might have expected; knowing nothing of liberty, caring nothing for it, he has remained inactive as the domestic animals around him, impelled, perhaps, by the same unconscious instinct of dependence upon the providence of a master wiser and stronger than himself. A child always in the scale of development, he may have had some child's consciousness that the boon of liberty so ostentatiously offered him by his over-zealous friends might prove to him fatal as the shirt of Nessus or the box of Pandora, and he still hesitates and hugs his chains.

I have no hope of the negro yet, though, God knows, I would have him free, free as I am myself, if freedom be his choice, through the strife and agony by which he, as all men, must purchase it. Eternal vigilance and continual struggle is the price of liberty.

On May 2, 1862, James R. Doolittle [Rep.], of Wisconsin, spoke in the Senate upon the limitations in the Constitution upon the punishment for treason.

AGAINST CONFISCATION OF REAL ESTATE OF TRAITORS

SENATOR DOOLITTLE

When the Constitution was formed it was a serious question whether there should be any power given to the United States Government to punish treason against it. Under the old Articles of Confederation no such power existed. It, however, is given by the Constitution of the United States, and the same language which gives it puts a limitation upon it. There is the power and there its limitation. There they stand side by side, put into the Constitution in the same clause. We cannot close our eyes to one and open them to the other.

The power to suppress insurrection is a distinct and substantive power, without limitation, except that whatever law shall be passed by Congress and whatever shall be done by the Executive in suppressing insurrection should not go beyond the powers usually exercised according to the modern usage of nations in carrying on civilized warfare—the laws of necessity and of humanity.

Under this Constitution Congress is not prohibited from declaring that personal estate shall be forfeited upon the conviction of a traitor, but that his real estate cannot be forfeited beyond his life upon the attainder for treason. I have received a copy of an able argument written by Joel Parker, who stands at the head of the law school of Harvard University. I find he makes the same distinction. He assumes it to be almost too clear for an argument. He says:

"The attainder spoken of in the clause cited from the Constitution being such attainder as, according to the common law, results from a judgment, it seems clear that the forfeiture, which is limited by the Constitution to an estate for life, relates to the same general kind of property which was forfeited by the attainder at common law; and the language of the constitutional provision indicates that this was *real* and not *personal property*. A forfeiture of a *life estate in personal property*, of which the traitor had the absolute title, would certainly be *an anomaly*. But it is clear that the forfeiture on attainder of treason was of real property only, lands, and interests in or rights to lands, and could be no other; for the forfeiture of the personal property of the traitor was the result of the conviction which preceded the judgment and the attainder.''

I will also read a sentence or two from Chitty's Criminal Law:

''There is this difference between conviction and judgment, that if the traitor die after conviction and before judgment he may pass his real estate, but not his personal property, because the goods and chattels are forfeited on the verdict of guilty, but the lands are not divested uutil the attainder, which is the pronouncing of the sentence of the court.''

See, also, Coke's ''Commentaries on Littleton,'' Vol. 2, Sec. 745.

It is clear, therefore, that, under this clause of the Constitution, giving to Congress the power to declare the punishment of treason, we may declare the absolute forfeiture of every dollar of the traitor's personal estate upon his conviction; but, when we come to touch his real estate, we can forfeit it for his life, and for his life only.

I am aware that Senators here have contended that in other countries of the world, upon a conviction of treason, men have had not only their personal property confiscated absolutely, but their real property also. I agree to that. Such was the law among the Persians, the Macedonians, the Greeks, the Romans, and in England, too, until they passed a law, to take effect after the death of the Pretender, to restrain its effect. The same power was exercised in this country in most if not all of the colonies during the Revolution; but not under this Constitution. That power was exercised before this Constitution was formed, when there was no such limitation upon them, when the common law was in full force, and the judgment of attainder forfeited all his real estate absolutely, as his personal estate was forfeited upon conviction.

It was with all these facts before them that our ancestors who formed the Constitution placed this limitation in it. They had been in rebellion themselves. In their own experience they had learned all there is in the passions which dictate and the consequences which follow attainders, forfeitures, and confiscations. They knew it all. With all the lights of human history before them, under the old and under the new dispensation, before and after Christ, when they met in convention to form this Constitution, to found this new Government to be the light and the example of nations, they determined to limit the power of confiscating real estate to the life of the guilty party, even in this highest of political crimes. They determined that, to the extent of the homes and lands of the family, the rule should be, *punish the guilty*, but *spare the innocent*.

On May 6 Senator Trumbull's bill was referred to a select committee of seven. The chairman, Daniel Clark [N. H.], duly reported the committee's bill, which merely authorized the President, at his discretion, to proclaim free all slaves of persons who shall be found in arms against the United States thirty days after such proclamation. It came up for discussion on May 16, and Garrett Davis [Ky.] tried to amend it by providing that the confiscated slaves be sold, the proceeds accruing to the Treasury. This amendment failing (only 7 votes being recorded in its favor), he then moved that no slave should be emancipated unless provision had been made for his immediate colonization out of the country; this amendment received only 6 votes. The bill was then put aside in favor of the House [Eliot] bill.

The Confiscation and Emancipation Bills

House of Representatives, April 30-May 26, 1862

This bill had been referred in the House to the Judiciary Committee, and was there reported against by John Hickman [Pa.], the chairman, because the President had already the power that it sought to confer. It was then referred to a select committee of seven, of which Mr. Eliot was made chairman. By this committee it was separated into two bills, one providing for confiscating the property of persistent rebels, and the other providing for emancipating their slaves, and these were reported on April 30. The debate on these measures lasted for several days. Judge Benjamin F. Thomas [Mass.], a conservative Republican, opposed them as a violation both of the Constitution and the law of nations.

"The duty of obedience to that Constitution was never more imperative than now. I am not disposed to deny that I have for it a superstitious reverence. I have 'worshipped it from my forefathers.' In the school of rigid discipline by which we were prepared for it, in the struggles out of which it was born, the seven years of bitter conflict, and the seven darker years in which that conflict seemed to be fruitless of good; in the wisdom with which it was constructed and first administered and set in motion; in the beneficent government it has secured for more than two generations; in the blessed influences it has exerted upon the cause of freedom and humanity the world over, I cannot fail to recognize the hand of a guiding and loving Providence. But not for the blessed memories of the past only do I cling to it. He must be blinded 'with excess of light,' or with the want of it, who does not see that to this nation, trembling on the verge of dissolution, it is the only possible bond of unity.''

Samuel S. Cox [Dem.], of Ohio, asked:

"Must these Northern fanatics be sated with negroes, taxes, and blood, with division North and devastation South, and peril to constitutional liberty everywhere, before relief shall come? They will not halt until their darling schemes are consummated. History tells us that such zealots do not and cannot go backward."

Said John Law [Dem.], of Indiana:

"The man who dreams of closing the present unhappy contest by reconstructing this Union upon any other basis than that prescribed by our fathers, in the compact formed by them, is a madman—aye, worse, a traitor—and should be hung as high as Haman. Sir, pass these acts, confiscate under these bills the property of these men, emancipate their negroes, place arms in the hands of these human gorillas, to murder their masters and violate their wives and daughters, and you will have a war such as was never witnessed in the worst days of the French Revolution, and horrors never exceeded in St. Domingo, for the balance of this century at least."

Mr. Eliot closed the debate on May 26 with a most radical speech in favor of the bills. Of the Confiscation Bill he said:

This bill seeks to condemn the property of the leading rebels, and to place the proceeds in the treasury for the purpose of helping to defray the expenses of the war, and also in aid of those who have been robbed by the Confederate Government. All laws of this kind, gentlemen must be aware, must be in their terms severe. The rebels began to confiscate a year ago. They passed confiscation laws, and under those laws there is but little property of loyal men left in their States. We are slow in following their example. I am surprised that, after a year's experience of the effects of their confiscation schemes, and after they have used the property taken from loyal citizens against the Government of the United States, gentlemen should come here and speak of this bill as being too severe. There is not a rebel of the classes mentioned in the bill who does not deserve to be hanged by the neck until he is dead.

I believe, Mr. Speaker, that this bill will accomplish good in the border States. It will strengthen the hands and hearts of loyal men. If made effectual, it will deprive the enemy of his means of carrying on the war. It will help to weaken and subdue him. It will increase our strength. It will, in part, indemnify us against the cost of this rebellion. It will give the property of rebels, first, to their creditors in loyal States; and, secondly, it will provide a means of indemnity for loyal men whose property, owned in rebellious States, has been taken from them.

Sir, when it is argued that this bill affects men who are dupes of ambitious leaders, I cannot but be struck with the audacity of such a proposition. Who are the dupes named in the first section of the bill? Are the President and Vice-President of this rebel Confederacy dupes? Are the members of Congress, members of the cabinet, members of the legislatures, members of conventions, high officers of the Confederacy or of different States, dupes? Have they not good sense enough to know what they are doing? Are they not conscious and willful rebels, and enemies against their Government? Are they not at war with us? Does any sane man believe they do not mean what they are doing, and that they do not know what they mean? Are they dupes? Sir, if we are deceived by such arguments against our bills we shall be the dupes, and the enemy, as they wage this war and confiscate our property, will hold us in derision.

The Confiscation Bill was passed by a vote of 82 to 68. The Emancipation Bill was next taken up and defeated by a vote of 74 yeas (all Republican) to 78 nays (15 of which were Republicans). It was then reconsidered, and, after elimination of its harsher features, was passed by a vote of 82 to 54.

· The House Confiscation Bill was amended in the Senate on motion of Daniel Clark [N. H.] by the addition of provisions under certain conditions of emancipation of slaves, and, on June 28, passed by a vote of 28 to 13. The House refused by a vote of 8 yeas to 124 nays to concur in this action, whereupon a joint conference of the two Houses was brought about, which presented a combined Confiscation and Emancipation Bill.

This bill passed the House by 82 yeas to 42 nays, and the Senate by 27 yeas to 12 nays, and was approved by the President on July 17. In its final form the bill contained the following provisions:

The slaves of the person convicted of treason performed after the passage of the act should be set free, and he himself should either suffer death, or be imprisoned not less than five years and fined not less than $10,000, at the discretion of the court. A person convicted of assisting rebellion was to have his slaves liberated, and himself be imprisoned not less than ten years, or fined not over $10,000, or suffer both penalties, all at the discretion of the court. Persons convicted under the act were permanently disqualified to hold office under the United States. The President was authorized to confiscate for the support of the army the property of any one of several enumerated classes of persons, namely: (1) rebel military and naval officers; (2) officers of the Confederate government; (3) officers of Confederate State governments; (4) all other citizens of seceded States who do not within sixty days after the President's proclamation of this act return to their allegiance to the United States; and (5) those citizens of loyal States and Territories who assist rebellion. Fugitive and captured slaves of rebels were deemed captives of war by the act, and ordered to be set free. Fugitive slaves of loyal owners were to be returned to them on their taking oath that they had not aided the rebellion; the civil authorities were to return these slaves—in no case the military or naval authorities. The President was authorized at his discretion to employ negroes to suppress the rebellion; and to colonize free negroes in some tropical country beyond the limits of the United States, as well as to proclaim amnesty to rebels.

At the end of the rebellion there were no prosecutions for treason. Says Alexander Johnston, in his "American Political History":

It has been roundly asserted that the reason for this was the consciousness of the Government of the United States that it had been illegally suppressing a misnamed rebellion, that treason could only hold against a State, and that Jefferson Davis and his associates had committed no crime and engaged in no treason, in any sense known to the Constitution or its framers. Those who so argue forget that Mr. Davis, at least, was no prisoner of war; that his surrender was unconditional and in a territory under military occupation; and that, if there had been any such impotent spite against him as this theory assigns to the Government, a drum-head court-martial and a file of men would quickly have made it patent, treason or no treason. The fact seems to be that his escape was due entirely to lack of spite. The collapse of the rebellion had been too complete to allow of spite. The nation stood aghast as it realized the thoroughness of its work; and its controlling impulse was to efface as rapidly as possible all evidences of the conflict. Treason trials would have been a festering sore in the body politic, and they were avoided.

CHAPTER VIII

EMANCIPATION

Union Victory at Antietam [Sharpsburg], Md.—President Lincoln Issues
the Emancipation Proclamation—He Forestalls Objections to It in an
Address on Colonization to Negro Deputation; in a Letter to Horace
Greeley, Replying to His "Prayer of Twenty Millions," and in an
Address on Emancipation to a Religious Delegation—The Preliminary
Proclamation—Its Reception by the Country and Europe—The Final
Proclamation—Second Annual Message of the President; It Treats of
Compensated Emancipation and the Relative Advantages of Retaining
Freedmen in the Country and Deporting Them; and Pleads That Con-
gress and the Country Aid Him in His Plan for Saving the Union—
Reply of William A. Richardson (Dem.), of Illinois, to the Message:
"Enslaving the Whites to Free the Blacks."

THE Union victory at Antietam [Sharpsburg], Md.,
on September 18-19, 1862, precipitated the emancipation proclamation of President Lincoln.

By the advice of William H. Seward, Secretary of
State, Lincoln had only been waiting for a Union victory
to declare an emancipation proclamation applying to
slaves in the disloyal States. Not only did he believe
that, as commander-in-chief of the army and navy of
the Republic, he had a constitutional right to issue the
proclamation as a war measure, but he was fortified by
the special authorization of Congress to do so at his
discretion. Late in July or early in August he had
announced to the Cabinet his determination to issue such
a proclamation.

After the President had determined to issue the
proclamation he set himself to forestall the objections
which he knew the document would call forth, such as:
that it was intended to establish negro equality; that
it proved the insincerity of the declared purpose of the
Administration to save the Union by showing this to

211

have been from the beginning to free the slave, etc. On
August 14, addressing a deputation of negroes on the
subject of colonization, he said, in regard to the vexed
question of race equality:

Why should the people of your race leave the country? It
is because you and we are different races. We have between us
a broader physical difference than exists between any other two
races. Whether this is right or wrong I need not discuss; but
this physical difference is a great disadvantage to us both. Your
race suffer greatly, many of them, by living among us, while ours
suffer from your presence. This affords a reason why we should
be separated. Your race is suffering, in my judgment, the greatest wrong inflicted on any people. But, even when you cease to
be slaves, you are yet far remote from being placed on an equality with the white race. You are cut off from many of the advantages which the other race enjoys. The aspiration of men is
to enjoy equality with the best when free, but on this broad continent not a single man of your race is made the equal of a single man of ours. Go where you are treated the best, and the ban
is still upon you. I do not propose to discuss this—but to present it as a fact with which we have to deal. I cannot alter it if
I would. . . . I believe in its general evil effects on the white
race. See our present condition—white men cutting one another's throats—none knowing how far it will extend. . . . But
for your race among us there could not be war, although many
men engaged on either side do not care for you one way or the
other. . . . It is better for us both, therefore, to be separated.

On August 19, 1862, Horace Greeley, in his paper,
the New York *Tribune*, addressed a letter to the President some weeks after this, entitled ''The Prayer of
Twenty Millions,'' exhorting Mr. Lincoln not to proclaim
all the slaves in our country free, but to execute the laws
of the land which operated to free large classes of the
slaves of rebels. It concluded as follows:

''On the face of this wide earth, Mr. President, there is not
one disinterested, determined, intelligent champion of the Union
cause who does not feel that all attempts to put down the rebellion, and at the same time uphold its inciting cause, are preposterous and futile—that the rebellion, if crushed out to-morrow, would be renewed within a year if slavery were left in full

vigor—that army officers, who remain to this day devoted to slavery, can at best be but halfway loyal to the Union—and that every hour of deference to slavery is an hour of added and deepened peril to the Union. I appeal to the testimony of your embassadors in Europe. It is freely at your service, not mine. Ask them to tell you candidly whether the seeming subserviency of your policy to the slaveholding slavery-upholding interest is not the perplexity, the despair of statesmen of all parties; and be admonished by the general answer!

What an immense majority of the loyal millions of your countrymen require of you is a frank, declared, unqualified, ungrudging execution of the laws of the land, more especially of the Confiscation Act. The rebels are everywhere using the late anti-negro riots in the North—as they have long used your officers' treatment of negroes in the South—to convince the slaves that they have nothing to hope from a Union success—that we mean in that case to sell them into a bitter bondage to defray the cost of the war. Let them impress this as a truth on the great mass of their ignorant and credulous bondmen, and the Union will never be restored—never. We cannot conquer ten millions of people united in solid phalanx against us, powerfully aided by Northern sympathizers and European allies. We must have scouts, guides, spies, cooks, teamsters, diggers, and choppers, from the blacks of the South—whether we allow them to fight for us or not—or we shall be baffled and repelled. As one of the millions who would gladly have avoided this struggle at any sacrifice but that of principle and honor, but who now feel that the triumph of the Union is indispensable not only to the existence of our country but to the well-being of mankind, I entreat you to render a hearty and unequivocal obedience to the law of the land.

The President replied to this appeal by telegraph on August 22, 1862.

As to the policy which I "seem to be pursuing," as you say, I have not meant to leave anyone in doubt. I would have the Union. I would have it in the shortest way under the Constitution.

The sooner the national authority can be restored, the nearer the Union will be the Union as it was.

If there be those who would not save the Union unless they could at the same time save slavery, I do not agree with them.

If there be those who would not save the Union unless they

could at the same time destroy slavery, I do not agree with
them.

*My paramount object is to save the Union, and not either
to save or destroy slavery.*

If I could save the Union without freeing any slave, I would
do it—if I could save it by freeing all the slaves, I would do it—
and if I could do it by freeing some and leaving others alone, I
would also do that.

LINCOLN CROSSING NIAGARA

[Suggested by a feat of Blondin, the tight-rope walker]

What I do about slavery and the colored race I do because
I believe it helps to save this Union; and, what I forbear, I
forbear because I do not believe it would help to save the
Union.

I shall do less whenever I shall believe what I am doing
hurts the cause! and I shall do more whenever I believe doing
more will help the cause.

I shall try to correct errors when shown to be errors; and I
shall adopt new views so fast as they shall appear to be true
views.

I have here stated my purpose according to my views of official duty; and I intend no modification of my oft-expressed personal wish that all men everywhere could be free.

But the most astute of the President's preparatory statements was his reply, on September 13, to a committee from the religious denominations of Chicago asking him to issue a proclamation of emancipation. In this he reviewed the arguments for the proclamation as if he were an opponent of them, and so, by admitting their cogency, he put himself, when ultimately he did issue the proclamation, in the politically advantageous position of being forced to do so. Also, by bringing expediency as a consideration to the fore, he prepared the country for an indefinite postponement of emancipation, which would be the case if there was delay in achieving the victory upon which its promulgation depended. The President said:

The subject presented in the memorial is one upon which I have thought much for weeks past, and I may even say for months. I am approached with the most opposite opinions and advice, and that by religious men who are equally certain that they represent the Divine will. I am sure that either the one or the other class is mistaken in that belief and perhaps in some respects both. I hope it will not be irreverent for me to say that, if it is probable that God would reveal his will to others on a point so connected with my duty, it might be supposed He would reveal it directly to me; for, unless I am more deceived in myself than I often am, it is my earnest desire to know the will of Providence in this matter. And if I can learn what it is I will do it. These are not, however, the days of miracles, and I suppose it will be granted that I am not to expect a direct revelation. I must study the plain physical facts of the case, ascertain what is possible, and learn what appears to be wise and right. . . .

What good would a proclamation of emancipation from me do, especially as we are now situated? I do not want to issue a document that the whole world will see must necessarily be inoperative, like the Pope's bull against the comet! Would my word free the slaves, when I cannot even enforce the Constitution in the rebel States? Is there a single court, or magistrate, or individual that would be influenced by it there? And what reason is there to think it would have any greater effect upon the slaves than the late law of Congress, which I approved, and which offers protection and freedom to the slaves of rebel masters who come within our lines? Yet I cannot learn that that law has caused a single slave to come over to us. And suppose they could be induced by a proclamation of freedom from me to throw themselves upon us, what should we do with them? How can we feed and care for such a multitude? General Butler wrote me a few days since that he was issuing more rations to the slaves who have rushed to him than to all the white troops under his command. They eat, and that is all; though it is true General Butler is feeding the whites also by the thousands; for it nearly amounts to a famine there. If, now, the pressure of the war should call off our forces from New Orleans to defend some other point, what is to prevent the masters from reducing the blacks to slavery again; for I am told that whenever the rebels take any black prisoners, free or slave, they immediately auction them off! They did so with those they took from a boat that was aground in the Tennessee River a few days ago. And then I am very ungenerously attacked for it! For instance, when, after the late battles at and near Bull Run, an expedition went out from Washington under a flag of truce to bury the dead and bring in the wounded, and the rebels seized the blacks who went along to help, and sent them into slavery, Horace Greeley said in his paper that the Government would probably do nothing about it. What could I do?

Now, then, tell me, if you please, what possible result of good would follow the issuing of such a proclamation as you desire? Understand, I raise no objections against it on legal or constitutional grounds, for, as commander-in-chief of the army and navy, in time of war I suppose I have a right to take any measure which may best subdue the enemy; nor do I urge objections of a moral nature, in view of possible consequences of insurrection and massacre at the South. I view this matter as a practical war measure, to be decided on according to the advantages or disadvantages it may offer to the suppression of the rebellion.

The committee at this point replied to the President's objection that the measure was inexpedient, by contending that it would secure at once the sympathy, heretofore in suspense, of England and France, and, indeed, of the whole civilized world; further, that, as slavery was clearly the root of the rebellion, it must be eradicated if the war was to be decisively ended. The President said:

I admit that slavery is at the root of the rebellion, or at least its *sine qua non*. The ambition of politicians may have instigated them to act, but they would have been impotent without slavery as their instrument. I will also concede that emancipation would help us in Europe, and convince them that we are incited by something more than ambition. I grant, further, that it would help somewhat at the North, though not so much, I fear, as you and those you represent imagine. Still, some additional strength would be added in that way to the war, and then, unquestionably, it would weaken the rebels by drawing off their laborers, which is of great importance; but I am not so sure we could do much with the blacks. If we were to arm them, I fear that in a few weeks the arms would be in the hands of the rebels; and, indeed, thus far, we have not had arms enough to equip our white troops. I will mention another thing, though it meet only your scorn and contempt. There are fifty thousand bayonets in the Union army from the border slave States. It would be a serious matter if, in consequence of a proclamation such as you desire, they should go over to the rebels. I do not think they all would—not so many, indeed, as a year ago, or as six months ago—not so many to-day as yesterday. Every day increases their Union feeling. They are also getting their pride enlisted, and want to beat the rebels. Let me say one thing more: I think you should admit that we already have an important principle to rally and unite the people, in the fact that constitutional government is at stake. This is a fundamental idea, going down about as deep as anything.

In dismissing the committee he said assuringly:

Do not misunderstand me because I have mentioned these objections. They indicate the difficulties that have thus far prevented my action in some such way as you desire. I have not decided against a proclamation of liberty to the slaves, but hold the matter under advisement. And I can assure you that the subject is on my mind, by day and night, more than any other. Whatever shall appear to be God's will, I will do. I trust that in the freedom with which I have canvassed your views I have not in any respect injured your feelings.

Already the President had laid the event in the hands

of God by vowing to issue the proclamation if Lee were driven back over the Potomac. This result of the battle of Antietam was not at once apparent. As Lincoln said to George S. Boutwell: ''The battle of Antietam was fought Wednesday, and until Saturday I could not find out whether we had gained a victory or lost a battle. It was then too late to issue the proclamation that day, and . . . I fixed it up a little Sunday, and Monday (September 22) I let them have it.''

In accordance with the request of Mr. Lincoln Secretary Seward suggested a few minor changes in the document, which were indorsed by his colleagues and accepted by the President. The proclamation then received the unqualified approval of the entire Cabinet except Postmaster-General Blair, who, while personally in favor of it, expressed apprehension of its evil effect on the border States and the army, which contained many opponents of Abolition. He asked leave to file a paper which he had prepared on the subject with the proclamation. This the President readily granted. Secretary Blair, however, changed his mind over night, and next morning withdrew his objections. The proclamation was published in the newspapers of the 23d. As the President said in response to a serenade from approving Washington citizens at the White House that evening: ''It [was] now for the country and the world to pass judgment, and, may be, take action upon it.''

The Emancipation Proclamation

The proclamation, after solemnly affirming that the purpose of the war was, and should continue to be, the restoration of the Union, and promising measures of compensated emancipation to those slave States which should adhere or return to the Union, and of colonization to the freedmen, declared that on January 1, 1863, ''all persons held as slaves within any State, or designated part of a State, the people whereof shall then be in rebellion against the United States, shall be then, thenceforward, and forever free.''

The country quickly gave its approval of the proclamation in the most official way possible at the time. When Confederate invasion of Pennsylvania was imminent Governor Andrew G. Curtin of that State had invited the governors of the Northern States to meet at Altoona on September 24 to consult on emergency measures for the common defence. Before this date arrived the defeat of Lee had removed the original purpose of the convocation, and the governors, after spending a day or so at Altoona in a helpful exchange of information upon military methods employed by their several States, proceeded to Washington and presented a written address to the President, pledging their support in suppressing the rebellion, with the recommendation that an army of 100,000 men be held in reserve at home ready for such emergencies as that which had recently occurred. To this was added an indorsement of the new proclamation. All the governors of the loyal States, those who were present, and the absentees to whom it was shortly sent, signed that portion relating to the suppression of rebellion, and all but the governors of New Jersey, Delaware, Maryland, Kentucky, and Missouri signed the indorsement of the proclamation.

The measure was acclaimed by the newspapers in general and by men of prominence all over the country. Nevertheless the President deplored the absence of material results. On September 28 he wrote to Vice-President Hamlin in reply to his congratulation upon the proclamation:

It is six days old, and, while commendation in newspapers and by distinguished individuals is all that a vain man could wish, the stocks have declined and troops come forward more slowly than ever. This, looked soberly in the face, is not very satisfactory. We have fewer troops in the field at the end of the six days than we had at the beginning—the attrition among the old outnumbering the addition by the new. The North responds to the proclamation sufficiently in breath; but breath alone kills no rebels.

The passage of the Emancipation and Confiscation

'Acts of Congress, followed as these were by the Emancipation Proclamation of the President, converted the Opposition, which had hitherto with few exceptions supported every other measure for the suppression of the rebellion, into a peace party. A number of Democrats continued to support the Administration in the vigorous prosecution of the war, and, in order to admit these into their ranks without committing them to other than the war issues, the Republicans assumed temporarily the character and designation of a "Union" party. "Union League" clubs for the support of the Administration began to spring up in the large cities of the country. By strenuous appeals to patriotism the Union party, in the congressional elections of the fall of 1862, retained its majority of Representatives, although with greatly decreased pluralities.

Abroad the proclamation secured immediately and enduringly the sympathy of the common people and their representative statesmen for the Northern cause, and so sounded the knell of Southern expectations of foreign aid and intervention.

Lincoln's Proposed Emancipation Amendments to the Constitution

In his annual message of December 1, 1862, the President proposed amendments to the Constitution which would provide compensation in the form of United States bonds to those States or loyal individuals which should free the slaves under their control at any time before January 1, 1900, and which would authorize Congress to colonize freedmen abroad. The articles he discussed at length, advocating them as embodying a plan of mutual concession between loyal and honest slaveholders and loyal and honest Abolitionists.

Doubtless some of those who are to pay, and not to receive, will object. Yet the measure is both just and economical. In a certain sense the liberation of slaves is the destruction of property—property acquired by descent or by purchase, the same as any other property. It is no less true for having been often said that the people of the South are not more responsible than are the people of the North; and when it is remembered how unhesitatingly we all use cotton and sugar and share the profits of dealing in them, it may not be quite safe to say that the South has been more responsible than the North for its continuance. If, then, for a common object this property is to be sacrificed, is it not just that it be done at a common charge?

Of the economic advantage of this plan the President said, prophesying a population at the end of the century of 100,000,000:

The proposed emancipation would shorten the war, perpetuate peace, insure this increase of population, and proportionately of the wealth of the country. With these we should pay all the emancipation would cost, together with our other debt, easier than we should pay our other debt without it.

On the subject of the competition of the freedmen with white laborers the President remarked at length, presenting economic arguments as to the relative advantages of retaining the freedmen in the country and of deporting them.

I cannot make it better known than it already is that I strongly favor colonization. And yet I wish to say there is an objection urged against free colored persons remaining in the country which is largely imaginary if not sometimes malicious.

It is insisted that their presence would injure and displace white labor and white laborers. If there ever could be a proper time for mere catch arguments, that time surely is not now. In times like the present men should utter nothing for which they would not willingly be responsible through time and in eternity. Is it true, then, that colored people can displace any more white labor by being free than by remaining slaves? If they stay in their old places, they jostle no white laborers; if they leave their old places, they leave them open to white laborers. Logically, there is neither more nor less of it. Emancipation, even without deportation, would probably enhance the wages of white labor, and very surely would not reduce them. Thus, the customary amount of labor would still have to be performed; the freed people would surely not do more than their old proportion of it, and very probably for a time would do less, leaving an increased part to white laborers, bringing their labor into greater demand, and consequently enhancing the wages of it. With deportation, even to a limited extent, enhanced wages to white labor is mathematically certain. Labor is like any other commodity in the market—increase the demand for it and you increase the price of it. Reduce the supply of black labor by colonizing the black laborer out of the country, and by precisely so much you increase the demand for, and wages of, white labor.

But it is dreaded that the freed people will swarm forth and cover the whole land? Are they not already in the land? Will liberation make them any more numerous? Equally distributed among the whites of the whole country, and there would be but one colored to seven whites. Could the one in any way greatly disturb the seven? There are many communities now having more than one free colored person to seven whites, and this without any apparent consciousness of evil from it. The District of Columbia and the States of Maryland and Delaware are all in this condition. The District has more than one free colored to six whites; and yet in its frequent petitions to Congress I believe it has never presented the presence of free colored persons as one of its grievances. But why should emancipation south send the free people north? People of any color seldom run unless there be something to run from. Heretofore colored people, to some extent, have fled north from bondage; and now, perhaps, from both bondage and destitution. But, if gradual emancipation and deportation be adopted, they will have neither to flee from. Their old masters will give them wages at least until new laborers can be procured; and the freedmen, in turn, will gladly give their labor for the wages till new homes can be found for them in congenial climes and with people of their own blood and race. This proposition can be trusted on the mutual interests involved. And, in any event, cannot the North decide for itself whether to receive them?

He said in conclusion:

It is doubted, then, that the plan I propose, if adopted, would shorten the war, and thus lessen its expenditure of money and of blood? Is it doubted that it would restore the national authority and national prosperity, and perpetuate both indefinitely? Is it doubted that we here—Congress and Executive—can secure its adoption? Will not the good people respond to a united and earnest appeal from us? Can we, can they, by any other means so certainly or so speedily assure these vital objects? We can succeed only by concert. It is not "Can any of us imagine better?" but "Can we all do better?" Object whatsoever is possible, still the question occurs, "Can we do better?" The dogmas of the quiet past are inadequate to the stormy present. The occasion is piled high with difficulty, and we must rise with the occasion. As our case is new, so we must think anew and act anew. We must disenthrall ourselves, and then we shall save our country.

Fellow citizens, we cannot escape history. We of this Congress and this administration will be remembered in spite of ourselves. No personal significance or insignificance can spare one or another of us. The fiery trial through which we pass will light us down, in honor or dishonor, to the latest generation. We say we are for the Union. The world will not forget that we say this. We know how to save the Union. The world knows we do know how to save it. We—even we here— hold the power and bear the responsibility. In giving freedom to the slave we assure freedom to the free—honorable alike in what we give and what we preserve. We shall nobly save or meanly lose the last, best hope of earth. Other means may succeed; this could not fail. The way is plain, peaceful, generous, just—a way which, if followed, the world will forever applaud, and God must forever bless.

Acts of Congress

Congress failed to legislate upon the subject of compensated emancipation; the Senators and Representatives from the border States holding that Congress under the Constitution had no authority to appropriate public money for such a purpose.

In other respects Congress loyally upheld the hands of the President. It ratified his suspension of the writ of *habeas corpus* in the cases of persons suspected of treason, and broadly authorized him to suspend the writ in the future "at such times, and in such places, and with regard to such persons, as in his judgment the public safety may require." An act was passed to enroll and draft in the national service the militia of the whole country, each State contributing its quota in the ratio of its population. By this the nation's power to compel the military services of its citizens was for the first time declared and maintained.

Of the attacks made by the opposition upon the President's message the following, delivered in the House on December 8 by William A. Richardson [Ill.], is typical:

ENSLAVING THE WHITES TO FREE THE BLACKS

ATTACK ON THE PRESIDENT'S MESSAGE

BY WILLIAM A. RICHARDSON, M. C.

Sir, it is a remarkable document. It is an extraordinary message, when we come to think of its sum and substance. To feed, clothe, buy, and colonize the negro we are to tax and mortgage the white man and his children. The white race is to be burdened to the earth for the benefit of the black race.

A friend of mine from New England the other day made a mathematical analysis of the message. He said, one from one and naught remains. Naught from naught and the message is the result. [Laughter.]

So far as it relates to the white race, that mathematical calculation is right. So far as it relates to the negro, or, in the court language of the President, the "free American of African descent," rivers of blood and countless millions of treasure are not enough for his benefit and advantage.

Now, sir, when our people have anxiously looked to the message from the President of the United States to learn what they have to hope of a restored Union, and a return of the blessings of peace once more to their firesides, by inference we learn, if not directly, that, if we will carry out all of the President's plans, if we will carry out his schemes, thirty-seven years from now the people may again behold the restoration of the Union and the return of peace. True, the message states that at the end of those thirty-seven years but few of us will then be living to enjoy the blessings we once enjoyed in this now distracted and divided country.

But, Mr. Chairman, there are a few passages in the message so extraordinary, so wonderful, that they require at least a passing notice. There has been, and still is, a great anxiety felt and expressed by our people that this negro population shall not interfere with them; that it shall not jostle them in the occupations they have heretofore pursued in the various indus-

trial pursuits of life in the great fertile regions of the West.
The President tells our people, those who supported him because
they believed he and his party intended to keep the non-slaveholding States and all the Territories of the Union for the sole
occupation of the white race, if you do not like my plan of
disposing of this black race; if you fear from their introduction among you that their labor will be brought into competition with that of your own, all you have to do to avoid this
competition is to quietly leave your present fields of labor, homes
to which, perhaps, you may be attached, and the graves of
your kindred, and emigrate southward, and occupy the places
made vacant by the exodus of what His Excellency terms the
"free Americans of African descent." That is the sum and
substance of it.

But, for sake of argument, admit, if you choose, that all the
plans of the President touching emancipation and colonization
of the negro were to-day successfully carried out, what would
it accomplish in the great work of restoring the Union? Nothing—worse than nothing.

The President recommends in his annual message three propositions to amend the Constitution of the United States. The
first, second, and third are for the benefit of the negro. The
people are sick and tired of this eternal talk upon the negro,
and they have expressed that disgust unmistakably in the recent
elections. The President's proposed amendments as a whole, or
either of them, could not receive the suffrages of a majority of
the people of more than two States of this Union.

While upon this subject I desire to call the attention of the
committee to a single feature in relation to these amendments.
In the message he recommends an amendment to the Constitution as follows:

"ART. —. Congress may appropriate money, and otherwise provide
for colonizing free colored persons, with their own consent, at any place or
places without the United States."

In this recommendation he seeks to give power to do what
he claims he has the power to do without it; and by this recommendation he admits he has been exercising unauthorized and
illegal authority. Is not this in itself an admission that the
Constitution, unamended, grants no power to Congress or the
Executive to appropriate or use the money of the people for
any purposes contemplated in this amendment? He calls upon
us to compromise. What compromise is that? For whom does
he propose a compromise? What for? In order that you may
VI—15

have more power to advance the negro. That is all there is to it, and there is nothing less of it. He tells us there are differences of opinion among the friends of the Union "in regard to slavery and the African race among us." He says, to all of those who differ with him, surrender your convictions and come to my plan—and he calls that compromise! Compromise! Yes, I trust in God the day is not far distant when the people of this country will compromise and save the Constitution and the Union for the white people, and not for the black people. Our people are for no other compromise than that.

There are other portions of the message upon which I should like to bestow some attention, but I will forbear to do so now, for I desire to call the attention of the committee to another proposition of the President which is connected with this subject.

The proclamation of the 22d of September last, issued by the President, took the country by surprise, and no one of the citizens more than myself. I had fondly hoped and been anxious that the President of the United States should so conduct himself in his high office as Chief Magistrate that I could lend him my support. I have been driven, with thousands of others, into opposition to the policy contained in that proclamation, for reasons which must commend themselves to every reflecting man sincerely desirous of terminating this war and suppressing the rebellion.

Mr. Lincoln, on the 4th of March, 1861, on the east portico of this Capitol, took a vow, which he said was registered in Heaven, to support the Constitution of the United States. In his inaugural address delivered on that occasion he said he had no lawful authority or inclination to interfere with the institution of slavery in the States where it exists. In his proclamation of the 22d of September last he assumes that he has power to forever free "all persons held as slaves within any State, or designated part of a State, the people whereof shall be in rebellion against the United States," thus violating the pledge so solemnly made in his inaugural address.

If the object of the proclamation was not to aid the rebellion, its effect was. It has strengthened the rebellion by driving into their army every person in the South that it was possible to drive there. Was its intent to affect those alone in rebellion? Certainly not. The slaves of every man in a rebellious State were to be free. The loyal man owning twenty slaves and the man in the rebel army owning a like number were by that proclamation to be affected precisely the same. The object of the proclamation was to benefit the negro, not to restore the Government or preserve the Constitution. It was nothing more, nothing less. It goes a bow-shot beyond anything done by this House at the last session of Congress.

But again. If the proclamation is to be carried into effect, the war must continue until every slave is free. If every rebel should lay down his arms on the 2d day of January next, or any subsequent day, and submit himself to the laws and Constitution of the United States, the war would still have to go on, unless the slaves were all free, for the proclamation declares that "the executive Government of the United States, including the military and naval authorities thereof, will recognize and maintain the freedom of such persons." It strengthens the arm of the rebellion, and postpones the time of restoring peace to this country, by the declaration of the purpose for which the executive power shall be used. In what respect has our cause —the cause of the Union—been advanced? Up to that time, throughout the great Northwest, you had but to call for volunteers and they rushed to the army. Since then you have had no volunteering. Prior to that time it was not necessary, as the Secretary of War—as I am told, for I have not read his report— now declares it is necessary, to have provost marshals in every county to arrest deserters from the army.

We are informed that but a few days before the issuing of this proclamation the President himself declared, in a conference with some gentlemen who were urging him to this step, that it would not only be wholly inoperative in the object sought, but would directly weaken us in the border States, but significantly added that it might increase our strength in the North. I pause here to inquire where that additional strength in the North was to be obtained; not certainly from the Democratic element in the North. If additional vigor was infused into the service, it must come from some other quarter which until then had not heartily sustained the policy of the Administration. I need not particularize what class of individuals were to be thus induced to lend their support—the country well knows the baleful influences of this class, and the ends they seek to accomplish.

But this is not all. The record of the military operations shows to-day almost conclusively what the country had for some considerable time suspected: that success in a military point of view was not so much the object sought as the bringing about a condition of things when a proclamation of this sort could be urged as the only means of securing to us success.

Here the speaker went on to prove that on two occasions General McClellan could have captured Richmond had he not been interfered with by the Administration, and that finally McClellan had been removed from command because, in his orders to the army, he had failed to indorse the President's Emancipation Proclamation, intended as it was to enslave the white man by freeing the black.

"THE TRUE ISSUE"

[McClellan stopping the division of the country by Lincoln and Davis]

From the collection of the New York Historical Society

The speaker then adverted to the despotic acts of the Administration.

Arrests of thousands of men in loyal States, without due process of law, by the order of the executive officers of this Government, at the times and places where, in all cases, courts of justice were entirely open and the execution of the laws wholly unobstructed. The most remarkable page in the history of our race is the fact that, while these outrages have been committed upon the rights of our people, no resistance has been offered, no violence done, and no life has been taken as the penalty for the wrong. The desire of the people to preserve the peace in their own midst has restrained them thus far from the commission of violence.

But they are in earnest. They mean to preserve their liberties and their rights. The results of the last elections were of no temporary character. Such a triumph has never before been witnessed in this country. There is not a man who voted the Democratic ticket last fall throughout the country who is not prepared, when the proper time comes, to lay down his life rather than sacrifice his liberty. Do not misunderstand us. We are for union. We are for liberty—constitutional liberty. Our ancestors, in all times past, have vindicated it; and their descendants, after long suffering, will, if need be, vindicate it before God and the world. They do not wish to be slaves, and do not mean to be made slaves.

Perhaps I should not anticipate the course of the President of the United States in regard to his proclamation. I trust that he will reconsider it; that he will pause and not go forward with it. This Government cannot be restored by the sword alone. You must carry with it the olive branch. The President says we are making history. I trust we are not making such history as the incendiary[1] who swung his lighted torch in the air to burn the temple of Diana at Ephesus, and who has left his name behind, while the name of him who reared that temple has perished from our memories. I think we may expect that, under a change of policy, the blessings of the Union may yet be restored and made perpetual.

[1] Herostratus.

CHAPTER IX

NEGRO SOLDIERS

Negro Soldiers in the Revolution—In the War of 1812—Organization of Negro Companies by Union Generals in 1862—Jefferson Davis Orders Execution for Felony of Union Officers Engaged in Such Organization—Congress Passes Act of July 17, 1862, Accepting Negroes for General Service in the Army—Thaddeus Stevens [Pa.] Introduces Bill in the House Specifically Employing Negroes as Soldiers—Debate: in Favor, Mr. Stevens, John Hickman [Pa.], Thomas M. Edwards [N. H.], Alexander S. Diven [N. Y.]; Opposed, John J. Crittenden [Ky.], Samuel S. Cox [O.]—Bill Is Passed by the House, and Rejected by the Senate as Conferring Power Already Granted—History of Negro Troops in the War—Employment of Negroes by the Rebels—Retaliation.

CRISPUS ATTUCKS, a mulatto and a fugitive slave, led the patriot mob at the Boston massacre. It was Peter Salem, one of the enfranchised negroes who fought at Bunker Hill, that shot dead Major Pitcairn, leader of the British marines, as he leaped over the breastworks crying, "The day is our own."

The Revolutionary Committee of Safety, feeling that it was inconsistent with the principles of the conflict and reflecting dishonor on the colonies to employ slaves as soldiers, decreed, on May 20, 1775, that only those negroes who were free should be admitted into the army. Many patriots thereupon freed their slaves that these might be permitted to fight.

In the Continental Congress Mr. Edward Rutledge, of South Carolina, moved, on September 26, 1775, that all negroes be dismissed from the patriot armies, but the opposition was so formidable and so determined that the motion did not prevail. Negroes, instead of being expelled from the service, continued to be received, often as substitutes for ex-masters or their sons; and, in Vir-

230

ginia especially, it gradually became a custom to give a slave his freedom on condition of his taking his master's place at the front.

The Congressional Committee of Conference with General Washington before Boston, headed by Benjamin Franklin, ordered on October 23, 1775, that negroes, "especially such as are slaves," should no longer be enlisted; but, on Washington's representation that the negro soldiers whose time had expired were much dissatisfied with the order, and that he feared some might show their resentment by deserting to the enemy, Congress, on January 16, 1776, permitted these to reënlist.

Already (in November, 1775) Lord Dunmore, Royal Governor of Virginia, in order to "reduce" the colonists "to a proper sense of their duty to His Majesty's crown and dignity," had invited slaves to enter the British army, offering them freedom if they would do so.

The Virginia patriots, to offset the effect of this proclamation, called the attention of the slaves to the fact that enlistment in the British army would leave their families at the mercy of "an enraged and injured people." Many enlisted, however, though almost all were destroyed by a malignant fever contracted in the camps.

On August 24, 1778, 775 negroes were enrolled in the Continental army. On August 29 a black regiment, all of whose members had been freed by the Rhode Island legislature on condition they enter the State militia, fought with notable gallantry at the battle of Rhode Island. The legislatures of other Northern States followed the example of that of Rhode Island, and in the South this policy was urged by leading patriots. It is highly probable, says Horace Greeley in his "American Conflict," that had the Revolutionary War lasted a few years longer slavery would have been abolished throughout the country.

So great was the fear of the British commanders that negroes would be set free and enrolled in the patriot army, that Sir Henry Clinton, on June 30, 1779, issued a proclamation offering protection and employment to all slaves who should enter the British lines. Lord Cornwallis, in his Southern campaign, proclaimed freedom to all slaves who should join him. Thomas Jefferson, in a letter to Dr. Gordon, from Paris, on July 16, 1788, estimated that this policy in one year cost Virginia 30,000 slaves, most of whom died of small-pox and camp-fever. Thirty of these were his own, and he characteristically said: "Had this been to give them freedom he (Lord Cornwallis) would have done right."

In the beginning of the War of 1812 the policy was generally adopted of not enlisting negroes, but toward its close, under the stress of military necessity, the restriction was abandoned. Thus the New York legislature, on October 24, 1814, authorized in several quarters the raising of two regiments of negroes, freeing those who were slaves, and compensating their owners with the negroes' pay. On September 21, 1814, Gen. Andrew Jackson, in a proclamation from Mobile, Ala., vigorously denounced the "mistaken policy" of excluding negroes from the army, and gave high praise to the bravery of those who had fought under him, which was shortly afterward confirmed in the defence of New Orleans (January 8, 1815), where a number of negroes fought side by side with the white soldiers, repelling from behind the breastworks the advance of the trained British soldiers under Pakenham with the same ardor which Peter Salem and his black companions had displayed at Bunker Hill.

In the Civil War, before Gen. David Hunter's proclamation of military emancipation had been revoked [see page 130], he had organized some of the slaves of his department into companies.

In his report to the Secretary of War [Edwin M. Stanton], on June 23, 1862, General Hunter gave this testimony to their efficiency:

The experiment of arming the blacks, so far as I have made it, has been a complete and even marvelous success. They are sober, docile, attentive, and enthusiastic; displaying great natural capacities for acquiring the duties of the soldier. They are eager beyond all things to take the field and be led into action;

and it is the unanimous opinion of the officers who have had charge of them that, in the peculiarities of this climate and country, they will prove invaluable auxiliaries—fully equal to the similar regiments so long and successfully used by the British authorities in the West India Islands.

On July 16, 1862, Congress passed an act authorizing the President to accept negroes for "any war service for which they may be found competent," though not specifying fighting as one of these services. The act was approved by the President on July 17.

On August 25, 1862, Secretary Stanton issued a special order to Gen. Rufus Saxton, military governor of the sea islands off the coast of South Carolina, to enlist and drill not over 5,000 negroes and to give them the pay of white soldiers. Saxton was ordered to cultivate the plantations with other negroes, and in every way to "withdraw from the enemy their laboring force and population."

Brigadier-General J. W. Phelps, a Vermont Abolitionist serving under Benjamin F. Butler at New Orleans during the summer of 1862, organized five companies of negroes, who, he announced to his chief, were "all willing and ready to show their devotion to our cause in any way it may be put to the test." He recommended that they be used as soldiers under the command of recent graduates of West Point and the more promising non-commissioned officers and privates.

General Butler, in response, instructed General Phelps to employ his "contrabands" upon the fortifications instead of organizing them as soldiers. This General Phelps peremptorily declined to do, saying, "I am not willing to become the mere slave-driver you propose, having no qualifications that way," and thereupon he threw up his commission.

Later (on July 31, 1862) General Butler felt constrained by the necessities and perils of his position to appeal to the free colored men of New Orleans to take up arms in the national service, which appeal was responded to with alacrity and enthusiasm, and a first regiment, 1,000 strong, was filled within 14 days—all its line officers being colored, as well as the rank and file. His next regiment, filled soon afterward, had its two highest officers white, all the rest colored. His third was officered by the best men that could be had, regardless of color. His two batteries were officered by whites only; for the simple reason that there were no others who had any knowledge of artillery.

On the reception at Richmond of tidings of General Hunter's and General Phelps's proceedings with reference to the enlistment of negro soldiers for the Union armies, President Jefferson Davis issued an order directing that said generals be no longer regarded as public enemies of the Confederacy, but as outlaws; and that, in the event of the capture of either of them, or of any other commissioned officer employed in organizing, drilling, or instructing slaves, he should not be treated as a prisoner of war, but held in close confinement for execution as a felon, at such time and place as he should order. It is not recorded that anyone was ever actually hung under this order.

Employment of Negro Soldiers

House of Representatives, January 29-February 2, 1863

On January 27, 1863, Thaddeus Stevens [Pa.] introduced in the House a bill authorizing the President to raise and equip 150,000 negro soldiers, and as many more as he deemed it expedient; to receive the same pay and treatment as white soldiers; to serve for five years, if necessary; the officers to be white or black; commissioned by the President; recruiting stations to be established in both free and slave States; all the slaves among the negroes to become free at discharge, the Government purchasing those belonging to loyal citizens.

The bill was hotly opposed by Representatives from the border States, and by the "Peace" Democrats of the North. Of the speeches of the former class that by John J. Crittenden, made on January 29, is representative.

You propose by this bill to raise a force of one hundred and fifty thousand slaves as soldiers. You include, to be sure, and permit to be enlisted, free men of color. How can you approve of it? You say the war is a contest for freedom, a contest for liberty; and shall we, sir, stigmatize our constituents, our brothers, the white free-born men of this land, as being so degenerate as to shrink from this contest, and compel you to appeal to your own black men to defend the liberties of the white man?

The bill proposes to raise one hundred and fifty thousand Americans of African descent. You stigmatize them, while you invite them into the field. You employ them as soldiers to fight your battle, but give them only one-half pay and exclude them from command to a great extent.

This distinction which the white race makes in its own favor against the negro may be an unjust one. It is not necessary for me to enter into that question or to define exactly the degree of superiority on the one side or of inferiority on the part of the other race. We know that it exists; it exists North, it exists South, and it exists everywhere. The feelings of our people in reference to it are founded upon instincts that have come down from one generation to another. There is not one of you here who would admit a black man to social equality or to any species of equality. Yet what are you striving to do? You propose to enlist the negro for five years. We are engaged in a mighty war now, a war caused by revolution and pregnant with revolution. What will be the result if we do not conquer a peace shortly? Before long the term of service of your white troops will have expired. Is the nation to be left to a standing black army, with the President at its head, clothed with almost illimitable war powers? Would anyone dare to propose such a policy as that to the American people—to leave the defence of the country and the lives and liberties of its people in the guardianship of any President with one hundred and fifty thousand myrmidons like these, without a knowledge of the simplest principles upon which our Government depends, and without any possibility of their being able to appreciate that liberty for which you are willing to fight and to send your sons to fight? The janizaries are safer depositaries of the liberties of the Ottoman than would be this army of slaves to protect our liberties.

All nations which have held slaves have been found to reject their services for military purposes in time of war. My learned friend from Ohio [Samuel Shellabarger], who the other day was comparing these rebels to Catiline, is well enough acquainted with his history, and can bear testimony that he, that bold conspirator, had Roman pride enough left in the midst of his vices to reject the assistance, even in his extremest hour of peril, of slaves and gladiators, although they were white slaves, men who had been born free, men who had been made captives in war, and reduced by the inhuman policy of that age to the condition of slavery; they had been tainted and marked with that degradation, and that was enough; even Catiline would not be their leader, and preferred to face the perils of the battle alone. And what a spectacle is here presented! The representatives of a nation which has ever boasted of its readiness to shed the last drop of its blood in defence of the liberties of its people are calling upon slaves to defend it and to defend them! Sir, it is a mockery—a mockery of the American people. It is a policy unlike that of any other nation. It is an insult to your army. It is a crime against the civilization of the age. It is a crime against the Constitution. It is an act of hostility against the Union. These are the sentiments with which I am compelled to regard this measure.

I say it is a crime against the Constitution. You send out your recruiting officer, and you authorize him to go into the State of Maryland, for instance, and to any gentleman's house and seduce away his slave and persuade him to enlist by the promise of his freedom, or, perhaps, the promise of a captaincy, and that slave the property of the master! Mr. Lincoln says the owner has property in his slave; that, he says, is plain and cannot be contested. And yet your recruiting officer is authorized to enlist the slave; to take from the lawful ownership of a loyal man his slave and put him in the army. Did injustice ever go further than this?

JOHN HUTCHINS [Pa.].—I would like to ask the gentleman from Kentucky a question. Do not the Government of the United States take minors and apprentices, whose services by law belong to the father or master, and put them into the army of the United States?

MR. CRITTENDEN.—Sir, if the gentleman can mislead himself by any such ideas as those that his question suggests, I cannot help him. I tell him now that the free-born boy owes no obligation of slavery to anyone. His father is his guardian; the owner of the slave is his master. To those who cannot understand that distinction I can make no explanation that will enable them to understand it.

Mr. Speaker, your law is impracticable. My friends, just

think of what you are doing! One hundred and fifty thousand negroes are to be enlisted. I say your army will consider it an insult and a degradation.

I remember that the distinguished gentleman from Pennsylvania, last session of Congress, was in favor of this same measure. The topics of our conversation then were the battles near Richmond, and there was much sympathy over the great slaughter there. It was then that he introduced this idea of a negro army; they would have saved so many of our dear sons. It seems to me that the gentleman's idea, fairly translated, amounted to this: that he wanted a negro to march before every white man in the field of battle. What a shame it is that proud Republicans, who talk so much about their liberties, should require to have poor negroes held before them in battle as a sort of shield! Do you want this negro army for such a purpose? Sooner advise your sons and brothers to desert. That may escape the attention of history. But, if you want to make the cowardice of our army memorable and historical, bring out your one hundred and fifty thousand black men, put them in the front of the battle, and shelter your white soldiers behind them.

Whenever the American sinks so low; whenever that pusillanimous policy is adopted by him, the liberties of such men are not worth much. The pride and heroism of the American name will have all gone. Let not the man who wants such a defence as that go forth to battle. Let him stay at home. That is not the way to train up a great people. Sparta had her slaves. So had Athens. Did they ever send these slaves into the battle? They were small republics, and were often greatly harassed by war, but they never used their slaves as soldiers. Shall we alone voluntarily degrade ourselves below the condition of other nations? Have not our citizens the courage and strength to defend the country? Have they not the public virtue that is absolutely necessary for the defence of their national existence and of their public liberties? When we shall abandon that defence to slaves we ought to give up our country.

Sir, you cannot execute such a law, and you know it. If you want to make war directly in Kentucky, I assure you, much as I deprecate and deplore it, that this will produce it. It is not in the power of the Government, State or Federal, to prevent actual hostilities there on the very day this sort of recruiting shall be entered on. Your recruiting officers will be driven pell-mell out of the State, or they will be hung, just as the temper of the people may happen to be. I tell you that this is a fact, and that the passage of this measure, instead of assisting to restore the Union, will enlarge and embitter the war. I do not believe that you can, by any measure, drive Kentucky to go out of the Union, and to make alliance with the secessionists and rebels of the South; but the people of Kentucky will resist oppression, come from where it will. They are for the Constitution and are against the rebels, because the rebels are the enemies of the Constitution; and they will be against you, too, whenever you resort to unconstitutional measures. We are fighting so that when peace comes our Constitution and liberties will be restored to us with it. But for that hope there would be no heart for the fight. But if, while we are carrying on a war against the rebellion, the Constitution of our country is to be destroyed piece by piece behind us, and we are to have nothing but the ruins of it left, why should we not be hostile to those who have done this work of destruction?

Sir, this plan of bringing black men into your military service will prove an act of cruelty to the slaves, but of profit to no one. Can they sympathize with us in the motives that actuate us in carrying on this war? That Constitution for which we are fighting makes them slaves; and yet you now call upon them to assist you in restoring its supremacy. What claim have you upon their services in any such cause? What do you bring them to the field for? Do you believe in your hearts you can ever make soldiers of them? There may have been brave seamen in the Pacific Ocean of the African race, and there may have been a brave company of black men which General Jackson saw fit to compliment after the battle of New Orleans; but do you expect your army of one hundred and fifty thousand blacks will prove to be of that class? Let me tell you that if you do you will be disappointed. You will gain no strength to your army by such means. For every black soldier you may muster into the service, you will disarm more brave soldiers who will think you have degraded them by this sort of military association. You cannot carry into the field, I repeat, an army made up of the African race. The slave is not a soldier, and he cannot be a soldier. It is not in the nature of things.

I protest, then, against the President, Mr. Lincoln, undertaking to garrison our important posts with negro soldiers. They are not safe, and never will be safe. I care not though the forts are in New York or Massachusetts; they are as much mine as they are yours. They belong to the United States, and I protest against their being placed in the hands of such defenders.

But, sir, I do not care so much about the employment of these men in respect to their inefficiency as soldiers as I do in respect to the character their employment will give to the war itself. You put one white man to command a thousand negroes at the South, and will he restrain them? Will it not result in servile war? It will be a servile war led by white men.

The speech of Samuel S. Cox [O.] is representative of the views of the Northern Democrats. On January 30 he spoke against the bill. He declared that those who promoted it were, in so doing, not the true friends of the negro, but rather his enemies.

The Confederate States will not treat our black soldiers as the equals of their white soldiers or of our white soldiers; and the result will be, as many negroes at the North are shrewd enough to foresee, that they will, if captured, receive none of the advantages of the laws of war, but all the terrible consequences of being outlawed from the international code, slavery, imprisonment, and perhaps death. And how, sir, can we retaliate for any such injuries or outrages? As the gentleman from Kansas argued the other day, and as Vattel argued before him, a rebellion, when formidable, demands, in the name of humanity, the observance of the laws of civilized warfare, the laws of moderation and honor. There is a distinct society, organized *de facto*, in the South; and the laws of war obtain the same as between two nations with regard to prisoners of war. These men in the South have the power, and, although it may have been obtained wrongfully and outrageously, we must legislate on the facts as they exist. We must not shut our eyes to the fact that they are a power so formidable that we cannot, as an act of humanity to our soldiers, refuse to observe the laws of war, not as we would interpret them, but as they also may interpret them. No genuine friend of the negro would try to persuade him to take the position of a soldier in our army, knowing how the Confederate Government has determined to treat negro soldiers. The men who would try to dragoon him into that position are not his friends. The poor negro, if he survive this conflict, will bitterly curse the very men who seem most to champion him, but whose championship has in it more of political consideration than of generous feeling.

THOMAS M. EDWARDS [N. H.].—I understand the gentleman

to say that, if these black soldiers in our army should be captured by the enemy and be handed over to the civil authorities to be treated as felons and their lives taken, or any other consequence visited them not known to the rules of civilized warfare, the United States Government would have no remedy.

MR. COX.—What is your remedy?

MR. EDWARDS.—Retaliation.

MR. COX.—Retaliation—that is a rule which will soon turn this into a barbarous war. It has no limit—no law. It has but one end—bloody extermination.

MR. EDWARDS.—I would hang or shoot one of their soldiers every time they hung or shot one of ours.

MR. COX.—Would you have the President retaliate upon white rebels because they abuse the captured negroes? You will answer yes. Then what? Retaliation again from them upon our white soldiers, and so on, until the war becomes unbearable to the Christian world and an outrage upon all civilized codes.

Furthermore, the measure is inadvisable because many white soldiers will not serve when black soldiers are enlisted. We can never eradicate from the great body of the white people of America that prejudice against the black race which has been carried from private life into the public service, and which, if you run counter to it, will destroy the vigor and *esprit* of the army.

Why, Mr. Speaker, perhaps one-third of our present army is made up of Irishmen. I tell you, sir, these Irishmen will not fight side by side with the negro. You would listen to such warnings if indeed you wished the army to succeed and the Union restored.

The bill was stoutly defended by Republicans, the most typical speech being by Mr. Stevens, mover of the bill, made on February 2.

It is said that we have already so large an army that we have no need of more soldiers, and that this bill will cause a needless expense. Let us look at this. It will require some three or four months to raise one hundred and fifty thousand. By that time, about June, the time of the two years' men of New York and of the nine months' men will expire. They will take from the army, I think, at least three hundred thousand men. How are you to supply their place except by colored soldiers? It is said by our opponents that in the present temper of the country you could not raise in the whole North fifty thousand men by voluntary enlistment, and that to enforce conscription is out of the question. It may be so; and, if it be, it is useless, perhaps, to inquire what has produced this condition of the public mind. No doubt the unhappy management of the war, and want of successful battles, have done something toward it. An unsuccessful war is always unpopular.

Another great cause is the conduct of partisan demagogues. The Democratic leaders—and when I speak of Democrats in these remarks I beg to be understood as not including those true Democrats who support the war and give their aid to the Administration—the Democratic leaders, I say, have been busy for the last year in denouncing the war and the Administration. They tell the people that this is an Abolition war, a war for the negro and not for the Union; that our Southern brethren have been injured and that we ought to lay down our arms and compromise. During the last electioneering campaign throughout Pennsylvania, and I suppose the whole North, when the new volunteers were called for, Democratic leaders traveled everywhere and advised that no Democrat should volunteer, but stay at home and carry the election and regain power. The masses followed their advice; scarcely any Democrats joined the volunteers.

Another thing that has cooled the ardor of the people is the rivalry among the officers and the evident sympathy of a large portion of them with the rebels. Our armies have been in the hands of men who had no heart in the cause and who have demoralized the army; and such demoralization has been transferred to their friends at home. Hence, if we are to continue this war, we must call in the aid of Africans, slaves as well as freemen.

But gentlemen speak boastfully of the power of the white men of the North, and that we have a million men in the field, and need no other aid. Sir, I have as high an opinion of the valor of Northern men as any man can have; but, instead of having a million, I do not believe we have now half that number of effective soldiers. Sickness, the sword, and absenteeism have taken half our troops; and in four months one-fourth more will be taken by the expiration of their time.

But suppose we could recruit our armies by white volunteers, is that any argument against employing blacks? Why should our race be exposed to suffering and disease when the African might endure his equal share of it? Is it wise, is it humane, to send your kindred to battle and to death, when you might put the colored man in the ranks and let him bear a

VI—16

part of the conflict between the rebel and his enfranchised slave? Why should these bloody graves be filled with our relatives rather than with the property of traitors slain by their own masters, who, in their turn, would fall by the hands of the oppressed? I have but little respect for the Northern man who would save the rebels' property at the expense of the life of white men.

We have heard repeated the usual slang of Democrats, so freely and falsely used by them to prejudice the minds of the people, that Republicans are trying to make the black man equal in all things to the white. The distinguished gentleman from Kentucky [Charles A. Wickliffe] and his allies from Ohio have talked of Sambo's commanding white men. Sir, the bill contains no such provisions. They are to be employed only as soldiers or non-commissioned officers as is provided by the original bill and by the amendments as now proposed. I do not expect to live to see the day when, in this Christian land, merit shall counterbalance the crime of color. True, we propose to give them an equal chance to meet death on the battlefield. But even then their great achievements, if equal to those of Dessalines, would give them no hope of honor. The only place where they can find equality is in the grave. There all God's children are equal.

But it is said that our soldiers would object to their employment in arms. It would be a strange taste that would prefer themselves to face the death-bearing heights of Fredericksburg, and be buried in trenches at the foot of them, than to see it done by colored soldiers. I do not believe it. My colleague [Hendrick B. Wright] said that he had heard some of our officers say that if we thus used them they would lay down their arms and retire from the army. In God's name let them go. They are rebels in heart, and ought to be in the Confederate army rather than in ours, to demoralize our soldiers. My colleague ought to report their names to the proper department, that they may be tried and inexorably shot.

The gentleman from Kentucky [Mr. Crittenden] objects to their employment lest it should lead to the freedom of the blacks. He says that he fights *only* for the freedom of his own white race. That sentiment is unworthy the high reputation of the friend and compeer of the great statesman of the West [Henry Clay]. That patriotism that is wholly absorbed by one's own country is narrow and selfish. That philanthropy which embraces only one's own race, and leaves the other numerous races of mankind to bondage and to misery, is cruel and detestable. But we are not fighting for the freedom of the slaves; we are fighting for the life of the nation; and, if in the heat of such strife the chains of the bondman are melted off, I shall thank God all the more. The distinguished, and, I would fain believe, the learned, gentleman from Kentucky exclaimed, "when before did any civilized country call on slaves to fight their battles? When did Sparta, or Athens, or Rome?" I must attribute this interrogative assertion to lack of memory.

I ask when did any civilized nation refuse to use their slaves in the defence of their country when its exigencies required it? Never! All have used them, and uniformly given them their freedom for their services. Sparta and Athens on many occasions armed their Helots. They were always their armor-bearers. That I may not be suspected of speaking without authority I will read a few passages from Roman history. In Arnold's "Rome" it is said:

"But there is no reason to doubt that Gracchus gained an important victory; and it was rendered famous by his giving liberty to the volunteer slaves, by whose valor it had mainly been won. The soldiers marched back to Beneventum in triumph, and the people poured out to meet them, and entreated Gracchus that they might invite them all to a public entertainment. Tables were set out in the streets, and the freed slaves attracted every one's notice by their white caps, the well-known sign of their enfranchisement. The whole delighted the generous and kind nature of Gracchus; to set free the slave and to relieve the poor, appear to have been hereditary virtues in his family."—Page 205.

How different was the heart of the pagan Gracchus from the heart of the Christian Kentuckian!

But we are told that Kentucky will resist; that our recruiting officers will be driven pell-mell from the State; that the proclamation is unconstitutional; and that we and the President are doing mischief and aggravating the South. Sir, that sounds so exactly like what I was accustomed to hear from that side of the House some years ago, when those seats were occupied by those who are now officers in the rebel army, that I am fain to inquire whether their spirit has not been left behind them.

Two years ago, when I had occasion to address this House, I declared my conviction that neither Congress, nor the Administration, nor the people, realized the magnitude of the war in which we were engaged, and the difficulty of its suppression; that the rebels were as brave as we, and had better generals, who were more in earnest than our own; that men who, after a deliberation of thirty years, had entered upon so perilous an enterprise, involving property, wife and children, and their own lives, would never submit until they were totally exhausted and unable to continue the war; and that that would never be done until you took from them their support—the slaves. I have seen no reason to change my opinion. I have seen two years of bloody war elapse with balanced success. I have seen our debt accumulate to a grievous amount. I have seen many a bleeding heart, many a mother weeping for her slaughtered son, tens of thousands of our neighbors gone to an untimely grave, and the rebels are not yet subdued. And yet we are told that we must not stop the further effusion of white blood by the employment of the oppressed slave against his oppressor. Sir, to which side do such men belong? Are they with the Republic or are they like Cethegus and Lentulus, sitting in the Roman senate, while their associate, Catiline, was with the rebel army outside the walls?

But they say this tends to excite servile war. I believe no such thing. Disciplined troops under the articles of war do not engage in insurrection. But suppose it were so: which is the most cruel, which the most to be deprecated—an exterminating war between the oppressed and his oppressor or a murderous warfare by uninjured citizens against the unoffending Government which had protected them and was the hope of the freedom of the world? Can servile war produce more inhuman scenes than are now enacted by the rebels?

Here the speaker cited murders of innocent negroes committed in cold blood by rebel soldiers.

If a servile war were the only means to save this Republic, I should welcome it as a measure of humanity.

It is said that colored soldiers are cowardly and unfit for battle. But all history contradicts it, from the time of Juba and Syphan and the terrible Numidian cavalry down through our Revolution and the armies of General Jackson to the present time. I send you living evidence in the letter of General Saxton, which the Clerk will please read.

The Clerk read as follows:

BEAUFORT, SOUTH CAROLINA, January 25, 1863.
DEAR SIR: I have the honor to report that the organization of the first regiment of South Carolina volunteers is now completed. In no regiment have I ever seen duty performed with so much cheerfulness and alacrity; and as sentinels they are peculiarly vigilant. I have never seen, in any body of men, such enthusiasm and deep-seated devotion to their officers as

exist in this; they will surely go wherever they are led. Every man is a volunteer, and seems fully persuaded of the importance of his service to his race.

ALEXANDER S. DIVEN [N. Y.].—Mr. Speaker, in connection with the testimony furnished in favor of the employment of the slave I desire to supply the testimony of the most remarkable man of modern Italy, who, while an exile from his beloved country, with all the ardor of his nature, entered the service of the republicans of Brazil, who were seeking to extricate themselves from the tyranny of the Brazilian emperor. In the description of one of the battles between the republican and imperial parties I find this passage:

"The terrible lancers of Canabarro had already made a movement forward, confusing the right flank of the enemy, which was therefore obliged to change front in confusion. The brave freedmen, proud of their force, became more firm and resolute, and that incomparable corps presented to view a forest of lances, being composed entirely of slaves liberated by the republic and chosen from the best horse tamers in the province, and all of them blacks, even the superior officers. The enemy had never seen the backs of those true sons of liberty. Their lances, which were longer than the common measure, their ebony faces and robust limbs, strengthened by perennial and laborious exercise, and their perfect discipline, struck terror into the enemy.''

A MEMBER.—What do you read from?

MR. DIVEN.—From the "Life of Garibaldi," by himself, page 63.

MR. STEVENS.—I believe that if the course which we now propose had been adopted eighteen months ago we should now have peace and universal liberty on this continent. But the timidity of conservatives, the clamor of Democratic demagogues, and the insidious counsels of Kentucky prevented our excellent and kind-hearted President from making stern resolves and using every legitimate means to crush the rebels. Sir, I would not have on my conscience the blood of the tens of thousands who have thus been sacrificed, and which must rest on the souls of its authors, for all the spoils of office, for all the allurements of the presidential chair, nor for all the diamonds that ever glittered in Golconda.

The bill was passed on February 2 by a vote of 83 to 54. The bill then went to the Senate, where it was referred to the Committee on Military Affairs. On February 12 Henry Wilson [Mass.] stated that the committee reported it back to the Senate with the recommendation that it do not pass, because the authority intended to be given by it to the President was already conferred on him by the act of July 17, 1862.

Bravery of Negro Soldiers

President Lincoln from this time on devoted a large part of his energy to enlisting negro troops, his old fear that the former slaves would make inefficient soldiers having been outweighed by consideration of the great moral force of the policy. To Governor Andrew Johnson of Tennessee, who was contemplating the raising in his State of a negro military force, he wrote on March 26, 1863:

In my opinion the country now needs no specific thing so much as some man of your ability and position to go to this work. When I speak of your position I mean that of an eminent citizen of a slave State and himself a slaveholder. The colored population is the great available and yet unavailed of force for restoring the Union. The bare sight of fifty thousand armed and drilled black soldiers upon the banks of the Mississippi would end the rebellion at once; and who doubts that we can present that sight if we but take hold in earnest? If you have been thinking of it, please do not dismiss the thought.

As we have seen, General David Hunter had already organized negro troops in his department. From the beginning the experiment was an unqualified success. It was a pleasure to the President that he could now write a letter of congratulation to the Abolitionist general whom less than a year before he had been compelled to reprimand for his premature act of emancipation.

I am glad to see the accounts of your colored force at Jacksonville, Fla. I see the enemy are driving at them fiercely, as is to be expected. It is important to the enemy that such a force shall not take shape and grow and thrive in the South, and in precisely the same proportion it is important to us that it shall. Hence the utmost caution and vigilance are necessary on our part. The enemy will make extra efforts to destroy them, and we should do the same to preserve and increase them.

In all their subsequent battles the negro soldiers acquitted themselves with such valor that in the war reports the sentence, "the colored troops fought bravely," became a stock expression.

On the occasion of their soldierly conduct at the assault of Port Hudson late in May, 1863, George Henry Boker wrote a poem called "The Black Regiment," in which he extolled their patriotism and pleaded for their recognition as comrades by the white soldiers.

"Freedom!" their battlecry,—
"Freedom! or leave to die!"
Ah! and they meant the word,
Not as with us 'tis heard,
Not a mere party shout;
They gave their spirits out,

. . . . .

Hundreds on hundreds fell;

. . . . .

Oh, to the living few,
Soldiers, be just and true,
Hail them as comrades tried;
Fight with them side by side;
Never, in field or tent,
Scorn the black regiment!

On June 1, 1863, through Senator Charles Sumner of Massachusetts, the President made a tentative offer to General Frémont to place him in command of all the negro troops to be raised. The offer was not accepted. Had it been, Frémont at the close of the war would have commanded an army of almost 200,000 men, second in number only to Grant's.

Employment of Negroes by the Confederates

As early as June 1, 1861, negroes were employed by the secessionists in constructing fortifications at Charleston, S. C. As soon as Virginia went out of the Union free negro volunteers were accepted in that State.

On June 28, 1861, after the legislature of Tennessee had formed a military alliance with the Confederacy, it authorized the governor, Isham G. Harris, "to receive into the military service of the State all male free persons of color, between the ages of 15 and 50," paying each $8 per month, with clothing and rations. It was further enacted that, if sufficient volunteers did not present themselves the sheriffs should *press* enough of such persons to make up the required number. Early in September it was announced in the Memphis *Ava-*

"O MASSA JEFF, DIS SECESH FEVER WILL KILL DE NIGGER!"
From the collection of the New York Historical Society

lanche that many negroes had volunteered for such service, and, armed and equipped with shovels, axes, blankets, etc., and under the leadership of white officers, were marching through the streets shouting for Jeff. Davis and singing war songs. In very sinister fashion the paper added: "Their destination is unknown, but it is supposed that they are on their way to the 'other side of Jordan.'"

About this time Alabama organized free negro volunteers, one regiment consisting of as many as 1,400.

In February, 1862, the Confederate legislature of

Virginia passed a bill to enroll in the military service all the free negroes in the State.

RETALIATION

In despite of these acts, when President Lincoln's preliminary emancipation proclamation appeared on September 22, 1862, the Confederate authorities exhibited great indignation over what they charged to be a deliberate purpose of the Union Government to incite a servile insurrection in the South. On October 13 General Pierre G. T. Beauregard wrote to a Confederate congressman at Richmond:

Has the bill for the execution of abolition prisoners, after January next, been passed? Do it, and England will be stirred into action. It is high time to proclaim the black flag after that period. Let the execution be with the garrote.

On December 23 Jefferson Davis, President of the Confederacy, proclaimed the outlawry of the Union generals who had enlisted negroes as soldiers, and decreed that all slaves and their white officers captured in arms be turned over to the State governors to be dealt with according to law. In his third annual message to his Congress on January 12, 1863, he stigmatized the final proclamation as a violation of President Lincoln's inaugural pledge and the platform on which he had been elected. He added:

It has established a state of things which can lead to but one of three possible consequences—the extermination of the slaves, the exile of the whole white population of the Confederacy, or absolute and total separation of these States from the United States. This proclamation is also an authentic statement by the Government of the United States of its inability to subjugate the South by force of arms, and, as such, must be accepted by neutral nations, which can no longer find any justification in withholding our just claims to formal recognition. It is also, in effect, an intimation to the people of the North that they must prepare to submit to a separation, now become inevitable; for that people are too acute not to understand that a restitution of the Union has been rendered forever impossible by the adoption of a measure which, from its very nature, neither admits of retraction nor can coexist with union.

But the passage which more especially concerns negro soldiers is the following:

We may well leave it to the instincts of that common humanity which a beneficent Creator has implanted in the breasts of our fellowmen of all countries to pass judgment on a measure by which several millions of human beings of an inferior race—peaceful and contented laborers in their sphere—are doomed to extermination, while at the same time they are encouraged to a general assassination of their masters by the insidious recommendation to abstain from violence unless in necessary self-defence. Our own detestation of those who have attempted the most execrable measures recorded in the history of guilty man is tempered by profound contempt for the impotent rage which it discloses. So far as regards the action of this government on such criminals as may attempt its execution, I confine myself to informing you that I shall—unless in your wisdom you deem some other course more expedient—deliver to the several State authorities all commissioned officers of the United States that may hereafter be captured by our forces in any of the States embraced in the proclamation, that they may be dealt with in accordance with the laws of those States providing for the punishment of criminals engaged in exciting servile insurrection. The enlisted soldiers I shall continue to treat as unwilling instruments in the commission of these crimes, and shall direct their discharge and return to their homes on the proper and usual parole.

The Confederate Congress took up the subject soon afterward, and, after protracted consideration, ultimately disposed of it by passing the following resolution:

Sec. 1. That, in the opinion of Congress, the commissioned officers of the enemy ought *not* to be delivered to the authorities of the respective States, as suggested in the said message, but all captives taken by the Confederate forces ought to be dealt with and disposed of by the Confederate Government.

Sec. 2. That, in the judgment of Congress, the proclamations of the President of the United States and the other measures of

Jeff. Davis

the Government of the United States and of its authorities, commanders, and forces, designed or tending to emancipate slaves in the Confederate States, or to abduct such slaves, or to incite them to insurrection, or to employ negroes in war against the Confederate States, or to overthrow the institution of African slavery, and bring on a servile war in these States, would, if successful, produce atrocious consequences, and that they are inconsistent with the spirit of those usages which, in modern warfare, prevail among civilized nations; they may, therefore, be properly and lawfully repressed by retaliation.

By Section 3 President Davis was authorized to ''cause full and ample retaliation to be made for every such violation, in such manner and to such extent as he may think proper.''

By Sections 4, 5, and 6 white officers of negro troops in the service of the Union, or those inciting the slaves to rise against their masters, were, if captured, to be put to death, or be otherwise punished at the discretion of the court.

SEC. 7. All negroes taken in arms against the Confederate States or who shall give aid or comfort to the enemies of the Confederate States shall, when captured, be delivered to the State authorities, to be dealt with according to the present or future laws of such State.

Some of the leading rebel journals, says Horace Greeley in his ''American Conflict,'' on reflection admitted that this was unjustifiable—that the Confederacy could not prescribe the color of citizens of the free States, never in bondage at the South, whom our Government might justifiably employ as soldiers. But the resolve nevertheless stood for years, if not to the last, unrepealed and unmodified, and was the primary, fundamental impediment whereby the exchange of prisoners between the belligerents was first interrupted; so that tens of thousands languished for weary months in prison-camps, where many thousands died of exposure and starvation.

Secretary Stanton, having learned that three Union black soldiers captured with the gunboat *Isaac Smith* at Stone River had been placed in close confinement, ordered three South Carolinian prisoners to be treated likewise, and the fact to be communicated to the Con-

federate leaders.   The Richmond *Examiner,* comment-
ing on this resolution, said:

It is not merely the pretention of a regular government
affecting to deal with rebels, but it is a deadly stab which they
are aiming at our institutions themselves—because they know
that, if we were insane enough to yield this point, to treat black
men as the equals of white, and insurgent slaves as equivalent
to our brave soldiers, the very foundation of slavery would be
fatally wounded.

After one of the conflicts before Charleston an immediate exchange of prisoners was agreed on, but when
the Union prisoners came to be received only whites
made their appearance.   A remonstrance against this
breach of faith was met by a plea of want of power to
surrender blacks taken in arms because of the resolve
of the Confederate Congress just quoted.   This caused
President Lincoln, on July 30, 1863, to issue a general
order:

"It is the duty of every government to give protection to its
citizens, of whatever class, color, or condition, and especially to
those who are duly organized as soldiers in the public service.
The law of nations and the usages and customs of war, as carried on by civilized powers, permit no distinction as to color in
the treatment of prisoners of war as public enemies.   To sell or
enslave any captured person on account of his color, and for
no offence against the laws of war, is a relapse into barbarism,
and a crime against the civilization of the age.

"The Government of the United States will give the same
protection to all its soldiers; and, if the enemy shall sell or
enslave anyone because of his color, the offence shall be punished by retaliation upon the enemy's prisoners in our possession.

"It is therefore ordered that, for every soldier of the United
States killed in violation of the laws of war, a rebel soldier shall
be executed; and for every one enslaved by the enemy or sold
into slavery, a rebel soldier shall be placed at hard labor on
public works, and continued at such labor until the other shall
be released and receive the treatment due to a prisoner of war."

Either the threat of the Confederates was an idle
one, or Lincoln's order deterred them from putting it

into execution, for with but one important exception they gave negroes captured in battle the same treatment that was accorded white prisoners. At the storming of Fort Pillow, Tennessee, on April 12, 1863, the Confederate General Forrest massacred at least three hundred of the garrison, most of them negroes and their white officers, after these soldiers had thrown down their arms.

A rumor of this act came to the President just before he delivered an address at a sanitary fair in Baltimore on April 18, 1864, and in his speech he solemnly promised that if the charge against Forrest proved upon investigation to be true retribution would be surely executed. He said:

There seems to be some anxiety in the public mind whether the Government is doing its duty to the colored soldier, and to the service, at this point. At the beginning of the war and for some time the use of colored troops was not contemplated; and how the change of purpose was wrought I will not now take time to explain. Upon a clear conviction of duty I resolved to turn that element of strength to account; and I am responsible for it to the American people, to the Christian world, to history, and in my final account to God. Having determined to use the negro as a soldier, there is no way but to give him all the protection given to any other soldier. . . . If, after all that has been said it shall turn out that there has been no massacre at Fort Pillow, it will be almost safe to say there has been none, and will be none, elsewhere. If there has been the massacre of three hundred there, or even the tenth part of three hundred, it will be conclusively proved; and, being so proved, the retribution shall as surely come. It will be a matter of grave consideration in what exact course to apply the retribution; but in the supposed case it must come.

A congressional investigation found that the rumor was true, and had not been exaggerated. Yet the brutality revealed was so monstrous that the tender-hearted President refrained, in spite of his promise, from a retribution which, to be effective, would have to be coextensive with the offence, and, because visited in cold blood upon innocent prisoners, would be even more brutal than the massacre, which was perpetrated in the blood-lust of conquest.

Accordingly, the public interest being concentrated at the time on the bloody Wilderness campaign of Grant in Virginia, the Fort Pillow incident was allowed by the Government to pass without action upon it.

Toward the end of the war, when the collapse of the rebellion was in plain sight, the Confederate Government debated the question of arming the slaves; the measure failed by one vote. Mr. Lincoln expressed his sentiments upon this unique phase of the conflict begun in defence of slavery in a speech on the occasion of a presentation of a captured rebel flag to Governor Morton of Indiana.

While I have often said that all men ought to be free, yet would I allow those colored persons to be slaves who want to be, and next to them those white people who argue in favor of making other people slaves. I am in favor of giving an appointment to such white men to try it on for these slaves. I will say one thing in regard to the negro being employed to fight for them. I do know he cannot fight and stay at home and make bread too. And, as one is about as important as the other to them, I don't care which they do. I am rather in favor of having them try them as soldiers. They lack one vote of doing that, and I wish I could send my vote over the river so that I might cast it in favor of allowing the negro to fight. But they cannot fight and work both. We now see the bottom of the enemy's resources.

CHAPTER X

"The War Is a Failure"

Clement L. Vallandigham [O.] Speaks in the House on the Failure of the War, and Demands Armistice with the Confederacy to Arrange Terms of Peace—Reply by John A. Bingham [O.] Declaring the Union Is Worth the Costliest Sacrifice of Blood and Treasure to Maintain It—Lincoln's Gettysburg Speech: "These Dead Shall Not Have Died in Vain"—Second Election of Lincoln—His Inaugural Address on the Prosecution of the War: "The Almighty Has His Purposes."

THE Union disaster at Fredericksburg (December 11-12, 1862) and the strong resistance of the Confederates at Vicksburg, overweighing in popular opinion the costly Union victory at Stone River (December 30, 1862–January 4, 1863), caused the Opposition in Congress to inaugurate its peace policy—the view that the "war is a failure," "the South cannot be conquered," and therefore that the Government should speedily make the best terms it could with the enemy.

On January 14, 1863, Clement L. Vallandigham [O.] spoke as follows in the House:

Peace and Reunion

Clement L. Vallandigham, M. C.

Sir, twenty months have elapsed, but the rebellion is not crushed out; its military power has not been broken; the insurgents have not dispersed. The Union is not restored; nor the Constitution maintained; nor the laws enforced. A thousand millions have been expended and three hundred thousand lives lost or bodies mangled; and to-day the Confederate flag is still near the Potomac and the Ohio, and the Confederate Government stronger, many times, than at the beginning. Not a State has been restored, not any part of any State has voluntarily re-

255

turned to the Union. And has anything been wanting that Congress, or the States, or the people in their most generous enthusiasm, their most impassioned patriotism, could bestow? Was it power? And did not the party of the Executive control the entire Federal Government, every State government, every county, every city, town, and village in the North and West? Was it patronage? All belonged to it. Was it influence? What more? Did not the school, the college, the church, the press, the secret orders, the municipality, the corporation (railroads, telegraphs, express companies), the voluntary association, all, all yield it to the utmost? Was it unanimity? Never was an Administration so supported in England or America. Five men and half a score of newspapers made up the opposition. Was it enthusiasm? The enthusiasm was fanatical. There has been nothing like it since the Crusades. Was it confidence? Sir, the faith of the people exceeded that of the patriarch. They gave up Constitution, law, right, liberty, all at your demand for arbitrary power that the rebellion might, as you promised, be crushed out in three months and the Union restored. Was credit needed? You took control of a country, young, vigorous, and inexhaustible in wealth and resources, and a Government almost free from public debt, and whose good faith had never been tarnished. Your great national loan bubble failed miserably, as it deserved to fail; but the bankers and merchants of Philadelphia, New York, and Boston lent you more than their entire banking capital. And when that failed, too, you forced credit by declaring your paper promises to pay a legal tender for all debts. Was money wanted? You had all the revenues of the United States, diminished, indeed, but still in gold. The whole wealth of the country, to the last dollar, lay at your feet. Private individuals, municipal corporations, the State governments, all in their frenzy gave you money or means with reckless prodigality. The great Eastern cities lent you $150,000,000. Congress voted first $250,000,000 and next $500,000,000 more in loans; and then first $50,000,000, then $10,000,000; next $90,000,-000, and in July last $150,000,000 in treasury notes; and the Secretary has issued also a paper "postage currency," in sums as low as five cents, limited in amount only by his discretion. Nay, more: already since the 4th of July, 1861, this House has appropriated $2,017,864,000, almost every dollar without debate and without a recorded vote. A thousand millions have been expended since the 15th of April, 1861; and a public debt or liability of $1,500,000,000 already incurred. And to support all this stupendous outlay and indebtedness a system of taxation, direct and indirect, has been inaugurated, the most onerous and unjust ever imposed upon any but a conquered people.

Money and credit, then, you have had in prodigal profusion. And were men wanted? More than a million rushed to arms! Seventy-five thousand first (and the country stood aghast at the multitude), then eighty-three thousand more were demanded; and three hundred and ten thousand responded to the call. The President next asked for four hundred thousand, and Congress, in its generous confidence, gave him five hundred thousand; and, not to be outdone, he took six hundred and thirty-seven thousand. Half of these melted away in their first campaign; and the President demanded three hundred thousand more for the war, and then drafted yet another three hundred thousand for nine months. The fabled hosts of Xerxes have been outnumbered. And yet victory strangely follows the standards of the foe. From Great Bethel to Vicksburg, the battle has not been to the strong. Yet every disaster, except the last, has been followed by a call for more troops, and every time so far they have been promptly furnished. From the beginning the war has been conducted like a political campaign, and it has been the folly of the party in power that they have assumed that numbers alone would win the field in a contest not with ballots but with musket and sword. Yet after nearly two years of more vigorous prosecution of war than ever recorded in history; after more skirmishes, combats, and battles than Alexander, Cæsar, or the first Napoleon ever fought in any five years of their military career, you have utterly, signally, disastrously —I will not say ignominiously—failed to subdue ten millions of ''rebels,'' whom you had taught the people of the North and West not only to hate but to despise. Rebels, did I say? Yes, your fathers were rebels, or your grandfathers. He who now before me on canvas looks down so sadly upon us, the false, degenerate, and imbecile guardians of the great Republic which he founded, was a rebel. And yet we, cradled ourselves in rebellion, and who have fostered and fraternized with every insurrection in the nineteenth century everywhere throughout the globe, would now, forsooth, make the word ''rebel'' a reproach. Rebels certainly they are; but all the persistent and stupendous efforts of the most gigantic warfare of modern times have, through your incompetency and folly, availed nothing to crush them out, cut off though they have been by your blockade from all the world, and dependent only upon their own courage and resources. And yet they were to be utterly conquered and subdued in six weeks or three months! Sir, my judgment was

VI—17

made up and expressed from the first. I learned it from Chatham: "My lords, you cannot conquer America." And you have not conquered the South. You never will. It is not in the nature of things possible; much less under your auspices. But money you have expended without limit, and blood poured out like water. Defeat, debt, taxation, sepulchers, these are your trophies. In vain the people gave you treasure and the soldier yielded up his life. "Fight, tax, emancipate, let these," said the gentleman from Maine [Frederick A. Pike] at the last session, "be the trinity of our salvation." Sir, they have become the trinity of your deep damnation. The war for the Union is, in your hands, a most bloody and costly failure. The President confessed it on the 22d of September, solemnly, officially, and under the broad seal of the United States. And he has now repeated the confession. The priests and rabbis of abolition taught him that God would not prosper such a cause. War for the Union was abandoned; war for the negro openly begun, and with stronger battalions than before. With what success? Let the dead at Fredericksburg and Vicksburg answer.

And now, sir, can this war continue? Whence the money to carry it on? Where the men? Can you borrow? From whom? Cau you tax more? Will the people bear it? Wait till you have collected what is already levied. How many millions more of "legal tender"—to-day forty-seven per cent. below the par of gold—can you float? Will men enlist now at any price? Ah, sir, it is easier to die at home. I beg pardon; but I trust I am not "discouraging enlistments." If I am, then first arrest Lincoln, Stanton, and Halleck, and some of your other generals; and I will retract; yes, I will recant. But can you draft again? Ask New England—New York. Ask Massachusetts. Where are the nine hundred thousand? Ask not Ohio—the Northwest. She thought you were in earnest, and gave you all, all—more than you demanded.

> "The wife whose babe first smiled that day,
>   The fair, fond bride of yester eve,
>   And aged sire and matron gray,
>   Saw the loved warriors haste away,
>   And deemed it sin to grieve."

Sir, in blood she has atoned for her credulity; and now there is mourning in every house and distress and sadness in every heart. Shall she give you any more?

But ought this war to continue? I answer, no—not a day, not an hour. What then? Shall we separate? Again I answer, no, no, no! What then? And now, sir, I come to the grandest and most solemn problem of statesmanship from the beginning of time; and to the God of Heaven, Illuminer of hearts and minds, I would humbly appeal for some measure, at least, of light and wisdom and strength to explore and reveal the dark but possible future of this land.

CAN THE UNION OF THESE STATES BE RESTORED? HOW SHALL IT BE DONE?

And why not? Is it historically impossible? Sir, the frequent civil wars and conflicts between the states of Greece did not prevent their cordial union to resist the Persian invasion; nor did even the thirty years' Peloponnesian war, springing in part, from the abduction of slaves, and embittered and disastrous as it was—let Thucydides speak—wholly destroy the fellowship of those states. The wise Romans ended the three years' social war after many bloody battles and much atrocity by admitting the states of Italy to all the rights and privileges of Roman citizenship—the very object to secure which these States had taken up arms. The border wars between Scotland and England, running through centuries, did not prevent the final union, in peace and by adjustment, of the two kingdoms under one monarch. Compromise did at last what ages of coercion and attempted conquest had failed to effect. England kept the crown, while Scotland gave the king to wear it; and the memories of Wallace and the Bruce of Bannockburn became part of the glories of British history. I pass by the union of Ireland with England—a union of force, which God and just men abhor; and yet precisely "the Union as it should be" of the abolitionists of America. Sir, the rivalries of the houses of York and Lancaster filled all England with cruelty and slaughter; yet compromise and intermarriage ended the strife at last, and the white rose and the red were blended in one. Who dreamed a month before the death of Cromwell that in two years the people of England, after twenty years of civil war and usurpation, would, with great unanimity, restore the house of Stuart in the person of its most worthless prince, whose father but eleven years before they had beheaded? And who could have foretold in the beginning of 1812 that within some three years Napoleon would be in exile upon a desert island and the Bourbons restored? Armed foreign intervention did it; but it is a strange history. Or who, then, expected to see a nephew of Napoleon, thirty-five years later, with the consent of the people, supplant the Bourbon and reign Emperor of France? **Sir,** many states and people, once separate, have become united in the course of ages through natural causes and without conquest, but I remember a single instance only in history of states or people once united, and speaking the same language, who have been forced permanently asunder by civil strife or war, unless they were separated by distance or vast natural boundaries. The secession of the Ten Tribes is the exception: these parted without actual war; and their subsequent history is not encouraging to secession. But when Moses, the greatest of all statesmen, would secure a distinct nationality and government to the Hebrews, he left Egypt and established his people in a distant country. In modern times the Netherlands, three centuries ago, won their independence by the sword; but France and the English Channel separated them from Spain. So did our Thirteen Colonies; but the Atlantic Ocean divorced us from England. So did Mexico and other Spanish colonies in America; but the same ocean divided them from Spain. Cuba and the Canadas still adhere to the parent government. And who now, North or South, in Europe or America, looking into history, shall presumptiously say that because of civil war the reunion of these States is impossible? War, indeed, while it lasts, is disunion, and, if it lasts long enough, will be final, eternal separation first and anarchy and despotism afterward. Hence I would hasten peace now, to-day, by every honorable appliance.

Are there physical causes which render reunion impracticable? None. Where other causes do not control, rivers unite; but mountains, deserts, and great bodies of water—*oceani dissociabiles*[1]—separate a people. Vast forests originally and the lakes now also divide us—not very widely or wholly—from the Canadas, though we speak the same language and are similar in manners, laws, and institutions. Our chief navigable rivers run from north to south. Most of our bays and arms of the sea take the same direction. So do our ranges of mountains. Natural causes all tend to Union, except as between the Pacific Coast and the country east of the Rocky Mountains to the Atlantic. It is "manifest destiny." Union is empire. Hence, hitherto we have continually extended our territory, and the Union with it, south and west. The Louisiana purchase, Florida, and Texas all attest it. We passed desert and forest, and scaled even the Rocky Mountains, to extend the Union to the Pacific. Sir, there is no natural boundary between the North and the South, and no line of latitude upon which to separate; and if ever a line

[1] "Friendship-barring oceans."

of longititude shall be established it will be east of the Mississippi valley. The Alleghanies are no longer a barrier. Highways ascend them everywhere, and the railroad now climbs their
summits and spans their chasms, or penetrates their rockiest
sides. The electric telegraph follows, and, stretching its connecting wires along the clouds, there mingles its vocal lightnings
with the fires of heaven.

And now, sir, is there any difference of race here so radical
as to forbid reunion? I do not refer to the negro race, styled
now, in unctuous official phrase by the President, "Americans
of African descent." Certainly, sir, there are two white races
in the United States, both from the same common stock, and
yet so distinct—one of them so peculiar—that they develop different forms of civilization, and might belong, almost, to different types of mankind. But the boundary of these two races
is not at all marked by the line which divides the slaveholding
from the non-slaveholding States. If race is to be the geograph-
ical limit of disunion, then Mason and Dixon's can never be the
line.

Speaking of the natural causes which had formed the
Union, Mr. Vallandigham said:

And now, sir, what one of them is wanting? What one
diminished? On the contrary, many of them are stronger to-
day than in the beginning. Migration and intermarriage have
strengthened the ties of consanguinity. Commerce, trade, and
production have immensely multiplied. Cotton, almost unknown
here in 1787, is now the chief product and export of the country.
It has set in motion three-fourths of the spindles of New England, and given employment, directly or remotely, to full half
the shipping, trade, and commerce of the United States. More
than that: cotton has kept the peace between England and
America for thirty years; and, had the people of the North been
as wise and practical as the statesmen of Great Britain, it
would have maintained Union and peace here. But we are being
taught in our first century and at our own cost the lessons
which England learned through the long and bloody experience
of eight hundred years. We shall be wiser next time. Let
not cotton be king, but peacemaker, and inherit the blessing.

A common interest, then, still remains to us. And union
for the common defence, at the end of this war, taxed, indebted,
impoverished, exhausted, as both sections must be, and with
foreign fleets and armies around us, will be fifty-fold more essen-

tial than ever before. And finally, sir, without union, our domestic tranquility must forever remain unsettled. If it cannot
be maintained within the Union, how, then, outside of it, without an exodus or colonization of the people of the one section
or the other to a distant country? Sir, I repeat that two governments so interlinked and bound together every way by physical and social ligaments cannot exist in peace without a common arbiter. Will treaties bind us? What better treaty than
the Constitution? What more solemn, more durable? Shall
we settle our disputes, then, by arbitration and compromise?
Sir, let us arbitrate and compromise now, inside of the Union.
Certainly it will be quite as easy.

And now, sir, to all these original causes and motives which
impelled to union at first must be added certain artificial ligaments which eighty years of association under a common Government have most fully developed. Chief among these are
canals, steam navigation, railroads, express companies, the postoffice, the newspaper press, and that terrible agent of good and
evil mixed—''spirit of health, and yet goblin damned''—if free,
the gentlest minister of truth and liberty; when enslaved, the
supplest instrument of falsehood and tyranny—the magnetic telegraph. All these have multiplied the speed or the quantity of
trade, travel, communication, migration, and intercourse of all
kinds between the different States and sections; and thus, so
long as a healthy condition of the body-politic continued, they
became powerful cementing agencies of union. The numerous
voluntary associations, artistic, literary, charitable, social, and
scientific, until corrupted and made fanatical; the various ecclesiastical organizations, until they divided; and the political
parties, so long as they remained all national and not sectional,
were also among the strong ties which bound us together. And
yet all of these, perverted and abused for some years in the
hands of bad or fanatical men, became still more powerful instrumentalities in the fatal work of disunion; just as the veins
and arteries of the human body, designed to convey the vitaliz-
ing fluid through every part of it, will carry also, and with
increased rapidity, it may be, the subtle poison which takes life
away.

Nor is this all. It was through their agency that the imprisoned winds of civil war were all let loose at first with
such sudden and appalling fury; and, kept in motion by political
power, they have ministered to that fury ever since. But, potent
alike for good and evil, they may yet, under the control of the
people, and in the hands of wise, good, and patriotic men, be

made the most effective agencies, under Providence, in the re-union of these States.

Other ties also, less material in their nature, but hardly less persuasive in their influence, have grown up under the Union. Long association, a common history, national reputation, treaties and diplomatic intercourse abroad, admission of new States, a common jurisprudence, great men whose names and fame are the patrimony of the whole country, patriotic music and songs, common battlefields, and glory won under the same flag. These make up the poetry of union; and yet, as in the marriage rela-tion and the family with similar influences, they are stronger than hooks of steel. He was a wise statesman, though he may never have held an office, who said, "Let me write the songs of a people and I care not who makes their laws." Why is the "Marseillaise" prohibited in France? Sir, "Hail Columbia" and the "Star Spangled Banner"—Pennsylvania gave us one and Maryland the other—have done more for the Union than all the legislation and all the debates in this Capitol for forty years; and they will do more yet again than all your armies, though you call out another million men into the field. Sir, I would add "Yankee Doodle"; but first let me be assured that Yankee Doodle loves the Union more than he hates the slave-holder.[1]

What, then, I ask, is the immediate, direct cause of dis-union and this civil war? Slavery, it is answered. Sir, that is the philosophy of the rustic in the play—"that a great cause of the night is lack of the sun." Certainly slavery was in one sense—very obscure indeed—the cause of the war. Had there been no slavery here, this particular war about slavery would never have been waged. But far better say that the negro is the cause of the war; for, had there been no negro here, there would be no war just now. What then? Exterminate him? Who demands it? Colonize him? How? Where? When? At whose cost? Sir, let us have an end of this folly.

But slavery is the cause of the war. Why? Because the South obstinately and wickedly refused to restrict or abolish it at the demand of the philosophers or fanatics and demagogues of the North and West. Then, sir, it was abolition, the purpose to abolish or interfere with and hem in slavery, which caused disunion and war. Slavery is only the *subject,* but abolition the *cause,* of this civil war. I will not be stopped by that cry of mingled fanaticism and hypocrisy about the sin and barbarism

---

[1] In truth, the song was written in derision, by a British officer, and not by an American.

of African slavery. Sir, I see more of barbarism and sin, a thousand times, in the continuance of this war, the dissolution of the Union, the breaking up of this Government, and the enslavement of the white race by debt and taxes and arbitrary power. The day of fanatics and sophists and enthusiasts, thank God, is gone at last; and though the age of chivalry may not, the age of practical statesmanship is about to return. Sir, there is fifty-fold less of anti-slavery sentiment to-day in the West than there was two years ago; and, if this war be continued, there will be still less a year hence. The people there begin, at last, to comprehend that domestic slavery in the South is a question, not of morals, or religion, or humanity, but a form of labor, perfectly compatible with the dignity of free white labor in the same community, and with national vigor, power, and prosperity, and especially with' military strength. They have learned, or begin to learn, that the evils of the system affect the master alone, or the community and State in which it exists; and that we of the free States partake of all the material benefits of the institution, unmixed with any part of its mischiefs. They believe also in the subordination of the negro race to the white where they both exist together, and that the condition of subordination, as established in the South, is far better every way for the negro than the hard servitude of poverty, degradation, and crime to which he is subjected in the free States. All this, sir, may be "pro-slaveryism," if there be such a word. Perhaps it is; but the people of the West begin now to think it wisdom and good sense. We will not establish slavery in our own midst; neither will we abolish or interfere with it outside of our own limits.

Sir, you cannot abolish slavery by the sword; still less by proclamations, though the President were to "proclaim" every month. Of what possible avail was his proclamation of September? Did the South submit? Was she even alarmed? And yet he has now fulmined another "bull against the comet"— *brutum fulmen*—and, threatening servile insurrection with all its horrors, has yet coolly appealed to the judgment of mankind, and invoked the blessing of the God of peace and love! But declaring it a military necessity, an essential measure of war to subdue the rebels, yet, with admirable wisdom, he expressly exempts from its operation the only States and parts of States in the South where he has the military power to execute it.

Neither, sir, can you abolish slavery by argument. As well attempt to abolish marriage or the relation of paternity. The South is resolved to maintain it at every hazard and by every sacrifice; and if "this Union cannot endure part slave and part free," then it is already and finally dissolved. Talk not to me of "West Virginia." Tell me not of Missouri, trampled under the feet of your soldiery. As well talk to me of Ireland. Sir, the destiny of those States must abide the issue of the **war**. But Kentucky you may find tougher. And Maryland—

"E 'en in her ashes live their wonted fires."

Nor will Delaware be found wanting in the day of trial.

But I deny the doctrine. It is full of disunion and civil war. It is disunion itself. Whoever first taught it ought to be dealt with as not only hostile to the Union, but an enemy of the human race. Sir, the fundamental idea of the Constitution is the perfect and eternal compatibility of a union of States "part slave and part free"; else the Constitution never would have been framed nor the Union founded; and seventy years of successful experiment have approved the wisdom of the plan. In my deliberate judgment a confederacy made up of slaveholding and non-slaveholding States is, in the nature of things, the strongest of all popular governments. African slavery has been, and is, eminently conservative. It makes the absolute political equality of the white race everywhere practicable. It dispenses with the English order of nobility, and leaves every white man, North and South, owning slaves or owning none, the equal of every other white man. It has reconciled universal suffrage throughout the free States with the stability of government.

What, then, sir, with so many causes impelling to reunion, keeps us apart to-day? Hate, passion, antagonism, revenge, all heated seven times hotter by war. Sir, these, while they last, are the most powerful of all motives with a people, and with the individual man; but fortunately they are least durable. They hold a divided sway in the same bosoms with the nobler qualities of love, justice, reason, placability; and, except when at their height, are weaker than the sense of interest, and always, in States at least, give way to it at last. No statesman who yields himself up to them can govern wisely or well; and no State whose policy is controlled by them can either prosper or endure. But war is both their offspring and their ailment, and while it lasts all other motives are subordinate. The virtues of peace cannot flourish, cannot even find development in the midst of fighting; and this civil war keeps in motion the centrifugal forces of the Union, and gives to them increased strength and activity every day. But such, and so many and powerful, in my judgment, are the cementing or centripetal agencies impelling us together that nothing but perpetual war and strife can keep us always divided.

And now, sir, if it be the will of all sections to unite, then upon what terms? Sir, between the South and most of the States of the North, and all of the West, there is but one subject in controversy—slavery. It is the only question, said Mr. Calhoun twenty-five years ago, of sufficient magnitude and potency to divide this Union; and divide it it will, he added, or drench the country in blood if not arrested. It has done both. But settle it on the original basis of the Constitution, and give to each section the power to protect itself within the Union, and now, after the terrible lessons of the past two years, the Union will be stronger than before, and, indeed, endure for ages. Woe to the man, North or South, who, to the third or fourth generation, should teach men disunion.

And now the way to reunion: what so easy? Behold to-day two separate governments in one country, and without a natural dividing line; with two presidents and cabinets, and a double congress; and yet each under a constitution so exactly similar, the one to the other, that a stranger could scarce discern the difference. Was ever folly and madness like this? Sir, it is not in the nature of things that it should so continue long.

But why speak of ways or terms of reunion now? The will is yet wanting in both sections. Union is consent and good will and fraternal affection. War is force, hate, revenge. Is the country tired at last of war? Has the experiment been tried long enough? Has sufficient blood been shed, treasure expended, and misery inflicted in both the North and the South? What then? Stop fighting. Make an armistice—no formal treaty. Withdraw your army from the seceded States. Reduce both armies to a fair and sufficient peace establishment. Declare absolute free trade between the North and South. Buy and sell. Agree upon a *zollverein*. Recall your fleets. Break up your blockade. Reduce your navy. Restore travel. Open up railroads. Reëstablish the telegraph. Reunite your express companies. No more *Monitors* and ironclads, but set your friendly steamers and steam ships again in motion. Visit the North and West. Visit the South. Exchange newspapers. Migrate. Intermarry. Let slavery alone. Hold elections at the appointed times. Let us choose a new President in sixty-four. And when the gospel of peace shall have descended again from

Heaven into their hearts, and the gospel of abolition and of hate been expelled, let your clergy and the churches meet again in Christian intercourse, North and South. Let the secret orders and voluntary associations everywhere reunite as brethren once more. In short, give to all the natural and all the artificial causes which impel us together their fullest sway. Let time do his office—drying tears, dispelling sorrows, mellowing passion, and making herb and grass and tree to grow again upon the hundred battlefields of this terrible war.

"But this is recognition." It is not formal recognition, to which I will not consent. Recognition now, and attempted permanent treaties about boundary, travel, and trade, and partition of Territories, would end in a war fiercer and more disastrous than before. Recognition is absolute disunion; and not between the slave and the free States, but with Delaware and Maryland as part of the North and Kentucky and Missouri part of the West. But wherever the actual line, every evil and mischief of disunion is implied in it. And for similar reasons, sir, I would not at this time press hastily a convention of the States. The men who now would hold seats in such a convention would, upon both sides, if both agreed to attend, come together full of the hate and bitterness inseparable from a civil war. No, sir; let passion have time to cool and reason to resume its sway. It cost thirty years of desperate and most wicked patience and industry to destroy or impair the magnificent temple of this Union. Let us be content if within three years we shall be able to restore it.

But certainly what I propose is informal, practical recognition. And that is precisely what exists to-day, and has existed, more or less defined, from the first. Flags of truce, exchange of prisoners, and all your other observances of the laws, forms, and courtesies of war are acts of recognition. Sir, does any man doubt to-day that there is a Confederate Government at Richmond, and that it is a "belligerent"? Even the Secretary of State has discovered it at last, though he has written ponderous folios of polished rhetoric to prove that it is not. Will continual war, then, without extended and substantial success, make the Confederate States any the less a government in fact?

"But it confesses disunion." Yes, just as the surgeon who sets your fractured limb in splints, in order that it may be healed, admits that it is broken. "But the Government will have failed to 'crush out the rebellion.'" Sir, it has failed. You went to war to prove that we had a Government. With what result? To the people of the loyal States it has, in your hands, been the Government of King Stork, but to the Confederate States, of King Log. "But the rebellion will have triumphed." Better triumph to-day than ten years hence. But I deny it. The rebellion will at last be crushed out in the only way in which it ever was possible. "But no one will be hung at the end of war." Neither will there be, though the war should last half a century, except by the mob or the hand of arbitrary power. But really, sir, if there is to be no hanging, let this Administration, and all who have done its bidding everywhere, rejoice and be exceeding glad.

And now, sir, allow me a word upon a subject of very great interest at this moment, and most important it may be in its influence upon the future—FOREIGN MEDIATION. I speak not of armed and hostile intervention, which I would resist as long as but one man was left to strike a blow at the invader. But friendly mediation—the kindly offer of an impartial power to stand as a daysman between the contending parties in this most bloody and exhausting strife—ought to be met in a spirit as cordial and ready as that in which it is proffered. It would be churlish to refuse. Certainly it is not consistent with the former dignity of this Government to ask for mediation; neither, sir, would it befit its ancient magnanimity to reject it. As proposed by the Emperor of France,[1] I would accept it at once. Now is the auspicious moment. It is the speediest, easiest, most graceful mode of suspending hostilities. Let us hear no more of the mediation of cannon and the sword. The day for all that has gone by. Let us be statesmen at last.

Very grand, indeed, would be the tribunal before which the great question of the union of these States and the final destiny of this continent for ages should be heard, and historic through all time the embassadors who should argue it. And, if both belligerents consent, let the subjects in controversy be referred to Switzerland, or Russia, or any other impartial and incorruptible power or state in Europe. But at last, sir, the people of these several States here, at home, must be the final arbiter of this great quarrel in America; and the people and States of the Northwest, the mediators who shall stand, like the prophet, betwixt the living and the dead, that the plague of disunion may be stayed.

The speech of Mr. Vallandigham was replied to by John A. Bingham [O.].

[1] Napoleon III.

THE UNION WORTH THE COSTLIEST SACRIFICE

JOHN A. BINGHAM, M. C.

My colleague tells us that the war ought to stop; that it should not continue a day nor an hour. He is for the Union, he tells us, and against the employment of the only means by which the Union can be this day maintained, the armed power of the people themselves. There can be no Union as it was, unless by arms you sustain, over all the Republic, the Constitution as the supreme law of the land; and yet the gentleman says the war ought to stop; that it should not continue a day nor an hour. Half of his speech is devoted to the task of satisfying the people that he is for the Constitution as it is and the Union as it was. Let us see. He tells us frankly that he voted neither men nor money to carry on the war. Suppose all the representatives in this hall had followed his example, had acted as he declares he has acted in the cause of the Union, what would have been the result? No bill authorizing the enlistment of volunteers in defence of your flag, no appropriation of money for arming, equipping, and keeping in the field six hundred thousand defenders of the Union, no arm lifted to support the tottering pillars of the Republic, shaking in this wild storm of rebellion. All would have been abandoned. The gentleman who says he is for the Union as it was would have abandoned all to the tender mercies of this armed rebellion, which has multiplied those graves all over the land to which the gentleman refers with so much tenderness, and so much regret for those who fill them; fallen, as he says, by reason of this unconstitutional war. The gentleman could not find it in his heart to denounce the rebellion as unconstitutional, but only the war on the part of the Government for the suppression of that rebellion is unconstitutional.

This is the last phase of that democracy which has brought this ruin upon the country. I do not say that everybody of the party to which the gentleman belongs was of his mind; but I do say, and I challenge contradiction in saying it, that, but for the aid and comfort which that gentleman and his party have given to this rebellion from its inception to this hour, this ruin, to which he points so significantly to-day, wrought by this terrible conflict of arms, and which has reached almost every hearthstone in the land, never had been. In my judgment, the gentleman, and those of his party who have agreed and coöperated with him, are not clear of the blood shed in this war. I am as tolerant of conflicting opinions as the gentleman or any other man; but I cannot be expected to be tolerant of the charge made by the gentleman this day, that those who stand by the country and by the Constitution, by reason of their fidelity to duty, violate the Constitution; nor can I be tolerant of the demand that the only means by which the Government can be maintained shall be withdrawn from its support, and the country left naked to its enemies. That is the point I make with the gentleman to-day. He seems to assume that there is no difficulty in the way to a restoration, a speedy restoration of peace and of the Union, if your armies are disbanded, if the war for the Union only ceases, and ceases at once. There is not a word of denunciation from the gentleman's lips against this rebellion, and he assumes and takes it for granted that secession is a constitutional right; and by way of glorifying these infernal architects of our country's ruin inquires, were not our fathers rebels like unto them? I thank him for his candor in so plainly announcing his opinion, though constrained to differ with him in his opinions and his conclusions.

My colleague, who talks to-day about the Union as it was, is the same gentleman who introduced, in February, 1861, in aid of this rebellion, the proposition to "divide the United States into four sections," and to arm, by an amendment to the Constitution, the rebellious section of country—the fifteen slave States—with the power to legalize secession, in utter disregard of every free State in the Union, and without the consent of any of them. I do not think that a gentleman occupying that position upon the records of the country has a right to denounce anybody as opponents of the Constitution and the Union; much less do I suppose it becomes him to assume that he is the special guardian of the "Constitution as it is and the Union as it was."

The gentleman was very correct in remarking that it would be a most singular spectacle, indeed, to have two separate governments within the limits of territory which God and nature had designed should be under one government, and be the common heritage of one people. I agree with him; and yet the gentleman managed and contrived a device by which the American people, if they had accepted the proposition, would have consented that that very result might be accomplished.

And yet the gentleman is for "the Union as it was." The gentleman seems to be horrified by the thought of two separate governments existing upon this common heritage of one people, which God, by its mountains, and its lakes, and its magnificent rivers, has declared shall never be partitioned. His premises and his conclusions are strangely at fault with each other. The gentleman is for the Union, and at the same moment for disunion. Disband your armies, and let the war for the Union cease, says the gentleman.

What then? The South would be independent of the North, and the South would be triumphant over your violated Constitution and shattered Union. The gentleman so assumed, and hence his resolutions of this session contemplate and speak of ''a final treaty of peace'' with these rebels as a foreign and independent power. The gentleman further assumes—and I would like to know by what authority—that if we withdraw our armies, if we lay down our arms, if we cease to make war upon the rebels, they will come back into the Union under a treaty of peace. I would like to know by what authority he says so. If he knows it, he ought to give the House the benefit of his information. If it is a mere matter of speculation with him, why, of course, he has a right to indulge in his speculations, but we may be pardoned if we question the correctness of them. Has he any definite information? The gentleman is silent upon that subject.

Mr. Vallandigham.—Will you allow me time to finish my speech?

Mr. Bingham.—That is an unreasonable request.

Mr. Vallandigham.—Then I have said all I desire to say to the gentleman.

Mr. Bingham.—I supposed the gentleman had. I have this to say in reply to the gentleman, that I doubt very much whether the gentleman is authorized to speak for these rebels to that extent. To whatever extent he may be their mouthpiece, I venture to doubt his authority to say for them that if we lay down our arms and surrender to them, and allow them to proclaim their independence and their triumph over us and over our common Government, they will then consent to come back and be governed by the Constitution and the laws. I have no doubt that the gentleman may say many things by their authority, but that is one thing I do not think he is allowed to say by his master, Jefferson Davis, yet.

Here the speaker discussed the conduct of President Buchanan's Administration as based on the policy proposed by Mr. Vallandigham, and charged that this conduct had brought on the war.

And with such a rôle as was thus played in the capital of the nation by that Democratic cabinet council, this gentleman who helped to put them there has the effrontery to come here and arraign men for making war on these innocent, unoffending rebels. According to his logic we should have sat silent, and allowed those gentlemen to plunder the people of the money in their treasury on the one hand, and to rob them of the means of self-defence and self-preservation on the other. The suggestion of the gentleman is in perfect keeping with the conduct of that Cabinet. Disband your army, he says. Leave the field to these rebels. Allow them to proclaim themselves to all the world independent of your authority. Allow the Union to be dissevered, and thereupon go to work and settle the difficulty, in the language of the gentleman's resolution, by "a final treaty of peace." That would be a spectacle for gods and men to look on with wonder—the Government of the United States engaged in a final treaty of peace with Robert Toombs and Jefferson Davis, and John B. Floyd and John Letcher of Virginia, and John Slidell and James Mason, with the gentleman from Ohio chief in their counsel.

But the gentleman, not content with simply making this suggestion, comes here to-day to discredit the Government in the face of the world, and says, with an air of triumph, "how can you carry on the war? Can it continue? Can you borrow more money? Can you obtain any more revenue by taxation?" And he undertakes to answer, for all the loyal people of this great country, "no." I ask him again for his authority. I deny the correctness of his conclusion. I would despair of the Republic if I thought that the millions who people all this broad land of ours, from the rock-bound coast of New England to the golden gates of the Pacific, were, like the gentleman from Ohio, ready to lay their hands upon their mouths, and their mouths in the dust,[1] crying before these armed rebels and thieves, "unclean, unclean, unclean." The people, sir, occupy no such position, thank God, and I trust they never will; because I believe that the spirit of the Puritans, at which the gentleman affects to sneer to-day, runs through their veins. "Ah," says my colleague, "you can borrow no more money; you can raise no more revenue by taxation." I take it that, in this instance, the wish of my colleague is father to the thought. He would, if he could, have those who hold the purse-strings in this land withhold from the Government the means of support. I have the right to infer, from his words, that he would, if he

[1] See speech of Geo. E. Pugh, Vol. V, page 242.

could, induce the loyal people of the land to withhold the payment of taxes in support of their own Government. And yet he is for the Union as it was and for the Constitution as it is!

The gentleman refers to Washington, whose bones, he says, are disturbed by this unconstitutional war for the Union. Has the gentleman, when he talks thus—suggesting to the people a disregard of law, a withholding of taxes, a refusal to support their Government—forgotten those grand words of Washington, which ought to be written to-day over the lintel of every door in the land: "the Constitution which at any time exists is sacredly obligatory on all until changed by the act of the whole people"? I think that admonition of Washington a sufficient response to the suggestions of the gentleman to the good people of this land to pay no more taxes, not to submit to their own laws, to allow the Union to be dismembered, and the heritage, which God himself has declared should be the common heritage of one people, to be divided. And for what purpose? Why, that it may be united again. I suppose the gentleman's philosophy is that the best way to preserve a man's life is to kill him, in the first place, merely for the purpose of showing his skill in restoring him to life again. He would destroy the Union to-day by disbanding the army; he would destroy the Union to-day by destroying the public confidence in the Government; he would destroy it by withholding from the Government the revenues necessary to carry on the war. And after that is done, he would restore it by some strange machinery, by some curious power of enchantment which he possesses. I warn the gentleman to lay no such flattering unction to his soul. He who would put out the light now burning on your altars had better be careful, before he does that work, to inquire what earthly power shall that light relume.

My colleague would consent that the pillars of the temple of our liberties should be shaken down, in the vain belief that he has the power to rear them again in all their just and beautiful proportions. I trust in God that my colleague's day-dream is not to be realized. I feel the conviction that those who reared the proportions of this beautiful fabric of American empire were mighty men, whom God taught to build for glory and for beauty. They were men who are not seen in every generation, or in every century. They were men of that large discourse that looks before and after. They were men fitted of God to accomplish the great work of laying the foundations of a great and free commonwealth.

In this hour of peril my colleague tells us to follow the example of Moses. He said he was one of the greatest statesmen that ever lived. I think it most likely. He wants us to follow the example of Moses; but what he meant by the suggestion I am not sure that I fully comprehend.

OWEN LOVEJOY [Ill.].—To lead the slaves out of the house of bondage.

MR. BINGHAM.—He informed us that Moses, when he wanted to do justice to his people, when he wanted to restore the authority of good government, took care to leave the land of Egypt, and lead them out of that country. Does the gentleman mean by that suggestion that we ought to follow the lead of some Moses—himself for example—get up and leave this goodly heritage of ours to be occupied exclusively by those rebels in arms, who have sworn that they will not have this Government of the people to rule over them? I cannot infer anything else. And if that be what he means, then I have this to say to him: that the right of expatriation is a right secured under the Constitution and laws of the United States to all its citizens; and if it be according to his mind to gather up his bundle under his arm, and to go into distant parts in order to accommodate these rebels, he has a perfect right to exercise his privilege. But I beg leave to suggest that those of us who think otherwise shall be permitted to stand by the old flag, and to remain on our native heath undisturbed, so long as it shall please God to let us live.

If he meant anything else than this bright suggestion, I would like to know what he did mean? My friend on my left suggests that he meant to lead the people out of their bondage into the land of their liberty. [Laughter.]

I hope the gentleman will not repudiate the law of his great law-giver—and he is also my great law-giver and model statesman. If we have any respect for Moses's law, in my belief the first act to be done by the nation should be to proclaim to these rebels, in the words uttered by this great law-giver, which he received from the Almighty himself in the midst of the darkness and earthquake of the mountain: "Thou shalt not steal." [Laughter.] They are attempting to steal your country and mine; they are attempting to steal your property and mine; they are attempting to steal the heritage of your children and mine. I ask my colleague whether he will consent that they shall steal any portion of this common territory of our country or not?

MR. VALLANDIGHAM.—I will consent that my colleague may volunteer to prevent it, if he wishes.

Mr. Bingham.—Will my colleague really consent that I may volunteer? [Laughter.]

Mr. Vallandigham.—Yes, sir. My colleague and myself will be in the same category, at leisure after the 4th of March, and perhaps we may volunteer together.

Mr. Bingham.—I take courage from that, for the inference to be drawn, both from the spoken arguments of my colleague and his official conduct in this House, is that he would permit nobody to volunteer. [Applause in the gallery.]

The gentleman would disband your army, withhold all supplies, and permit me alone to volunteer against all these rebels in arms. That is magnanimity. Talk about volunteering, sneeringly, when you, who have sworn to support the Constitution of the United States, stand by and see it torn and rent in tatters, and deny the right to maintain it by arms. When violent hands are laid upon the old flag of the Union, stained, as it is, all over with the blood of its defenders, shed by their assassins and murderers, you deny the right to uphold it, and refuse to vote supplies to your citizen soldiery, who peril all things earthly for the majesty of the law and in defence of their own institutions. You talk about volunteering! [Applause in the galleries.]

My colleague said that you cannot maintain this Union, or the authority of this Government, by force of arms; that you must do it by compromise; and he undertakes to make this good by some carefully considered references to history. There is one thing in the history of the world which he has overlooked, and that is this great fact, that there is not a single well-authenticated instance upon record of a great government, assailed by internal dissensions and armed rebellion, which submitted and surrendered to the rebellion and survived—not one. Yet the gentleman would have us, in the light of that great warning, lay down our arms, disband our armies, submit to the rebellion for the time being, and undertake to settle this great controversy afterward in favor of republican institutions by compromise! No government can survive a base surrender of its own authority to armed rebels. The rebels in that event become the government.

Mr. Speaker, I know the effect of such an appeal to the people of the country. I know that the good people of this land, who have given the first born of their homes for the defence of the Union and the Constitution and the suppression of the rebellion, love their noble sons and cherish them as they do the apple of their eye. I know that after their day's work is done, in the quiet twilight of the evening they mourn over their absence and the broken circle of their homes. I beg them to remember that, though by disbanding your army they may for the moment make whole again the golden circle of their homes, they may thereby lose to themselves and their children a country. I ask them to remember that beautiful utterance, than which none more beautiful ever fell from human lips, of one of the dying Fathers of the Republic, "I commit my spirit to God and my daughter to my country." How could he, how could any man, die in peace while leaving his child without a country and a government to shelter and protect it when he was gone?

No, sir, there is something more important to be considered here to-day than the question whether this life or that life, even though it be the noblest and the most promising in the land, shall survive this war, and that question is, shall the Republic live immortal among the nations, and cover with the ægis of its protection your children and mine, and all the children of this land, when we ourselves shall be no more upon the earth? Yes, sir, the great question of to-day is, shall the Republic live? Any sacrifice of blood, any present loss to us of "this intellectual being," is not too great to be made, if thereby we may maintain intact that Constitution which our fathers gave us.

The theme of Mr. Bingham's speech received simpler and briefer but even more effective treatment by the President a few months later.

On November 19, 1863, the National Cemetery of soldiers killed at the battle of Gettysburg was dedicated in the presence of a vast array of people assembled from all parts of the Union upon the battlefield. The orator of the day was Edward Everett. At the close of his long address, composed in the finished periods of that "classic" order of American oratory of which he was the greatest living master, when the thunder of applause that it evoked had ceased, President Lincoln rose and spoke a few heart-felt words which so moved the deeps of emotion in his hearers that many sat spell-bound and silent after the speaker had finished. As the President's letter to Mr. Everett, written on the following day, indicates Mr. Lincoln inferred from this reception that the speech was a "failure," but he was quickly disabused of that idea by evidences coming from every part of the Union of the deep impression it had made on the hearts of his countrymen.

"These Dead Shall Not Have Died in Vain"

Speech of President Lincoln at Gettysburg

Fourscore and seven years ago our fathers brought forth on this continent a new nation, conceived in liberty, and dedicated to the proposition that all men are created equal.

Now we are engaged in a great civil war, testing whether that nation, or any nation so conceived and so dedicated, can long endure. We are met on a great battlefield of that war. We have come to dedicate a portion of that field as a final resting-place for those who here gave their lives that that nation might live. It is altogether fitting and proper that we should do this.

But, in a larger sense, we cannot dedicate—we cannot consecrate—we cannot hallow—this ground. The brave men, living and dead, who struggled here, have consecrated it far above our poor power to add or detract. The world will little note nor long remember what we say here, but it can never forget what they did here. It is for us, the living, rather, to be dedicated here to the unfinished work which they who fought here have thus far so nobly advanced. It is rather for us to be here dedicated to the great task remaining before us—that from these honored dead we take increased devotion to that cause for which they gave the last full measure of devotion; that we here highly resolve that these dead shall not have died in vain; that this nation, under God, shall have a new birth of freedom; and that government of the people, by the people, for the people, shall not perish from the earth.

The declaration that "the war is a failure" was embodied in the next national platform of the Democracy [1864], but the party's candidate for President, General George B. McClellan, virtually repudiated it. Lincoln was triumphantly reëlected, and in his second inaugural address, on March 4, 1865, justified the prosecution of the war until slavery, the curse from which it sprang, should forever be abolished.

"THE ALMIGHTY HAS HIS PURPOSES"

SECOND INAUGURAL OF PRESIDENT LINCOLN

Neither party expected for the war the magnitude or the duration which it has already attained.   Neither anticipated that the cause of the conflict might cease with, or even before, the conflict itself should cease.   Each looked for an easier triumph, and a result less fundamental and astounding.   Both read the

LITTLE MAC. IN HIS GREAT TWO-HORSE ACT, IN THE PRESIDENTIAL CANVASS
OF 1864

From the collection of the New York Historical Society

same Bible, and pray to the same God; and each invokes his aid against the other.   It may seem strange that any men should dare to ask a just God's assistance in wringing their bread from the sweat of other men's faces; but let us judge not, that we may be not judged.   The prayers of both could not be answered—that of neither has been answered fully.

The Almighty has his own purposes.   "Woe unto the world because of offences! for it must needs be that offences come, but woe to that man by whom the offence cometh."   If we shall suppose that American slavery is one of those offences which, in the providence of God, must needs come, but which, having continued through his appointed time, he now wills to remove, and that he gives to both North and South this terrible war, as the woe due to those by whom the offence came, shall we discern therein any departure from those divine attributes which the believers in a living God always ascribe to him? Fondly do we hope—fervently do we pray—that this mighty scourge of war may speedily pass away. Yet, if God wills that it continue until all the wealth piled by the bondman's two hundred and fifty years of unrequited toil shall be sunk, and until every drop of blood drawn with the lash shall be paid by another drawn with the sword, as was said three thousand years ago, so still it must be said, ''The judgments of the Lord are true and righteous altogether.''

With malice toward none; with charity for all; with firmness in the right, as God gives us to see the right, let us strive on to finish the work we are in; to bind up the nation's wounds; to care for him who shall have borne the battle, and for his widow, and his orphan—to do all which may achieve and cherish a just and lasting peace among ourselves, and with all nations.

CHAPTER XI

CONSCRIPTION

Henry Wilson [Mass.] Proposes in the Senate Bill to Draft Soldiers—His
Speech on the Bill—It Is Passed—Debate in the House on the Bill:
in Favor, William M. Davis [Pa.], James H. Campbell [Pa.], John H.
Bingham [O.]; Opposed, Charles J. Biddle [Pa.], Chilton A. White
[O.], Clement L. Vallandigham [O.], James C. Robinson [Ill.], Samuel
S. Cox [O.], Daniel W. Voorhees [Ind.]—Bill Is Passed—Conscription
by the South.

ON February 16, 1863, Henry Wilson [Mass.]
brought before the Senate a bill for a draft of
soldiers between the ages of twenty and forty-
five to prosecute the war.

It was passed upon the same day after considerable
debate and amendment. After a long and heated discussion in the House it was passed by that body, with
various amendments, on February 25. The House
amendments were accepted by the Senate on March 2,
and the bill was approved by President Lincoln on
March 3.

In its final form its preamble read as follows:

Whereas there now exist in the United States an insurrection
and rebellion against the authority thereof, and it is, under the
Constitution of the United States, the duty of the Government
to suppress insurrection and rebellion, to guarantee to each State
a republican form of government, and to preserve the public
tranquillity; and, whereas, for these high purposes, a military
force is indispensable, to raise and support which all persons
ought willingly to contribute; and, whereas, no service can be
more praiseworthy and honorable than that which is rendered
for the maintenance of the Constitution and Union, and the consequent preservation of free government; be it enacted, etc.

The Conscription Act

Congress, February 16-25, 1863

Senator Wilson.—The needs of the nation demand that we should fill the regiments now in the field, worn and wasted by disease and death, by enrolling and drafting the population of the country under the constitutional authority "to raise and support armies."

That grant of power carries with it, in the language of "The Federalist," "all the powers requisite to the complete execution of its trust."

Sir, this grant to Congress of power "to raise and support armies" carries with it the right to do it by voluntary enlistment or by compulsory process. If men cannot be raised by voluntary enlistment then the Government must raise men by involuntary means, or the power to raise and support armies for the public defence is a nullity. James Monroe said, in a letter to the chairman of the Military Committee of the House of Representatives, in 1814, that—

"It would be absurd to suppose that Congress could not carry this power into effect otherwise than by accepting the voluntary service of individuals. It might happen that an army could not be raised in that mode, whence the power would have been granted in vain."

It is a high and sacred duty, resting alike upon all the citizens of the Republic, upon the sons of toil and misfortune and the more favored few, to labor, to suffer, ay, to die, if need be, for their country. Never since the dawn of creation have the men of any age been summoned to the performance of a higher or nobler duty than are the men of this generation in America. The passage of this great measure will clothe the President with ample authority to summon forth the sons of the Republic to the performance of the high and sacred duty of saving their country, now menaced, and the periled cause of civilization and freedom in America, and of winning the lasting gratitude of coming ages, and that enduring renown which follows every duty nobly and bravely done. The enactment of this bill will give confidence to the Government, strength to the country, and joy to the worn and weary soldiers of the Republic around their camp fires in the land of the rebellion.

There was unanimous acceptance by the Senate of the principles of the bill, the discussion being upon its details. In the House, however, the principle was strenuously opposed, chiefly by the Northern "Peace" Democrats, when the bill came up for discussion on February 23. A provision to punish by fine or imprisonment any one who should violently resist the draft or who should counsel or aid any person to resist it was the particular object of attack.

Charles J. Biddle [Pa.] objected to the bill. He said the effect of it was to turn the militia, the constitutional defence of the people against any aggression of their rights, into a regular army, the unquestioning instrument of the Government.

The Executive, empowered, as the very word shows, only to execute known laws, establishes "martial law," that is, "the will of a conqueror," over all the people of the North. I feel a personal interest, an interest as a citizen, that things should not go on thus; for I believe it is at the constant risk of lighting up the flame of social revolution around your hearthstones and mine. Let us be warned in time. Have you noted the significant circumstance of men fresh from unjust imprisonment in Federal dungeons being received with high public honors and elevated to high positions?

WILLIAM M. DAVIS [Pa.].—Will the gentleman inform the House who it is that will inaugurate a revolution in the North— the Republican party or the party with which the gentleman acts?

MR. BIDDLE.—I think, sir, it will be an outraged people, without respect to party. I believe that the spirit which animated Hampden and the men of the English Revolution is not extinct in the age in which we live. That flame was brightened by the great example of the men of our own Revolution.

James H. Campbell [Pa.] replied to his colleague (Mr. Biddle).

Mr. Speaker, in the early stages of this rebellion it became necessary to exercise an extreme power to arrest the traitors who were circulating through the Northern States hatching treason and poisoning the minds of the people, because at that time the life of this nation was in daily and hourly peril; no man knew the extent of the conspiracy against the Union; we were surrounded by spies and traitors everywhere. They were in the legislative bodies of the country; they were with the armies in the field; they were in every town, village, and hamlet of the North; and I commend the President and War Department for the vigor with which they caused traitors to be arrested and incarcerated, until it could be ascertained where the country stood, and proper measures could be perfected for their trial and conviction.

Sir, in all ages and under all civilized governments there have been instances of the exercise of extreme power whenever the life of the nation has been in peril. Extreme peril makes extreme necessity; and nations, like individuals, must act accordingly. When the assassin enters your house at night you do not pause to take the ordinary measures that might be resorted to in broad daylight and under ordinary circumstances. You first defend the life of your family, and afterward take the necessary measures to convict and punish the culprit.

Let me tell gentlemen on the other side that, so far from condemning these arrests, it would be better for them if they could read the writing on the wall, and make their peace with liberty and their country while there is yet time. If they cannot see the evidence of a healthy reaction among the masses they are blind to the signs of the times. The error of the Government has been *leniency*. If it had given to traitors a drum-head court-martial and hempen cord, it would better have pleased the loyal men in the United States. [Applause in the galleries.] If I mistake not, the day is not far distant when the people will be so aroused against rebellion that traitors, their aiders and abettors, will call upon the rocks and mountains to cover them.

Now, sir, there was an intimation thrown out by my colleague —often repeated from that side of the House—that if we proceed with proper measures—measures which they are pleased to call unconstitutional—to make arrests and put down the rebellion, we will stir up revolution at the North. I am not afraid of any social or political revolution in the free States. If gentlemen see proper to inaugurate social or political armed revolution at the North, I hope they will do it at once; the sooner the traitorous effort is made the better. There is loyalty enough in the North to take care of any treason that can be found among the free States. Our soldiers in the army can take care of the rebels in front, and loyal men enough will rise up in the free States to dispose of the rebels within their limits. [Applause in the galleries.]

Until the last traitor is compelled to submit to lawful authority, to the Constitution and laws, we can have no peace; till that is done peace is infamy, peace is anarchy, peace is destruction, and no loyal and judicious man will advocate it. The rebels scout and scorn all propositions of peace, even if we were disposed to listen to them. There is no alternative but to conquer or be conquered; to live freemen or die slaves. And I am one of those who are ready to vote the last man and the last dollar for the accomplishment of the great object before us. I am ready to fight it out by land and by sea, as long as may be necessary to crush out the rebels themselves, and all their sympathizers at home and abroad. [Applause in the galleries.]

Chilton A. White [O.] followed Mr. Campbell in a speech against the bill.

This bill provides for the appointment of a provost marshal in every congressional district in the United States. It provides for the appointment of persons for taking the census of those who are subject to military duty. It provides for the appointment of draft commissioners. All these officers will be appointed by the executive officer of the United States, and they will be violent political partisans, holding the personal liberty and the personal security of every citizen within the congressional districts of the United States, as it were, in the hollow of their hands. These provost marshals are armed with the power to arrest for treasonable practices. In God's name, what does that mean? This is the most singular definition of crime I have ever seen embodied into any statutory enactment of this or any other country. What are treasonable practices? Who are to determine what they are? Are these provost marshals, many of them unskilled in the law, to determine that question? Why, it will have as many definitions and as many meanings as there are provost marshals to construe the statute. If a man gets up and argues upon the stump against this wicked, this corrupt, and this usurping Administration, he will be denounced as engaged in treasonable practices, according to the view of these political partisans, who are made the judges of the loyalty of every man in this country.

Why, sir, if the devil himself were to tax his ingenuity he could not invent a more complete device for destroying the liberty and happiness of the people than this bill, as illustrated in the light of the history of this country for the past eighteen months.

Treasonable practices! Why, sir, in the opinion of many of those gentlemen upon this floor who assume to be the especial

guardians of the loyalty of the country, I have no doubt I would
be considered as engaged in treasonable practices while denouncing this measure and this scheme, as I do denounce it here and
now.

Oh, but it is said that these men are only to be arrested and
detained for a short period of time, and for a temporary purpose, which will pass away with the occasion, and that after the
draft is all over they are to be delivered over to the judicial
tribunals of the country. Delivered over! what for? Is there
any man here who ever expects that anybody will ever be tried
for treasonable practices? No, sir; it is a device; it is a catch;
it is an excuse; it is an apology, to afford some justification for
this monstrous and outrageous provision. No trial is intended,
and no judicial tribunal will ever hear of any of these treasonable practices. This clause is incorporated here to afford an
apology for illegal arrests. Men will be arrested without oath,
and without show of probable cause. They will be detained without the benefit of a speedy and public trial by an impartial jury
of the country. It is but the renewal of that reign of terror
which we passed through but a few days before our election last
fall.

But another new kind of trial is established and invented by
this bill. If any person shall dissuade another from the performance of military duty he is to be considered as guilty of
crime and subject to summary arrest and trial. What does that
mean? Does it mean that if a man denounces the policy of this
Administration as wicked, corrupt, and dangerous to the liberties
of the people; if he denounces the acts of usurpation of which
it has been guilty; if he denounces the monstrous policy upon
which it at present conducts the war in open and flagrant violation of the Constitution, and in derogation of the rights and established institutions of the States, is he to be taken and held
as discouraging persons from the performance of military duty?
If so, then I suppose he would be held guilty, and would be subject to military arrest.

We all know what construction will be placed upon this provision. They are unjust and ingenious devices by which the
people are to be deprived of this last vestige of liberty. All this
might be borne if the injured citizen could appeal to the local
State judicial tribunals for the redress of injuries thus inflicted
upon him; but by your indemnity bill provision is made for taking all this class of cases, by a novel and unusual mode of appeal, to the United States courts; and when thus appealed you
have provided that under the plea of the general issue evidence

may be offered to show that the wrong was committed upon probable cause, or under color of authority derived from the President or a law of Congress, and such proof shall constitute a good and valid defence to the action, and the court shall so charge the jury, and the jury shall so find. Thus you declare by law what shall be a defence; you put the charge to the jury in the mouth of the court, and compel the jury to find accordingly. What more effectual immunity could be granted for the commission of these wrongs upon the rights and the liberties of the citizen than are here given? Not only the independence, but the very existence of the local State judicial tribunals is struck down so far as this class of cases is concerned, and it is sought to dog him into submission to these wrongs by compelling him to seek redress in distant courts, under circumstances of great inconvenience and at great cost; and as a further penalty for seeking redress it is provided that if he is non-suited, or fails in the action, he shall pay double costs.

When you have overthrown the constitutions of the States; when you have overthrown the judicial authorities of the States; when you have removed from the citizens every possible means for the protection of their personal liberty and property; when you have done all this, the only refuge which is left, the only appeal which the injured and outraged citizen can make, is to the God of justice and the God of right. And if these outrages are carried to the extent I apprehend they will be, that appeal, as God reigns in heaven, will be made. I tell you that in my section of the State of Ohio the spirit of our citizens will no longer tolerate these things. They will defend the rights of the citizen; and, if you close all the judicial tribunals and every mode of legal redress to them, they will plant themselves upon the constitution of their States and of the United States, and defend themselves in the possession of the rights and liberties guaranteed to them by those instruments, with and by all the means which God and nature have placed in their possession. They have already borne too much, and I tell you they will not bear more.

Why, gentlemen upon the other side of the House say there has not been enough of this thing; that there have not been as many political arrests as should have been made. And they talk about liberty, about free government, and about republican institutions. My God! what ideas of republican institutions, of free government, and of liberty must such men have! What do they mean by these words? Is it that kind of license which permits one party, because they have the power, to seize, without authority of law, condemn without trial, and imprison without process the partisans of another party? Is that the kind of free government they want? Is that the kind of republican institutions which it is desired to perpetuate in this country? Is that the liberty of which you boast so much? Sir, I want liberty, but I want it regulated by law, not by license, not subject to the capricious will of any one man. This bill strikes at the very roots of every immunity that belongs to the citizen. It not only affects his personal liberty, but it even affects the freedom of his speech; it puts a gag in his mouth and will subject him to arrest and imprisonment for words spoken. Why, sir, the theory of our Government is that even error of opinion may be tolerated so long as reason is left free to combat it, or until it seeks to perpetuate itself by force.

We are willing to extend to you, without let or hindrance on our part, all the rights we claim for ourselves. We invite you into the arena before the people, to a full, fair, and unrestrained discussion of the questions at issue between us. Bring to your aid every argument and every reason you can to support your sinking cause; and let it be understood that these same rights which we concede to you we claim and intend to exercise for ourselves, and no earthly power shall prevent us from doing so. God, by a law of His own making, made thought free and left each individual free to select his own form and mode for its expression; and it is not for you, gentlemen, to ascend the throne of the Almighty and attempt to set boundaries to the range of opinion or prescribe the forms of speech in which it shall be expressed, and to denounce your judgments upon men who do not think and speak according to prescribed forms. When God made man in His own image, the noblest of all sublunary beings, a creature endowed with reason and free will, an intellectual being, it became his high prerogative, each one for himself and not one for another, to exercise these faculties; not as he must answer to you, but as he must answer to his Creator, for himself, so he must use and improve his talents for himself; and it is only when opinion seeks to perpetuate itself by force, and not by argument and consent, that it may be met with force. In these respects our Government is but a reflex of the divine mind, and while we on our side support our cause by the persuasive influences of truth, reason, and argument, you on your side have no right to resort to coercive measures against us. If you do, I warn you that an eye for an eye and tooth for tooth will be the law. We intend to walk in the light of our own reason, forming our own judgments and pursuing our own conclusions, supporting them by the inherent power of truth, illustrated by such reason and argument as we can bring to bear. Were we, on all fitting and proper occasions, to refuse to do so, we would violate a trust reposed in us by God himself, and prove ourselves unworthy of our divine Master, fit subjects for degradation and slavery.

Now, sir, I wish to say that I believe this to be a bill that would strike down the rights of the States and the liberties of the citizen, and that, if attempted to be enforced and executed, it will lead to results and calamities in this country which will sadden all our hearts and the hearts of right-minded men everywhere. The time has passed when the people of this country will submit longer to the state of things which has been inaugurated by the party now in power. They know their rights, and, knowing them, they are bent and determined upon maintaining them at all costs and at all hazards. Gentlemen on the other side may take all the comfort they can from any apparent reaction they see going on in the country. We have suffered imprisonment; we have suffered wrongs, and insults, and indignities; our motives of patriotism have been impugned; thousands of our citizens are to-day languishing in your prisons and bastiles, snuffing the damp vapors of solitary dungeons, separated from their families, their business, and all the associations and endearments that cluster around home; and all, sir, for no other crime or offence than that their views and opinions do not exactly correspond with your own; men whose ruling passions are an uncompromising devotion to the Constitution and the Union, but differ with you as to the best means to be employed for their maintenance and support.

Clement L. Vallandigham [O.] followed his colleague in opposing the bill.

Mr. Speaker, I do not propose to discuss this bill at any great length in this House. I am satisfied that there is a settled purpose to enact it into a law, so far as it is possible for the action of the Senate and House and the President to make it such. I appeal, therefore, from you, from them, directly to the country; to a forum where there is no military committee, no previous question, no hour rule, and where the people themselves are the masters. I commend the spirit in which this discussion was commenced by the chairman of the Military Committee [Abraham B. Olin, of New York]. Only let me caution him that he cannot dictate to the minority here what course they shall pursue. But, sir, I regret that I cannot extend the commendation to the gentleman from Pennsylvania [Mr. Campbell] who addressed the House a little while ago. If he or any other gentleman of the majority imagines that any one here is to be deterred by threats from the expression of his opinions, or from giving such votes as he may see fit to give, he has utterly misapprehended the temper and determination of those who sit on this side of the chamber. His threat I hurl back with defiance into his teeth. I spurn it. I spit upon it. That is not the argument to be addressed to equals here; and I therefore most respectfully suggest that hereafter we shall be spared personal denunciation and insinuations against the loyalty of men who sit with me here; men whose devotion to the Constitution and attachment to the Union of these States are as ardent and immovable as yours, and who only differ from you as to the mode of securing the great object nearest their hearts.

Mr. Campbell.—The gentleman will allow me——

Mr. Vallandigham.—I yield for explanation.

Mr. Campbell.—Mr. Speaker, it is a significant fact that the gentleman from Ohio has applied my remarks to himself and others on his side of the House. Why was this done? I was denouncing *traitors* here, and I will denounce them while I have a place upon this floor. It is my duty and my privilege to do so. And, if the gentleman from Ohio chooses to give my remarks a personal application, he can so apply them.

Mr. Vallandigham.—That is enough.

Mr. Campbell.—One moment.

Mr. Vallandigham.—Not another moment after that. I yielded the floor in the spirit of a gentleman, and not to be met in the manner of a blackguard. [Applause and hisses in the galleries.]

Mr. Campbell.—The member from Ohio is a blackguard. [Renewed hisses and applause in the galleries.]

James C. Robinson. [Ill.].—I rise to a question of order. I demand that the galleries be cleared. We have been insulted time and again by contractors and plunderers of the Government in these galleries, and I ask that they be now cleared.

Samuel S. Cox [O.].—I hope my friend from Illinois will not insist on that. Only a very small portion of those in the galleries take part in these disturbances. The fool-killer will take care of them.

Mr. Vallandigham.—I have already said that it is not my purpose to debate the general merits of this bill at large, and for the reason that I am satisfied that argument is of no avail

VI—19

here. I appeal, therefore, to the people. Before them I propose to try this great question—the question of constitutional power, and of the unwise and injudicious exercise of it in this bill. We have been compelled, repeatedly, since the 4th of March, 1861, to appeal to the same tribunal. We appealed to it at the recent election. And the people did pronounce judgment upon our appeal.

Talk to me, indeed, of the leniency of the Executive! too few arrests! too much forbearance by those in power! Sir, it is the people who have been too lenient. They have submitted to your oppressions and wrongs as no free people ought ever to submit. But the day of patient endurance has gone by at last. Mistake them not. They will be lenient no longer. Abide by the Constitution, stand by the laws, restore the Union if *you* can restore it—not by force; you have tried that and failed—Try some other method now—the ancient, the approved, the reasonable way— the way in which the Union was first made. Surrender it not now—not yet—never. But unity is not union; and attempt not, at your peril—I warn you—to coerce unity by the utter destruction of the Constitution and of the rights of the States and the liberties of the people. Union is liberty and consent: unity is despotism and force. For what was the Union ordained? As a splendid edifice to attract the gaze and admiration of the world? As a magnificent temple—a stupendous superstructure of marble and iron, like this Capitol, upon whose lofty dome the bronzed image—hollow and inanimate—of freedom is soon to stand erect in colossal mockery, while the true spirit, the living goddess of liberty, veils her eyes and turns away her face in sorrow, because, upon the altar established here and dedicated by our fathers to her worship, you, a false and most disloyal priesthood, offer up, night and morning, the mingled sacrifices of servitude and despotism? No, sir. It was for the sake of the altar, the service, the religion, the devotees that the temple of the Union was first erected; and, when these are all gone, let the edifice itself perish. Never—never—never will the people consent to lose their own personal and political rights and liberties to the end that you may delude and mock them with the splendid unity of despotism.

Sir, what are the bills which have passed, or are still before, the House? The bill to give the President entire control of the currency—the purse—of the country. A tax bill to clothe him with power over the whole property of the country. A bill to put all power in his hands over the personal liberties of the people. A bill to indemnify him, and all under him, for every act of oppression and outrage already consummated. A bill to enable him to suspend the writ of *habeas corpus* in order to justify or protect him, and every minion of his, in the arrests which he or they may choose to make—arrests, too, for mere opinions' sake. Sir, some two hundred years ago men were burned at the stake, subjected to the horrors of the Inquisition, to all the tortures that the devilish ingenuity of man could invent—for what? For opinions on questions of religion—of man's duty and relation to his God. And now, to-day, for opinions on questions political, under a free Government, in a country whose liberties were purchased by our fathers by seven years' outpouring of blood and expenditure of treasure—we have lived to see men, the born heirs of this precious inheritance, subjected to arrest and cruel imprisonment at the caprice of a President, or a Secretary, or a constable. And, as if that were not enough, a bill is introduced here to-day, and pressed forward to a vote, with the right of debate, indeed—extorted from you by the minority—but without the right to amend, with no more than the mere privilege of protest—a bill which enables the President to bring under his power, as Commander-in-Chief, every man in the United States between the ages of twenty and forty-five—three millions of men. And, as if not satisfied with that, this bill provides, further, that every other citizen, man, woman, and child, under twenty years of age and over forty-five, including those that may be exempt between these ages, shall be also at the mercy—so far as his personal liberty is concerned —of some miserable ''provost marshal'' with the rank of a captain of cavalry who is never to see service in the field; and every congressional district in the United States is to be governed—yes, governed—by this petty satrap—this military eunuch—this Baba—and he even may be black—who is to do the bidding of your Sultan, of his Grand Vizier. Sir, you have but one step further to go—give him the symbols of his office— the Turkish bow-string and the sack.

What is it, sir, but a bill to abrogate the Constitution, to repeal all existing laws, to destroy all rights, to strike down the judiciary and erect upon the ruins of civil and political liberty a stupendous superstructure of despotism. And for what? To enforce law? No, sir. It is admitted now by the legislation of Congress, and by the two proclamations of the President, it is admitted by common consent that the war is for the abolition of negro slavery, to secure freedom to the black man. You tell me, some of you, I know, that it is so prosecuted because this is the only way to restore the Union; but others openly and candidly confess that the purpose of the prosecution of the war is to abolish slavery. And thus, sir, it is that the freedom of the negro is to be purchased, under this bill, at the sacrifice of every right of the white men of the United States.

Sir, I am opposed, earnestly, inexorably opposed, to this measure. If there were not another man in this House to vote against it, if there were none to raise his voice against it, I, at least, dare stand here alone in my place, as a Representative, undismayed, unseduced, unterrified, and heedless of the miserable cry of "disloyalty," of sympathy with the rebellion and with rebels, to denounce it as the very consummation of the conspiracy against the Constitution and the liberties of my country.

Where, now, are your taunts and denunciations, heaped upon the Confederate Government for its conscription, when you, yourselves, become the humble imitators of that government and bring in here a conscription act more odious even than that passed by the Confederate Congress at Richmond? What is this bill? A confession that the people are no longer ready to enlist; that they are not willing to carry on this war longer, until some effort has been made to settle this great controversy in some other way than by the sword. And yet, in addition to the one million two hundred and thirty-seven thousand men who have voluntarily enlisted, you propose now to force the entire body of the people, between the ages of twenty and forty-five, under military law and within the control of the President as Commander-in-Chief of the army for three years, or during the war—which is to say "for life"; aye, sir, for life, and half your army has already found, or will yet find, that their enlistment was for life, too.

Sir, what does all this mean? You were a majority at first; the people were almost unanimously with you, and they were generous and enthusiastic in your support. You abused your power and your trust, and you failed to do the work which you promised. You have lost the confidence, lost the hearts of the people. You are now in a minority at home. And yet what a spectacle is exhibited here to-night! You, an accidental, temporary majority, condemned and repudiated by the people, are exhausting the few remaining hours of your political life in attempting to defeat the popular will, and to compel, by the most desperate and despotic of expedients ever resorted to, the submission of the majority of the people, at home, to the minority, their servants here. Sir, this experiment has been tried before in other ages and countries and its issue always, among a people born free or fit to be free, has been expulsion or death to the conspirators and tyrants.

Have a care, have a care, I entreat you, that you do not press these measures too far. I shall do nothing to stir up an already excited people—not because of any fear of your contemptible petty provost marshals, but because I desire to see no violence or revolution in the North or West. But I warn you now, that whenever, against the will of the people, and to perpetuate power and office in a popular Government which they have taken from you, you undertake to enforce this bill, and, like the destroying angel in Egypt, enter every house for the first-born sons of the people—remember Poland. You cannot and will not be permitted to establish a military despotism.

What do you propose to make the duty of each provost marshal in carrying out the draft? Among other things, that he shall "inquire into and report to the provost marshal-general" —what? Treason. No. Felony? No. Breach of the peace, or violation of law of any kind? No; but "treasonable practices"; yes, *treasonable practices.* What mean you by these strange, ominous words? Whence come they? Sir, they are no more new or original than any other of the cast-off rags filched by this Administration from the lumber-house of other and more antiquated despotisms. The history of European tyranny has taught us somewhat of this doctrine of constructive treason. Treasonable practices! Sir, the very language is borrowed from the old proclamations of the British monarchs some hundreds of years ago. It was this that called forth that English act of Parliament of twenty-fifth Edward III, from which we have borrowed the noble provision against constructive treason in the Constitution of the United States. Arbitrary arrests for no crime known, defined, or limited by law, but for pretended offences, herded together under the general and most comprehensive name of "treasonable practices," had been so frequent in the worst periods of English history, that in the language of the act of Henry IV, "no man knew how to behave himself or what to do or say for doubt of the pains of treason." The statute of Edward III had cut all these fungous, toadstool treasons up by the root; and yet, so prompt is arbitrary power to denounce all opposition to it as treasonable that, as Lord Hale observes—

"Things were so carried by parties and factions in the succeeding reign of Richard II, that this statute was but little observed but as this or that party got the better. So . . . it came to pass that almost every offence that was *or seemed to be* a breach of the faith and allegiance due to the king was, by *construction, consequence, and interpretation*, raised into the offence of high treason.''

But steadily, in better times, the people and the Parliament of England returned to the spirit and letter of the act of Edward III, passed by a Parliament which now, for five hundred years, has been known and honored as *Parliamentum benedictum,* the ''blessed Parliament''—just as this Congress will be known, for ages to come, as ''the accursed Congress.'' Among many other acts, it was declared by a statute, in the first year of the fourth Henry's reign, that *''in no time to come* any treason be judged, otherwise than as ordained by the statute of King Edward III.'' And for nearly two hundred years it has been the aim of the lawyers and judges of England to adhere to the plain letter, spirit, and intent of that act, ''to be extended,'' in the language of Erskine in his noble defence of Hardy, ''by no new or occasional constructions—to be strained by no fancied analogies—to be measured by no rules of political expediency—to be judged of by no theory—to be determined by the wisdom of no individual, however wise—but to be expounded by the simple, genuine letter of the law.''

Such, sir, is the law of treason in England to-day ; and so much of the just and admirable statute of Edward as is applicable to our form of government was embodied in the Constitution of the United States. And yet what have we lived to hear in America daily, not in political harangues or the press only, but in official proclamations and in bills in Congress! Yes, your high officials talk now of ''treasonable practices'' as glibly ''as girls of thirteen do of puppy dogs.'' Treasonable practices! Disloyalty! Who imported these precious phrases and gave them a legal settlement here? Your Secretary of War. He it was who by command of our most noble President authorized every marshal, every sheriff, every township constable, or city policeman in every State in the Union to fix, in his own imagination, what he might choose to call a treasonable or disloyal practice, and then to arrest any citizen at his discretion, without any accusing oath and without due process or any process of law. And now, sir, all this monstrous tyranny, against the whole spirit and the very letter of the Constitution, is to be deliberately embodied in an act of Congress! Your petty provost marshals are to determine what treasonable practices are and ''inquire into,'' detect, spy out, eavesdrop, insnare, and then inform, report to the chief spy at Washington. These, sir, are now to be our American liberties under your Administration. There is not a crowned head in Europe who dare venture on such an experiment. How long, think you, this people will submit? But words, too—conservation or public speech—are to be adjudged "treasonable practices." Men, women, and children are to be haled to prison for free speech. Whoever shall denounce or oppose this Administration; whoever may affirm that war will not restore the Union, and teach men the gospel of peace, may be reported and arrested upon some old grudge, and by some ancient enemy, it may be, and imprisoned as guilty of a treasonable practice.

Sir, there can be but one treasonable practice under the Constitution in the United States. "Treason against the United States," says the Constitution, "shall consist *only* in levying war against them, or in adhering to their enemies, giving them aid and comfort." [Here a Republican member nodded several times and smiled.] Ah, sir, I understand you. But was Lord Chatham guilty of legal treason, treasonable aid and comfort, when he denounced the war against the colonies and rejoiced that America had resisted? Was Burke, or Fox, or Barré guilty when defending the Americans in the British Parliament and demanding conciliation and peace? Were even the Federalists guilty of treason, as defined in the Constitution, for "giving aid and comfort" to the enemy in the war of 1812? Were the Whigs in 1846? Was the Ohio Senator liable to punishment, under the Constitution, and by law, who said, sixteen years ago, in the Senate chamber, when we were at war in Mexico: "If I were a Mexican as I am an American, I would greet your volunteers with bloody hands and welcome them to hospitable graves?" Was Abraham Lincoln guilty because he denounced that same war while a Representative on the floor of this House? Was all this "adhering to the enemy, giving him aid and comfort" within the meaning of this provision?

A MEMBER.—The Democratic papers said so.

MR. VALLANDIGHAM.—Sir, I am speaking now as a lawyer and as a legislator to legislators and lawyers acting under oath and the other special and solemn sanctions of this chamber, and not in the loose language of the political canvass.

The speaker here denounced the treatment accorded those who had been arrested by the Government.

Newspapers, the Bible, letters from home, except under surveillance, a breath of air, a sight of the waves of the sea, or of the mild blue sky, the song of birds, whatever was denied to the prisoner of Chillon, and more, too; yes, even a solitary lamp in the casemate, where a dying prisoner struggled with death, all have been refused to the American citizen accused of disloyal speech or opinions by this most just and merciful Administration.

Says the Constitution:

"The accused shall enjoy the right to have the assistance of counsel for his defence."

And yet your Secretary of State, the "conservative" Seward —the confederate of Thurlow Weed, that treacherous, dissembling foe to constitutional liberty and the true interests of his country—forbade his prisoners to employ counsel, under penalty of prolonged imprisonment.

And here is another order to the same effect, signed by William H. Seward himself, and read to the prisoners at Fort Warren on the 29th of November, 1861:

"Discountenancing and repudiating all such practices"—

The disloyal practice, forsooth, of employing counsel—

"the Secretary of State desires that all the State prisoners may understand *that they are expected to revoke all such engagements now existing and avoid any hereafter,* as they can only lead to new complications and embarrassments to the cases of prisoners on whose behalf *the Government might be disposed to act with liberality.*"

Most magnanimous Secretary! Liberality toward men guilty of no crime, but who, though they had been murderers or pirates, were entitled by the plain letter of the Constitution to have "the assistance of counsel for their defence." Sir, there was but one step further possible, and that short step was taken some months later when the prisoners of state were required to make oath, as the condition of their discharge, that they would not seek their constitutional and legal remedy in court for the wrongs and outrages inflicted upon them.

Sir, incredible as all this will seem some years hence, it has happened, all of it, and more yet untold, within the last twenty months in the United States. Under executive usurpation and by virtue of presidential proclamations and cabinet orders it has been done without law and against Constitution; and now it is proposed to sanction and authorize it all by an equally unconstitutional and void act of Congress. It is a vain thing to seek to cloak all this under the false semblance of law. Liberty is no more guarded or secured and arbitrary power no more hedged in and limited here than under the executive orders of last summer. We know what has already been done, and we will submit to it no longer. Away, then, with your vain clamor about disloyalty, your miserable mockery of treasonable practices. We have read with virtuous indignation in history ages ago of an Englishman whose favorite buck the king had killed and who suffered death as a traitor for wishing, in a fit of vexation, that the buck, horns and all, were emboweled in the body of the king. But what have we not lived to see in our own time? Sir, not many months ago this Administration, in its great and tender mercy toward the six hundred and forty prisoners of state, confined for treasonable practices at Camp Chase near the capital of Ohio, appointed a commissioner, an extra-judicial functionary, unknown to the Constitution and laws, to hear and determine the cases of the several parties accused and with power to discharge at his discretion or to banish to Bull's Island in Lake Erie. Among the political prisoners called before him was a lad of fifteen, a newsboy upon the Ohio River, whose only offence proved, upon inquiry, to be that he owed fifteen cents—the unpaid balance of a debt due to his washer-woman—possibly a woman of color—who had him arrested by the provost marshal as guilty of "disloyal practices." For four weary months the lad had lain in that foul and most loathsome prison, under military charge, lest, peradventure, he should overturn the Government of the United States; or, at least, the administration of Abraham Lincoln!

And yet, Senators and Representatives, catching up the brutal cry of a bloodthirsty but infatuated partisan press, exclaim "the Government has been too lenient, there ought to have been more arrests!"

Well did Hamilton remark that "arbitrary imprisonments have been in all ages the favorite and most formidable instruments of tyranny"; and, not less truly, Blackstone declares that they are "a less public, a less striking, and therefore *a more dangerous engine* of arbitrary government" than executions upon the scaffold. And yet, to-night, you seek here, under the cloak of an act of Congress, to authorize these arrests and imprisonments, and thus to renew again that reign of terror which smote the hearts of the stoutest among us, last summer, as "the pestilence which walketh in darkness."

Sir, if your objects are constitutional, you have power abundantly under the Constitution, without infraction or usurpation. The men who framed that instrument made it both for war and peace. Nay, more, they expressly provide for the cases of insurrection and rebellion. You have ample power to do all that of right you ought to do—all that the people, your masters, permit under their supreme will—the Constitution. Confine, then, yourselves within these limits, and the rising storm of popular discontent will be hushed.

Here the speaker denounced arbitrary arrests as illegal even under the suspension of *habeas corpus*.

The gentleman from Rhode Island [William P. Sheffield] said, very justly, that the suspension of the writ of *habeas corpus* does not authorize arrests except upon sworn warrant, charging some offence known to the law and dangerous to the public safety. He is right. It does not; and this was so admitted in the bill which passed the Senate in 1807. The suspension only denies release upon bail, or a discharge without trial, to parties thus arrested. It suspends no other right or privilege under the Constitution—certainly not the right to a speedy public trial by jury in a civil court. It dispenses with no "due process of law," except only that particular writ. It does not take away the claim for damages to which a party illegally arrested, or legally arrested, but without probable cause, is entitled.

And yet it has been assumed by the party in power that a suspension of the writ of *habeas corpus* is a suspension of the entire Constitution and of all laws, so far as the personal rights of the citizen are concerned. Why, then, sir, stop with arbitrary arrests and imprisonments? Does any man believe that it will end here? Not so have I learned history. The guillotine! the guillotine! the guillotine follows next.

Sir, when one of those earliest confined in Fort La Fayette —I had it from his own lips—made complaint to the Secretary of State of the injustice of his arrest and the severity of the' treatment to which he had been subjected in the exercise of arbitrary power, no offence being alleged against him, "why," said the Secretary, with a smile of most significant complacency, "my dear sir, you ought not to complain; *we might have gone further.*" Light flashed upon the mind of the gentleman and he replied: "Ah! that is true, sir; you had just the same right to behead as to arrest and imprison me."

Sir, it is this which makes revolutions. A gentleman upon the other side asked this afternoon which party was to rise now in revolution. The answer of the able and gallant gentleman from Pennsylvania [Mr. Biddle] was pertinent and just—

"No party, but an outraged people." It is not, let me tell you, the leaders of parties who begin revolutions. Never. Did any one of the distinguished characters of the Revolution of 1776 participate in the throwing of the tea into Boston Harbor? Who was it? Who, to-day, can name the actors in that now historic scene? Good men agitate; obscure men begin real revolutions; great men finally direct and control them. And if, indeed, we are about to pass through the usual stages of revolution, it will not be the leaders of the Democratic party—not I, not the men with me here to-night—but some man among the people, now unknown and unnoted, who will hurl your tea into the harbor; and it may even be in Boston once again; for the love of liberty, I would fain believe, lingers still under the shadow of the monument on Bunker Hill. But, sir, we seek no revolution—except through the ballot-box. The conflict to which we challenge you is not of arms but of argument. Do you believe in the virtue and intelligence of the people? Do you admit their capacity for self-government? Have they not intelligence enough to understand the right, and virtue enough to pursue it? Come then: meet us through the press, and with free speech and before the assemblages of the people and we will argue these questions, as we and our fathers have done from the beginning of the Government—"Are we right or you right, we wrong or you wrong?" And by the judgment of the people we will, one and all, abide. We have a Constitution yet, and laws yet. To them I appeal. Give us our rights; give us known and fixed laws; give us the judiciary; arrest us only upon due process of law; give us presentment or indictment by grand juries; speedy and public trial; trial by jury and at home; tell us the nature and cause of the accusation; confront us with witnesses; allow us witnesses in our behalf, and the assistance of counsel for our defence; secure us in our persons, our houses, our papers, and our effects; leave us arms, not for resistance to law or against rightful authority, but to defend ourselves from outrage and violence; give us free speech and a free press; the right peaceably to assemble; and, above all, free and undisturbed elections and the ballot; take our sons, take our money, our property, take all else; and we will wait a little, till, at the time and in the manner appointed by Constitution and law, we shall eject you from the trusts you have abused and the seats of power you have dishonored, and other and better men shall reign in your stead.

John A. Bingham [O.] replied to his colleague.

The argument to which we have listened to-night, with what degree of patience we could, has been characterized by two most remarkable assumptions. The one is that the gentleman from Ohio, who addressed the House [Mr. Vallandigham], and those whom he is supposed to represent, are the sole guardians of the Constitution of the United States of America. And the other is that, when he and his especial associates will it, that great instrument will perish in the fierce breath of revolution. In my judgment, sir, these assumptions are unworthy of my colleague, as they are unworthy of any man who has grown to man's estate under the shelter of the Constitution of the United States. The care of that Constitution is in the hands of the people, the whole people, who ordained it for the establishment of justice and the security of liberty. That great people the gentleman no more represents than I do. When they choose basely to surrender the sacred trust of the Constitution it will fall; but, so long as it pleases them to stand by it, it will be maintained.

If this be so, how comes it that the gentleman should assume that he is sole interpreter and protector of the Constitution, and that, by a breath of his mouth, it may be destroyed? Why, sir, it is but a few days ago that, upon this floor, in the very spirit of the speech which he has made to-night, my colleague undertook to demonstrate, by mutilating a letter of the Secretary of State, that the Constitution of the United States does not allow the American people to protect and maintain by force of arms their Government and their nationality against armed treason.

MR. VALLANDIGHAM.—I have spoken many times here; I have never referred to the gentleman; yet, since the beginning of this session, he has felt himself called upon not only to attempt to reply to what I have said, but to draw me into a wrangle upon this floor, a thing for which he is eminently qualified but for which I have the most sovereign contempt and of which I shall take no notice whatever.

MR. BINGHAM.—As the gentleman interrupted me for no purpose of denial or explanation he has no right to interrupt me either to question my motives or announce his contempt for all who choose to dissent from his arrogant assumptions. I suppose, from the tone and temper of my colleague's interruption, that he deems me guilty of the great *crimen læsæ majestatis*,[1] if I dare to lisp when his majesty rises in his place here and assumes to speak the law of the land.

He is not clothed, sir, with any such power over either my

[1] Crime of contemning majesty.

person as a citizen or my right as a Representative. The gentleman makes a virtue of necessity and, after rambling through half an hour of his speech to show that we were breaking through the intrenchments of the Constitution, that we were trampling upon the right of *habeas corpus,* of freedom of speech, of freedom of the press, and of the right of trial by jury; after denouncing us in set phrases for all this, he now rises and complains that I should venture to strike back, and says that I seek to draw him into a wrangle. Why, the gentleman is the last man on this footstool that I would want to have any wrangle with. [Laughter.] Now, that expression may be a little ambiguous, and the gentleman may have the benefit of it. [Laughter.] Perhaps the gentleman felt that the world would understand, when he calls attention to the fact that I once before in my life, and I believe only once, ventured to reply to a speech of his, I thereby sought to immortalize myself by coupling my name with so distinguished a person as himself! If that is the gentleman's idea, I beg him to count me out. [Laughter.] But, sir, whatever false motives the gentleman may attribute to me, I wish him to understand that I shall not sit silent here when I see a deliberate attempt made on this floor to convince this House, on the one hand, and the people of this country, on the other, that we have no right by law to authorize, and compel, if you please, the employment of all the able-bodied men of the country to crush out rebellion against the supremacy of the Government, the Constitution, and the laws. Go read those words that the gentleman dwelt upon with such emphasis the other day, and feel the blush of shame mount to your cheek that any American citizen of this Republic should utter such a sentiment.

Talk about freedom of speech, talk about the right of trial by jury, talk about personal liberty, talk about the privilege of the writ of *habeas corpus,* talk about your construction of 25 Edward III, and then come here and proclaim to this House that "only an imperial or despotic government could subjugate thoroughly disaffected and insurrectionary members of the State!"

The gentleman to-night has sought to justify this remarkable utterance. Hence his elaborate argument to show the limitation of the provision of the Constitution, that "treason against the United States shall consist only in levying war against them, or in adhering to their enemies, giving them aid and comfort."

Mr. Speaker, I do not desire to take up any unnecessary time in the discussion of this great and important question; but, as the gentleman has seen fit to attempt to justify his words that the United States Government has not the constitutional right to subjugate traitors and suppress armed rebellion by force, I deem it my duty to refer the House to the construction of the statute of 25 Edward III, which the gentleman says is literally the same as the treason clause of the Constitution of the United States. Let this construction of the statute of Edward go out with the gentleman's argument, in order that the antidote may go along with the poison which he attempts to infuse into the public mind. The construction of that statute before the Constitution was made, and, therefore, before its provisions were incorporated into the Constitution, was that the words "adhering to the enemy," etc., applied to cases only of adherence to a *foreign*, not a domestic, enemy. What then? Whoever adheres to a domestic enemy engaged in rebellion is, according to the legal construction of that great statute, instead of being indictable under the second clause thereof, indictable under the first clause, and to be held chargeable with levying war. That is all there is of it.

For the sake of the argument, grant it that words encouraging treason and inciting to treason do not constitute the crime of treason, does it result that such utterances are not a crime, and, as such, to be so declared and punished under the Constitution of the United States? I know, sir, that by a high authority it is said: "It seems clearly to be agreed that, by the common law and the statute of Edward III, words spoken amount only to a high misdemeanor and no treason." Grant this to be the true construction of the statute of Edward III, as the same stand incorporated in the treason clause of our Constitution, what comfort can my colleague derive from that construction in support of his argument against the bill now under discussion, that you may not provide, as in this bill is provided, to punish, not as treason but as "a high misdemeanor," the utterance of words spoken, written, or printed, with intent to counsel and advise resistance to the laws, or to dissuade drafted soldiers from the performance of their duty?

I suppose that the reference of my colleague to the provision of the statute of 25 Edward III, defining treason, was to proclaim in advance that all of this legislation which provides for punishing as a crime those who, in any way, aid in encouraging desertion or forcible resistance to the laws is unconstitutional; that you cannot punish persons who favor this rebellion, except those who actually take up arms and levy war against the Republic. I do not believe it. I wish to say, in addition, that, notwithstanding his suggestion that the Supreme Court would declare this law unconstitutional and deny the power of the Government to punish and restrain the "treasonable practices" defined in and prohibited by this bill, in my opinion that court will never so decide; never, sir. The gentleman says that, if you pass this and kindred bills for the suppression of this rebellion, then we must have revolution. The people only can make revolution. I rather think that my colleague is not well informed about the purposes of the people to say that they will rush into revolution. He may be ready for revolution, and, doubtless, he may wish to lead that revolution; but are the people ready to assent to that? So long as the people are faithful to the great trust of maintaining free representative government they will take care of a revolution either inaugurated by him or any of his associates who howl against the Executive for protecting and defending that Government against armed rebellion.

What is the gentleman's argument against this bill? One objection by him urged is that the bill provides for what he is pleased to call arbitrary arrests. What is the provision? Simply that whoever shall resist any draft of men enrolled under this act, or counsel or aid any person to resist such draft, or assault any officer in making such draft, shall, for the time being, be subject to summary arrest by the provost marshal, and shall be delivered to the civil authorities, and, upon trial and conviction, be subject to fine and imprisonment. That is what my colleague calls arbitrary arrests. His logic, I suppose, is that men may resist a lawful draft, may aid resistance thereto, may brutally assault drafting officers, but shall not be interrupted in their crime until affidavit is made before and warrant obtained from some United States commissioner or judge, remote, it may be, hundreds of miles. He would not allow the marshals of the United States to be the conservators of the public peace, nor even the judges of the United States to be conservators of the peace, though the steps of the temple of justice and the laws may be stained by the blood of the citizen shed by lawless violence in their presence, and in forbidden resistance to the laws which they are sworn to support and execute. The gentleman's argument means, though he has not the candor plainly to declare it, that traitors and all their aiders have the right to go on with their crime and murder until legally arrested upon complaint and warrant in due form of law, and only after such legal arrest to be made to answer for their crimes upon the verdict of an impartial jury of the State and district in which they may have committed their offences.

We are not to arrest them summarily, for that is arbitrary, he argues, but we are to proceed literally according to the provisions of the Constitution.

If the argument is good for such aiders of the rebellion it is of equal force as to the rebels, for they are persons as well as their aiders, and, like them, are included in the provisions of the Constitution cited. What sort of logic and reason is this upon a question of this sort when three hundred thousand rebels are in arms? Does not the gentleman himself see that there is a hiatus in his logic wide enough to drive a coach and six through?

Now, let us see how this rule, as stated by him, would work practically. Jefferson Davis has three hundred thousand rebels drawn up in line of battle before the capital of the United States, and you are mustering your forces under this conscription act to beat back this rebel host. While this is going on, the gentleman from Ohio stands with the Constitution in hand and calls out to the people all over the North to refuse to come to the rescue of their imperiled capital and violated Constitution because the act under which they are summoned is unconstitutional. By such utterances would my colleague keep back from the field all the loyal people of this land, while traitors in arms were seizing their capital, burning their towns, laying waste their fields, and setting at defiance and overthrowing their Government and laws. While this ruin is being wrought the people are to be greeted with the cry of my colleague: "Hold back! these rebels are citizens, and, though they may be guilty of treason, you must not interfere with them, nor with those who aid them, except you act strictly under the warrants and indictments known to the law." That is the substance of his argument.

The gentleman, not content with his endeavor to fetter the Government by requiring the jury rather than the army to try traitors, complains that we are interfering with the freedom of speech, and again he quotes the Constitution and attempts to hold it up as a shield between these men who commit or aid and abet this great treason against the Republic, and the right and duty of the people to crush them by force under the express sanction of law. I understand that the freedom of speech which is guaranteed by the Constitution is not that freedom of speech which consists in saying that these rebels in arms "ought to be induced to invade the Northern States," and rob and burn the habitations of Northern people. My colleague is learned in the reading of the Constitution, and I would be glad to have him point out a single line ever written by an American citizen or uttered by an American jurist whose opinion is entitled to any consideration which ever gave any such interpretation as that to the guaranties of the Constitution of the United States. No, sir; freedom of speech is the inborn right of every man, whether citizen or stranger, but it is a right which he may not exercise to the detriment of the commonwealth, and, therefore, for its abuse he is to be held responsible, as he is to be held responsible for the abuse of any other element of his personal liberty. The right of locomotion is as sacredly guarded under your Constitution as is the right of freedom of speech; but, if a citizen, in the exercise of his right of locomotion, sees fit to creep burglariously into the habitation of his neighbor and thereby commit felony it is in vain that he holds up the Constitution as a shield and tells us that that secures him the right of liberty and property. He has the right to play the honest man and loyal citizen, but he has not the liberty to play the part of a common thief or a burglar.

So it is with this guaranteed freedom of speech. I say it is the right of the people to punish and imprison every man in this land who, either by oral, written, or printed words, urges or advises any portion of the American people to quench in blood this last, great experiment of republican government. If there is any man here now who has the effrontery to deny that proposition, I should like to hear him.

The gentleman says that *habeas corpus* can only be suspended within the limits of the rebellion. That is a remarkable suggestion. I suppose, according to that doctrine, that when this rebellion was confined to the corporate limits of Charleston and Sullivan's Island, it would have been highly improper to have suspended the privilege at Columbia or Georgetown in South Carolina, where they were beating up recruits to swell their cowardly cohorts to ten thousand strong, designed to do murder on the seventy brave men within the walls of Fort Sumter. Who ever heard before of such an interpretation as that being put upon your Constitution? I say here, and I challenge contradiction, that the fair construction of that provision is this, that the people, through their representatives, are the sole judges of the extent to which the privilege of the writ may be suspended in time of rebellion or invasion; and if, in their opinion, the public safety in time of such rebellion or invasion requires a suspension of the privilege of the writ in all cases throughout the limits of the Republic, it is their right to declare it and their duty to execute it.

Well, sir, the gentleman says that the suspension of the privilege of the writ does not confer the power of arrest. I answer that the power to suspend the privilege of the writ for the public safety necessarily implies the power of arrest and detention. But the gentleman says you must give all persons charged with conspiracy a speedy trial. Does not he know that by the provision of the Constitution, if a citizen commit treason or other crime against the United States, in South Carolina or North Carolina, he must be tried within the State and district in which he commits the offence? Meantime you have no courts there to try such offenders, and, according to the gentleman's argument, you must not restrain them of their liberty by summary arrest, but allow them to go at large and practice their treason and conspiracy, and give aid and comfort to the enemy, until such time as your civil process and courts are again restored and the supremacy of your laws acknowledged or enforced within the limits of such jurisdiction! Does any man fail to see that such objections to this needful legislation are, after all, disguise it as you may under professions of love for the Constitution and the rights of the people guaranteed under the Constitution, but another attempt to aid this rebellion and secure to it an easy triumph over the Constitution and laws?

Ah, but, says the gentleman, your bastiles are open to receive these victims of executive despotism. I should have been glad if the gentleman had particularized who these persons are that have such a claim upon his sympathy. There was a man arrested for inciting the mob at Baltimore. The gentleman was careful not to name him. It is a name that is in bad association. It is the name by which was designated the first of murderers, on whose brow was set the damning blotch of fratricide. This man was arrested and sent to the "bastile"; and my colleague arises in his place and cries out: "A violation of the Constitution." According to his logic, Kane should have been left at large to incite men to cast iron bars from the tops of their houses in Baltimore upon the heads of our citizen soldiery.

There was another arrest made, to which I suppose the gentleman refers, although he was not pleased to name the party, in our own State. I remember well, Mr. Speaker—who does not remember?—that, about the time that arrest was made in Ohio, for seven long days a battle raged before Richmond. During that protracted struggle, while that field of conflict was covered with the thick darkness of battle and the shadow of death, and in all the loyal homes of our people hands were raised in silent prayer for the Republic and its defenders, a cry came up from the banks of the York and the James Rivers:

Help! help! help! brothers of the free North and West, or we perish, and our banner of glory and of beauty goes down before the armed legions of treason. In response to that call the people rushed to the conflict from the hills of New England to the golden sands of California, filling the continent with their shout—

> "We are coming, we are coming,
> Six hundred thousand more."

It was in the presence of this sublime uprising of the freemen of this land for the defence of their homes and country, and the rescue from an unequal struggle of your gallant army, that a partisan in Ohio, it is said, dared to outrage and disgrace humanity by saying to his neighbors: "Stop, brother Democrats, stay at home and vote; and let the army of the Union perish." It is said that man was arrested by order of the President.

SEVERAL MEMBERS.—Who was he?

MR. BINGHAM.—I prefer to let history, the avenger, name him.

SAMUEL S. COX [O.].—Will my colleague yield to me for a moment?

MR. BINGHAM.—I do not yield.

MR. COX.—I know my colleague will oblige me.

MR. BINGHAM.—This does not affect my colleague.

MR. COX.—It affects one of my constituents.

MR. BINGHAM.—I have said, Mr. Speaker, that such an utterance is said to have been made and published, and that the author of it was arrested.

MR. COX.—Why was he not tried?

MR. BINGHAM.—I now submit to the country that, if there were any such utterance made, the author of it should not only be arrested and imprisoned, but that the man who, in such an hour of peril, would attempt to keep back citizens from the defence of their homes and the relief of their brothers in arms, should not only be imprisoned, but should be hung by the neck, without judge or jury, till he be dead. [Applause.]

Daniel W. Voorhees [Ind.] closed the debate.

Mr. Speaker, it is either my good fortune or my bad fortune never to have been a member of a legislative body until I took my seat in this Congress. Consequently, I may not be so familiar with the rules of propriety that obtain among members of deliberative bodies as others who have had more experience. But, I must confess, Mr. Speaker, that, with my limited experience, I have observed the course of this debate with amazement, and with some degree of honest indignation.

This debate was opened by the gentleman from New York [Mr. Olin] with a lecture to this side of the House, informing us how he desired we should discuss this question. We were desired to behave ourselves and to pursue a certain line of conduct marked out for us in advance by his magisterial authority. The air of a testy, domineering pedagogue pervaded the style and substance of all his remarks.

After him comes the strap-and-button gentleman from Pennsylvania [Mr. Campbell], who howled forth his threats on this floor like some angry animal in pursuit of prey. Possibly it has affected somebody's nerves. Doubtless it did affect his own. I must say, however, that it did not affect mine at all, except as a gust of harsh and discordant sound is always more or less jarring to my nervous system. It passed by this side of the House as mere wind, somewhat unpleasant and disgusting, but entirely harmless. I submit that the military and malicious gentleman from Pennsylvania has no right thus to afflict and annoy the persecuted minority in this hall.

After him, in the order of debate, on the other side, comes that strange and eccentric gentleman from Ohio [Mr. Bingham] who so often holds this House and these galleries in listening and wondering suspense and attention. In his private intercourse he is one of the kindest and most amiable gentleman whom I ever had the good fortune to meet; but on this floor a stranger would take him to be, not merely Cato the Censor, for I believe Cato was very dignified, and certainly the gentleman from Ohio hardly ever is [laughter], but some furious actor in a play, whose part required him to scold and rave at every human being who was so unfortunate as to fall beneath his dreadful scowl. He is stormy and terrible to those who know him not, but to those who know him well gentle as summer and as tender as the dove who woos his mate. I am apologizing for his manner to those who do not understand him. His terrific outbreaks here against the minority may be regarded as a sort of pleasant episode to the grave proceedings of this House, a little ridiculous, but perfectly innocent. It is only his manner that is severe, not his matter. He starts out by telling us that the language of the distinguished gentleman from Ohio [Mr. Vallandigham], who held spell-bound this House from the position in which I stand, with one of the ablest arguments I ever heard, was all unworthy of a member of this body. Who constituted him a judge of his colleagues? Where does he find the authority to arraign his

peers on this floor?   Sir, there is but one reply to language and
conduct like this.   We reject with scorn your unasked advice;
we spurn your offensive lectures; we despise your puerile threats;
we defy the malice which actuates them; we hold you and your
outrageous insolence in sovereign and most unmitigated contempt.

Sir, it ill becomes gentlemen who have met with repudiation
at the hands of their people; who, for their policy and conduct
on this floor, have been rejected by their own constituents, and
who stand condemned before the country, to come here and lecture Democratic members.   In common decency you ought to
keep silent, as mere cumberers of the ground whose days are
numbered.   Popular majorities have been piled up against you
by thousands and tens of thousands.   Loyal people have spoken
your knell; the funeral bell has been tolled over your political
graves by patriotic hands; the grass is growing green on the sod
which covers you.   And yet you dare come here to lecture living
men!   We bear in our bodies political vitality; you are political
ghosts, specters from political graveyards, where the people
buried you last fall, and wrote on your tombstones: "No resur-
rection."   How dare you lecture the living, who yet stand on
the shores of time, and who have something to do with earthly
affairs?   [Laughter.]   I invoke the spell of decency and of regard for propriety, and, in the name of that spell, I exorcise
these spirits, and tell them "down, down, to whence you came."
[Laughter.]

You talk about what is worthy and unworthy.   Shall I accept gibbering and squeaking political ghosts, who will troop
home on the 4th of March to the vast charnel-house of repudiated
politicians, as my masters?   I own but one master in this Government—it is the sovereign people.

The days of this Congress are drawing to a close and we
may as well have a plain talk among ourselves before we part.
If you propose at this time, with Government credit at sixty
per cent. below par; if you propose, with $2,500,000,000 of in-
debtedness; if you propose, with a distracted country, with the
agricultural pursuits depressed, and the whole land groaning
from the effects of this war; if you propose, in full view of all
these things, to tax the people, in addition to what is necessary to
sustain the Government, to an unlimited extent—perhaps hundreds of millions—for the purpose of accomplishing compensated emancipation, for the purpose of flooding the free States
with free negroes, then you may make up your minds for trouble.
The money will not be paid, and you cannot compel it.   You will
find at last who owns and controls this Government.   The people

will assert the original divine right of the oppressed and outraged. They will say to you, in the language of the Constitution: "We, the people, made this Government; you are not our masters, but our servants."

A strange error has crept into the public mind. Men talk as if they could force and coerce public sentiment. The very theory of our Government forbids it. The theory of our Government is that, not Abraham Lincoln, not his Cabinet, not you men whose lingering footsteps are just departing from these places forever, constitute this Government, but that the people made it all, and constitute all its parts. They made it and they will uphold it in the mode which satisfies themselves. But not only that; they will make you obey the Constitution in its spirit, which is the concentrated will of the people.

For the purpose of uniting public sentiment and of prosecuting the war with unity of purpose I presume comes the proclamation of the President of September. Ten days before he issued it he said, himself, to the Chicago ministers that he had not the power to promulgate such a document and that it would do no good if he did. In that he was right, for once. But I suppose he gave way to pressure. He was pressed. By whom? By Horace Greeley, that political harlot, who appeared in a praying attitude in behalf of twenty million people. He gave way to pressure brought to bear, too, by the Governor of Massachusetts [John A. Andrew]. He gave way to the pressure and, I have no doubt, experienced relief. This was Jacksonian, very. It showed what is known as backbone. I have an immense respect for an Executive who violates his oath under the pressure of impertinent meddlers. But the President was told of the moral and military effect of such a proclamation, and I presume he believed all he heard was true. But the gentleman from Ohio [Mr. Bingham] was unfortunate in his musical recitation of the New England song a few minutes ago:

> "We are coming, Father Abraham,
> Six hundred thousand strong."

for if anybody is on the way here to swell the broken ranks of the army under the inspiration of that proclamation he is tarrying long. His arrival has not been noticed in the papers.

Lo! the mountain had labored, and the mouse came forth! Massachusetts, this hour, instead of crowding the highways and byways with her sons, has her Senator [Henry Wilson] in the other end of the Capitol, the chairman of the Committee on Military Affairs, pressing a conscript bill through the Senate, when his own State stands in defiance of the call made upon her last summer. To-day her quota is not full, and her Governor has become an itinerant recruiting sergeant in search of negroes to fill up the regiments of Massachusetts troops under the call made last fall by the President of the United States. This is the response of Massachusetts to the proclamation.

And the gentleman from New York, the chairman of the Committee on Military Affairs of this House [Abraham B. Olin], comes here and has to admit his State is delinquent thirty thousand troops, under the calls already made upon her.

Mr. Olin.—And that deficiency is principally owing to a deficiency of troops which ought to have been sent from the city of New York, where the Democracy of the Five Points has held undisputed sway. [Laughter.]

Mr. Voorhees.—You propose to put the black man alongside of the loyal white soldier. You propose to buy negroes, steal negroes, fight for negroes, obtain negroes in any way, and then humiliate and disgrace the white soldier by his presence and contact in the ranks.

You have thus outraged and insulted all classes of citizens, but the soldier most of all. Is it strange, then, that no more volunteers come to the standard of war? You have betrayed the loyal heart of the country, and that betrayal rises up in judgment against you; and its offspring, the birth of that betrayal, is this fearful, odious, and despotic conscription bill.

No conservative general can stand before the consuming flames that emanate from the seething caldron, the boiling cesspool of fanaticism which controls this Administration. Aye, sir, you struck down McClellan at the head of the army. You struck him down because he was in the way of your radical abolition schemes. It was another step in the betrayal of the people. Go with me to the townships in Indiana, Mr. Speaker; go to the hamlets, go to the school-houses and meet there the loyal farmers who pay their taxes from their well-worn pocketbooks—not your flash speculators in stocks on Wall street; not your political or banking gamblers and swindling contractors, who control this Government and who surround this Capitol like jackals and unclean beasts, like kites and carrion crows, watching and snuffing for plunder amid the misfortunes that have befallen the country; not that class of men, but men who are devoted to the old Constitution, who worship reverently after the old forms of religion, who love their country and maintain their own honor—go and ask these men, upon whom you have to rely for this Government, what they think of the removal of George B.

McClellan from the command of their sons. They will tell you that their sons love him as no chieftain was ever loved by his troops since the days of the great Napoleon. They will tell you that, in spite of all jealousies and assailants, he is the only man who has ever gained a battle at the head of the army of the Potomac; and, as plain people, they will tell you that, in their minds, his removal was caused by the machinations, the mischievous machinations, of the radical element which prevails here, and which is now running the Government to destruction in this Capitol. This, sir, is the firm belief of the country, and you will have to meet it.

You may call us disloyal if it will ease your hearts any, but our opinion upon this side of the House is just as firm, just as sharply and clearly made up, that the majority of this House has been disloyal in the acts I have enumerated and in the general scope of its conduct to the Constitution of the country as if you had been convicted of overt treason, and stood ready to be executed according to law.

But there is another feature in the conduct of this Administration and its supporters that goes as a reason why troops cannot now be brought into the field as volunteers, and a despotic conscription bill has to be passed. The people of the country have seen public economy disregarded. They have seen thieves and plunderers in the high places of the Government not only unrebuked, but rewarded by promotion to higher honors in place and profit. They have seen fortunes more than mountain high made in a single night by political favorites. No, sir; keep still, sir. The gentleman from Pennsylvania [John Covode, who made a remark in his seat] can speak feelingly and knowingly and understandingly, I have no doubt, upon the subject to which I allude. He has his friend, the late Secretary of War, the late minister to Russia, the late candidate for United States Senator in Pennsylvania, I presume, in his mind. I have no doubt it is a delicate point with him. I have by my side, however, my very distinguished and reliable friend from Massachusetts [Henry L. Dawes], who always comes to my relief, and, if I cannot prove by him that Simon Cameron and some of his friends are plunderers and public thieves, I will give up the case. [Laughter.]

These contractors and lobby thieves surrounding this Capitol, creating a swell mob in these galleries, the greediest of the greedy, the hungriest of all animals that ever infested in droves and packs the haunts of political offal, are the men who are loudest and most persistent for the continued prosecution of this war,

No abuse can be denounced that we do not hear the cry of treason from their hungry lips. What does it matter to them that the poor soldier lies stiff in the snow upon his thin blanket? They go upon the motto, "Put money in thy purse." If you think that

COPPERHEADS WORSHIPPING THEIR IDOL

[McClellan supported by Vallandigham and Seymour]

From the collection of the New York Historical Society

the people are blind to this state of affairs you are mistaken. They know that these loathsome cormorants are encamped here to eat out their substance. They know that they are the Hessians of this war, and that no peace will be permitted to revisit this bleeding land so long as villainy can find pay in the coffers of the Government, if this evil brood can prevent it.

But, sir, I thank God that the hand-writing is on the wall. The corrupt and impious feast of Belshazzar, the king, his princes, his parasites and concubines, is about over. The fingers of the American people are busily engaged in writing a doom against those who have turned the temple of our fathers into a den of thieves.

The people have seen other things, however, to discourage them in the prosecution of this war. They have seen you take advantage of the political condition of the country—you men who represent the spindles and looms of New England; they have seen you coming here and forcing on the agricultural portions of the country a tariff which is a robbery, a direct plunder on honest labor; they have seen you develop the most selfish, greedy, degrading element of the human heart—the love of gain by unfair means—taxing the whole country for the purpose of carrying out merely personal interests. To-day the Western farmer, the Western mechanic, pays three or four times the ordinary price for the articles which he has to buy from you and which he can buy nowhere else.

The people understand it well. They know that this increase of price does not go into the treasury of their beloved country; that it does not go even into the coffers "where thieves break through and steal"; but that it goes directly into the pockets of the millionaire, the nabob, the monopolist of the manufacturing districts. They know all that. It makes them tired of war. They are sore at heart and see no hope of success, justice, union, or constitutional liberty at your hands.

Further, I say to you, gentlemen, that, as the Lord God reigns in heaven, you cannot go on with your system of provost marshals and police officials arresting free white men for discharging what they conceive to be their duty within the plain provisions of the Constitution and maintain peace in the loyal States. Blood will flow. You cannot and you shall not forge our fetters on our limbs without a struggle for the mastery.

The great American heart is fired anew with the love of liberty, and the people are arousing like the giant after his sleep. They have erected their heads and warn you not to lay the weight of your finger, of your smallest finger, on one of the great muniments of personal freedom which adorn the history of the world. If you do, it is at your most deadly peril.

CONSCRIPTION BY THE SOUTH

Conscription in the Southern States, says Alexander Johnston in his "American Political History," preceded, and, to some extent, compelled, the adoption of conscription by the Federal Government. The act of

SOUTHERN VOLUNTEERS

From the collection of the New York Historical Society

April 16, 1862, with the amendment of September 27, 1862, was rather a levy *en masse* than a conscription. It made no provision for draft, but placed all white men between the ages of eighteen and forty-five, resident in the Confederate States, and not legally exempt, in the Confederate service.

July 18, 1863, by proclamation, President Jefferson Davis put the conscription law into operation, and directed the enrolment to begin at once. February 17, 1864, a second conscription law was passed. It added to the former conscript ages those between seventeen and eighteen, and between forty-five and fifty, who were to do duty as a garrison and reserve corps. It excepted certain classes, such as one editor to each newspaper, one apothecary to each drug store, and one farmer to each farm employing fifteen able-bodied slaves, and provided that all persons who should neglect or refuse to be enrolled should be placed in the field service for the war. No substitutes were or could be accepted, for every person able to do military duty was himself already conscripted.

Very little resistance was made to this sweeping levy, for the Government of the Confederate States showed little mercy to opposition of any kind. Only through the conscription were the Southern armies filled for the last two years of the war, and its enforcement was so rigorous and inquisitorial that toward the end of the war the Confederacy generally had more men in the field than it could provide with arms.

CHAPTER XII

Civil vs. Military Authority

Draft Riots in New York City—The President's Controversy with Gov. Horatio Seymour [N. Y.] on the Constitutionality of the Draft—Gen. Ambrose E. Burnside Imprisons, by Martial Law, Clement L. Vallandigham [O.] for Inciting Resistance to the Draft—The President Changes the Sentence to Exile into the Confederacy—Democratic Resolutions of Protest—The President Replies Justifying Military Arrests—Vallandigham, in Exile in Canada, Is Nominated by Ohio Democrats as Governor—Reply of the President to Committee of Ohio Democrats—Speeches against the Administration by Franklin Pierce and Gov. Horatio Seymour [N. Y.]—Vallandigham Is Overwhelmingly Defeated by Aid of the National Administration—Republican Victories in State Elections—Address of the President to Illinois Voters Justifying His Acts—His Replies to Mayor Fernando Wood, of New York City, and Others Volunteering to Mediate with the South—His Refusal to Accept Alexander H. Stephens [Ga.] as Envoy of the Confederacy.

THE draft ordered by the conscription met with little resistance outside of New York City and a few Democratic counties in Ohio.

In New York the law was put into operation on July 11, 1863. On the following Monday a mob broke into the office of the provost marshal, destroyed the wheel which contained the names of possible conscripts, and, setting fire to the building and preventing the firemen from extinguishing the flames, caused it to be burned to the ground. On the Superintendent of Police endeavoring to enforce order, he was set upon and barely escaped with his life. The police being unable to cope with the disorder, New York City regiments at the front were telegraphed for; they were unable to arrive for four days, and during this time the mob, increasing in number, committed many outrages, hanging negroes, and, after driving the little inmates into the street, pillaging and burning a colored orphan asylum. Collecting in Printing House Square on Monday they were about to destroy the offices of the newspapers which supported the Administration—particularly the *Tribune*—when Governor Horatio Seymour caused them to desist temporarily from executing their design by speaking to them from the steps of the City Hall. On Tuesday he issued a proclamation against rioting, but this had no effect. On the return of the troops the mob dispersed.

The draft, however, was not enforced in the city for some time. On August 3 Governor Seymour appealed to the President to suspend execution of the law until the courts could decide on its constitutionality, which had been questioned. The President replied that the draft must go on, leaving the question of constitutionality to be decided later.

My purpose is to be in my action just and constitutional, and yet practical, in performing the important duty with which I am charged: of maintaining the unity and the free principles of our common country.

The draft was resumed on August 19, and was concluded in an orderly fashion.

ARREST OF VALLANDIGHAM

A less tragic yet politically more important development of Northern resistance to military authority occurred in Ohio during the summer and fall of 1863. General Ambrose E. Burnside in his new department (headquarters Cincinnati) issued an edict known as "General Order No. 38," forbidding acts committed for the benefit of the enemy, and stating that persons committing such offences would be tried as spies or traitors, or sent over into the lines of their friends, the rebels.

Clement L. Vallandigham, whose term in Congress had expired in March, and who had been defeated for reëlection, repeated in various public speeches the sentiments he had uttered in the House of Representatives, assailing such acts of the Administration as the conscription law as unconstitutional and despotic.

On May 4 General Burnside arrested Mr. Vallandigham at his home in Dayton, and brought him to headquarters at Cincinnati for trial by court-martial. His counsel, ex-Senator George E. Pugh, applied for a writ of *habeas corpus,* which the judge refused, on the ground that the action of General Burnside was in the interest of public safety. Mr. Vallandigham was tried on the 6th, found guilty, and sentenced to imprisonment in a Federal fortress. General Burnside designated Fort Warren in Boston Harbor as the place of incarceration. The President, however, changed this sentence into the alternative presented by Order No. 38, and sent the prisoner over into the Confederate lines. From the South Mr. Vallandigham ran through the blockade, finally arriving in Canada.

Public meetings were held all over the country to denounce the Administration for its despotic act. General Burnside, fearing that he had been unwise in bringing this storm of criticism upon the Government, offered his resignation. In reply the President telegraphed him on May 29 as follows:

When I shall wish to supersede you I will let you know. All the Cabinet regretted the necessity of arresting, for instance, Vallandigham, some perhaps doubting there was a real necessity for it; but, being done, all were for seeing you through with it.

The brunt of seeing Burnside through, however, fell on the President, and ably did he fulfil the difficult task. Opposed to him were some of the shrewdest constitutional lawyers in the country. At their instigation able resolutions in denunciation of Vallandigham's arrest as unconstitutional were passed at various public meetings. The President chose to reply to the resolutions passed at Albany, N. Y., on May 19. To this Governor Seymour had sent an address, in which he said: "If this proceeding is approved by the Government, and sanctioned by the people, it is not merely a step toward revolution—it is revolution; it will not only lead to military despotism—it establishes military despotism.'' The resolutions closed with a denunciation of ''the blow struck at a citizen of Ohio'' as ''aimed at every citizen of the North,'' and ''against the spirit of our laws and Constitution.'' They earnestly called on the President ''to reverse the action of the military tribunal which has passed a cruel and unusual punishment upon the party arrested, prohibited in terms by the Constitution,'' and to restore him to liberty.

The President took his time in preparing a reply, with the result that the letter, when it was finished on June 12, proved to be one of his notable papers, comparable for its cogent argument to his Cooper Union address.

Military Arrests Justifiable

President Lincoln

He began by analyzing the resolutions of the meeting and showing that their movers and himself had a common purpose, the maintenance of the nation, differing only in the choice of measures for effecting that object. ''The meeting, by their resolutions, assert and argue that certain military arrests, . . . for which I am ultimately responsible, are unconstitutional. I think they are not.'' He then argued that these arrests were not made for ''treason,'' as charged, but on ''totally different grounds,'' *i. e.*, for purely military reasons. He narrated the manner in which the enemy with which the country was in open war had, under cover of ''liberty of speech,'' ''liberty of the press,'' and *''habeas corpus,''* kept a corps of spies in the North, which had aided the secessionist cause in a thousand ways. ''Yet,'' said the President, ''thoroughly imbued with a reverence for the guaranteed rights of individuals, I was slow to adopt the strong measures which by degrees I had been forced to regard as being within the exceptions of the Constitution, and as indispensable to the public safety.'' But the evil had to be dealt with, and by more effective means than afforded by the civil courts, on whose juries sympathizers with the accused were apt to sit, "more ready to hang the panel than to hang the traitor." And again, said Lincoln, there are crimes against the country which may be so conducted as to evade the cognizance of a civil court, such as dissuading a man from volunteering or inducing a soldier to desert. These are cases clearly coming under that clause of the Constitution which permits suspension of the writ of *habeas corpus* "when, in cases of rebellion or invasion, public safety may require it."

The President then proceeded to draw a distinction between civil and military law. He said:

The former is directed at the small percentage of ordinary and continuous perpetration of crime, while the latter is directed at sudden and extensive uprisings against the Government, which, at most, will succeed or fail in no great length of time. In the latter case arrests are made not so much for what has been done, as for what probably would be done. The latter is more for the preventive and less for the vindictive than the former. In such cases the purposes of men are much more easily understood than in cases of ordinary crime. The man who stands by and says nothing when the peril of his Government is discussed cannot be misunderstood. If not hindered, he is sure to help the enemy; much more if he talks ambiguously—talks for his country with "buts," and "ifs," and "ands."

The President showed how greatly the country had suffered through deferring arrests for treason, by citing the cases of John C. Breckinridge, Robert E. Lee, Joseph E. Johnston, and other commanders in the Confederate service who had all been within the power of the Government after the outbreak of the war, and who were well known to be traitors at the time. Said the President:

In view of these and similar cases, I think the time not unlikely to come when I shall be blamed for having made too few arrests rather than too many.

Mr. Lincoln then examined the contention of the committee that even during a war military arrests were unconstitutional outside of the region of hostilities. To this the President replied:

Inasmuch, however, as the Constitution itself makes no such distinction, I am unable to believe that there is any such constitutional distinction. I concede that the class of arrests complained of can be constitutional only when, in cases of rebellion or invasion, the public safety may require them; and I insist that in such cases they are constitutional wherever the public safety does require them, as well in places to which they may prevent the rebellion extending as in those where it may be already prevailing; as well where they may restrain mischievous interference with the raising and supplying of armies to suppress the rebellion, as where the rebellion may actually be; as well where they may restrain the enticing men out of the army, as where they would prevent mutiny in the army. . . .

Mr. Vallandigham's arrest was made because he was laboring, with some effect, to prevent the raising of troops, to encourage desertions from the army, and to leave the rebellion without an adequate military force to suppress it. He was not arrested because he was damaging the political prospects of the Administration or the personal interests of the commanding general, but because he was damaging the army, upon the existence and vigor of which the life of the nation depends. He was warring upon the military, and this gave the military constitutional jurisdiction to lay hands upon him. If Mr. Vallandigham was not damaging the military power of the country, then his arrest was made on mistake of fact, which I would be glad to correct on reasonably satisfactory evidence.

With an argument appealing even more to the hearts than the heads of his critics, Mr. Lincoln continued:

I understand the meeting whose resolutions I am considering to be in favor of suppressing the rebellion by military force— by armies. Long experience has shown that armies cannot be maintained unless desertion shall be punished by the severe penalty of death. The case requires, and the law and the Constitution sanction, this punishment. Must I shoot a simple-minded soldier boy who deserts, while I must not touch a hair of a wily agitator who induces him to desert? . . . I think that, in such a case, to silence the agitator and save the boy is not only constitutional, but a great mercy.

In fine, said the President:

I can no more be persuaded that the Government can constitutionally take no strong measures in time of rebellion, because it can be shown that the same could not be lawfully taken in time of peace, than I can be persuaded that a particular drug is not good medicine for a sick man because it can be shown not to be good food for a well one. Nor am I able to appreciate the danger apprehended by the meeting, that the American people will by means of military arrests during the rebellion lose the right of public discussion, the liberty of speech and the press, the law of evidence, trial by jury, and *habeas corpus* throughout the indefinite peaceful future which I trust lies before them, any more than I am able to believe that a man could contract so strong an appetite for emetics during temporary illness as to persist in feeding upon them during the remainder of his healthful life.

The President gently rebuked the memorialists for introducing partisan politics into the affair by designating themselves as "Democrats" rather than "American citizens." Nevertheless he accepted the challenge, and showed that Andrew Jackson, the idol of the Democratic party, had made a military arrest of the author of a denunciatory newspaper article, and refused the service upon himself of a writ of *habeas corpus,* being fined for so doing; thirty years later, after a full discussion of the constitutional aspects of the case, a Democratic Congress refunded him principal and interest of the fine.

At the conclusion of his letter the President stated that he had been pained when he learned of Mr. Vallandigham's arrest, and he promised to release him with pleasure when he felt assured that the public safety would not suffer by it.

TREASON MADE ODIOUS

On June 11 the Ohio Democratic convention nominated Vallandigham for governor of the State upon a platform which protested against the emancipation proclamation, military arrests in loyal States, and, in particular, the banishment of Vallandigham. A committee presented these resolutions to the President, and on June 29 he replied to them in the tenor of his letter to the Albany meeting, elaborating the constitutional argument, and closing with the following proposition:

Your nominee for governor . . . is known . . . to declare against the use of an army to suppress the rebellion. Your own attitude, therefore, encourages desertion, resistance to the draft, and the like, because it teaches those who incline to desert and to escape the draft to believe it is your purpose to protect them and to hope that you will become strong enough to do so. . . .

I cannot say I think you desire this effect to follow your attitude; but I assure you that both friends and enemies of the Union look upon it in this light. It is a substantial hope, and, by consequence, a real strength to the enemy. If it is a false hope, and one which you would willingly dispel, I will make the way exceedingly easy. I send you duplicates of this letter, in order that you, or a majority, may, if you choose, indorse your names upon one of them, and return it thus indorsed to me, with the understanding that those signing are thereby committed to the following propositions, and to nothing else:—

1. That there is now rebellion in the United States, the object and tendency of which is to destroy the national Union; and that, in your opinion, an army and navy are constitutional means for suppressing that rebellion.

2. That no one of you will do anything which, in his own judgment, will tend to hinder the increase, or favor the decrease, or lessen the efficiency of the army and navy, while engaged in the effort to suppress that rebellion; and,—

3. That each of you will, in his sphere, do all he can to have the officers, soldiers, and seamen of the army and navy, while engaged in the effort to suppress the rebellion, paid, fed, clad, and otherwise well provided for and supported.

And with the further understanding that upon receiving the letter and names thus indorsed I will cause them to be published, which publication shall be, within itself, a revocation of the order in relation to Mr. Vallandigham.

The committee, put upon the defensive by this clever device of the President, took the only attitude which was possible short of capitulation, and rejected the proposition as an insult to their loyalty.

Distinguished members of the Democratic party in other States took the same position as the Ohio committee. Ex-President Franklin Pierce delivered a carefully prepared oration at a great Democratic meeting held in Concord, N. H., in midsummer. He said:

"Moral Force, Not Arms, Will Save the Union"

Franklin Pierce

Do we not all know that the cause of our calamities is the vicious intermeddling of too many of the citizens of the Northern States with the constitutional rights of the Southern States, coöperating with the discontents of the people of those States? And now, war! war, in its direst shape—war, such as it makes the blood run cold to read of in the history of other nations and of other times—war, on a scale of a million of men in arms —war, horrid as that of barbaric ages, rages in several of the States of the Union, as its more immediate field, and casts the lurid shadow of its death and lamentation athwart the whole expanse, and into every nook and corner of our vast domain. Nor is that all; for in those of the States which are exempt from the actual ravages of war, in which the roar of the cannon, and the rattle of the musketry, and the groans of the dying are heard but as a faint echo of terror from other lands, even here in the loyal States, the mailed hand of military usurpation strikes down the liberties of the people and its foot tramples on a desecrated Constitution. Aye, in this land of free thought, free speech, and free writing—in this Republic of free suffrage, with liberty of thought and expression as the very essence of republican institutions—even here, in these free States, it is made criminal . . . for that noble martyr of free speech, Mr. Vallandigham, to discuss public affairs in Ohio—aye, even here, the temporary agents of the sovereign people, the transitory administrators of the government, tell us that in time of war the mere arbitrary will of the President takes the place of the Constitution, and the President himself announces to us that it is treasonable to speak or to write otherwise than as he may prescribe; nay, that it is treasonable even to be silent, though we be struck dumb by the shock of the calamities with which evil counsels, incompetency, and corruption, have overwhelmed our country.

This fearful, fruitless, fatal civil war has exhibited our amazing resources and vast military power. It has shown that, united, even in carrying out, in its widest interpretation, the Monroe Doctrine, on this continent, we could, with such protection as the broad ocean which flows between ourselves and European powers affords, have stood against the world in arms. I speak of the war as fruitless; for it is clear that, prosecuted upon the basis of the proclamations of September 22 and September 24, 1862, prosecuted, as I must understand those proclamations, to say nothing of the kindred brood which has followed, upon the theory of emancipation, devastation, subjugation, it cannot fail to be fruitless in everything except the harvest of woe which it is ripening for what was once the peerless Republic.

Now, fellow citizens, after having said thus much, it is right that you should ask me, What would you do in this fearful extremity? I reply, From the beginning of this struggle to the present moment my hope has been in moral power. There it reposes still. When, in the spring of 1861, I had occasion to address my fellow citizens of this city, from the balcony of the hotel before us, I then said I had not believed, and did not then believe, aggression by arms was either a suitable or possible remedy for existing evils. All that has occurred since then has but strengthened and confirmed my convictions in this regard. I repeat, then, my judgment impels me to rely upon moral force, and not upon any of the coercive instrumentalities of military power. We have seen, in the experience of the last two years, how futile are all our efforts to maintain the Union by force of arms; but, even had war been carried on by us successfully, the ruinous result would exhibit its utter impracticability for the attainment of the desired end. Through peaceful agencies, and through such agencies alone, can we hope to 'form a more perfect Union, establish justice, insure domestic tranquillity, provide for the common defence, promote the general welfare, and secure the blessings of liberty to ourselves and our posterity': the great objects for which, and for which alone, the Constitution was formed. If you turn round and ask me, What if these agencies fail, what if the passionate anger of both sections forbids, what if the ballot-box is sealed? Then, all efforts, whether of war or peace, having failed, my reply is, You will take care of yourselves; with or without arms, with or without leaders, we will, at least, in the effort to defend our rights as a free people, build up a great mausoleum of hearts, to which men who yearn for liberty will, in after years, with bowed heads and reverently, resort, as Christian pilgrims to the sacred shrines of the Holy Land.

Governor Horatio Seymour [N. Y.] addressed a large gathering in New York City about the same time. He said:

THE REVOLUTIONARY DOCTRINE OF PUBLIC NECESSITY

GOVERNOR SEYMOUR

A few years ago we stood before this community to warn them of the dangers of sectional strife; but our fears were laughed at. At a later day, when the clouds of war overhung our country, we implored those in authority to compromise that difficulty: for we had been told by that great orator and statesman, Burke, that there never yet was a revolution that might not have been prevented by a compromise opportunely and graciously made. [Great applause.] Our prayers were unheeded. Again, when the contest was opened, we invoked those who had the conduct of affairs not to underrate the power of the adversary—not to underrate the courage, and resources, and endurance of our own sister States. This warning was treated as sympathy with treason. You have the results of these unheeded warnings and unheeded prayers; they have stained our soil with blood; they have carried mourning into thousands of homes; and to-day they have brought our country to the very verge of destruction. Once more I come before you to offer again an earnest prayer, and beg you to listen to a warning. Our country is not only at this time torn by one of the bloodiest wars that has ever ravaged the face of the earth, but, if we turn our faces to our own loyal States, how is it there? You find the community divided into political parties, strongly arrayed, and using with regard to each other terms of reproach and defiance. It is said by those who support more particularly the Administration that we, who differ honestly, patriotically, sincerely, from them with regard to the line of duty, are men of treasonable purposes and enemies to our country. ["Hear, hear."] On the other hand, the Democratic organization look upon this Administration as hostile to their rights and liberties; they look upon their opponents as men who would do them wrong in regard to their most sacred franchises. I need not call your attention to the tone of the press, or to the tone of public feeling, to show you how, at this moment, parties are thus exasperated, and stand in defiant attitudes to each other. A few years ago we were told that sectional strife, waged in words like these, would do no harm to our country; but you have seen the sad and bloody results. Let us be admonished now in time, and take care that this irritation, this feeling which is growing up in our midst, shall not also ripen into civil troubles that shall carry the evils of war into our own homes.

Upon one point all are agreed, and that is this: Until we have a united North we can have no successful war. Until we have a united, harmonious North we can have no beneficent peace. How shall we gain harmony? How shall the unity of all be obtained? Is it to be coerced? I appeal to you, my Republican friends, when you say to us that the nation's life and existence hang upon harmony and concord here, if you yourselves, in your serious moments, believe that this is to be produced by seizing our persons, by infringing upon our rights, by insulting our homes, and by depriving us of those cherished principles for which our fathers fought, and to which we have always sworn allegiance. [Great applause.]

We only ask that you shall give to us that which you claim for yourselves, and that which every freeman, and every man who respects himself, will have—freedom of speech, the right to exercise all the franchises conferred by the Constitution upon American citizens. [Great applause.] Can you safely deny us these? Will you not trample upon your own rights if you refuse to listen? Do you not create revolution when you say that our persons may be rightfully seized, our property confiscated, our homes entered? Are you not exposing yourselves, your own interests, to as great a peril as that with which you threaten us? Remember this, that the bloody, and treasonable, and revolutionary doctrine of public necessity can be proclaimed by a mob as well as by a government. [Applause.]

To-day the great masses of conservatives who still battle for time-honored principles of government, amid denunciation, contumely, and abuse, are the only barriers that stand between this Government and its own destruction. If we should acquiesce in the doctrine that, in times of war, constitutions are suspended, and laws have lost their force, then we should accept a doctrine that the very right by which this Government administers its power has lost its virtue, and we would be brought down to the level of rebellion itself, having an existence only by virtue of material power. When men accept despotism they may have a choice as to who the despot shall be. The struggle then will not be, Shall we have constitutional liberty? But, having accepted the doctrine that the Constitution has lost its force, every instinct of personal ambition, every instinct of personal security, will lead men to put themselves under the protection of that power which they suppose most competent to guard their persons.

In conclusion he said:

We stand to-day amid new-made graves, in a land filled with mourning; upon a soil saturated with the blood of the fiercest conflict of which history gives us an account. We can, if we will, avert all these calamities and evoke a blessing. If we will do what? Hold that Constitution, and liberties, and laws are suspended?—shrink back from the assertion of right? Will that restore them? Or shall we do as our fathers did, under circumstances of like trial, when they combated against the powers of a crown? They did not say that liberty was suspended; that men might be deprived of the right of trial by jury; that they might be torn from their homes by midnight intruders? [Tremendous and continued applause.] If you would save your country and your liberties, begin right; begin at the hearthstones, which are ever meant to be the foundations of American institutions; begin in your family circle; declare that your privileges shall be held sacred; and, having once proclaimed your own rights, take care that you do not invade those of your neighbor. [Applause.]

The Ohio Democrats went into the campaign foredoomed to defeat. The Republican party determined to "make treason odious" by piling up an enormous majority of votes against him. They nominated John Brough, a "War Democrat," to make the issue as clear as possible. By a State law the soldiers in the field were permitted to vote, and they, as well as the citizens at home, cast their ballots under conditions which would be far from satisfactory to a ballot reformer of the present day. Brough won the election with over 100,000 votes to spare. Soon after his defeat, Vallandigham returned openly to Ohio, evidently daring the Government to arrest him again. The President, however, realizing that Vallandigham's power to injure the draft was broken, ignored his presence in the country. Undoubtedly he would have taken a similar course from the beginning, had not Burnside's action in arresting Vallan-

digham forced him to carry out an autocratic policy.
For Lincoln did not approve of supplying martyrs to
the opposition, and, therefore, when forced to do so,
he contrived to make them as unheroic, and even
ridiculous, as possible. Brilliant orator though he was,
Clement L. Vallandigham's connection with his party
became a positive detriment to it, and he soon retired
from politics to devote himself to law, in the practice
of which he met his death in a strange and tragic
fashion. In defending a man accused of murder he
shot himself, as he was illustrating the manner in which
his client might have discharged his pistol by accident
while drawing it from his pocket.

The political campaign of 1863 in other States as
well as in Ohio was waged along the lines laid down by
the President, with the result of sweeping gubernatorial victories for the Administration.

The President not only sounded the keynote of the
campaign, and formulated the Administration's platform, but wrote, as it were, the campaign text-book of
his party, reviewing the acts of the Administration and
supporting its policies so completely and cogently that
nothing essential could be added. All this he did in
an address which he sent to a mass-meeting of "unconditional Union men" at Springfield, Ill., and which
was there read on September 3 amid the greatest enthusiasm.

Justification of His Administration

President Lincoln

After tendering the nation's gratitude to those
"noble men whom no partisan malice or partisan hope
can make false to the nation's life," the President
plunged at once into a justification of his course.

There are those who are dissatisfied with me. To such I
would say: You desire peace, and you blame me that we do
not have it. But how can we attain it? There are but three
conceivable ways: First, to suppress the rebellion by force of
arms. This I am trying to do. Are you for it? If you are,

so far we are agreed. If you are not for it, a second way is to give up the Union. I am against this. Are you for it? If you are, you should say so plainly. If you are not for force, nor yet for dissolution, there only remains some imaginable compromise. I do not believe any compromise embracing the maintenance of the Union is now possible. All I learn leads to a directly opposite belief. The strength of the rebellion is its military, its army. That army dominates all the country and all the people within its range. Any offer of terms made by any man or men within that range, in opposition to that army, is simply nothing for the present, because such man or men have no power whatever to enforce their side of a compromise, if one were made with them.

To illustrate. Suppose refugees from the South and peace men of the North get together in convention and frame and proclaim a compromise embracing a restoration of the Union. In what way can that compromise be used to keep Lee's army out of Pennsylvania? Meade's army can keep Lee's army out of Pennsylvania, and, I think, can ultimately drive it out of existence. But no paper compromise to which the controllers of Lee's army are not agreed can at all affect that army. In an effort at such compromise we should waste time which the enemy would improve to our disadvantage; and that would be all. A compromise, to be effective, must be made either with those who control the rebel army, or with the people first liberated from the domination of that army by the success of our own army. Now, allow me to assure you that no word or intimation from that rebel army, or from any of the men controlling it, in relation to any peace compromise, has ever come to my knowledge or belief. All charges and insinuations to the contrary are deceptive and groundless. And I promise you that, if any such proposition shall hereafter come, it shall not be rejected and kept a secret from you. I freely acknowledge myself the servant of the people, according to the bond of service—the United States Constitution—and that, as such, I am responsible to them.

But to be plain. You are dissatisfied with me about the negro. Quite likely there is a difference of opinion between you and myself upon that subject. I certainly wish that all men could be free, while I suppose you do not. Yet I have neither adopted nor proposed any measure which is not consistent with even your view, provided you are for the Union. I suggested compensated emancipation, to which you replied you wished not to be taxed to buy negroes. But I had not asked you to be taxed to buy negroes, except in such way as to save you from greater taxation to save the Union exclusively by other means.

You dislike the emancipation proclamation, and perhaps would have it retracted. You say it is unconstitutional. I think differently. I think the Constitution invests its commander-in-chief with the law of war in time of war. The most that can be said—if so much—is that slaves are property. Is there—has there ever been—any question that, by the law of war, property, both of enemies and friends, may be taken when needed? And is it not needed whenever taking it helps us, or hurts the enemy? Armies, the world over, destroy enemies' property when they cannot use it; and even destroy their own to keep it from the enemy. Civilized belligerents do all in their power to help themselves or hurt the enemy, except a few things regarded as barbarous or cruel. Among the exceptions are the massacre of vanquished foes and non-combatants, male and female.

But the proclamation, as law, either is valid or is not valid. If it is not valid it needs no retraction. If it is valid it cannot be retracted, any more than the dead can be brought to life. Some of you profess to think its retraction would operate favorably for the Union. Why better *after* the retraction than *before* the issue? There was more than a year and a half of trial to suppress the rebellion before the proclamation was issued, the last one hundred days of which passed under an explicit notice that it was coming, unless averted by those in revolt returning to their allegiance. The war has certainly progressed as favorably for us since the issue of the proclamation as before.

I know as fully as one can know the opinions of others that some of the commanders of our armies in the field, who have given us our most important victories, believe the emancipation policy and the use of colored troops constitute the heaviest blows yet dealt to the rebellion, and that at least one of those important successes could not have been achieved when it was but for the aid of black soldiers.

Among the commanders who hold these views are some who have never had any affinity with what is called "abolitionism," or with "Republican party politics," but who hold them purely as military opinions. I submit their opinions as entitled to some weight against the objections often urged that emancipation and arming the blacks are unwise as military measures, and were not adopted as such in good faith.

You say that you will not fight to free negroes. Some of them seem willing to fight for you; but no matter. Fight you, then exclusively, to save the Union. I issued the proclamation on purpose to aid you in saving the Union. Whenever you shall have conquered all resistance to the Union, if I shall urge you to continue fighting, it will be an apt time then for you to declare you will not fight to free negroes. I thought that in your struggle for the Union, to whatever extent the negroes should cease helping the enemy, to that extent it weakened the enemy in his resistance to you. Do you think differently? I thought that whatever negroes can be got to do as soldiers leaves just so much less for white soldiers to do in saving the Union. Does it appear otherwise to you? But negroes, like other people, act upon motives. Why should they do anything for us if we will do nothing for them? If they stake their lives for us they must be prompted by the strongest motive, even the promise of freedom. And the promise, being made, must be kept.

The letter closed with a glowing exordium, such as those which, in the days of the fight for free territory, had roused his auditors to a frenzy of enthusiasm. In classic phrase it pictured the soldiers and sailors of the Union marching on to certain victory. It paid tribute to the courage of the negro troops, and with Cromwellian ire contrasted their patriotism with the hypocritical pretensions of the "malignants" of the peace party. Yet its oratorical fever was restrained from soaring into bombast by a ballast of common sense, and its tense feeling was relieved by a touch of grotesque humor, to which, as President even more than as citizen, Lincoln was wont to give loose in his most serious moments. Virtually his "last stump-speech," it was unquestionably his most characteristic and best one.

The signs look better. The Father of Waters again goes unvexed to the sea. Thanks to the great Northwest for it; nor yet wholly to them. Three hundred miles up they met New England, Empire, Keystone, and Jersey, hewing their way right and left. The sunny South, too, in more colors than one, also lent a helping hand. On the spot, their part of the history was jotted down in black and white. The job was a great national one, and let none be slighted who bore an honorable part in it. And, while those who have cleared the great river may well be proud, even that is not all. It is hard to say that anything has been more bravely and well done than at Antietam, Murfreesboro, Gettysburg, and on many fields of less note. Nor must Uncle Sam's web feet be forgotten. At all the watery margins they have been present. Not only on the deep sea, the broad bay, and the rapid river, but also up the narrow, muddy bayou, and wherever the ground was a little damp, they have been and made their tracks. Thanks to all: for the great republic—for the principle it lives by and keeps alive—for man's vast future—thanks to all.

Peace does not appear so distant as it did. I hope it will come soon, and come to stay, and so come as to be worth the keeping in all future time. It will then have been proved that among free men there can be no successful appeal from the ballot to the bullet, and that they who take such appeal are sure to lose their case and pay the cost. And then there will be some black men who can remember that with silent tongue, and clenched teeth, and steady eye, and well-poised bayonet, they have helped mankind on to this great consummation, while I fear there will be some white ones unable to forget that with malignant heart and deceitful speech they strove to hinder it.

Still, let us not be over-sanguine of a speedy final triumph. Let us be quite sober. Let us diligently apply the means, never doubting that a just God, in his own good time, will give us the rightful result.

That reference in the address to offers of compromise made by representatives of the Confederacy was evoked by various propositions made for self-advertisement by irresponsible parties such as Fernando Wood, a Democratic politician of New York, who boldly confessed his sympathy with the South and virtually offered himself as a mediator. To him Lincoln had replied (on December 12, 1862):

Understanding your phrase, "The Southern States would send representatives to the next Congress," to be substantially the same as that "the people of the Southern States would cease resistance, and would reinaugurate, submit to, and maintain the national authority within the limits of such States, under the Constitution of the United States," I say that in such case the war would cease on the part of the United States, and that if, within a reasonable time, ''a full and general amnesty'' were necessary to such end, it would not be withheld. I do not think it would be proper now for me to communicate this formally or informally to the people of the Southern States. My belief is that they already know it; and when they choose, if ever, they can communicate with me unequivocally. Nor do I think it proper now to suspend military operations to try any experiment of negotiation.

It is true, however, that a no less responsible party than Alexander H. Stephens, Vice-President of the Confederacy, had presented to the Navy Department on July 4, 1863, a request that he be permitted to come to Washington bearing ''a communication in writing from Jefferson Davis, Commander-in-Chief of the land and naval forces of the Confederate States, to Abraham Lincoln, Commander-in-Chief of the land and naval forces of the United States,'' but there was no statement of the nature of the communication. As the request studiously avoided recognition of the President in other than the military capacity of that office, Mr. Lincoln very wisely and properly ordered the Secretary of the Navy [Gideon Welles] to reply:

The request of A. H. Stephens is inadmissible. The customary agents and channels are adequate for all needful communication and conference between the United States forces and the insurgents.

CHAPTER XIII

"Bayonets at the Polls"

Lazarus W. Powell [Ky.] Introduces Bill in Senate to Prevent Military Interference with Elections—Debate: in Favor of Bill, Senator Powell, James A. McDougall [Cal.], Reverdy Johnson [Md.]; Opposed, Jacob M. Howard [Mich.], James Harlan [Ia.].

OWING to charges that there had been military interference by the order of the President with elections held in the border States during the summer and autumn of 1863, Lazarus W. Powell [Ky.] introduced in the Senate on January 5, 1864, a bill to prevent officers of the army and navy from interfering in elections in the States. This was finally referred to the Committee on Military Affairs, which reported against it, and presented an elaborate report justifying the action of the President. On March 3 Senator Powell's bill was brought before the Senate as in Committee of the Whole.

Military Interference with Elections

Senate, March 3-5, 1864

On March 3 and 4 Senator Powell spoke in favor of the bill.

It cannot be doubted that upon the keeping of the elective franchise absolutely free depends the very existence of our form of government and our republican institutions. Free States in all ages have regarded the purity of the elective franchise as of the greatest and most vital importance, and have enacted severe penal laws for the punishment of those who interfered by force or fraud to prevent free elections. I believe there is no government on the face of the earth in which elections have been carried on for the purpose of appointing any of the officers of the government, save and except the United States of

336

America, that has not had laws to punish, and severely punish, those who should interfere with the freedom of the elective franchise. All the republics of antiquity had the severest laws punishing those who interfered with the freedom of their elections.

By the laws of Great Britain persons convicted of bribery, force, or fraud at elections are punished severely. At the common law bribery and kindred offences were crimes, and the British statutes punished persons guilty of such offences on conviction with fines of £500, and deprived them of the privilege ever after of voting or holding any office of trust or honor under that government. One section of this bill provides that the soldiers of the army of the United States shall not be permitted to be kept within one mile of any poll where an election is going on, on the day of election. I find similar provisions in the English law.

Mr. Tucker, in his notes to Blackstone's Commentaries, in reference to the British law requiring soldiers to be removed from the place of voting, says, ''A similar regulation in the election of Representatives to Congress seems highly proper and necessary.'' It is strange to me that we have never had such a law on our statute book. I suppose the only reason for the absence of such a law is that our elections have been regulated heretofore by officers appointed by the States, and it is only very recently that the armies of the United States have attempted to interfere in our elections.

By the spirit of the Constitution of the United States, and by the constitution of every State in the Union, the military is to be kept in strict subordination to the civil power; and I suppose that those who went before us never thought we should have rulers so wicked and corrupt as to use the machinery of the Federal Government for the purpose of prostrating the freedom of elections in the States; otherwise, I am sure that such laws as the one before us would have been enacted long before this. I find upon examination that seven of the States of the Union have enacted statutes to prevent soldiers making their appearance on election day at the places where the elections are held—Maryland, Mississippi, New Jersey, New York, Pennsylvania, Maine, and Massachusetts. The constitution of the State of Maryland provides that, upon conviction for the offence of giving or receiving bribes or influencing any man to give an illegal vote, not only the man giving the bribe, but the man giving the illegal vote shall forever after be disqualified from voting and from holding any office of trust, honor, or profit under the

State government. Every State in the Union has severe penal laws, providing for the punishment of all who in any way interfere to prevent free elections.

With us, Mr. President, sovereignty resides in the people, and the people by the exercise of free suffrage declare their will and appoint their agencies to carry on the government. He who attempts to interfere with this most inestimable right, whether he be President, major general, or citizen, is an enemy to the Republic and deserves the harshest punishment. In order to have free elections, there must be free speech and a free press; the sovereign people must have an opportunity of forming an enlightened public opinion upon the questions at issue, which can only be done after full and free discussion. Free speech and a free press in a government like ours are the soul of republican institutions; free suffrage is the very heart-strings of civil liberty. To be free, the elections must be conducted in accordance with laws so framed as to prevent fraud, force, intimidation, corruption, and venality, superintended by election judges and officers independent of the executive or any other power of the Government; the military must not interfere, but be kept in strict subordination to the law, which should be so framed as to prevent absolutely such interference. The only duty of the Executive is to see that the law is faithfully executed. The Executive must not use the power intrusted to him to prevent free elections.

It is certainly a subversion of the very foundation of the Government for the Executive to use the force and the power that the Government has placed in his hands for defensive purposes to overthrow the free suffrages of the people and to appoint those to power who will be his truckling menials, his subservient agents to carry out his will, to aid him it may be to overthrow the liberties of the people whom they should represent, betray the Constitution that they should preserve and protect, destroy everything that makes the Government desirable and worthy of the support of an honest and free people. Yet, sir, such things have been done, and I regret to say that there are those in the Senate chamber who not only do not denounce, but who approve these usurpations, these plain, palpable violations of the Constitution of their country.

Mr. President, let us for a moment see what are the powers of the President of the United States. From whence does he derive this power to regulate elections and to appoint representatives of the people? for when stripped of its verbiage that is really what has been done in many parts of the States of

Maryland, Missouri, Kentucky, and Delaware. Where, I ask, does the Executive of the United States derive such power? He certainly does not derive it from the Constitution.

He is commander-in-chief of the armies of the United States, and under that clause I suppose those who oppose the bill claim that the President can rightfully exercise the power that he has exercised in overthrowing the freedom of elections in Maryland and other States. They claim it under the war power, which I will notice in another part of my remarks. The President is to "take care that the laws be faithfully executed." What laws are they that the President shall see faithfully executed? The Constitution declares that—

"This Constitution and the laws of the United States which shall be made in pursuance thereof, and all treaties made or which shall be made under the authority of the United States, shall be the supreme law of the land."

These are the laws that the President is to see faithfully executed. Whenever he goes beyond that he is a usurper. The President, under the Constitution, can exercise no implied power. All the implied powers that can be exercised under our Government must be exercised by another and a different body of magistracy, to wit, the legislative; and that is the express language of the Constitution.

In the States to which I have alluded, the President, or those acting under his orders, have prescribed the qualifications of voters and the qualifications of candidates for office, and that, too, in direct violation of the Constitution of the United States. This is a grave charge, but it is one that I will make good by testimony that none can doubt. Let us see who it is that has the right to prescribe the qualifications of voters. I suppose that no Senator will deny that as to all State offices the States have the power to prescribe the qualifications of the officer as well as of the voter. That power not having been delegated by the Constitution to the general Government, the States necessarily retain it. But there is an express provision of the Constitution. The tenth amendment, which declares "The powers not delegated to the United States by the Constitution, nor prohibited by it to the States, are reserved to the States respectively or to the people," and the Constitution very clearly indicate who are qualified voters for members of Congress. The second section of the first article of the Constitution declares who shall be qualified electors for members of Congress. It fixes the qualification as the one ordained by the State government for the members of the most numerous branch of their legislature. That is the fundamental law of the land; but in violation of that provision of the Constitution the military have seen fit, by military orders, to fix the qualifications of voters in the States. They have gone further, and fixed the qualifications for office. Not only the military have done this, but the President of the United States himself has done it. I am not going to waste all my time upon those who do the chief magistrate's bidding, but it is my purpose to-day to expose his atrocious violations of the Constitution. I trust that I shall speak of the President in a manner that is courteous, but I certainly shall do it in very plain language. The charges that I have to make I trust will not be misunderstood by anyone. I will not deal in innuendo, insinuation, or hint, but I will make the charge directly, and I have the proof to sustain it.

The Committee on Military Affairs, who made a very elaborate report, which I have before me, and which I shall presently review, justify the military in all they have done in controlling elections. The sole object of the committee in their report seems to be the justification and vindication of the military authorities for their atrocious assault on the rights of the States and the liberties of the people and their wicked and illegal interference in elections; and they assault every person who says or does anything tending to prove that the military have usurped powers that belong to the civil officers of the States and to the people. The committee justify the President and the military authorities for this interference in elections upon the ground that it was right and proper that the military arm should have been so used to protect the voters, "the loyal voters," as they are called in the report. The Constitution prescribes the duty of the chief magistrate on this subject in article four:

The President of the United States has no authority or power to send his military into one of the adhering States for the purpose of preventing domestic violence at the polls unless he has been invited to do so by the State authorities.

But for this provision of the Constitution a corrupt, venal, or ambitious President could by means of the military force, under some imaginary plea of domestic violence, invade any State in this Union on the eve of an election, and dictate the persons who should be returned as members of the other House of Congress, who should be returned as members of the legislature, who should be returned as governors of the States. In a word, if you allow him to use the army in this way without the invitation of the State authorities, a wicked and corrupt man would have it in his power to prostrate every State government in the Union, and to elect officers who would do his bidding, and thus overthrow the liberties of the people, and establish a consolidated despotism of which he would be the master.

The speaker referred in particular to military interference in the gubernatorial election in Kentucky, where Charles A. Wickliffe was the Democratic candidate.

The committee say that Mr. Wickliffe and the gentlemen who invited him to become a candidate desired rebels to vote.

The committee say that they invited those whose hands were red with the blood of Unionists, and who were loaded with the spoils of the plundered friends of the Union, to come to the polls. The committee were drawing upon their fancy for their facts in making such a statement, and a most distempered fancy it must have been. They could not have been deluded by the words "Southern rights," because this address states distinctly that the Southern rights men were not secessionists, and were not implicated in the rebellion.

The organization that put Mr. Wickliffe forward as a candidate was the Democratic party under its old name and under its old flag.

In this report the committee impugn the loyalty of Mr. Wickliffe; and upon what ground? Mr. Wickliffe was one of the first and stanchest Union men in the State of Kentucky. In the other end of this Capitol he voted men and money to carry on the war; and he never failed to do so until the last session, when he voted against an appropriation bill because the House would not insert a clause in it that the money should not be used for the purpose of freeing negroes and reducing States to provinces. It is well known that Mr. Wickliffe was a strong and warm friend of the war up to that time, until he thought the radical policy of the President was such as would destroy every hope of the restoration of the Union.

Well, sir, that sterling old patriot became the candidate of a party that were prevented from exercising the right of suffrage in Kentucky; and in order to justify that outrage and the striking of his name from the polls by the ruthless hand of the military, this committee say he is disloyal. I have no doubt if an angel of the Lord had appeared before the Committee on

Military Affairs and told them there had been military interference in the elections in Maryland and Kentucky, that it was
seen and known by all who were present at the polls, the writer
of the report of the committee would have asserted that the
angel was disloyal. Every man—I do not care how elevated
his position or upright his standing in society, or how devoted
he may have been in the past or the present to the Union—who
asserts that there was interference in the elections, the committee say is disloyal, or they impute some unworthy motive to
him.

General Burnside, on the 31st of July, issued an order
placing Kentucky under martial law, declaring that it was to
prevent the rebel troops interfering in the election. There was
no necessity for that order. At the time it was issued there
were not in Kentucky more than about a thousand rebel soldiers, and they were cavalry in one portion of the State in
rapid retreat; and on the day of election there were no Confederate soldiers in the State.

I will not now discuss the question as to whether General
Burnside had the power to declare martial law. It is well
known to the Senate that I hold there is no power in the Government, in the President, or any of his commanders, to declare
martial law; but if it did exist it should be confined to besieged
cities and localities occupied by the army. But certainly there
is no power to declare martial law in the adhering States, when
they are not occupied by the forces of the enemy.

General Burnside plainly and palpably violated the Constitution of his country when he issued that order interfering with
elections. Let me ask, did Kentucky invite General Burnside
to bring his forces there to protect the election? No, sir. The
legislature did not do it; the governor, in the language of the
day a loyal man, never invited him to do it.

What did General Burnside do? What were the orders issued by his subordinates? Here is an extract from one of
them:

"Judges and clerks so appointed are hereby directed not to place the
name of any person on the poll books to be voted for at said election who
is not a Union man, or who may be opposed to furnishing men and money
for a vigorous prosecution of the war."

There is appended to that order an oath which varies from
the oath prescribed by the law of Kentucky. The constitution
and laws of Kentucky do not require that a man shall be in

favor of furnishing men and money for a vigorous prosecution of the war to qualify him to hold office.

In many of the counties the name of the whole Democratic ticket was stricken from the poll book by the military authorities. In many voting places and in entire counties of Kentucky no man was allowed to vote for that ticket.

In many places the candidates were arrested. In the first congressional district Judge Trimble, the candidate for Con-

"BAYONETS AT THE POLLS"

From the collection of the New York Historical Society

gress, as loyal a man and as true to the Constitution and Union of his fathers as lives in the Union, was arrested by military authority. He was brought to the city of Henderson, a town just without his district, and there he was kept in military confinement near a month, until after the election was over. They told him that, if he would decline being a candidate for Congress, they would release him. He would not so degrade his manhood as to decline the canvass at the bidding of military tyrants and usurpers, and he was kept in prison. They found that he would be elected by a large majority notwithstanding his imprisonment, and then they sent the military over his district and had his name stricken from the polls in almost every voting precinct in the district. The gentleman who beat him got some four thousand votes in a district that polls about twenty thousand.

Mr. Anderson, who now occupies the seat in Congress from the first district in Kentucky, frankly acknowledges that he was elected by the bayonets.

Such were the terrorism and interference by the military that Mr. Wickliffe, the Democratic candidate for governor, in some six or seven of the strongest Democratic counties in the State, did not get a single vote, and in many other strong Democratic counties he received very few votes.

In the case of the Maryland election the speaker afforded proof that the President was directly responsible for military interference at the polls.

The Athenians were so watchful and so jealous of the right of free suffrage that a stranger who interfered in the assemblies of the people was regarded as a traitor, and was punished by their laws with death. Had President Lincoln and General Schenck lived in the time of the free commonwealth of Athens, and interfered with the assemblies of the people as they did with the right of free suffrage in Maryland, they would have been executed as traitors and felons, and would have justly deserved their fate.

The doctrine of those gentlemen who desire to clothe the Executive with this supreme power, with this absolute power, with this more than dictatorial power, places this great Republic in that humiliating attitude. I do not think that a citizen in a country governed by law was ever driven to the necessity of appealing to one man for protection. Sir, the citizen who for the time being fills the chief executive office is bound to see that the laws are faithfully executed: that is his sworn duty. There is no liberty save in the supremacy of the law. In all free governments the citizen appeals to the law for protection.

Mr. President, all usurpers and all tyrants that have gone before us, those who have overthrown the liberties of every people who have lost their liberties, claim their powers under this plea of necessity. Cæsar, when he led his army from Gaul, crossed the Rubicon, and overthrew the liberties of his country, did it upon the plea of necessity, and tyrants the world over have done the same thing. The President seems to me to follow in the footsteps of Cæsar, Pompey, and Cromwell. The Chief Magistrate, I regret to say, seems to copy all the faults, while he has exhibited none of the virtues of those distinguished men. Speaking of Cæsar Montesquieu says:

"He raised troubles in the city by his emissaries; he made himself master of all elections; and consuls, prætors, and tribunes purchased their promotions at their own price."

"He made himself master of all elections." That is what is being done here.

Mr. President, from the authorities I have read it seems that we are following in the footsteps of nations whose liberties have been overthrown and trampled down beneath the iron heel of military despotism.

Allow me to tell you, Senators, that one reason why the people have submitted so quietly, so uncomplainingly, to the many usurpations of the Executive is that they hoped in a short time to have the privilege of relieving themselves of the President by means of free suffrage; but if you allow the military to prevent free elections you not only stab the Republic in its very vitals, but you will by that means cause many persons who think that these usurpations of power ought to be resisted only at the ballot box to look about for other means to redress their grievances. If you do not wish blood to flow in this land, if you wish to preserve our institutions, allow the people the privilege of turning out every four years their President if they desire to do so.

Sir, the President and his satraps had better beware. A brave' people will not stand these things always. A day of reckoning will come, and an awful day it will be to those guilty men who have overthrown and trodden under foot the Constitution and laws of their country, and unlawfully deprived the people of their dearest rights.

It is pleasant when we see that a gleam of light has broken in upon persons from whom we expected little good. I hold in my hand an extract from a speech of the most distinguished radical in America—a man of learning, a man of eloquence, indeed of rare elocution. I had thought that his whole soul was fully absorbed in this negro question, and that he could not talk without bringing it in. I mean Wendell Phillips. But while I think him a fanatic of the deepest dye, he differs from others of his party; he sometimes has lucid intervals. Allow me to read an extract from a speech of that eloquent man on this very point:

"But let me remind you of another tendency of the time. You know, for instance, that the writ of *habeas corpus*, by which government is bound to render a reason to the judiciary before it lays its hands upon a citizen, has been called the high-water mark of English liberty. The present Napoleon, in his treatise on the English Constitution, calls it the germ of English institutions. Lieber says that that, with free meetings like this, and a free press, are the three elements which distinguish liberty from despotism, and all that Saxon blood has gained in the battles and toils of two hundred years are these three things. Now, to-day, every one of these—*habeas corpus*, the right of free meeting, and free press—is annihilated in every square mile of the Republic. We live to-day, every one of us, under martial law or mob law. The Secretary of State puts into his bastile, with a warrant as irresponsible as that of Louis, any man whom he pleases; and you know that neither press nor lips may venture to arraign the government without being silenced.

''We are tending with rapid strides—you say, inevitable; I don't deny it, necessarily; I don't question it; we are tending to that strong government which frightened Jefferson; toward that unlimited debt, that endless army. We have already those alien and sedition laws, which, in 1798, wrecked the Federal party and summoned the Democratic into existence. For the first time on the continent we have passports, which even Louis Bonaparte pronounced useless and odious. For the first time in our history, government spies frequent our great cities.''

That, sir, is a very graphic and truly eloquent picture of the times in which we are, and I hope the country will take warning. We seem to have yielded everything to the military power, and I regret to say with a tameness and submission which, in my judgment, are unbecoming members of an American Congress.

A military republic we have, and we have a republic but in name—the animating principle, the security of the citizen in life, liberty, and property is gone.

There never was a time, it does not exist now, and has not existed since this unfortunate civil war commenced, in which it was necessary for the President to overthrow the Constitution and elevate the military above the civil power. There is power enough in the Constitution to furnish the President every dollar and every man needed for this war. Congress can give him the sword and the purse. What more can you confer? Nothing. Where, then, the necessity and the excuse for these wanton violations of the Constitution, this reckless overthrow of the liberties of the people, this setting at naught the laws and the constitutions of the States, this regulating of elections by the sword? None. None. The genius of our Government is founded upon the principle that the military shall be kept in strict subordination to the civil power. But the friends of the President claim it as a matter of necessity to save the life of the nation, when they must see that the President is trampling under his feet the Constitution, and crushing out the liberties of the people, and destroying every vital principle that gives value to free government.

But, sir, we have had other great chieftains before. There was a man who lived in this Republic that I suppose was thought by all wise and good men to be almost as great as Abraham Lincoln is thought to be by his cringing, truckling, and obsequious followers; that man was George Washington. He led our armies through a seven years' war in most trying times, when the organization of the civil authority was very defective; when there was great difficulty in procuring men for the army and money to defray the necessary expenses of the Government, many of the States failing to furnish their quotas of men and money. Did Washington, during that long and arduous struggle, ever think it necessary to subordinate the civil to the military authority? No, sir; no. In 1783, when he resigned his commission at Annapolis, Thomas Mifflin, President of the Continental Congress, addressed him as follows:

"You have conducted the great military contest with wisdom and fortitude, invariably regarding the rights of the civil power through all disasters and dangers."

This I regard as the highest and most deserved compliment that was ever bestowed upon mortal man.

Sir, I would that this vacillating, dissembling, weak, and I fear wicked and corrupt man in the White House had been infused with the wisdom, virtue, and patriotism that animated the soul and prompted the actions of the great Washington in our revolutionary struggle. Washington and his compatriots were engaged in a struggle for civil liberty; the sword was used only to resist the encroachment of tyrants, and was subordinated to the civil power. The resistance was successful. They then laid broad, deep, and strong the foundation of civil and religious liberty. They proclaimed the Constitution as the fundamental law, and threw it as a strong and impenetrable shield around the rights of the States and the liberties of the people. The Executive is now using the sword which should only be directed against the armed enemies of the Republic for the sacrilegious purpose of suppressing free speech, free press, and free suffrage, and the overthrow of the Constitution, the rights of the States, and the liberties of the people of the adhering States.

On March 23 Jacob M. Howard [Mich.] spoke against the bill.

This measure is brought forward at an unpropitious time, at a time when the country is engaged in a struggle against an immense armed rebellion which calls for the exertion of all the faculties, all the power of the Government, all its means, and for the exercise of every patriotic quality which belongs to American freemen. In the strictest sense of the law of nations it is a civil war, it has been so adjudged to be by the Supreme Court of the United States.

The two governments being, in respect to each other, not foreign and independent, but their citizens being citizens of the same common government, and in law subject to the same authority, there cannot be drawn between them that exact line of distinction which exists between the subjects of two belligerent foreign governments at war with one another; yet there is, because there must be somewhere, a test, recognized by the law of war, which is to determine the treatment that one party may exercise toward the subjects of the other, and by which one party may be known from the other. It is that line of demarcation which divides the loyal from the disloyal. It is the test and touchstone by which the heart of every citizen is to be tried and by which it is to be determined whether he is in favor of the old Government or whether he is opposed to it. All those who in their hearts are friendly to the old Government, who are willing to support and uphold it, are loyal— they have the rights of loyal belligerents; while all those who in their hearts are opposed to the old Government, or even indifferent to its preservation, who are willing to destroy and overthrow it, or to see it destroyed or overthrown, and especially those who directly or indirectly give actual aid and comfort to the rebellion, are disloyal, and are to be treated as enemies. I know of no other rule by which a distinction can be established between the two classes, those who are loyal and those who are disloyal.

In the midst of this clash of arms, while the whole hemisphere is lighted up by the lurid flames of war, extending from the Atlantic Ocean far west to the Rocky Mountains, while every loyal man is filled with anxiety for the final result of the contest, while along this frontier, marked by a line of bristling bayonets for more than fifteen hundred miles, the war is waging with fury, and the line itself constantly fluctuating, the Senator from Kentucky brings forward a bill prohibiting the military authorities, in any case, in any manner, to interfere with what he calls the freedom of election in the States, severely punishing military men for fighting battles, in certain cases, as well as for preventing the enemy himself from participating in State elections!

That honorable Senator will admit that for a measure so novel in its provisions, so extraordinary in the results which it aims to accomplish, there should be evidence of some great and intolerable evil which may be cured by such a measure. It is not sufficient that there may be a few trifling instances of wrong and misuse of military power; the evil should be so enormous as to address itself to the conscience of every member of the Senate, and the evidence of it so clear and overwhelming as to leave no doubt or hesitation in the mind. I shall show, I think, before I conclude my remarks, that there is no such evil; and that, if there be any evil of even considerable magnitude, the evidence of its existence has not been presented to us by the honorable Senator from Kentucky or any other member in such form as to deserve our serious attention.

And, sir, *in limine*, I have to say, in respect to this bill, that it contains a provision which, in my judgment, is utterly unsupported by any clause of the Constitution of the United States, and is as clearly obnoxious to the objection of unconstitutionality as any bill which has ever been presented to the Senate.

I beg to know from what provision of the Constitution it is that the Senator from Kentucky derives the power of employing the courts or other authorities of the United States to punish persons who may violate a State law regulating elections or defining the qualifications of State voters? Whence does he derive the power to punish by Federal sentences in Federal courts violations of a law which it is competent for a State and a State only to enact?

Will the Senator tell me in reply that Congress have a right to inflict this punishment upon a man because he is in the military or naval service of the United States? Such a proposition is not capable of argument. Men are placed in the military service of the United States for the purpose of acting in that capacity; and the power of Congress in such cases only goes to the extent of controlling and regulating their conduct according to the code of war; and there it stops. It cannot be pretended that because a man is a soldier in the army and goes home and commits a murder in the State to which he belongs Congress therefore may declare by a law that he shall be tried and punished for the murder in a Federal court. The crime in such a case is committed against the peace and dignity of the State, not against the peace and dignity of the United States;

and, although if committed by him while in actual service and in the ranks, he might be punished by court-martial, yet the offence would be against the code of war and not the laws of the State.

Let us, then, sir, hear something less, if the Senator pleases, of these continued, bitter denunciations against the majority of this body for violations of the Constitution. For one, sir, I say to that Senator, I do not acknowledge him as a safe teacher. *"Non tali auxilio, nec defensoribus istis."* Give us no such aid, no such defenders.

Mr. President, we are told by the Senator from Kentucky that the Government of the United States have no power to restrain persons who are rebels, or who are suspected to be rebels, from voting in the States. I do not agree with the Senator as to the power of the Government to prevent disloyal men voting at a State poll. In the present state of things every man who is not for us is against us. Every man, as I said before, who is not friendly to the Government of the United States in his heart is opposed to it. Every man who is not willing to use reasonable and ordinary means, military means, for defending and upholding it at such a moment as this, is an enemy of the United States, and deserves to be treated as an enemy.

Sir, I stand by the doctrine laid down in the report of the Committee on Military Affairs. I hold that these persons whose hearts are against their Government, who are willing that the Government should be destroyed—and I go as far as to declare that those who are unwilling in such a crisis as this to come to the support of the Government and render it their aid, and even those who affect to occupy a position of mere indifference toward it, are also within the category of enemies of their country—ought not, in justice, to be suffered to go to the polls. There must be a distinction somewhere, in this war, between enemies and friends. A friend is the man whose heart is attached to the Government and who is willing, according to his means, to do something to uphold it. He is not the only enemy who takes up arms or furnishes supplies to those in arms, but who looks upon this struggle with indifference, whose heart has no pulsation in favor of the cause, but who is ready whenever an occasion presents itself to go over and join the rebels, or to welcome them when they come as invaders into our midst.

The Senator tells us that the military authorities have no right whatever to interfere in a State election; and if I understood him rightly he went so far as to declare that every person who is not prohibited by the laws of the State itself from voting has a right to vote, and that the United States have no authority to intervene for the purpose of preventing it, although he may be a rebel, stained from the crown of his head to the soles of his feet with the blood of loyal men. I am about to quote an authority which will perhaps have some weight with that Senator. I believe the first example of such interference in a State election was set by General McClellan while commander of the army of the Potomac. In response to a letter of request, addressed to him by Governor Hicks of Maryland, dated October 26, 1861, he issued the following order, dated October 29, 1861, to General N. P. Banks:

> GENERAL: There is an apprehension among Union citizens in many parts of Maryland of an attempt at interference with their rights of suffrage by disunion citizens on the occasion of the election to take place on the 6th of November next.
>
> In order to prevent this the major-general commanding directs that you send detachments of a sufficient number of men to the different points in your vicinity where the elections are to be held *to protect the Union voters,* and to *see that no disunionists are allowed* to intimidate them, or in any way to interfere with their rights.
>
> He also desires you to arrest and hold in confinement until after the election all disunionists who are known to have returned from Virginia recently, and *who show themselves at the polls,* and to guard effectually against any invasion of the peace and order of the election. For the purpose of carrying out these instructions *you are authorized to suspend the habeas corpus.*

If this power exists in the Government of the United States in any of its departments, in time of war, then no State can interfere with its exercise, but the citizens of the State must submit it as to the exercise of any other Federal power, because it acts upon those citizens as individuals. In short, if the Government have this tutelary authority, if they have the right to treat rebels or rebel sympathizers, or those who aid and abet the rebellion, *as enemies,* as they undoubtedly have, then they may use it through the military arm or any other instrumentality to which they see fit to resort. They may thus prevent those enemies from exercising any of the rights of citizens in the State. For this we have at least the sanction of General McClellan—certainly, with a certain portion of the members of this body, a high authority; and I am very happy to be able for once to concur fully in the opinions of the general. The power is thus, as we see, sanctioned by that distinguished military leader, the heir-apparent of the Democratic party to the next Presidency, and the promising help and support, I suppose, of the cause of the Union as they would restore it. At all events, it is sufficient for my purpose that I have his complete sanction of the principle that it is the right of the military arm to interfere in State elections so far as to prevent traitors from voting, although they may happen to possess the formal qualifications of electors of the State. I think he was entirely right, and I am free to give him that praise.

If we have that power, as General McClellan agrees we have, then it belongs to us exclusively, and the States have nothing to do but to permit its exercise. It is a power peculiarly pertaining to the United States, and as much to be respected and obeyed as the judicial power of the Government. The two jurisdictions are here as separate and distinct as in any other case. The States have just as much right to trespass on any other constitutional power belonging to the Government as upon this.

Sir, in my judgment, the case comes clearly and distinctly within the principle laid down by the Supreme Court of the United States in the case of Booth, in which the decision of the court was delivered by the present chief justice [Roger B. Taney]. (See 21 Howard's Reports, p. 524.)

And I say here that, whenever a military officer has issued an order for the purpose of keeping traitors away from the polls, and the order is regular in form, no State has in a time of rebellion or civil war any right to dispute or obstruct its operation; and whenever the governor of a State, a judge of election, or other State magistrate, undertakes to resist such an order, he brings himself within the principle laid down by the Supreme Court, asserting that such interference may be resisted even by violence. It is nothing more nor less than this, that the authority of the United States is supreme; and it rests with the Senator from Kentucky, and those who entertain his views, to establish the principle that the Government of the United States is not supreme in the treatment of its enemies. The Senator has not argued that question. He has assumed that it is not. It is with him a mere *petitio principii*, the assumption of the truth of a proposition that remains to be proved. Let him by fair and candid argument, by reference to the books of authority, show, if he can, that the Government of the United States in the prosecution of a war is not supreme and has no right to define and declare who are enemies of the United States and who are friends. He will find it a vain task; and I indulge the fancy that he will not be swift to undertake it.

Sir, the rebels on this subject have been our instructors.

They have found no constitutional difficulty in treating persons within their limits attached to the Government of the United States, and acknowledging their allegiance to it as enemies. Without scruple or hesitation they proceeded at an early day to enact a statute, now in force among them, by which every Union man born in a State still adhering to the Union is proscribed and expelled from their territorial limits.[1]

But, sir, the Senator from Kentucky has made another novel discovery in the field of constitutional law, to which I must be indulged in paying some slight attention. He tells the Senate in his speech on this bill that the Government of the United States has no right whatever to send troops into any State unless it be at the request of the legislature while in session, or of the Executive when the legislature cannot be convened; and he is extremely earnest and confident on this point. He flatters himself that he has at length discovered the great touchstone by which this whole war is proved to be unconstitutional, and "coercion" a tyranny and an outrage. This is the first time in my professional life that I ever heard it asserted by a gentleman professing to be a judge of the principles of the Constitution, and a good lawyer, that the right of the Government of the United States to employ military force to put down an insurrection was derived from and is solely dependent upon that clause of the Constitution to which he refers. The clause declares that the Government of the United States shall protect each State against domestic violence when called upon by the State. The very language itself shows that the violence against which the State is to be protected is violence not against the authority of the United States, but against the authority of the State, and of the State only.

Domestic violence in a State is violence against the authority of the State, and that violence may be in perfect consistency with the loyalty of the persons who commit it to the Government of the United States.

It is merely local violence against the regular government of the State, and does not embrace an insurrection or rebellion against the Federal Government. And such is the meaning given to the clause in "The Federalist," if the Senator will see fit to consult it. It may be entirely consistent with the authority of the United States, like the Dorr rebellion, in Rhode Island, or the more ancient insurrection of Shay, in Massachusetts. The present war is a rebellion against the authority of the United States, not that of any one particular State, and is not there-

"An act respecting alien enemies," approved August 8, 1861.

fore a case of mere domestic violence as mentioned in the clause on which the Senator relies.

This, however, is the Senator's logic: the States in rebellion are agitated by domestic violence; in such cases the Government of the United States cannot interpose, except upon the request of the legislature of the State when in session, or of the Executive when the legislature cannot be convened; and because the legislature and Executive of all the seceded States have omitted to apply to the Government of the United States for aid to put down this violence; *ergo,* the Government of the United States has no right to march its troops into those States; *ergo,* the whole war is unconstitutional, and we who are engaged in prosecuting this war within the limits of these seceded States are guilty of a perpetual violation of our oaths and of the Constitution of our country. Such is the Senator's logic.

The Senator seemed to forget that, aside from this particular clause, there is given to Congress in express terms power to suppress rebellion and insurrection against the Federal Government itself. We are now acting under this broader and general power. We are acting under a power by no means necessary to have been incorporated in the Constitution—the power to suppress rebellion and insurrection—because from the very nature of Government itself, from the very necessity of its being, the Federal Government, like every other government, must be held to have the right of self-defence, the right to put down resistance to its authority, the right to enforce its own laws, for that cannot be called a government which has no power to carry its own enactments into execution. It is of the very essence of all governments to command, and if a government may command, it is the duty of those who are commanded to obey; so that even without the clause expressly giving to Congress the power to put down an insurrection they would have plenary power so to do.

But the framers of the instrument saw fit to grant the power in express terms, as if in anticipation of this "State rights" objection. (See "The Federalist," 43.)

My conscience will not be troubled by the fanciful constitutional objection that the Government of the United States have no right to "subjugate a State." We have, sir, the same right to subjugate a State in insurrection as to subjugate a foreign country with which we are at war; and the Senator from Kentucky will find it impossible, I apprehend, to draw anything like a sensible distinction between the two cases.

The report of the committee alleges that at the date of a certain letter, which is included in the pamphlet, addressed to Mr. Wickliffe, of Kentucky, and dated June 13, 1863, the business of recruiting blacks was in active progress. It is against that policy that the letter is particularly denunciatory. The writers of the letter used the following language:

"We hold this rebellion utterly unjustifiable in its inception, and a dissolution of the Uuion the greatest of calamities.

"We would use all just and constitutional means adapted to the suppression of the one and the restoration of the other."

Again they say:

"It is now obvious that the fixed purpose of the administration is to arm the negroes of the South to make war upon the whites, and we hold it to be the duty of the people of Kentucky to enter against such a policy a solemn and most emphatic protest."

What is the plain implication from this language addressed to Mr. Wickliffe, that the writers hold the rebellion unjustifiable "in its inception"? Is it not tantamount to a declaration that, although in its inception the rebellion was utterly unjustifiable, it had, nevertheless, become otherwise in consequence of the acts of the Administration, and particularly the act authorizing the recruiting of black troops?

And the Senator says that, at the very time this solemn protest was entered by these leading gentlemen of Kentucky, there was no such thing in Kentucky as the recruiting of black troops.

What, then, is the pith and point of the declaration that the rebellion had become justifiable, although unjustifiable in its inception? Not because recruiting of black troops was going on in Kentucky, but because it was going on somewhere else, and because these troops were to be used as aids in suppressing the rebellion. Sir, this is an audacious presumption on the part of Kentucky. No, sir, I will not say Kentucky; I do not mean the people of Kentucky; I mean the demagogues who assume to be the leaders of the people of Kentucky. What right have they to dictate to the United States what troops they shall raise, or where they shall raise them, or how employ them, so long as the people of Kentucky are not affected by the proceeding?

Mr. President, if there ever was a necessity for the vigorous interposition of military authority to guard the polls against the intrusion of rebels, if there was ever a case in the history of the United States in which the strong arm of military power was invoked by every interest of community, it was the case of Kentucky; and I undertake to say that, without this interference, Kentucky, in all human probability, would to-day have been regularly installed as a member of the rebel confederation. Nothing but the loyal hearts and strong arms of Northern men who hurried from their homes has prevented that State, with all its glorious memories, going over to the rebellion.

I do not stand here to pretend, and I will not assert, that there may not have been abuses in the execution of some of the orders. But you may say the same of the execution of any law. Every power, every law is liable to be abused; but this is no reason for denying or extinguishing the power itself, for repealing it or for repealing the law.

The leader of the Democratic party, Mr. Wickliffe, was plainly unfriendly to the Government of the United States. He was their candidate for governor. The letter inviting him to stand as such declares that the writers "hold this rebellion utterly unjustifiable in its inception," plainly, as I have already remarked, intimating that it had become justifiable. The writers of the pamphlet observe: "Mr. Wickliffe, in accepting the nomination which had thus been tendered him, expressed his hearty concurrence in our view"; that is, his hearty concurrence in the statement that the rebellion had become no longer unjustifiable. I submit, sir, that a man who, at such a time, can so far forget what is due to his country as to intimate that this rebellion had become a justifiable one was not a fit person to be voted for at the polls. And I say boldly that I think the military authorities in Kentucky did exactly right when they instructed the judges of election not to permit Mr. Wickliffe's name to appear on the poll list as a candidate for governor, although, notwithstanding several orders of that kind, he received a very considerable vote in Kentucky.

But, sir, there is no allegation, even in the pamphlet itself, that any one single individual known to be a true and loyal man was hindered from voting at the election in Kentucky on the 3d of August, 1863. It is very true, as the writers of the pamphlet remark, that the aggregate vote at that election compared with the number of male persons over twenty-one years old in 1862 was small. But the smallness of the vote shows not so much that voters were excluded from the polls as that multitudes kept away because of their own disloyal proclivities, while thousands upon thousands had emigrated or gone into the rebel army or into the Union army.

The declarations of the authors of the pamphlet show a different kind of loyalty from mine. It is the loyalty of neutrality, which is no loyalty, and just as inconsistent with the duty which a State and its people owe to the Government of the United States as open rebellion.

Neutrality, sir, Kentucky neutrality, what is it in law, and what would it be if practically carried out there or elsewhere? If the agreement said to have been made by General McClellan with Buckner recognizing the neutrality of the State had been carried into execution practically Kentucky would have been as effectually out of this Union as is now the State of South Carolina. Neutrality, let me say to the Senator, is an attribute belonging exclusively to a sovereign power, an independent nation. You cannot predicate neutrality of any community that does not possess the right of sovereignty as an independent nation, for there are certain rights and duties pertaining to neutrality which can be exercised only by an independent nation, and with which any subordinate or dependent condition is totally incompatible.

Sir, let us contemplate for a moment the condition that Kentucky would have been in if she had carried out effectually her idea of neutrality. The Government of the United States would have been disabled from recruiting a single man within her limits, such recruiting being forbidden by the laws of war and nations within neutral territory. Again, the United States could not have marched a single platoon across the border of Kentucky, although the enemy had been in her midst. The Ohio and the Mississippi would have been sealed up against the navigation of the United States. Kentucky would have been flourishing in all the peace and comfort of neutrality, keeping the Union forces away upon the one side and possibly inviting the rebels upon the other, while at the same time she would have been at complete liberty to carry on trade and commerce in everything not contraband of war with both the belligerent parties.

In short, she would have been enjoying a harvest of profits in her trade with the rebels, and a like harvest in her trade with the Union armies, and at the same time feeling none of the inconveniences of the war. Such, sir, was manifestly the idea at the bottom of Kentucky neutrality.

Is it founded upon the Constitution? Will the gentleman say that under that instrument it is the right of any one of the States to set up to be neutral in a war, whether a civil or a foreign war? No, sir. It is as plainly prohibited as open rebellion, and the claim is as incompatible with fidelity to the Government as the claim of nullification or secession.

Sir, it is amazing that a gentleman who has so much to say about the violation of the Constitution of the United States, a gentleman who has not hesitated to say upon this floor that if justice had been done to Abraham Lincoln for his imputed unconstitutional interference in State elections he would have been hanged like those who were denounced as traitors by the laws of Greece for voting at elections where they had no right— it is amazing that such a Senator can stand up here and advocate in the same breath the right of a State to assume the condition of neutrality in a war. It is nothing more nor less than actual secession, because it implies an utter repudiation of the obligations of the State to the general Government. Sir, I thank Heaven that the President of the United States at an early day rebuked this pretension.

The speaker then turned to the Maryland election. Referring to the proclamation of Governor Bradford he said:

This proclamation was a direct invitation to the judges of election and the people of Maryland to disregard the order [of Gen. Schenck], and, if need be, to resort to violence in resisting it. It was a threat to produce an insurrection, and to drive out the United States troops by force. The report of the Military Committee holds that the governor had no right to issue it, or to instruct the judges in this manner. The Senator from Kentucky, in his emphatic reply to this part of the report, tells us that the Governor of Maryland had "a right to issue a proclamation concerning elections." Who denies it? The Senator was combating a proposition the committee had not made.

Undoubtedly, sir, the Governor of Maryland, like any other governor, has a right to issue a proclamation on any subject connected with his duties; but neither the Governor of Maryland nor any other governor has the right to say to the judges of elections, "Your duties are such and such, and you must do so and so." The law, not the governor's proclamation, regulates their duties. And whatever may be that law, whether in the shape of a State statute or the order of a military man for the protection of the polls, such as that of General Schenck, it is nevertheless law, and Governor Bradford had no more right to say to the judges that they were not to obey General

Schenck's order than to tell them they were not to obey a statute of the United States. It did not lie in the mouth of the Governor of Maryland to dispense them from that obligation.

Sir, if the judges of election had been as hasty as the governor, if they had resorted to the power of the county or other force for the purpose of resisting the execution of this order, it is easy to see that before the sun of the 3d of November went down below the western horizon the soil of ancient Maryland would have been stained with fraternal blood, and hundreds, perhaps thousands, of her sons would have been weltering in their gore; for it would inevitably have led to a violent collision between the troops of the United States and the people of Maryland.

The Senator alleges that the judges were prevented from executing the laws. In many cases, he says, they were imprisoned. Let me say, with the utmost personal respect for that Senator, that I have discovered no case, from the beginning to the end of this vast amount of written testimony, which shows or conduces to show that the judges of election were prevented in any case from executing the laws. If there be any such case, I hope the honorable Senator will be able to lay it before the Senate. There are but two cases in which the judges of election were arrested; the one the case in Kentucky, where the judges of election openly and contemptuously refused to recognize the military authority and to execute the orders, and were therefore placed under arrest; the other in Maryland, where an investigation ordered by the President showed that the persons arrested were not judges, but citizens, who had abandoned their posts as officers.

As I said in the beginning, Mr. President, in order to justify Congress in passing this bill, the proof of existing evils should be plain, indubitable, and irresistible. The times especially require it. Were it a time of peace, I admit the military authorities of the United States would have no power to interfere with State elections; but it is not a time of peace, but of war; a time in which the feelings of every man in the nation are taking a fixed direction, either in favor of the Government or against it; a time when it is absolutely necessary for the preservation not only of the Federal Government, but of the State governments, that a line of demarcation should be drawn between the loyal and the disloyal, between men who are friendly and men who are unfriendly; and I insist that, in view of the evidence before us, there is no sufficient reason for the passage of this bill had we even the power to pass it.

The bill was debated at various times until June 22, when, through the persistent efforts of Senator Powell, it was finally brought to a vote. Several amendments, however, were first offered by the Senator himself; the most important of which was one providing that soldiers may be stationed at the polls if "it shall be necessary to repel the armed enemies of the United States." This and other amendments were adopted.

Samuel C. Pomeroy [Kan.] then moved to add to Senator Powell's amendment the words: "or to keep the peace at the polls."

Senator Powell, James A. McDougall [Cal.] and others objected to this amendment as destroying the effect of the bill. It expressed, they declared, the very pretext upon which the recent outrage against the free ballot had been committed. This amendment, however, was adopted by a vote of 16 to 15. The bill was then passed by a vote of 19 to 13.

James Harlan [Ia.] moved to reconsider the passage of the bill. The motion was entered.

On June 23 Senator Howard spoke in favor of reconsidering the measure.

This bill gives permission for the employment of the military forces of the United States at elections only where there shall be armed enemies of the Federal Government at the polls, or where it shall be necessary to employ a military force to keep the peace. It therefore leaves the implication perfectly irresistible that in all other cases it shall not be lawful for the military authorities to employ their forces, although there might be thronging around the polls rebels who had just left the field of battle, and whose hands were crimsoned with the blood of loyal men. This bill allows notorious rebels to come to the polls and cast their ballots without the slightest fear of interference on the part of the military authorities.

It is said, Mr. President, that it is the exclusive privilege of the States to protect their own polls. But this is true only in a time of peace. For in a time of war a State government is not competent to extend to a person who is a public enemy of the National Government, and against whom and against whose class or community the United States as a nation is waging war, any political right or privilege whatever; and I do assert that such a person is in all respects and at all times subject to the laws of the Federal Government relating to him as a public enemy, and subject to those laws in exclusion of any conflicting law of a State. For a State cannot legally be engaged in war; the whole of the war power pertains exclusively to the Federal Government.

Reverdy Johnson [Md.] replied to Senator Howard.

Who is to ascertain what men are public enemies of the United States? Shall a citizen of Maryland, for instance, decide that I am not entitled to vote at an election in my own State? There is but one subject upon which the Federal Government has any authority to interfere with elections. Over the times, the places, and the manner, the Constitution gives to the several States the exclusive authority with two exceptions, which have nothing in the world to do with the manner in which the franchise is to be exercised or with the parties who are to exercise it. Upon all other subjects, therefore, than of time and manner, the jurisdiction of the States is just as paramount and exclusive as it was before the Constitution was adopted.

Mr. President, we hold our rights under the Constitution consecrated by the blood of our ancestors. We have proved ourselves worthy to enjoy them by meeting the enemies of our country upon the field and the ocean, and we are doing it now. Oh, save us, save us in the name of freedom, from the rule of military despotism!

On June 28 the motion to reconsider the vote on the bill was defeated by a vote of 19 to 23.

CHAPTER XIV

The Thirteenth Amendment

[CONSTITUTIONAL ABOLITION OF SLAVERY]

Lyman Trumbull [Ill.] Moves in the Senate a Constitutional Amendment Abolishing Slavery—Debate: in Favor, Sen. Trumbull, Henry Wilson [Mass.], Daniel Clark [N. H.], Timothy O. Howe [Wis.], Reverdy Johnson [Md.], John P. Hale [N. H.], Charles Sumner; Opposed, Garrett Davis [Ky.], Willard Saulsbury [Del.], James A. McDougall [Cal.]—Resolution Is Carried in the Senate, and Defeated in the House—It Is Passed at the Next Session.

ON March 28, 1864, Lyman Trumbull [Ill.] introduced in the Senate, from the Committee on the Judiciary, the following proposed amendment to the Constitution:

ARTICLE XIII

Sec. 1. Neither slavery nor involuntary servitude, except as a punishment for crime, whereof the party shall have been duly convicted, shall exist within the United States, or any place subject to their jurisdiction.

Sec. 2. Congress shall have power to enforce this article by appropriate legislation.

Abolition of Slavery

Senate, March 28-April 8, 1864

SENATOR TRUMBULL.—Without stopping to inquire into all the causes of our troubles, and of the distress, desolation, and death which have grown out of this atrocious rebellion, I suppose it will be generally admitted that they sprung from slavery. If a large political party in the North attribute these troubles to the impertinent interference of Northern philan-

thropists and fanatics with an institution in the Southern
States with which they had no right to interfere, I reply, if
there had been no such institution there could have been no
such alleged impertinent interference; if there had been no
slavery in the South, there could have been no Abolitionists in
the North to interfere with it. If, upon the other hand, it be
said that this rebellion grows out of the attempt on the part of
those in the interest of slavery to govern this country so as to
perpetuate and increase the slaveholding power, and failing in
this that they have endeavored to overthrow the Government
and set up an empire of their own, founded upon slavery as its
chief corner-stone, I reply, if there had been no slavery there
could have been no such foundation on which to build. If the
freedom of speech and of the press, so dear to freemen everywhere, and especially cherished in this time of war by a large
party in the North who are now opposed to interfering with
slavery, has been denied us all our lives in one-half the States
of the Union, it was by reason of slavery. If these halls have
resounded from our earliest recollections with the strifes and
contests of sections, ending sometimes in blood, it was slavery
which almost always occasioned them.

Senator Trumbull here reviewed the acts of the
President and Congress relating to negroes, previously
to the Emancipation Proclamation.

But, sir, had these laws, all of them, been efficiently executed they would not wholly have extirpated slavery. They
were aimed only at the slaves of rebels. Congress never undertook to free the slaves of loyal men; no act has ever passed for
that purpose.

At a later period, the President by proclamation undertook
to free the slaves in certain localities. Notice of this proclamation was given in September, 1862, and it was to become effective in January, 1863. Unlike the acts of Congress, which undertook to free the slaves of rebels only, and of such as came
under our control, the President's proclamation excepted from
its provisions the regions of country subject to our authority,
and declared free the slaves only who were in regions of country from which the authority of the United States was expelled,
enjoining upon the persons proposed to be made free to abstain
from all violence unless in necessary self-defence, and recom-
mending them in all cases, when allowed, to labor faithfully for
reasonable wages.

The force and effect of this proclamation are understood very differently by its advocates and opponents. The former insist that it is and was within the constitutional power of the President, as commander-in-chief, to issue such a proclamation; that it is the noblest act of his life or the age; and that by virtue of its provisions all slaves within the localities designated become *ipso facto* free; while others declare that it was issued without competent authority, and has not and cannot effect the emancipation of a single slave. These latter insist that the most the President could do, as commander of the armies of the United States, would be, in the absence of legislation, to seize and free the slaves which came within the control of the army; that the power exercised by a commander-in-chief, as such, must be a power exercised in fact, and that beyond his lines where his armies cannot go his orders are mere *brutum fulmen*,[1] and can work neither a forfeiture of property nor freedom of slaves; that the power of Frémont and Hunter, commanders-in-chief for a certain time in their departments, who assumed to free the slaves within their respective commands, was just as effective within the boundaries of their commands as that of the commander-in-chief of all the departments, who as commander could not draw to himself any of his presidential powers; and that neither had or could have any force except within the lines and where the army actually had the power to execute the order; that to that extent the previous acts of Congress would free the slaves of rebels, and if the President's proclamation had any effect it would be only to free the slaves of loyal men, for which the laws of the land did not provide.

I will not undertake to say which of these opinions is correct, nor is it necessary for my purposes to decide. It is enough for me to show that any and all these laws and proclamations, giving to each the largest effect claimed by its friends, are ineffectual to the destruction of slavery. The laws of Congress if faithfully executed would leave remaining the slaves belonging to loyal masters, which, considering how many are held by children and females not engaged in the rebellion, would be no inconsiderable number, and the President's proclamation excepts from its provisions all of Delaware, Maryland, Kentucky, Tennessee, Missouri, and a good portion of Louisiana and Virginia—almost half the slave States.

If then we are to get rid of the institution, we must have some more efficient way of doing it than by the proclamations

[1] Idle thunder.

that have been issued or the acts of Congress which have been passed.

Some, however, say that we may pass an act of Congress to abolish slavery altogether, and petitions are sent to Congress asking it to pass such a law. I am as anxious to get rid of slavery as any person; but has Congress authority to pass a law abolishing slavery everywhere, freeing the slaves of the loyal, the slaves of the friends of the Government as well as the slaves of the disloyal and of the enemies of the Government? Why, sir, it has been an admitted axiom from the foundation of this Government, among all parties, that Congress had no authority to interfere with slavery in the States where it existed. But it is said this was in a time of peace, and we are now at war, and Congress has authority to carry on war, and in carrying on war we may free the slaves. Why so? Because it is necessary; for no other reason. If we can do it by act of Congress it must be because it is a necessity to the prosecution of the war. We have authority to put down the enemies of the country; we have the right to slay them in battle; we have authority to confiscate their property; but, mark you, does that give any authority to slay the friends of the country, to confiscate the property of the friends of the country, or to free the slaves of the friends of the country?

But it said that freeing slaves would aid us in raising troops; that slaves are unwilling to volunteer and enter the public service unless other slaves are made free, and that we could raise troops better, sooner, and have a more efficient army if slavery were declared abolished. Suppose that were so, is it a necessity? Can we not raise an army without doing this? Has not the Congress of the United States unlimited authority to provide for the raising of armies by draft, by force to put any and every man capable of bearing arms into its service? Have we not already passed a law compelling men to enter the service of the Government in its defence and for the putting down this rebellion? Then there is no necessity to free the slaves in order to raise an army.

But it is a convenience, perhaps some will say. Sir, it is not because a measure would be convenient that Congress has authority to adopt it. The measure must be appropriate and needful to carry into effect some granted power, or we have no authority to adopt it. I can imagine a thousand things that would aid us to raise troops, which no one would contend Congress had authority to do. We now find that it is costing us a large sum of money to carry on this war. There are apprehensions in some quarters that the finances of the country will not be sufficient to prosecute it to the end. A measure that would enable us to carry on the war cheaper would certainly be one in aid of this war power. In consequence of the prosperity which prevails in the country, wages at this time are very high. Men are unwilling to enlist without large bounties and large pay, because they get high wages at home. Suppose we introduce a bill that no man shall be paid in any manufacturing establishment, at any mechanic art, or for his daily labor, more than ten cents a day, and we visit with penalties and punishment any man who shall give to his employee more than that sum; do you not think that would hold out an additional inducement to volunteer? But who would contend that Congress had any such authority? Manifestly it has not. Nor can I find the constitutional authority to abolish slavery everywhere by act of Congress as a necessity to prosecuting the war.

Then, sir, in my judgment, the only effectual way of ridding the country of slavery, and so that it cannot be resuscitated, is by an amendment of the Constitution forever prohibiting it within the jurisdiction of the United States. This amendment adopted, not only does slavery cease, but it can never be reëstablished by State authority, or in any other way than by again amending the Constitution. Whereas, if slavery should now be abolished by act of Congress or proclamation of the President, assuming that either has the power to do it, there is nothing in the Constitution to prevent any State from reëstablishing it. This change of the Constitution will also relieve us of all difficulty in the restoration to the Union of the rebel States when our brave soldiers shall have reduced them to obedience to the laws.

Henry Wilson [Mass.] followed in a speech, entitled "The Death of Slavery Is the Life of the Nation."

I think it is reasonable to suppose that if this proposed amendment passes Congress it will within a year receive the ratification of the requisite number of States to make it a part of the Constitution. That accomplished, and we are forever freed of this troublesome question. We relieve Congress of sectional strifes, and, what is better than all, we restore to a whole race that freedom which is theirs by the gift of God, but which we for generations have wickedly denied them.

Slavery is the conspirator that conceived and organized this mighty conspiracy against the unity and existence of the Republic. Slavery is the traitor that madly plunged the nation into the fire and blood and darkness of civil war. Slavery is the criminal whose hands are dripping with the blood of our murdered sons. Yes, slavery is the conspirator, the traitor, the criminal that is reddening the sods of Christian America with the blood of fathers and husbands, sons and brothers, and bathing them with the bitter tears of mothers, wives, and sisters.

Sir, slavery—bold, proud, domineering, with hate in its heart, scorn in its eye, defiance in its mien—has pronounced against the existence of republican institutions in America, against the supremacy of the Government, the unity and life of the nation. Slavery, hating the cherished institutions that tend to secure the rights and enlarge the privileges of mankind; despising the toiling masses as mudsills and white slaves; defying the Government, its Constitution and its laws, has openly pronounced itself the mortal and unappeasable enemy of the Republic. Slavery stands to-day the only clearly pronounced foe our country has on the globe. Therefore, every word spoken, every line written, every act performed, that keeps the breath of life in slavery for a moment, is against the existence of democratic institutions, against the dignity of the toiling millions, against the liberty, the peace, the honor, the renown, and the life of the nation. In the lights of to-day that flash upon us from camp and battlefield, the loyal eye, heart, and brain of America sees and feels and realizes that the death of slavery is the life of the nation! The loyal voice of patriotism pronounces, in clear accents, that American slavery must die that the American Republic may live!

Sir, under the Constitution, framed to secure the blessings of liberty, slavery strode into the chambers of legislation, the halls of justice, the mansions of the Executive, and, with menaces in the one hand and bribes in the other, it awed the timid and seduced the weak. Marching on from conquest to conquest, crushing where it could not awe, seduce, or corrupt, slavery saw institutions of learning, benevolence, and religion, political organizations and public men, aye, and the people, too, bend before it and acknowledge its iron rule. Seizing on the needed acquisitions of Louisiana and of Florida to extend its boundaries, consolidate its power, and enlarge its sway, slavery crossed the Mississippi and there established its barbarous dominion against the too feeble resistance of a not yet conquered people. Controlling absolutely the policy of the South, swaying the policy of the nation, impressing itself upon the legislation, the sentiments, and opinions of the North, slavery moved on to assured dominion. Under its aggressive advances emancipation societies, organized by the men of the revolutionary era in the first bright ardor of secured liberty, one by one disappeared; presses and churches forgot to remember those in bonds as bound with them, and recreant sons disowned the sentiments, opinions, and principles of a glorious ancestry. And slavery, in the pride of power, proclaimed itself in the halls of Congress, through its apostles and champions, its Calhouns and McDuffies, "a positive good," "the only stable basis of republican institutions," "the corner-stone of the republican edifice."

But amid this general defection from the faith of the statesmen and heroes of the revolutionary age, a fearless and faithful few clung to the teachings of Washington and Franklin, Jefferson and Jay, and their illustrious compeers. Unawed by its power, unseduced by its blandishments, they opposed to the aggressions of slavery—aye, to slavery itself—a stern and unyielding resistance. They proclaimed emancipation to be the duty of the master and the right of the slave. To advance the cause of emancipation and to improve the condition of free people of color they avowed their readiness to use "all means sanctioned by law, humanity, and religion." Slavery marked and branded these heroic men as political and social outlaws; compelling them, in the words of John G. Whittier, "to hold property, liberty, and life itself at the mercy of lawless mobs." Slavery cast its malign influence over all the land, maddening the brain and firing the heart of a deluded people against the fearless few who opposed its aggressions and pitied its hapless victims. Passion—blind, unreasoning passion—ruled the hour. Cities were lighted by the sacked and burning dwellings of a proscribed and hated race. Churches, institutions of learning, and presses were often forcibly closed or destroyed at the bidding of slavery by the lawless violence of "gentlemen of property and standing."

Slaves were held in the District of Columbia, and slave pens and the slave trade polluted and dishonored the national capital under the color of laws for which the people of America were responsible in the forum of nations and before the throne of Almighty God. Christian men and women, oppressed with the sin and shame, humbly petitioned Congress to relieve them from that sin and shame by making the national capital free. Slavery bade its tools—its Pattons, its Pinckneys, and its Athertons—violate the constitutional right of petition, and willing majorities hastened to register its decree. Slavery arraigned before the bar of the House of Representatives John Quincy Adams, the illustrious champion of the right of petition and the freedom of speech, and it expelled the fearless and faithful Giddings for the offence of daring to construe the Constitution of his country and interpret the law of nations. Slavery stepped upon the decks of Massachusetts ships in the harbor of Charleston, seized colored seamen, citizens of the commonwealth, and consigned them to prisons, to be fined, to be lashed, and to be sold into perpetual bondage. Massachusetts, mindful of the rights of all her citizens, sent Samuel Hoar, one of her most honored sons, to test the constitutional rights of her imprisoned citizens in the judicial tribunals. Slavery cast him violently from South Carolina, and enacted that whoever should attempt to defend the rights of colored seamen in the courts of that commonwealth should suffer the ignominy of imprisonment.

Slavery cast its devouring eye upon the broad, rich fields of Texas, and sent its pioneers to wrench them from the feeble grasp of the Mexican republic. By the pen of Calhoun, its great champion, slavery in the name of the nation demanded, in the face of Europe, the annexation of that slaveholding republic, to defeat ultimate emancipation there, and to tighten the fetters of the bondmen here. In obedience to the humiliating demand of slavery, Texas was forced into the Union by an unconstitutional joint resolution, and the nation plunged into a war with Mexico. When peace returned, it brought with it half a million square miles of free territory. The North, the humiliated North, timidly asked that this territory, made forever free by Mexican law, should be forever consecrated to freedom by national legislation; but slavery demanded the right to extend itself over these free Territories, and threatened the dismemberment of the Union if that claim was denied. California framed a constitution and asked admission as a free commonwealth, but slavery resisted her admission with menaces of disunion and civil war. To appease slavery, a pliant Congress organized Utah and New Mexico, so that slave masters could range over them with their fettered bondmen, gave fifteen thousand square miles of the free soil of New Mexico to slaveholding Texas, and with them $10,000,000, and enacted the unconstitutional, inhuman, and unchristian Fugitive Slave Act, that has dishonored and humiliated the nation before earth and heaven. Slavery then, in its hour of complete triumph, insolently demanded that the two great political parties, who had shrunk appalled before its menaces of disunion and civil war, who had betrayed the cause of freedom, humanity, and civilization in America, should now declare these its acts "finalities," and bid the people forever cease "agitation."

Having forced these parties to pronounce its legislation of 1850 a "finality in principle and substance," slavery strode like an imperial despot into these chambers and demanded the repeal of the Missouri prohibition of the 6th of March, 1820, and a faithless Congress and a subservient Executive hastened to open half a million square miles, in the central regions of the Republic, consecrated forever to freedom and free labor, to the footsteps of the bondman. Northern freemen went to that magnificent Territory to found there the institutions of freedom. Slavery made its brutal tools invade Kansas, seize the ballot box, elect a territorial legislature, enact inhuman and unchristian laws, bathe the virgin soil of that beautiful region with the blood of civil war, frame a slave constitution by fraud, and force it upon a free people. Faithfully did the propagandists of slavery labor in Kansas and in Congress, and in the executive departments of the Government, to execute its decrees. They invaded the Territory, they usurped the government, they enacted slave statutes, they robbed and burned, they murdered brave men contending for their lawful rights. In Congress, the champions of slavery were hardly less brutal than in the wilds of distant Kansas. My colleague [Mr. Sumner] portrayed the crimes of slavery against Kansas, and he was smitten down upon the floor of the Senate by "a brutal, murderous, and cowardly assault." The propagandists of slavery framed a slave constitution, sustained it by fraud and violence, and the weak and wicked administration of James Buchanan, in obedience to the imperative demands of slavery, attempted to force it by corruption through Congress upon an unwilling people, but for the first time slavery was baffled, defeated, dishonored. Freemen triumphed; Kansas came into the Union radiant with liberty.

Sir, slavery saw its waning power; it saw, too, that its criminal victories of the past were but barren and fruitless triumphs that turned to ashes on the lip. It then wrung from the Supreme Court the Dred Scott decision, by which it hoped to control the vast Territories of the Republic, even against the will of the actual settlers. It bade the legislature of New Mexico enact a slave code, and also a code for the enslavement of white laboring men. It sent Walker and his filibusters to Central America to win slave territory. It sighed for Cuba, which it could not clutch. It mobbed, flogged, expelled, and sometimes murdered Christian men and women in the South for no offence against law, humanity, or religion. It maddened the Southern brain and fired the Southern heart. It turned large masses of the people of the South against the institutions and the people of the North, against the Constitution and the old flag of their country. It came into the Thirty-sixth Congress threatening to dismember this Union of constellated commonwealths if the people of America should elect a President opposed to its admission into the Territories. It rushed into the Democratic national convention, and, as the first step toward disunion, severed the Democratic party. It then went into the presidential election, seeking defeat, yet threatening the vengeance of disunion and civil war if defeated. Regardless, however, of its treasonable menaces, the people went to the ballot boxes and made Abraham Lincoln President of the United States. Slavery instantly raised the banner of treason, dragged South Carolina with headlong haste into open rebellion, and forced other States swiftly to follow her example. Slavery organized conspiracies in the cabinet, conspiracies in Congress, conspiracies in the States, conspiracies in the army, conspiracies in the navy, conspiracies everywhere for the overthrow of the Government and the disruption of the Republic. At the bidding of slavery the oft-vaunted Southern Confederacy, the dream of slaveholding traitors for thirty years, rose upon the recognized basis that bondage was the normal condition of all men of the African race. Slavery bade those of its champions who were in the service of the nation leave cabinets and Senates, military posts and naval stations, for the service of the rebellion; and, at the bidding of slavery, Floyd, its truest exponent, left the cabinet when there seemed nothing more for him to steal; and Davis and Toombs, Slidell and Mason, Hunter and Benjamin, and their guilty compeers in treason, in solemn mockery left the chambers of Congress when the plots, conspiracies, treacheries, and perjuries imposed upon them by the great architect of ruin seemed accomplished.

Sir, not content with seizing forts, arsenals, arms, and public property everywhere within the rebel States, slavery bade the frowning batteries menacing Sumter fire upon the *Star of the West* sailing under the protecting folds of the national flag, and freighted with bread for starving soldiers; and when that act of armed treason failed to arouse to action an insulted but patient and forbearing country, slavery bade those rebel batteries open their fire on Sumter and its few starving but heroic defenders; and those consuming batteries, in obedience to its command, hurled shot and shell upon that devoted fortress till the glorious old flag of united America came down, and the rebel banner waved over the smoking ruins. And thus slavery, after an aggressive warfare of two generations upon the vital and animating spirit of republican institutions, upon the cherished and hallowed sentiments of a free and Christian people, upon the enduring interests and lasting fame of the nation, organizes a treasonable conspiracy, raises the standard of revolt, and plunges the nation into a bloody contest for the preservation of its menaced life. To the full comprehension of every man in America whose heart, brain, and soul have not been poisoned by its seductive arts and malign influence slavery is the cause, the whole cause, of this foul, wicked, and bloody rebellion. Every loyal American whose reason is unclouded sees that slavery is the prolific mother of all these nameless woes— these sunless agonies of civil war. He sees that every loyal soldier upon the cot of sickness, of wounds, and of death was laid there by slavery; that every wounded and maimed soldier hobbling along our streets was wounded and maimed by slavery; that the lowly grave of every loyal soldier fallen in defence of the country was dug by slavery; that mourning wives and sorrowing children were made widows and orphans by slavery. Before the tribunal of mankind of the present and of coming ages, before the bar of the ever-living God, the loyal heart of America holds slavery responsible for every dollar sacrificed, for every drop of blood shed, for every pang of toil, of agony, and of death, for every tear wrung from suffering or affection, in this godless rebellion now upon us. For these treasonable deeds, for these crimes against freedom, humanity, and the life of the nation, slavery should be doomed by the loyal people of America to a swift, utter, and ignominious annihilation.

But slavery, Mr. President, should not only be doomed to an ignominious death, to perish utterly from the face of the country, for the treasonable crime of levying war upon the Government, but the safety if not the existence of the nation demands its extermination. The experience of nearly three years of civil war has demonstrated to the full comprehension of every loyal and intelligent man in America that slavery is the motive power, the heart and soul and brain of the rebellion.

Sir, slavery not only fires the Southern heart, brain, and soul, and nerves the Southern arm in council hall and on the battlefield with its malignant hate and bitter scorn of Yankee laborers and Yankee institutions, its lofty contempt for the principles and policy of freedom, its haughty defiance of the authority of the national Government, and its gorgeous visions of the future power of the Southern Confederacy, extending its imperial sway over Cuba, Mexico, and Central America, and commanding the commerce of the world by its tropical productions and its millions of slaves, but it uses the bones and sinews of more than three millions of the bondmen of rebel masters in support of the rebellion. These slaves of rebel masters sow and reap, plant and gather the harvests that support rebel masters and feed rebel armies. By their ceaseless, unpaid toil, these millions of bondmen enable their traitorous masters and the poor white men of the rebel States to leave their fields and shops and rush to the battlefield to shed the blood of our loyal countrymen, of our neighbors and friends and brothers and sons. These bondmen throw up fortifications, dig trenches and rifle pits, make roads and bridges, fell forests and build barracks, drive teams, and relieve in many ways the toil of rebel soldiers, thus making more efficient the rebel armies. The spade and hoe of the slaves of rebels support the rifle and bayonet of rebel soldiers. Slavery is not only the motive power, the heart and soul of the rebellion, but it is the arm also. Therefore the preservation of the life of the country, and the lives of our brave soldiers battling for national existence, as well as the just punishment of conspiracy and treason, demand that the loyal men of the Republic shall swear by Him who liveth evermore that slavery in America shall die.

Not only the punishment of its appalling crimes, not only the lives of our countrymen and the preservation of the life of the nation, demand the utter extermination of slavery, but the future repose of the country also demands it. Slavery has poisoned the very fountains of existence in the South; it has entered into the blood and bone and marrow and the soul of our Southern countrymen. It has filled their bosoms with bitter, fierce, unreasoning hate toward their countrymen of the North, and the institutions, the Government, and the flag of their country. So long as slavery shall live, it will infuse its deadly and fatal poison into the Southern brain, heart, and soul. Then let slavery die a felon's death, and sink into a traitor's grave, amid the curses of a loyal nation. Then, when slavery shall sleep the sleep that knows no waking, in the grave of dishonor and infamy, reason will assume its mild sway again over our now maddened, poisoned, and intoxicated countrymen of the South. Take the maddening cup from the trembling hand of the drunkard, who, in his wild delirium, hates the mother who bore him, the wife of his bosom, and the children of his love, and that drunkard will be a man again, and love, cherish, and protect the mother, wife, and children he would smite down in his madness. Smite down slavery, strike the fetters from the limbs of its hapless victims, and slave masters will become loyal again, ready to pour out their blood for the Government they now hate and the country they now assail. They will recur to the recollections of the early days of the Republic with gratitude and patriotic pride, they will look forward with undoubting confidence in the future of their country. Their hearts will again throb with kindly regard for their countrymen of the North, and they will hail once more the beneficent institutions of a united country. The old flag, under which the men of the North and of the South fought and bled, side by side, on land and wave, will again be an object of affection and pride; its stars, now obscured to their vision, will gleam again with brighter luster and more radiant beauty.

Congress, not by the consent of the loyal States or loyal masters, but by the will and power of the nation, has made free at once and forever every slave who enlists into the military service. The Attorney-General pronounces the black man, who was said to have no rights that white men were bound to respect, a citizen of the United States. The Secretary of State gives the black man the passport of citizenship, which in every quarter of the globe is evidence that the bearer is a citizen of the North American Republic. The Secretary of War commissions a black man to be a surgeon in the military service of the United States, and the President organizes a hundred and twenty regiments, of eighty thousand black men, who are bearing upon their flashing bayonets the unity of the Republic and the destinies of their race.

Sir, slavery in America, though upheld by interests, customs, and usages, trenched about by inhuman statutes, and hedged around by passionate, vehement, and unreasoning prejudices, is fast crumbling to atoms beneath the blows rained upon it by a liberty-loving and patriotic people. But let anti-slavery men listen to no truce, to no compromise, to no cry for mercy. Let them now be as inflexible as justice, as inexorable as destiny. Whenever and wherever a blow can be dealt at the vitals of the retreating fiend, let that blow be struck in the name of the bleeding nation, and of the "dumb, toiling millions bound and sold." A truce with slavery is a defeat for the nation. A compromise with slavery is a present of disaster and dishonor and a future of anarchy and blood. Mercy to slavery is a crime against liberty. The death of slavery is the annihilation of the rebellion, the unity of the Republic, the life of the nation, the harmonious development of republican institutions, the repose, culture, and renown of the people.

The hideous Fugitive Slave Act still blackens the statutes of this Christian land, reminding us of the degradation and humiliation of our country when the heel of that master was on its neck. Justice and humanity, self-respect and decency, all demand that the lingering infamy shall be obliterated from the page it blackens.

If this amendment shall be incorporated by the will of the nation into the Constitution of the United States, it will obliterate the last lingering vestiges of the slave system.

Our country is now floating on the stormy waves of civil war. Darkness lowers and tempests threaten. The waves are rising and foaming and breaking around us and over us with ingulfing fury. But amid the thick gloom, the star of duty casts its clear radiance over the dark and troubled waters, making luminous our pathway. That duty is, with every conception of the brain, every throb of the heart, every aspiration of the soul, by thought, by word, and by deed to feel, to think, to speak, to act so as to obliterate the last vestiges of slavery in America, subjugate rebel slave masters to the authority of the nation, hold up the weary arm of our struggling Government, crowd with heroic manhood the ranks of our armies that are bearing the destinies of the country on the points of their glittering bayonets, and thus forever blast the last hope of the rebel chiefs.

Then shall the waning star of the rebellion go down in eternal night, and the star of peace shall ascend the heavens, casting its mild radiance over fields now darkened by the storms of this fratricidal war. Then, when "the war drums throb no longer and the battle flags are furled," our absent sons, with the laurels of victory on their brows, will come back to gladden our households and fill the vacant chairs around our hearthstones. Then the star of United America, now obscured, will reappear, radiant with splendor on the forehead of the skies, to illume the pathway and gladden the heart of struggling humanity.

On March 30 Garrett Davis [Ky.] spoke against the proposed amendment.

I am opposed to the pending proposition to amend the Constitution of the United States for several reasons intrinsic to the subject. In the first place, it strikes at one of the most essential principles of our commingled system of national and of State governments.

To maintain the Union, to hold it in its harmonious and perfect action, it is as essential that the existence of the authority and powers of the States within their reserved sovereignty should be upheld, maintained, and preserved as it is that the limited and delegated powers and sovereignty of the general Government should exist, be supported, defended, and exercised.

The absorption of the sovereignty not delegated by the Constitution to the general Government, and consequently reserved to the States, or any portion of it, by the President or Congress, would be revolutionary and destructive of our system, as would be the absorption by the States of the sovereignty, or any portion of it, delegated to the Government of the United States. The encroachment of either upon the other is equally unauthorized and criminal, and the persons engaged in making it are punishable for parallel offences by their respective judicial tribunals. Mr. President [Mr. Powell in the chair], it is clearly and imperatively the duty of you and myself to defend the reserved rights and sovereignty of Kentucky against the encroachments of Abraham Lincoln and his party, as it is to defend the limited sovereignty of the United States against the assaults of the rebels. To fail in either would be equally delinquent and criminal. Whoever, and by whatever command, has resisted by an array of force the execution of the laws of Kentucky has committed the offence of treason against that State, and should suffer the penalty denounced against the crime. The President of the United States, the Secretary of War, and generals high in command have moved armed bodies of men into Maryland, Delaware, Kentucky, and Missouri, to resist and defeat the execution of the election laws of those States, and have themselves, by the power of the sword, driven their free citizens from their own polls, and themselves virtually appointed the minions of executive power to seats in the House of Representatives of Congress and to State offices. Those high functionaries thereby committed treason against those States, and the most important and imperative duty of their authorities and people is to have those great delinquents arraigned and punished for their crimes by the judgment of the courts of the States against which they were committed. The punishment of Federal officers so high in authority for the commission of treason against the States, by the just and firm execution of the law in their civil courts, would be an example of the most salutary influence. To suppress the rebellion by force of arms, and to punish by the due administration of the law its most guilty authors, and also the great violators of the Constitution of the United States, who profess to be acting under its authority, and who have committed treason against States, would effect more in the support and preservation of constitutional liberty, and to vindicate the capacity of the people for self-government than the performance of any other duty or work.

But to the objection that the proposed amendment of the Constitution would infringe the right of the States to manage their local and domestic affairs, it may also be answered that slavery concerns all the States as well as those in which it exists. If there be truth in this position, it may be replied that there is no important property interest, pursuit, or institution in any State that does not, directly or indirectly, concern the people of every other State; and that argument would require the Constitution of the United States to be so amended as to give the Federal Government power over all of them, which would establish a perfectly consolidated Government and virtually annihilate the States.

There are many matters, the control of which is left by our Government wholly and exclusively with the States, and over which the people would not have confided to Congress and the President a particle of power when the Constitution was formed, that much more closely and momentously concern all the States than the continuance of slavery in some of them. Religious faith is one. The Federal Government has no power to interfere in any way with the subject of religion. The *entailment* of real and personal property, the principle of *primogeniture,* a system of railroads and other internal improvements in the several States connecting with the systems of other States— all these are subjects of domestic and local concern within every State, of which it has the exclusive management; and yet each one more nearly, and with larger interest and greater sympathy, would concern the people of all the other States than does slavery in the slave States the people of the free States.

Slavery, in this day and generation, has for the people of the United States a factitious but an absorbing interest; in the future, under altered circumstances, the others, and especially religion, may still more strongly possess them. If this proposed alteration of the Constitution be accepted it will be a precedent, and may establish a principle that may carry those other domestic concerns, and still others not now thought of, into the domain of an encroaching and centralized despotism, and which would be a very great stride.

If it were conceded that the power to amend the Constitution, as established and regulated by the fifth article, would by its terms and letter authorize the proposed change, it would be in fatal conflict with its intent and spirit, and, therefore, according to a universal rule of construction, void and of no effect. It never was the purpose of those who made it to subject many of its great principles to be expunged by the exercise of this power of amendment. The power to amend is but the power to improve, and any alteration to be legitimate should be an amendment. To this it may be said that as there is no certain test by which this question of amendment can be tried it is necessarily decided by the amending power. Granting this argument to be sound, still there is another and very important question connected with this power of amendment. Does it import the power of revolution? Of making such essential change in the nature, form, powers, and limitations of the Government as would be revolutionary of it—of its important structure, of its characteristic principles, of the great and essential rights and liberties assured by it to the citizen? The true and precise question is, does the proposed change, or *amendment*, carry a revolutionary principle and power? I hold that the framers of the Constitution did not intend it to be, and that it is not, in its nature or in fact, a revolutionary power; that there is a boundary between the power of revolution and the power of amendment, which the latter, as established in our Constitution, cannot pass; and that if the proposed change is revolutionary it would be null and void, notwithstanding it might be formally adopted. It would not be a part of the Constitution, and would consequently have no effect. An amendment proposing to abolish all the popular elective features of our Government, or that Representatives should hold their offices for life; that the place of Senator should be hereditary, coupled with a title and the privileges of nobility; that the President should be a king, and transmit his crown and throne as in England, would be revolutionary, and out of the power of the pale of amendment. Neither the legislative, executive, nor judicial branch of the Government could be swept away under the guise of the exercise of this power of amendment. The States and their governments are as essential and indispensable parts of our compound system of government as the United States and the Federal Government, and could not be expunged by this power of amendment. The retention by the States of their exclusive rights, and the right to ordain, manage, and control them, independent of all control or interference by the United States Government any more than of a foreign power, is a great and essential feature of our system, and it cannot be revolutionized, destroyed, by this power of amendment. If it can take cognizance of slavery, it may of every other local and domestic concern of the States. That would be revolutionary, and is therefore out of the domain of amendment. The power of amendment can only be made to embrace the forms and the provisions and principles of secondary importance.

If the principle involved by the proposed amendment be sound, and, it, if formally adopted, would be valid and obligatory, then in the same mode the terms of the members of the House could be extended for seven years; Senators could be metamorphosed into hereditary nobles, with titles, and the President into a monarch; and any other changes, utterly revolutionary and destructive of our Government and the popular freedom it establishes, could be made. No, sir, this power of amendment does not carry the power of revolution, in whole or in part, to be executed *in solido* or in detail, to burst forth at once in full-grown proportions, or to be cautiously developed from time to time and by gradual accumulation, like Mr. Lincoln's war policy, until the whole work is consummated. Neither the subversion of our free and popular Government, nor any of its great distinctive and essential features, or of those preëxisting and vital rights and liberties to secure and perpetuate which to the people were its object and its mission, is within the legitimate scope and operation of the power of amendment. That would be in both aspects, not amendment, but destruction and revolution.

Nor, sir, is the present condition of the country and the people at all propitious or fit to enter upon the most grave and important work of amending, altering the Constitution of our Government, the paramount law which regulates and controls within its orbit the constitutions, laws, and administrations of all the States and every official act of Congress, of the President, and of every other officer of the United States. The revision of the work of the preëminently great and patriotic men who put together that wonderful political structure, so admirably adjusted and balanced, so novel yet so complete, so free and yet possessed of all the necessary and proper powers and vigor, is one of the most delicate and important tasks which those who are to perform it can possibly undertake. They ought to be free from all sectional prejudice and excitement, and bring to it calm and unperturbed reason and broad and true patriotism and statesmanship. The condition of the country should be fixed, that of settled and stable repose, that any changes and modifications might be safely and wisely adapted to its permanent relations, interests, and tranquillity.

There is every probability that when the war is closed modifications of the Constitution will then be highly necessary and proper; but their nature, extent, and the features and powers of the Government in which they may be required cannot be possibly divined. Now to make any might mar rather than improve.

But when to this consideration, the unsettled condition of the country, is added the present state of the mind and passions of the people, nationally, sectionally, and individually, the position that now is not the proper time to intermeddle with the Constitution cannot, with any reason, be controverted. No man is free from apprehension and excitement, and with vast numbers it approximates frenzy, mania. Sectional opinions and prejudices were never before so rife and extreme. Hatred to slavery and slave owners by the members of the Republican party generally has demented them. They are wholly incapable of any fair and just consideration of the rights of slaveholders, in relation not only to that property, but all their other rights individually and collectively as slaveholding States. Extreme aversion and prejudice with both of those classes of the people have usurped the place of reason and truth. Neither entertains for the other any sentiments of kindness, fraternity, charity, or justice. I have no belief that there is in either House of the present Congress, or that there would be in the legislature or convention of any one of the States, a single member whose mind and passions are so little affected by the present condition of public affairs as not to be disqualified for the delicate and difficult work of revising and altering the common government of all the States and all the people of the United States. I believe with the most of them that unfitness would exist to such an extent as to make it impossible for them to deliberate and act, not only impartially and justly for their adversaries in politics and their sections, but also wisely and safely for themselves and their own States.

Another objection of overruling weight is that no revision of the Constitution in any form ought to be undertaken under the auspices of the party in power. Its leaders have always been hostile to the compromises on the subject of slavery, and the protection which it guarantees to the owners of that property. From a much earlier day than secession was thought of in the South, those leaders had determined on the destruction of slavery; and, if they could not succeed by any other means, even to revolutionize the Government to effect it. They did not bring on a general war to that end, though they had long assaulted it in every other form; and as soon as the rebellion broke forth they quietly decided, if possible, to make it the occasion and to furnish the means of the overthrow of slavery. Mr. Lincoln had been an extreme abolitionist from early life; and it was that consideration that procured him the nomination of the Chicago convention. When he and the chiefs of his party in Congress, at the commencement of the war, unanimously declared that their purpose and policy were not to attack slavery, or any other rights or institutions of the insurgent States, but only to vindicate the authority and laws of the United States over the rebels, they were dissembling, and then lying in wait to make an onset on slavery. They knew that their purpose could be effected only by breaking over constitutional guaranties, and by the power of the army to subdue all opposition to their scheme. There is no right of person or property that the President and Congress have not outrageously infracted and trampled out, under and by the agency of the iron heel of military despotism, to subjugate or awe every person disposed to offer even legal and peaceful resistance to their flagrant abuses and usurpations of power. As they progressed, and met with impunity in their nefarious work, their objects were enlarged. They determined not only to consummate the destruction of slavery, so that it could never be restored, but also to continue themselves and their party in place and power. The first they consider substantially as an accomplished fact; and they are, and have been for more than a year, moving with increasing energy and boldness toward the other as their now paramount object. They affect to adhere to the forms of the Constitution, while they utterly disregard not only its spirit, but also its express provisions and all the liberty and protection which it assures to the citizen. They have devised the boldest and most revolutionary measures under the guise of law and executive administration as the machinery of their operations. The first in time was the erection of West Virginia into a new State, and her admission into the Union in palpable violation of the Constitution, so admitted and avowed by many of their leaders both in and out of Congress; and attempted to be justified by them on the ground that the country was in a state of rebellion and revolution, and the Constitution of no obligation whatever. The President took the official opinion of the Attorney-General, which was that the measure was without constitutional authority, and yet he approved it.

After the congressional elections in the fall of 1862 it was apparent that, if those which were to take place in the other States in 1863 were to be decided by the free suffrages of their people, Mr. Lincoln and his party would be in a minority in the present House. The success of their projects and the retention of power by them made it necessary that they should have the majority in the House as well as in the Senate. He therefore ordered the military authorities to interfere and overthrow the freedom of elections, and to depose the State laws and officers for conducting them in Missouri, Kentucky, Maryland, and Delaware, to the extent of securing a majority for him in the House. To that extent he was equally a usurper with Cæsar, Cromwell, and Bonaparte.

But Mr. Lincoln has long since imbibed other views and projects of personal ambition. A desire for reëlection has seized upon him. It now possesses all the mind and heart and soul that he has. He is no statesman, but a mere political charlatan. He has inordinate vanity and conceit. He is a consummate dissembler, and an adroit and sagacious demagog. He has the illusion of making a great historical name for himself in connection with the total abolition of slavery in the United States. He also loves power and money. He has long foreseen that in his desire for reëlection he would have several competitors from his own party. He is not fierce or revengeful, or even boldly audacious and radical; and, though not marked by any sense of benevolence, humanity, or justice, he does not possess positively the opposite qualities, and, though a radical, is not reckless or rash. He is, and always has been, as uncompromisingly opposed to slavery as the most ultra radical, but preferred to overthrow it with some show of legal and constitutional authority; and that it should be effected gradually, and not by sudden and violent change. Such were his first and individual views and policy in relation to slavery; but, being rather of flexible but still obstinate nature, the pressure of the bold and more energetic radicals has pushed him pretty well nigh to their extreme position. As this "marshaled him the way he was going," he is well disposed to accept it, and, if it promised to aid him materially in his purpose of a reëlection, he would not hesitate to take it with alacrity. But he understands that most of the radicals prefer other men to himself, and, while he must manage to satisfy and win them if possible, and especially as their second choice, he must hold on to all the moderate men of the Republican party, and by some show of conservatism win others outside. This keeps him very busy at his favorite game of "playing for all the pockets."

But he regards, and with much truth, that his personal, official, and distinctive party consists of the officeholders and seekers, contractors and those seeking contracts, whose numbers are greater than our armies in the field. To those prætorian, not *cohorts*, but *legions*, he was determined to add others in his own especial interests. Hence he issued another edict, the effect of which was to demolish all the constitutions and governments of the rebel States, and among them Tennessee and Arkansas and other States whose constitutions have not been changed in a particle within many years before the rebellion; and to authorize one-tenth of as many people as voted in them at the last presidential election to reconstruct and to carry on their State governments. But he prescribed as the indispensable condition that all men who took part in the reconstruction must renounce their negro property and take an oath to support his war policy as embodied in all his proclamations and the laws of Congress passed by his party. He pledged his faith to support and defend these spurious State governments by the power of the United States armies and navies. All their elections were to be under the surveillance of the President's military subordinates; and consequently none but his minions and tools could vote or hold office. The reorganization of those States is to be virtually by him and for all his purposes. They were designed to be dependencies and he the autocrat. The world never witnessed a more lawless and daring political enterprise, and, except in the feature of blood, it comes up to the measure of the greatest usurpations. The people of the States are the only legitimate power to construct or reconstruct their civil governments; and Congress, and not the President, is the authority to admit them primarily, or secondarily, into the Union, and to guarantee to them *republican forms of government*. Mr. Lincoln seizes upon all this power. Under this presidential autocracy, old, or Eastern, as well as West Virginia, Louisiana, Arkansas, Tennessee, and other rebel States have been or are to be readmitted into the Union, and to take part with the other States in its government. By the present ratio all Virginia, east, west, and rebel, would be entitled to eleven Representatives in Congress. The new State has three, and it is a question what portion of the residue the few counties of the other division of the State within our military lines can rightfully have, and, a yet more difficult one, what number of electoral votes in the presidential election will be the right of those few counties. The new State having but three for her Representatives and two for her Senators, if those few counties can elect the residue for the whole of the remaining State, and also for its two Senators, the new State and a small fractional part of the remainder of the State would cast together fifteen electoral votes. That vote by those counties would give them a very undue and unconstitutional weight over the people of the other States in the presidential election. If that will be permitted may depend, I presume, upon the problem whether it would be necessary to reëlect Mr. Lincoln. To effect that object I believe a separate State could and would be organized out of East Tennessee, and two in Maryland, one upon the eastern and the other upon the western shore, without the least regard to constitutional difficulties. When Louisiana is readmitted she will be entitled to seven electoral votes, Tennessee to ten, Arkansas to five, and all Virginia to fifteen. So that by the organization of these four "rottenborough" and unauthorized States there would be secured to Mr. Lincoln not only thirty-seven electoral votes in the presidential election, but, what may be even of more importance, that number in the Republican nominating convention at Baltimore. I take it for true that these illegitimate States, being the progeny of Mr. Lincoln, will support him when and where and anyhow they can. They will also be ready to vote for this proposed amendment of the Constitution.

But Mr. Lincoln is a cautious and farseeing man. He has had still another provision made, first and mainly for his own personal success, subordinately for that of his party. The Territories of Colorado and Nevada have already, at the present session, been admitted as new States into the Union; and the chairman of the Committee on Territories has told us, and no doubt truly, that Nebraska will also be admitted. Thus there will be admitted three more new States, each with one Representative and two Senators, having an aggregate of eleven electoral votes and an equal strength in the Baltimore convention. I believe, both on principle and policy, that no Territory ought to be admitted as a State until it has a population equal to the ratio of representation. That ratio is now 127,000. By the census of 1860, Colorado had a population of 34,277; Nebraska, 28,841; and Nevada, 6,857.

Thus by military interference at elections, the destruction and reorganization of States, the admission of new States with but a small fraction of the ratio of population, all by infraction of the Constitution, and in opposition to right, justice, and policy, and chiefly by the power and under the supervision of Mr. Lincoln, a great and dangerous strength has been accumulated to him as President to be exercised to promote his own selfish and ambitious views in the first place; and, secondly, to continue his party in power to enable it to protract the aggrandizement of its leaders, the pecuniary advantages of its masses, and the complete consummation of its most wicked and destructive policy and measures.

Our own Government has become so abused and perverted, so unjust and oppressive to all who will not bow to those who administer it in unquestioning submission, so fruitful and general a source of evil and practical despotism, that hundreds of thousands and millions of the most loyal people of the United States are in doubt whether it, as administered, or the rebellion is the greatest national scourge. The assaults, wrongs, and oppressions of both on the border slave States is such as to be passing them, as it were, between the upper and nether millstone. The greatest good that could now fall to the lot of the people of those States would be the speediest suppression of the rebellion by all constitutional measures and means, and by the expulsion from power of the party that has possession of the Government and is ruling the country and so recklessly rushing both upon ruin. I look for the consummation of the first to the continued efforts of our brave and numerous soldiery and the submission of the rebels. For the second I still rely upon the peaceful remedy of the ballot-box, applied by the sovereign power of the United States; and, if it were applied so as to produce that great change, I believe that the cessation of the war, the submission and reconciliation of the rebels, the reconstruction of the Union, and the vindication of the laws and Constitution, with renewed guaranties and strength, would all speedily ensue. But if the dominant party can continue their power and rule, either by the will or acquiescence of the people or the exercise of the formidable powers which it has usurped, I am not able to see any termination of the present and still growing ills short of the ordeal of general and bloody anarchy.

On March 31 Willard Saulsbury [Del.] replied to Senator Trumbull.

Mr. President, we are told that the reason why this amendment should be made is that slavery has caused the present national difficulties; that if it had not been for the existence of slavery there would be no war. The honorable chairman of the Judiciary Committee tells us that even if the present troubles have been brought on by the interference of Northern fanatics with the institution of slavery, then if slavery had not existed there would have been nothing for them to interfere with, and the rebellion would not have taken place; that if it was brought on by the desire of the people of the South to strengthen and encourage the institution, then if it had not existed the rebellion would not have taken place; and he seems to think that to it we owe the loss of freedom of speech, freedom of the press, and most of the ills under which we are now suffering. He therefore proposes as the great remedy,—I presume not only to heal our present troubles, but as a bond of peace in the future—that the institution of slavery shall be wiped out by a change of the Constitution.

If there had been no fire, so large a portion of the city of New York as was burned down in 1835 would not have been burned down. If there was no water, there would be no overflowing floods. If there was no sun in the heavens, no man would fall prostrate to the earth and die from the heat of that sun. Let the Senator correct all the ills of life. Let him quench the fire that warms all the human race, and no incendiary then could burn our dwellings; let him dry up the fountains of the deep and close the windows of heaven, that there shall be no more water; let him pluck the sun from on high, that his heat shall no more cause death.

But, sir, I hold that if you adopt this amendment, and you could get three-fourths of the States to ratify it, it would not be obligatory upon the others for another reason; and that is that you cannot propose this amendment to all the States, as contemplated by the Constitution of the United States. There are confessedly some eight or nine of these States now out of the Union, over which the Federal Government does not pretend to exercise control. What is the meaning of the clause that the Congress of the United States may propose amendments which, when ratified by three-fourths of the States, shall become a part of the Constitution? It means that you shall propose those amendments, not to a portion of the States, but to all the States, so that all the States may have the power to act upon them.

The Constitution of the United States is the same as any

other contract. It is a contract between the States, who, in the language of Mr. Madison, are parties to it, and the plain, evident, honest import of this clause of the Constitution giving the power of ratification to three-fourths of the States is and must be so understood by all right-thinking men, that all the States shall have the power of passing upon that proposed amendment, of ratifying or rejecting it, and that, if that privilege is denied any State, if your amendment is not proposed to any State, it cannot operate upon that State, because it would be in violation of the just terms and fair interpretation of the Constitution.

If you wish to make an amendment to the Constitution of the United States which shall be binding and obligatory in all future time upon the parties to that Constitution, why not wait till peace is restored ; why not wait till passion ceases to inflame the breast and madness to warp the judgment and craze the brain of men ? The fundamental law of a great people should never be changed amid the shock of arms. Reason should sit calmly on her throne ; judgment should be brought to the ''line'' before acting on such a question.

But, sir, I oppose this proposed amendment on another ground. It is impossible for it to be ratified by a vote of three-fourths of the States. The Senator from Illinois,[1] the chairman of the Committee on the Judiciary, said it would require twenty-eight States, and he named the States which he supposed would vote to ratify it. He included all the adhering States with the exception of my own, and he thought she could not stand against it Let me tell the honorable Senator that, if the resolution is passed, I do not suppose my State will be in the way of it ; not because she will approve of it ; not because the majority of her people will not be honestly opposed to it and would not vote against it, but because you do not intend that they shall ever act upon it. The Senator said that Maryland had inaugurated this policy, and she would be in favor of it. I have some acquaintance with the people of that State. She will agree to it, just as the Senator, if met by a highwayman, solitary, alone, and unarmed, presenting a pistol at his head and demanding his purse, would agree to give it up.

But he expects to receive accessions from Arkansas, Tennessee, North Carolina, and Louisiana in favor of this proposed amendment. Does the Senator believe that, if the people of those States were free to act, and could pass upon his

[1] Lyman Trumbull.

proposed amendment according to their wish or judgment, there would be one man in ten who would vote to ratify it?

What is your government in Arkansas, in Louisiana, and in Tennessee? Take away your soldiers, and there would be scarcely one man in fifty in either of those States that would either approve your amendment or recognize your authority. And yet the Senator would affect the rights of nearly one-half of what was once this Union by going through—I say it in no disrespect to the honorable Senator, but I say it because I believe it and think it—going through the farce of an election under military control and restraint, and then come in the presence of the Senate of the United States and before the people of the country and of the world, and proclaim that the people of three-fourths of the States of the Union, in the spirit which their fathers intended them to act and in the free exercise of their judgments and their opinions as guaranteed to them by their fathers, have agreed to amend their Constitution and forever hereafter wipe out the foul blot of slavery!

Mr. President, nothing is to be gained by this except one thing, and that you may accomplish. You may succeed by such an amendment as this, by an election—no, not by an election, but by a farce enacted in the border States and by a worse farce enacted in some of the seceded States—you may succeed in abolishing slavery in the States of Delaware, Maryland, Kentucky, and Missouri. That is what you can do. You can succeed in injuring those who never tried to injure you; but, unless you conquer the South, unless you make them pass under the yoke as you avow your purpose to do, unless you take bodily hold of their slaves and draw them within your lines and keep them there, you have accomplished nothing. You have regarded them as belligerents, and consequently the slave you take to-day from them and put your uniform upon, if he is recaptured by them, is not free, though proclamations and legislative enactments may so declare, but is a slave still, and not only a slave by reason of the fact that he is in possession of his original master, but, by a sound principle of the law of nations, the *jus postliminii*, he reverts to his original owner.

Daniel Clark [N. H.] rebutted the argument that the time was not ripe for the amendment.

I am told that this is not the time for such an amendment of the Constitution. Pray when, sir, will it come? Will it be when the President has issued more and more calls for two or

three hundred thousand men of the country's bravest and best?
Will it be when more fathers and husbands and sons have
fallen, and their graves are thicker by the banks of the rivers
and streamlets and hillsides? Will it be when there are more
scenes like this I hold in my hand, of a quiet spot by the side
of a river, with the moon shining upon the water and a lonely
sentinel keeping guard, and here in the open space the head-
boards marking the burial places of many a soldier boy, and an
open grave to receive another inmate, and underneath the
words, "All quiet on the Potomac"? [Exhibiting a photograph
to the Senate.] Will it be when such scenes of quiet are more
numerous, not only along the Potomac but by the Rapidan, the
Chickahominy, the Stone, the Tennessee, the Cumberland, the
Big Black, and the Red? Sir, *now*, in my judgment, is the
time, and the fitting time. Never until now could this amendment have been carried, and now I hope and believe that it can
be carried. "Whom the gods would destroy they first make
mad."

Slavery's strongest and safest guaranties were in the Constitution, and its supporters were made when they cast away
and threw off those guaranties. Remaining in the Union, no
one would probably have moved for an amendment of the Constitution. Loyal to the Government, hostile armies would not
have set free their slaves, nor laws now necessary and expedient have authorized their employment against their masters
in arms.

But now, sir, every free State will gladly, it is hoped and
believed, vote for the proposed amendment. Most would rejoice to do it; while numbers of the slave States, aghast at the
miseries of secession and the horrors of this cruel Civil War,
recognizing slavery as the cause of all this disturbance and all
these woes, would be among the foremost to sweep it forever
away.

Now, sir, is the time to do it. And not only is now the
time, but the necessity and the duty of doing it are upon us.
We can have no permanent peace nor restored Union until it
is done.

There are those who cry, "The Union as it was and the
Constitution as it is!" But I am free and bold to confess
that I am for a Union without slavery, and an amended Constitution making it forever impossible. This revolt was to preserve slavery, and we shall fail of our whole duty if we do
not remove the inciting cause. To restore this Union with slavery in it when we have subdued the rebel armies would be

again to build your house on its smoking ruins when you had not put out the fire which burned it down.

If the dire calamities now befalling us be the "retributions of Providence upon a stupendous crime," what mad folly to hug that crime, and seek to avoid its future punishment! "Let my people go." But Pharaoh would not let them go; and then came sufferings, and plagues, and the smiting of the first-born. Oh! how many of our first-born have been smitten and fallen. Let us be wise and heed the teaching. There is a Providence in the great events now transpiring. The people see the hand. It points the way. They are filled with hope and faith. They follow the pillar and the cloud, and will struggle and endure.

I know, Mr. President, that the suppression of the rebellion will necessarily wound and maim slavery. I know that every victory over the rebels is a victory also over the cause of the rebellion, and I know, too, that the arming of the slaves will make the future enslaving of these men and their kindred well-nigh impossible; but slavery will still exist, not in much vigor or strength, but in the root and principle. This amendment will dig out the root and repudiate the principle.

Mr. President, in a quiet churchyard, near his home, is the grave of a soldier who returned to die. At the head of his grave is a marble slab, and on it these few but expressive words, "Mustered out." Let both Houses of Congress, by a two-thirds vote, recommend this amendment abolishing slavery, and let three-fourths of the States, burying slavery by their ratification, come and write its epitaph on the Constitution, "Mustered out."

The soldier was "mustered out," we trust, to enlist again in the shining cohorts in advance of earth's extreme picket line, but let this be "mustered out" to go, like Judas, to its own place.

On April 4 Timothy O. Howe [Wis.] spoke upon the likelihood of the border States accepting the amendment and upon the status of the seceded States.

The State of Delaware will adopt this amendment; her people will adopt it in the exercise of their free judgment. The Senator from Delaware [Mr. Saulsbury] shakes his head. I do not know but that he will oppose the amendment; that he will advise the people of Delaware not to adopt it; but his advice will not prevail, I humbly trust and I humbly believe.

Undertake to persuade that little State of Delaware not to enfranchise her few slaves when all the rest of the Union are crying for it! Dame Partington, Mr. President, standing on the beach of the Atlantic, trying to put back its waves with her mop, would be a model of practical sagacity compared with the Senator from Delaware if he should stand on the borders of that little State and undertake to persuade her not to let the deluge of freedom, which God has commanded to sweep the continent, flow over that little patch of His pasture.

Delaware will adopt the amendment, and so will Kentucky. Sir, Henry Clay sleeps in Kentucky. Let her people reject this proposition to amend the Constitution under the pressure of this great national necessity, and they would see the bones of the great hero rise from his grave and stalk indignantly from the borders; they would not rest there any longer. Kentucky will adopt this amendment. Every State will adopt it. I know that there are eleven States which have declared themselves independent of this Constitution and of all amendments to it. What are you going to do with them? There are those communities of people. They are States or they are not. It is a question that you ought to settle. In my judgment, there are no American States there. Decide the matter as you will: if they are States, they are going to vote upon this amendment, and they are going to vote for it; every man who votes at all upon it will vote to adopt the amendment. If they are not States, they are not to vote upon it, and their votes are not to be counted, and you still have a unanimous verdict from the States of the American Union in favor of this amendment to the Constitution.

On April 5 Reverdy Johnson [Md.] spoke in favor of the amendment.

To manumit at once nearly four million slaves who have been in bondage by hereditary descent during their whole lives, and who, because they were in bondage, and as one of the consequences of the condition in which they were placed, have been kept in a state of almost absolute ignorance, is an event of which the world's history furnishes no parallel. Whether if it succeeds it will be attended by weal or by woe the future must decide. That it will not be followed by unmixed good or by unmixed evil is perhaps almost certain; and the only question in my view that presents itself to statesmen is, first, whether the measure itself be right, independent of its consequences; and, secondly, whether those consequences may be such as render it inexpedient, because inhuman in other particulars, to do what is right.

There was a period in our own time when there was but one opinion upon the question of right. The men who fought through the Revolution, those who survived its peril and shared in its glory, and who were called to the convention by which the Constitution of the United States was drafted and recommended to the adoption of the American people, almost without exception thought that slavery was not only an evil to any people among whom it might exist, but that it was an evil of the highest character, which it was the duty of all Christian people, if possible, to remove, because it was a sin as well as an evil.

Its recognition in the Constitution (for it is idle, as I think, to deny that it is there recognized), the authority given by implication to a trade which might lead to its increase by immigration, was not because a large majority of the members of the convention, and a large majority of the people of the United States in the mass favored the institution, but because they believed that without provisions of that description it would be difficult to have a Union adopted. Whether they were right or wrong it is now useless to inquire. Judging by what was occurring at the time, it is possible, and perhaps even more than probable, that they were right; but, if they made a mistake as to that fact, if the Union could have been adopted without the recognition of the institution in the government which formed it, if its gradual extirpation could have been provided for, no one who is a spectator of the scenes around us will now fail to regret that it had not been done.

My private opinion has ever been that slavery is an evil. But in the public situation in which I now stand I have deemed it my duty to recognize the binding and paramount authority of the Constitution, to yield my moral convictions to the obligation of that instrument, and not to esteem myself as excusable or justified in construing it by any views of morality which I might entertain, or in construing out of it any provisions that might be found in it inconsistent with such views. With these views, I appeal to the authority of the Constitution itself as a justification for the vote which I shall give upon this measure.

I shall not stop to inquire whether slavery produced the war or not. One thing, in my judgment, is perfectly clear, now that that war is upon us, that a prosperous and perma-

nent peace can never be secured if the institution is permitted
to survive; and will it not survive unless a measure like that
upon your table shall receive the sanction which the Constitution requires? That brings me to inquire into the legality and
the effect of the other means by which it is proposed to get
rid of it.

First, can it be accomplished by the President? He does not
claim for himself—he has not gone to that extent—the authority to abolish slavery except as an incident of the military
power with which in the state of civil war in which we are
engaged he is vested as Commander-in-chief of the army. The
Supreme Court has asserted, what cannot be denied, because
your own legislation had recognized its existence, and because
the fact, independent of that recognition, was apparent, that
a state of war did exist. But in so saying, and in meeting
the objection that, although in one sense it was a war, yet in
another sense it was a mere rebellion in which each one of
the parties concerned in the seceded States was committing
from day to day, and as often as he denied the authority of
the United States and attempted to maintain his denial by
force of arms, treason, they said that these parties were not
the less to be considered as enemies because they were traitors.

The Supreme Court never pretended and never intimated,
as I read their opinion, that the existence of that belligerent
relation terminated all the civil obligations which the citizens
of the seceded States were under to the Government of the
United States; but, on the contrary, announced it as the inevitable inference, from the statement which I have just made,
that in their view they were enemies although traitors; that,
although they were enemies; they were not less so because they
were traitors; that in point of fact, as the parties then stood,
there was due from each one of the citizens or inhabitants of
the seceded States an allegiance and an obligation to fulfill it,
and of course to observe the laws and yield to the authority
of the United States, which, at the end of the war, if that
end should be so successful as to reinstate the Government of
the United States in authority, might proceed against them
under the laws of the land as traitors, and in the sense of the
Constitution which defined the crime of treason.

It would be monstrous, Mr. President, as I think, if it were
otherwise. There are now—I think the number has been less-
ened, and it is due to truth, as I think, so to state, by the policy
which has been adopted in the prosecution of the war—but
there are now in the rebellious States hundreds and thousands

of citizens just as devoted to the Union as any member of the Senate, and just as anxious to see its authority restored as any member of this body. These are entitled, therefore, to the protection of the Government. Their obedience in point of fact and their ostensible obedience to the eye of the power which is around them, in itself a government *de facto,* is an obedience which they have no power to resist, and upon the well-established principles of the laws of nations is an obedience in which there is no crime.

If it be true that it is a legal exercise of a belligerent right to manumit the slaves of the enemy, one thing is perfectly certain as a proposition equally applicable to a civil war, which in this aspect, with reference to the power which it confers on the President, stands precisely in the condition in which his power stands in the case of an international war, that he has no practical power to effect the manumission of slaves belonging to the enemy where he has not the physical power to attain that result. The President never uttered a truth more absolutely sound than when he stated that a proclamation of manumission or of freedom could have just as much effect upon the slaves of the enemy as a popish bull would have upon the course of a comet. All, therefore, in my view, that can be accomplished by means of presidential power derived from his being by the Constitution placed at the head of the armies of the United States in this war is that, if he can get the slave under the control of the Union, he can manumit him.

If these slaves come to the standard of the United States, or if that standard is carried within the territorial limits of the foe and the slaves are there within its control, discharged actually from the domination of their masters, the proclamation which declares them free may, and I am inclined to think will, have that effect. But just as sure as anything in the future can be said to be sure is it, in my judgment, that, if the war was to terminate without any provision being made for the condition of the slaves who have not come within the actual control of the military authority of the United States, they will be decided by the courts of the United States to be slaves still.

It is evident that the tendency of the President's own mind led to that result. In his proclamation of amnesty he says, in effect: When I offer to you an amnesty, coupled with the condition not only that you are to support the Constitution of the United States and the laws made in pursuance of the Constitution by Congress, but that you are to support any proclamations that may have been or may hereafter be issued by the Executive from time to time, I am willing that you shall take that oath subject to the right of having that question decided judicially in the future.

Second, can emancipation be accomplished by the legislative power? It is true that the Congress of the United States by the Constitution is clothed with an authority to declare war; and it is maintained that, under the authority to declare war, slaves may be emancipated. That may be true; but it may not be true so as to do away with the necessity of the measure upon your table. They may be emancipated, *quo modo?*[1] The power, like whatever emancipating power the President may be clothed with under his authority as Commander-in-chief executing the war power, is limited by the practical exercise of that war power. How far do your troops go? Against whom are they fighting? Get the slaves under the protection of your standard, and, if you think proper then is the time (and before then you are impotent to accomplish it), make them free; but until then the effort to accomplish it by the mere exercise of legislative authority, in my judgment, is just as futile as the effort to accomplish it by the mere exercise of executive authority.

That is not all. In order to gain the end which, in common with a majority of the Senate, I have at heart, the abolition of slavery by means of the exercise of this legislative war power must go a step further and show that it is a power which may be exerted over the loyal as well as the disloyal States. Will that proposition bear examination? The Constitution of the United States, as we all know, in a state of peace gives no power to any branch of the Government of the United States to interfere with slavery in the States. A few wild men, carried away by some loose and undefined notions of human liberty with which the Constitution does not deal, think that they find, in the principles of the Declaration of Independence and in the great principles which were the object for establishing the Constitution of the United States, principles so inconsistent with human slavery that the Constitution not only does authorize the legislative department of the Government to put an end to it, but makes that the duty of the Government; or rather that it is so inconsistent with the principles upon which the Government is founded that the judiciary, if called upon to decide, will decide that there can be no human slavery. I will not stop to examine that. I as-

---

[1] "In what manner?"

sume what, with the exception of a few persons to whom I have just alluded, has been the universal opinion—the opinion pronounced by the convention which nominated the present incumbent of the presidential chair, over and over again announced on the floor of Congress, announced upon the floor of Congress by overwhelming majorities since this rebellion commenced—that with the existence of human slavery in the States the Constitution of the United States in a time of peace has nothing whatever to do. If in time of war, the Government of the United States may in a certain condition of things effect the object of freeing slaves, putting an end to the institution under the military power, it can only be in those cases and against those people against whom they have a right to exert their power. Because one or more States have seceded and have carried their secession to an extent that they have become belligerents in a certain sense toward the United States, what right have the United States, in the exercise of the power which they are authorized to wield for the purpose of putting down the rebellion and reinstating the authority of the Government, to interfere with the loyal States of Maryland, or Kentucky, or Missouri? Have they any right to declare war upon Maryland, or upon either of the other States that I have named? Certainly not; and, if so far from having the authority to carry on war against a loyal State they are carrying on the war against the disloyal States by means of the power of the loyal States, including Maryland, Kentucky, and Missouri, it is a contradiction in terms that in the exercise of that war power they can, as against themselves, against the loyal States, exert an authority incident alone to the war power, when the war power itself is applicable alone to a state of war.

There remains a third method of emancipation—by an amendment to the Constitution. Now it is said it cannot be done in that mode. The honorable member from Kentucky [Mr. Davis], if I understand him correctly, in the very elaborate speech which he delivered upon the subject a few days since, full of all the learning which belongs to the question and pregnant with a very ingenious application of that learning, seems to think that there is something in the admitted sovereignty of the States which is inconsistent with the authority of the people of the United States to amend the Constitution so as to trench at all upon the existing authority of the States. The honorable member from Delaware [Mr. Saulsbury] takes another ground, and that is that, as slaves are made property by the laws of the States, that property, like every other description of property, is not the subject of government interference, except as that interference may be necessary for its protection. Now, a word or two upon each objection.

The honorable member from Kentucky is right in saying that in a certain sense the States are sovereign; but, if he means by that to say that the United States in another sense are not equally sovereign, he is mistaken. The school of which Mr. Calhoun was the head, and the antecedent school by whose teachings he professed to be governed, that which had for its head Mr. Madison, seemed to have been under the impression, and unfortunately succeeded in inculcating it upon the public mind too strongly for the peace of the country, the safety and prosperity of his own section, that the only sovereignty was that which belonged to the States. There never was a greater political heresy. The States, in the first place, were never disunited. As one they declared independence. As one they fought and conquered the independence so declared. As one, in order to make that independence fruitful of all the blessings which they anticipated from it, they made the Constitution of the United States. They met in convention, they adopted the Constitution in convention, and recommended it not to the States in the capacity of States, not to the governments of the States as governments, but to the people of the States for their adoption; and they could have submitted it in no other way. Any other mode of laying it before the country would have been inconsistent with the preamble to the instrument, which states that it is the work of the people as contradistinguished from the States. How the people were to assemble, where they were to assemble, what influences were to govern them in deciding for or against the Constitution is immaterial. When they once decided in its favor, the people of each State agreed as a people with the people of every other State that that should be the form of government. They consented in adopting the Constitution as a people that the Constitution, if adopted by the people of nine States, should be the Constitution of the people of those States in the aggregate.

So said the Supreme Court of the United States in the case of McCulloch vs. The State of Maryland in the opinion given by Mr. Chief Justice Marshall. So said the same court in the opion given, and it was the unanimous opinion, in the case of Booth vs. The United States by the present Chief Justice. They both announced as the clear operation of the Constitution, and as a fact ever to be borne in mind in construing the Constitution of the United States, that it was the adoption of the people of the United States, and that the sovereignty of the United States to the extent of the powers conferred upon the Government of the United States, and the sovereignty conferred upon the governments of the States by the people of the States respectively, was precisely the same and no more than it would have been if they had been framed and adopted at the same time. That is to say, each State, except so far as the people as a people had gone with other people in depriving themselves of the powers with which they were antecedently clothed, had no authority, as long as that other Constitution remained, to take any step inconsistent with the powers conferred by that Constitution; or, in the language of the court, that each, within the sphere of the authority with which it was clothed, was supreme. There was no absolute sovereignty; that is to say, there was no sovereignty coextensive with the whole scope of political power belonging to the government of either; but each was invested with a portion of the sovereignty which the people might create, and each therefore within the extent of the portion allowed it was to the extent of that portion supreme.

Now a word or two in answer to the honorable member from Delaware. He says that, with reference to the Constitution of the United States, the institution of slavery is not within the amendatory clause, because, with reference to the Government of the United States, it is not a subject for political interference. Let me ask the honorable member, and he can answer it hereafter if he thinks proper, could human slavery have been abolished by the Constitution originally? I suppose no one will doubt that. Then why is it that it cannot be done now under the clause which gives to the people of the United States the authority to amend the Constitution? It can only be that it has been taken entirely out of the scope of governmental power, the scope of the political power of the people, because it was not abolished by the Constitution. Why, Mr. President, what says the preamble to the Constitution? That justice might be established; that tranquillity might be preserved; that the common defence and general welfare might be maintained; and, last and, chief of all, that liberty might be secured. Is there no justice in putting an end to human slavery? Is there no danger to the tranquillity of the country in its existence? May it not interfere with the common defence and general welfare? And, above all, is it consistent with any notion which the mind of man can conceive of human liberty? The very clause under which we seek to put an end to the institution, the amendatory clause, may have been, and in all probability was, inserted into the instrument from a conviction that the time would come when justice would call so loudly for the extinction of the institution that her call could not be disobeyed, when the peace and tranquillity of the land would demand in thunder tones the destruction of the institution as inconsistent with such peace and tranquillity; and when the sentiment of the world would become shocked with the existence of. a condition of things in the only free government upon the face of the globe as far as the white man is concerned, and founded upon principles utterly inconsistent with any other form of government than a government which secures freedom.

On the following day Senator Saulsbury replied to Senator Johnson's argument based on the preamble of the Constitution. He said that a preamble to any instrument was effective in construing the meaning of the body of the instrument only when the latter was doubtful, and that the body of the Constitution was clear and plain upon the relative powers of the Federal Government and the States. But, accepting Senator Johnson's view of the bearing of the preamble of the Constitution upon the license allowed in the emendation of that instrument, he said:

That, because this Constitution was ordained "to form a more perfect Union, to establish justice, insure domestic tranquillity, provide for the common defence, promote the general welfare, and secure the blessings of liberty," it does not follow that any such amendment as this can be made, because the instrument itself shows for whom these blessings were intended to be preserved—to us and to our posterity. What connection had the slave population of the United States with the formation of this Constitution? Did they constitute any part of "us and our posterity" in the contemplation of the framers of this instrument? Not at all. Without elaborating this idea, I submit that no just or legitimate argument can be drawn from the preamble of the Constitution that the Congress of the United States have authority to propose this amendment, or that it would become binding in consideration of the ratification of three-fourths of the States.

John P. Hale [N. H.] followed Senator Saulsbury.

Our friends who oppose this resolution die hard, very hard. I remember reading that when the British Parliament sat in judgment upon Charles I, and sentenced him to lose his head, they were apprehensive that when it came to the last, and he was actually required to bow down and put his head under the axe, he might resist, and the Commons, with great prudence and prescience, had prepared pulleys and machinery by which, if he resisted, he should actually be drawn under the axe and his head severed from his body. That is history that I think is not without its teaching in the present day. I think that the judgment has gone forth that slavery must die. The commons have passed that sentence; and I tell you, sir, that, if slavery is refractory, and does not quietly submit, the Commons will prepare pulleys by which to bring the victim under the axe.

Mr. President, permit me to say that this is a day when the nation is to commence its real life, a day when the nation is to be disembarrassed of the inconsistencies which have marked its history and its career.

Sir, what is the truth? We have had upon the pages of our public history, our public documents, and our public records some of the sublimest truths that ever fell from human lips; and there never has been in the history of the world a more striking contrast than we have presented to heaven and earth between the grandeur and the sublimity of our professions and the degradation and infamy of our practice. That day is to pass away, and to pass away, I trust, right speedily.

But I desire to say a word, in all sincerity and in all kindness, to those gentlemen who still linger here, the representatives, or rather the administrators *de bonis non*,[1] of what was once the old Democratic party. [Laughter.] They pretend to think—and I am not the man to stand here and say they do not believe what they pretend to believe—that it is in their power, if they had the control, to save the country and restore the Union. I am willing to concede, for the purposes of all that I have to say, that they actually believe it; that that is their faith; and I apprehend, from some things that have fallen from some gentlemen even in this neighborhood, that my honorable and venerable friend from Kentucky [Mr. Davis] is not far from entertaining similar opinions, that the Democratic party might, by some possibility, save the country and save the Union; and, what is more than all that, save themselves, too. Sir, it is a delusion, an utter delusion. Let me ask their

[1] "Of no goods."

attention for a moment or two to some considerations which induce me to believe that it is an utter delusion.

How can they do it? Patrick Henry, the great orator of the Revolution—no offence to Massachusetts [laughter]—said that he knew of no other lamp to guide his feet but the light of experience. Taking that as a maxim or as a text, let me ask what there is in the history of this Democratic party that gives countenance to the idea that by any possibility, even if they had everything their own way, they could save the country and save the Union? This rebellion, revolution, or whatever you please to call it—I believe it has been judicially decided that we are not at war—commenced under James Buchanan, a Democratic President. They had a Democratic Senate, a Democratic House of Representatives, a super-Democratic Supreme Court of the United States, and a large majority of all the officers of every organization, moral and physical, in the country, including the army and navy and ministers. They could not keep the peace with all that. They lost it. Nay, more than that, they had a little love feast of their own down at Charleston; there was no Abolitionist, no Federalist there to vex and plague them; and they could not keep family peace. They could not keep national peace, and they could not keep family peace, but split, broke, went asunder, every man his own way, and the present is the result of it.

How are they going to do any better now than they did then? They lost eleven States at one slide that they had then. They are all gone; and I say it with great respect and great kindness to them they have lost, besides, pretty nearly every respectable man they had in the free States that gave character and stability to their party. I need not go out of the Senate chamber to prove that. Well, sir, they have lost all that; and now, in the days of their dissolution and weakness, when their preaching here sounds in one respect something similar to that of John the Baptist—"the voice of one crying in the wilderness" [laughter]; for there is only here and there one of them—they are still impressed with that insane delusion that if they had the power they could save the country and save the Union and save themselves.

It is said to be a hard thing for an individual to find out when his mental faculties begin to fail him. It is not difficult for him to find out when his physical strength fails him, but it is very rare that a man finds out when his mental vigor begins to fail him. I suppose what is true of individuals is true of parties and of collections of men. But let me ask my friends,

VI—26

do they not feel in their own experience that the day of the strength of the Democracy has departed, that it has gone or is going? It seems to me that they must. I appeal, then, to all who hear me, is it not the part of wisdom to submit to what is inevitable? Charles I did not compel the Commons to put the pulleys on to haul him under the axe; but when he found the axe was up and that the Commons had decreed that his head should go under it and the axe should come down, like a sensible and well-bred gentleman as he was, he put his head under.

Mr. President, what is to be cannot be avoided; and if there is any one thing which, it seems to me, the indications from every side everywhere teach us, it is that the day of this power is over; and there is no indication more conclusive of it than the Christian and statesmanlike effort made by the honorable Senator from Maryland yesterday. I ask everybody who hears me, do you not rejoice that the day has come? Are you not glad that this nation, blind and deaf so long to the teachings of history and the commands of God, has at length aroused itself from its lethargy, listened to the voices which heaven and earth, God and nature, are proclaiming, and is preparing to put itself in alliance with the Power which cannot be resisted and whose fiat will most surely be executed.

Whenever, unconditionally and without equivocation, we come up to the mark and place ourselves on the high standard of Christian duty, and resolve that, despite of all extraneous circumstances, of all doubtful contingencies, of all questions of expediency, we will place ourselves firmly upon the everlasting rock of duty and our action shall be in accordance with our conscientious convictions, then, and not till then, will that pillar of cloud by day and of fire by night which led the chosen people from the house of bondage to the land of promise be ours. Then we shall indeed and in truth be worthy of our genealogy and our history. Then the sublime teachings of the Pilgrim Fathers, who left everything behind them that they might come hither and plant in this wilderness a temple of liberty and throw wide open its doors for the oppressed of earth to enter and be at rest—then will all that be realized. Then without shame, without reproach, and without apology, we can stand in this nineteenth century, soldiers of the new civilization and of an old Christianity, going forth to battle with every impulse of our hearts and every purpose that we entertain in full accordance with the best wishes and hopes of the good on earth and of the God in heaven; when we take this position and take it firmly and ably, then and not until then shall we triumph; then and not till then shall we see the beginning of the end.

Mr. President, let me say one word more.   When the Savior of man, with the sympathy and pathos with which He loved the chief city of His native land, wept over Jerusalem His lamentation was, "If thou hadst known in this thy day the things that belong to thy peace!"   Sir, that is what this nation ought to know; that is what the nation ought to understand. It is what I believe; and by a vigorous prosecution of this measure we shall evidence to heaven and earth that we do understand and mean to perform the things which belong to our nation's peace.

On April 8 Charles Sumner [Mass.] closed the debate in a long and brilliant speech in favor of the amendment.

Under the influences of the present struggle for national life, and in obedience to its incessant exigencies, the people have already changed, and in nothing so much as slavery.   Old opinions and prejudices have dissolved, and that traditional foothold which slavery once possessed has been gradually weakened until now it scarcely exists.   Naturally this change must sooner or later show itself in the interpretation of the Constitution.   But it is already visible even there, in the concession of powers over slavery which were formerly denied.   The time, then, has come when the Constitution, which has been so long interpreted for slavery, may be interpreted for freedom. This is one stage of triumph.   Universal emancipation, which is at hand, can be won only by complete emancipation of the Constitution itself, which has been degraded to wear chains so long that its real character is scarcely known.

Sometimes the concession is made on the ground of *military necessity*.   The capacious war powers of the Constitution are invoked, and it is said that in their legitimate exercise slavery may be destroyed.   There is much in this concession; more even than is imagined by many from whom it proceeds.   It is war, say they, which puts these powers in motion; but they forget that wherever slavery exists there is perpetual war—that slavery itself is a *state of war* between two races, where one is for the moment victor—pictured accurately by Jefferson when he described it as "permitting one-half of the citizens to trample on the rights of the other, transforming those into enemies and these into despots.'' Therefore, wherever slavery exists, even in seeming peace, the war power may be invoked to put an end to a condition which is internecine, and to overthrow pretensions which are hostile to every attribute of the Almighty.

But it is not on military necessity alone that the concession is made. There are many who, as they read the Constitution now, see its powers over slavery more clearly than before. The old superstition is abandoned; and they join with Patrick Henry when, in the Virginia convention, he declared that the power of manumission was given to Congress, (1) in the ''general welfare'' clause. He did not hesitate to argue against the adoption of the Constitution because it gave this power. And shall we be less perspicacious for freedom than this Virginia statesman was for slavery? Discerning this power, he confessed his dismay; but let us confess our joy.

2. Next comes the clause, ''Congress shall have power to declare war, to raise and support armies, to provide and maintain a navy.'' A power like this is from its very nature unlimited. In raising and supporting an army, in providing and maintaining a navy, Congress is not restrained to any particular class or color. It may call upon all and authorize that *contract* which the Government makes with an enlisted soldier. But such a contract would be in itself an act of manumission; for a slave cannot make a contract. And if the contract be followed by actual service, who can deny its completest efficacy in enfranchising the soldier-slave and his whole family? Shakespeare, immortal teacher, gives expression to an instinctive sentiment when he makes Henry V, on the eve of the battle of Agincourt, encourage his men by promising,

> ''For he to-day that sheds his blood with me
> Shall be my brother; *be he ne'er so vile*
> *This day shall gentle his condition.*''

3. There is still another clause: ''The United States shall guarantee to every State in this Union a *republican form of government.*'' But the question recurs, What is a republican form of government? John Adams, in the correspondence of his old age, says:

''The customary meanings of the words *republic* and *commonwealth* have been infinite. They have been applied to every government under heaven; that of Turkey and that of Spain, as well as that of Athens and of Rome, of Geneva and San Marino.''—*John Adams's Works,* Vol. 10, p. 378.

But the guaranty of a republican form of government must have a meaning congenial with the purposes of the Constitution. Evidently it must be construed so as to uphold the Constitution according to all the promises of its preamble, and Mr. Madison has left a record showing that this clause was originally suggested in part by the fear of slavery. But no American need be at a loss to designate some of the distinctive elements of a republic according to the idea of American institutions. These will be found first in the Declaration of Independence, by which it is solemnly announced "that all men are endowed by their Creator with certain inalienable rights; that among these are life, liberty, and the pursuit of happiness." And they will be found, secondly, in that other guaranty and prohibition of the Constitution, in harmony with the Declaration of Independence; *"no person* shall be deprived of life, *liberty,* or property *without due process of law."* Such are some of the essential elements of a "republican form of government," which cannot be disowned by us without disowning the very muniments of our liberties; and it is these which the United States are bound to guarantee. But all these make slavery impossible. It is idle to say that this result was not anticipated. It would be, then, only another illustration that our fathers "builded wiser than they knew."

4. But, independent of the clause of guaranty, there is the clause just quoted, which in itself is a source of power; *"no person* shall be deprived of life, *liberty,* or property *without due process of law."* This was a part of the amendments to the Constitution proposed by the first Congress, under the popular demand for a Bill of Rights. Brief as it is, it is in itself alone a whole Bill of Rights. Liberty can be lost only by "due process of law," words borrowed from the old liberty-loving common law.

Such is the protection which is thrown by the Constitution over every "person," without distinction of race or color, class or condition. There can be no doubt about the universality of this protection. Its natural meaning is plain; but there is an incident of history which makes it plainer still, excluding all possibility of misconception. A clause of this character was originally recommended as an amendment by two slave States —North Carolina and Virginia—but it was restrained by them to *freemen,* thus: "No *freeman* ought to be deprived of his life, *liberty,* or property but by the *law of the land."* But when the recommendation came before Congress the word "person" was substituted for "freeman," and the more searching phrase, "due process of law," was substituted for "the law of the land." In making this change, rejecting the recommendation of two slave States, the authors of this amendment revealed their purpose, that *no person* wearing the human form should be deprived of *liberty* without due process of law; and the proposition was adopted by the votes of Congress and then of the States as a part of the Constitution. Clearly on its face it is an express guaranty of personal liberty and an express prohibition against its invasion anywhere.

In the face of this guaranty and prohibition—for it is both —how can any "person" be held as a slave? But it is sometimes said that this provision must be restrained to places within the exclusive jurisdiction of the National Government. Let me say frankly that such formerly was my own impression, often avowed in this Chamber; but I never doubted its complete efficacy to render slavery unconstitutional in all such places, so that "no person" could be held as a slave at the national capital or in any national territory. Constitutionally slavery has always been an outlaw wherever that provision of the Constitution was applicable. Nobody doubted that it was binding on the national courts, and yet it was left unexecuted—a dead letter, killed by the predominant influence of slavery, until at last Congress was obliged by legislative act to do what the courts had failed to do, and to put an end to slavery in the national capital and national Territories.

But there are no words in this guaranty and prohibition by which they are restrained to any exclusive jurisdiction. They are broad and general as the Constitution itself; and since they are in support of human rights they cannot be restrained by any interpretation. There is no limitation in them, and nobody now can supply any such limitation without encountering the venerable maxim of law, *Impius ac crudelis qui libertati non favet*—"Impious and cruel is he who does not favor liberty." Long enough courts and Congress have merited this condemnation. The time has come when they should merit it no longer. The Constitution should become a living letter under the predominant influence of freedom. It is this conviction which has brought petitioners to Congress, during the present session, asking that the Constitution shall be simply executed against slavery and not altered. Ah! sir, it would be a glad sight to see that Constitution, which we have all sworn to support, interpreted generously, nobly, gloriously for freedom, so that everywhere within its influence the chains should drop from the slave. If it be said that this was not anticipated at the adoption of the Constitution, I remind you of the words of Patrick Henry at the time when he said, "the paper speaks to the point." No doubt. It does speak to the point. Cicero preferred to err with Plato rather than to think right with other men. And pardon me if, on this occasion, when my country is in peril from slavery, and when human rights are to be rescued, I prefer to err with Patrick Henry, the contemporary of the Constitution, rather than to think right with Senators who hesitate against slavery.

But all these provisions are something more than powers; *they are duties also.* And yet we are constantly and painfully reminded in this Chamber that pending measures against slavery are unconstitutional. Sir, this is an immense mistake. *Nothing against slavery can be unconstitutional.* It is only hesitation which is unconstitutional.

And yet slavery still exists—in defiance of all these requirements of the Constitution; nay, more, in defiance of reason and justice, which can never be disobeyed with impunity—it exists, the perpetual spoiler of human rights and disturber of the public peace, degrading master as well as slave, corrupting society, weakening government, impoverishing the very soil itself, and impairing the natural resources of the country. Such an outrage, so offensive in every respect, not only to the Constitution, but also to the whole system of order by which the universe is governed, is plainly a *national nuisance,* which, for the general welfare and in the name of justice, ought to be abated. But at this moment, when it menaces the national life, it will not be enough to treat slavery merely as a nuisance; for it is much more. It is a public enemy and traitor wherever it shows itself, to be subdued, in the discharge of solemn guaranties of Government and of personal rights, and in the exercise of unquestionable and indefeasible rights of *self-defence.* All now admit that in the rebel States it is a *public enemy and traitor,* so that the rebellion may be seen in slavery, and slavery may be seen in the rebellion. But slavery throughout the country, everywhere within the national limits, is a *living unit, one and indivisible*—so that even outside the rebel States it is the same public enemy and traitor, lending succor to the rebellion, and holding out "blue lights" to encourage and direct its operations. But whether regarded as national nuisance or as public enemy and traitor, it is obnoxious to the same judgment, and must be abolished.

If, in abolishing slavery, any injury were done to the just interests of any human being or to any rights of any kind, there might be something "to give us pause," even against these irresistible requirements. But nothing of the kind can ensue. No just interests and no rights can suffer. It is the rare felicity of such an act, as well outside as inside the rebel States, that, while striking a blow at the rebellion, and assuring future tranquillity, so that the Republic shall no longer be a house divided against itself, it will add at once to the value of the whole fee simple wherever slavery exists, will secure individual rights, and will advance civilization itself.

There is another motive to abolish slavery at this time. Embattled armies now stand face to face, on the one side fighting for slavery. The gauntlet that has been flung down we have yet taken up only in part. In abolishing slavery entirely we take up the gauntlet entirely. Then can we look with confidence to the blessings of Almighty God upon our arms. So long as we sustain slavery, so long as we hesitate to strike at it, the heavy battalions of our armies will fail in power. Sir Giles Overreach[1] found his sword, as he attempted to draw it, "glued with orphans' tears." Let not our soldiers find their swords "glued" with the tears of the slave.

There is one question and only one which rises in our path; and this only because the national representatives have so long been drugged and drenched with slavery, which they have taken in all forms, whether of dose or douche, that, like a long-suffering patient, they are not yet emancipated from its influence. I refer, of course, to the question of compensation under the shameful assumption that there can be property in man. Sir, there was a moment when I was willing to pay money largely, or at least to any reasonable amount, for emancipation; but it was *as ransom*, and never as compensation. Thank God! that time has now passed, never to return; and simply because money is no longer needed for the purpose. Our fathers under Washington never paid the Algerines for the emancipation of our enslaved fellow citizens, except as ransom, and they ceased all such tribute when emancipation could be had without it. Such must be our rule now. Any other rule would be to impoverish the treasury for nothing. The time has come for the old tocsin to sound, "Millions for defence, not a cent for tribute." Ay, sir; millions of dollars—with millions of strong arms also—to defend our country against slave-masters; but not a cent for tribute to slave-masters.

But if money is to be paid as compensation, clearly it cannot go to the master who for generations has robbed the slave

[1] A character in "A New Way to Pay Old Debts," by Philip Massinger.

of his toil and all its fruits, so that, in justice, he may be regarded now as the trustee of accumulated earnings with interest which he has never paid over. Any money paid as compensation must belong, every dollar of it, to the slave. If the case were audited in Heaven's chancery, there must be another allowance for the denial of inestimable rights. The loss of wages may be estimated, but where is the tariff or price-current by which those other losses which have been the lot of every slave shall be determined? Mortal arithmetic is impotent to assess the fearful sum total. In presence of this infinite responsibility the whole question must be referred to that other tribunal where master and slave will be equal, while infinite wisdom tempers justice with mercy.

But the proposition of compensation is founded on the intolerable assumption of property in man, an idea which often intrudes into these debates, sometimes from its open vindicators and sometimes from others who reluctantly recognize it, but allow it to influence their conduct which is thus "sicklied o'er" with slavery. Sir, parliamentary law must be observed; but if an outburst of indignant hisses were ever justifiable in a parliamentary assembly it ought to break forth at every mention of this proposition, whatever form it may take—whether of daring assumption or the mildest suggestion, or equivocation even. Impious toward God and insulting toward man, it is disowned alike by the conscience and the reason; nor is there any softness of phrase or argument by which its essential wickedness can be disguised. The fool hath said in his heart that there is no God; but it is kindred folly to say that there is no man. The first is atheism, and the second is like unto the first.

Again, we are brought by learned Senators to the Constitution, which requires that there shall be "just compensation" where "private property" is taken for public use. But plainly on the present occasion the requirement of the Constitution is absolutely inapplicable, for there is no "private property" to take. Slavery is but a bundle of barbarous pretensions, from which certain persons are to be released. At what price shall these pretensions be estimated? How much shall be paid for the controlling pretension of property in man? How much shall be allowed for that other pretension to shut the gates of knowledge and keep the victim from the book of life? How much shall be expended to redeem the pretension to rob a human being of all the fruits of his toil? And, sir, what "just compensation" shall be voted for the renunciation of that

Heaven-defying pretension, too disgusting to picture in its details, which despoils the slave of wife and child, and hands
them over to lust or avarice? Let these pretensions be re-
nounced, and slavery ceases to exist; but there can be no "just
compensation" for any such renunciation. The human heart,
reason, religion, the Constitution itself, rise in judgment
against it. As well vote "just compensation" to the hardened
offender who renounces his disobedience to the Ten Command-
ments and promises that he will cease to steal, that he will
cease to commit adultery, and that he will cease to covet his
neighbor's wife. Ay, sir, there is nothing in the Constitution
to sanction any such outrage. Such an appropriation would
be unconstitutional.

Putting aside, then, all objections that have been interposed,
whether proceeding from open opposition or from lukewarm
support, the great question recurs, that question which dominates this whole debate, How shall slavery be overthrown?
The answer is threefold: first, by the courts, declaring and
applying the true principles of the Constitution; secondly, by
Congress, in the exercise of the powers which belong to it;
and, thirdly, by the people, through an amendment to the
Constitution. Courts, Congress, people, all may be invoked,
and the occasion will justify the appeal.

1. Let the appeal be made to the courts. But, alas! one
of the saddest chapters in our history has been the conduct of
judges who have lent themselves to the support of slavery.
Injunctions of the Constitution, guaranties of personal liberty,
and prohibitions against its invasion have all been forgotten.
Courts which should have been asylums of liberty have been
changed into *barracoons,* and the Supreme Court of the United
States, by a final decision of surpassing infamy, became the
greatest *barracoon* of all. It has been part of the calamity of
the times that, under the influence of slavery, justice, like
Astræa of old, had fled. But now at last, in a regenerated
Republic, with the power of slavery waning, and the people
rising in judgment against it, let us hope that the judgments
of courts may be reconsidered, and that the powers of the Constitution in behalf of liberty may be fully exercised, so that
the blessed condition shall be fulfilled when

"Ancient frauds shall fail,
Returning justice lift aloft her scale."

Sir, no court can afford to do an act of wrong. Its business
is justice; and when under any apology it ceases to do justice

it loses those titles to reverence which otherwise are so willingly bestowed. There are instances of great magistrates who have openly declared their disobedience to laws "against common right and reason," and their names are mentioned with gratitude in the history of jurisprudence. There are other instances of men holding the balance and the sword, whose names have been gathered into a volume, as "atrocious judges." If our judges, who have cruelly interpreted the Constitution in favor of slavery, do not come into the latter class, they clearly can claim no place among those others who have stood for justice like the rock on which the sea breaks in idle spray. Doubtless the model decision of the American bench, destined to be quoted hereafter with the most honor, because the boldest in its conformity with the great principles of humanity and social order, was that of the Vermont judge who refused to surrender a fugitive slave *until his pretended master should show a title deed from the Almighty.*

But the courts have no longer any occasion for such boldness. They need not step outside the Constitution. It is only needed that they should follow just principles in its interpretation. Let them be guided by a teacher like Edmund Burke, who spoke as follows:

"*Men cannot covenant themselves out of their rights and their duties;* nor by any other means can arbitrary power be conveyed to any man. *Those who give to others such rights perform acts that are void as they are given.*" . . . "Those who give and those who receive arbitrary power are alike criminal, and there is no man but is bound to resist it to the best of his power, wherever it shall show its face in the world. It is a crime to bear it where it can be rationally shaken off."—*Speech on Impeachment of Warren Hastings.*

Or let them be guided by that other teacher, Lord Chatham, when he said:

"With respect to the decisions of the courts of justice I am far from denying their due weight and authority; yet, placing them in the most respectable view, I will consider them, not as law, but as an evidence of the law; and, before they can arrive even at that degree of authority, it must appear that they are founded in, and confirmed by, reason; that they are supported by precedents, taken from good and moderate times; that they do not contradict any positive law; that they are submitted to without reluctance by the people; that they are unquestioned by the legislature (which is equivalent to a tacit confirmation); *and, what in my judgment is by far the most important, that they do not violate the spirit of the constitution.*"—*Speech of Lord Chatham in 1770, with regard to the proceeding on the Middlesex election.*

If courts were thus inspired, it is easy to see that slavery would disappear under their righteous judgments.

2. But unhappily the courts will not perform the duty of the hour, and we must look elsewhere. An appeal must be made to Congress; and here, as has been fully developed, the powers are ample, unless in their interpretation you surrender in advance to slavery. By a single brief statute Congress may sweep slavery out of existence.

But, even if Congress be not prepared for that single decisive measure which shall promptly put an end to this whole question and strike slavery to death, there are other measures by which this end may be hastened. The towering Upas may be girdled, even if it may not be felled at once to the earth.

The Fugitive Slave bill, conceived in iniquity and imposed upon the North as a badge of subjugation, may be repealed.

The coastwise slave trade may be deprived of all support in the statute book.

The traffic in human beings, as an article of "commerce among States," may be extirpated.

And, above all, that odious rule of evidence, so injurious to justice and discreditable to the country, excluding the testimony of colored persons in national courts, may be abolished.

Let these things be done. In themselves they will be much. But they will be more as the assurance of the overthrow sure to follow.

3. But all these will not be enough. The people must be summoned to confirm the whole work. It is for them to put the cap-stone upon the sublime structure. An amendment of the Constitution may do what courts and Congress decline to do, or, even should they act, it may cover their action with its panoply. Such an amendment in any event will give completeness and permanence to emancipation, and bring the Constitution into avowed harmony with the Declaration of Independence. Happy day, long wished for, destined to gladden those beatified spirits who have labored on earth to this end, but died without the sight.

The founder of political science in modern times, writer as well as statesman, Machiavelli, in his most instructive work, the "Discourses on Livy," has a chapter entitled, "To have long life in a republic, it is necessary to draw it back often to its origin"; and in the chapter he shows how the original virtue in which a republic was founded becomes so far corrupted that, in the process of time, the body-politic must be destroyed; as in the case of the natural body, where, according to the doctors of medicine, there is something added daily which perpetually requires cure. He teaches under this head that republics are brought back to their origin, and the principles in which they were founded, by pressure without or prudence within, and he affirms that the destruction of Rome by the Gauls was necessary that the republic might have a new birth, and thus acquire new life and new virtue, all of which ensued when the barbarians had been driven back. The illustration, perhaps, is fanciful, but there is wisdom in the counsel, and now the time has come for its application. The Gauls are upon us, not, however, from a distance, but domestic Gauls; and we, too, may profit by the occasion to secure for the Republic a new birth, that it may acquire a new life and new virtue. Happily, in our case the way is easy, for it is only necessary to carry the Republic back to its baptismal vows, and the declared sentiments of its origin. There is the Declaration of Independence: let its solemn promises be redeemed. There is the Constitution: let it speak, according to the promises of the Declaration.

The amendment to the Constitution was passed by a vote of 38 to 6 (more than the two-thirds required), the negative votes being cast by Lazarus W. Powell and Garrett Davis, of Kentucky; Willard Saulsbury and George R. Riddle, of Delaware; James A. McDougall, of California, and Thomas A. Hendricks, of Indiana.

Upon announcement of the vote Senator Saulsbury rose in his seat "simply to say" that he now "bade farewell to any hope of the reconstruction of the American Union."

Senator McDougall objected to the decision of the Vice-President that the resolution had passed, saying that a two-thirds majority of a full Senate, counting two votes from each of the seceded States, was in his opinion necessary to pass a measure in which all the States were vitally concerned under the Constitution. The chair overruled the objection, and Senator McDougall did not contest the overruling.

The Senate resolution came before the House on May 31, and a motion to reject it was voted down by 55 yeas to 76 nays. It was thoroughly debated (the arguments being largely repetitions of those in the Senate) until June 15, when it was put to the vote, with the result of 93 yeas and 65 nays, 23 Representatives not voting. The measure thus failed of passage, not receiving the two-thirds majority required by the Constitution. It was not brought forward again during this session.

The subject was brought forward at the next session and, after considerable debate in which few new arguments were presented, a joint resolution submitting the amendment to the States for ratification was passed by Congress on January 31, 1865, and approved by the President on February 1. Upon ratification by the requisite three-fourths majority of the States it went into effect by proclamation on December 18, 1865.

ImTheStory.com

Personalized Classic Books in many genre's

Unique gift for kids, partners, friends, colleagues

Customize:

- Character Names

- Upload your own front/back cover images (optional)

- Inscribe a personal message/dedication on the
  inside page (optional)

Customize many titles Including
- Alice in Wonderland
- Romeo and Juliet
- The Wizard of Oz
- A Christmas Carol
- Dracula
- Dr. Jekyll & Mr. Hyde
- And more...

Printed by BoD™in Norderstedt, Germany